Nutshell

of

WEST PUBLISHING COMPANY

P.O. Box 64526

St. Paul, Minnesota 55164–0526

Accounting—Law and, 1984, 377 pages, by E. McGruder Faris, Late Professor of Law, Stetson University.

Administrative Law and Process, 2nd Ed., 1981, 445 pages, by Ernest Gellhorn, Former Dean and Professor of Law, Case Western Reserve University and Barry B. Boyer, Professor of Law, SUNY, Buffalo.

Admiralty, 2nd Ed., 1988, about 362 pages, by Frank L. Maraist, Professor of Law, Louisiana State University.

Agency-Partnership, 1977, 364 pages, by Roscoe T. Steffen, Late Professor of Law, University of Chicago.

American Indian Law, 1981, 288 pages, by William C. Canby, Jr., Adjunct Professor of Law, Arizona State University.

Antitrust Law and Economics, 3rd Ed., 1986, 472 pages, by Ernest Gellhorn, Former Dean and Professor of Law, Case Western Reserve University.

Appellate Advocacy, 1984, 325 pages, by Alan D. Hornstein, Professor of Law, University of Maryland.

Art Law, 1984, 335 pages, by Leonard D. DuBoff, Professor of Law, Lewis and Clark College, Northwestern School of Law.

Banking and Financial Institutions, 1984, 409 pages, by William A. Lovett, Professor of Law, Tulane University.

Church-State Relations—Law of, 1981, 305 pages, by Leonard F. Manning, Late Professor of Law, Fordham University.

Civil Procedure, 2nd Ed., 1986, 306 pages, by Mary Kay Kane, Professor of Law, University of California, Hastings College of the Law.

Civil Rights, 1978, 279 pages, by Norman Vieira, Professor of Law, Southern Illinois University.

Commercial Paper, 3rd Ed., 1982, 404 pages, by Charles M. Weber, Professor of Business Law, University of Arizona and Richard E. Speidel, Professor of Law, Northwestern University.

Community Property, 2nd Ed., 1988, about 420 pages, by Robert L. Mennell, Former Professor of Law, Hamline University and Thomas M. Boykoff.

Comparative Legal Traditions, 1982, 402 pages, by Mary Ann Glendon, Professor of Law, Harvard University, Michael Wallace Gordon, Professor of Law, University of Florida and Christopher Osakwe, Professor of Law, Tulane University.

Conflicts, 1982, 470 pages, by David D. Siegel, Professor of Law, St. John's University.

Constitutional Analysis, 1979, 388 pages, by Jerre S. Williams, Professor of Law Emeritus, University of Texas.

Constitutional Federalism, 2nd Ed., 1987, 411 pages, by David E. Engdahl, Professor of Law, University of Puget Sound.

Constitutional Law, 1986, 389 pages, by Jerome A. Barron, Dean and Professor of Law, George Washington University and C. Thomas Dienes, Professor of Law, George Washington University.

Consumer Law, 2nd Ed., 1981, 418 pages, by David G. Epstein, Dean and Professor of Law, Emory University and Steve H. Nickles, Professor of Law, University of Minnesota.

Contract Remedies, 1981, 323 pages, by Jane M. Friedman, Professor of Law, Wayne State University.

Contracts, 2nd Ed., 1984, 425 pages, by Gordon D. Schaber, Dean and Professor of Law, McGeorge School of Law and Claude D. Rohwer, Professor of Law, McGeorge School of Law.

Corporations—Law of, 2nd Ed., 1987, 515 pages, by Robert W. Hamilton, Professor of Law, University of Texas.

Corrections and Prisoners' Rights—Law of, 2nd Ed., 1983, 386 pages, by Sheldon Krantz, Dean and Professor of Law, University of San Diego.

Criminal Law, 2nd Ed., 1987, 321 pages, by Arnold H. Loewy, Professor of Law, University of North Carolina.

Criminal Procedure—Constitutional Limitations, 4th Ed., 1988, about 461 pages, by Jerold H. Israel, Professor of Law, University of Michigan and Wayne R. LaFave, Professor of Law, University of Illinois.

Debtor-Creditor Law, 3rd Ed., 1986, 383 pages, by David G. Epstein, Dean and Professor of Law, Emory University.

Employment Discrimination—Federal Law of, 2nd Ed., 1981, 402 pages, by Mack A. Player, Professor of Law, University of Georgia.

Energy Law, 1981, 338 pages, by Joseph P. Tomain, Professor of Law, University of Cincinnatti.

Environmental Law, 1983, 343 pages by Roger W. Findley, Professor of Law, University of Illinois and Daniel A. Farber, Professor of Law, University of Minnesota.

Estate and Gift Taxation, Federal, 3rd Ed., 1983, 509 pages, by John K. McNulty, Professor of Law, University of California, Berkeley.

Estate Planning—Introduction to, 3rd Ed., 1983, 370 pages, by Robert J. Lynn, Professor of Law, Ohio State University.

Evidence, Federal Rules of, 2nd Ed., 1987, 473 pages, by Michael H. Graham, Professor of Law, University of Miami.

Evidence, State and Federal Rules, 2nd Ed., 1981, 514 pages, by Paul F. Rothstein, Professor of Law, Georgetown University.

Family Law, 2nd Ed., 1986, 444 pages, by Harry D. Krause, Professor of Law, University of Illinois.

Federal Jurisdiction, 2nd Ed., 1981, 258 pages, by David P. Currie, Professor of Law, University of Chicago.

Future Interests, 1981, 361 pages, by Lawrence W. Waggoner, Professor of Law, University of Michigan.

Government Contracts, 1979, 423 pages, by W. Noel Keyes, Professor of Law, Pepperdine University.

Historical Introduction to Anglo-American Law, 2nd Ed., 1973, 280 pages, by Frederick G. Kempin, Jr., Professor of Business Law, Wharton School of Finance and Commerce, University of Pennsylvania.

Immigration Law and Procedure, 1984, 345 pages, by David Weissbrodt, Professor of Law, University of Minnesota.

Injunctions, 1974, 264 pages, by John F. Dobbyn, Professor of Law, Villanova University.

Insurance Law, 1981, 281 pages, by John F. Dobbyn, Professor of Law, Villanova University.

Intellectual Property—Patents, Trademarks and Copyright, 1983, 428 pages, by Arthur R. Miller, Professor of Law, Harvard University, and Michael H. Davis, Professor of Law, Cleveland State University, Cleveland-Marshall College of Law.

International Business Transactions, 2nd Ed., 1984, 476 pages, by Donald T. Wilson, Late Professor of Law, Loyola University, Los Angeles.

International Law (Public), 1985, 262 pages, by Thomas Buergenthal, Professor of Law, Emory University and Harold G. Maier, Professor of Law, Vanderbilt University.

Introduction to the Study and Practice of Law, 1983, 418 pages, by Kenney F. Hegland, Professor of Law, University of Arizona.

Judicial Process, 1980, 292 pages, by William L. Reynolds, Professor of Law, University of Maryland.

Jurisdiction, 4th Ed., 1980, 232 pages, by Albert A. Ehrenzweig, Late Professor of Law, University of California, Berkeley, David W. Louisell, Late Professor of Law, University of California, Berkeley and Geoffrey C. Hazard, Jr., Professor of Law, Yale Law School.

Juvenile Courts, 3rd Ed., 1984, 291 pages, by Sanford J. Fox, Professor of Law, Boston College.

Labor Arbitration Law and Practice, 1979, 358 pages, by Dennis R. Nolan, Professor of Law, University of South Carolina.

Labor Law, 2nd Ed., 1986, 397 pages, by Douglas L. Leslie, Professor of Law, University of Virginia.

Land Use, 2nd Ed., 1985, 356 pages, by Robert R. Wright, Professor of Law, University of Arkansas, Little Rock and Susan Webber Wright, Professor of Law, University of Arkansas, Little Rock.

Landlord and Tenant Law, 2nd Ed., 1986, 311 pages, by David S. Hill, Professor of Law, University of Colorado.

Law Study and Law Examinations—Introduction to, 1971, 389 pages, by Stanley V. Kinyon, Late Professor of Law, University of Minnesota.

Legal Interviewing and Counseling, 2nd Ed., 1987, 487 pages, by Thomas L. Shaffer, Professor of Law, Washington and Lee University and James R. Elkins, Professor of Law, West Virginia University.

Legal Research, 4th Ed., 1985, 452 pages, by Morris L. Cohen, Professor of Law and Law Librarian, Yale University.

Legal Writing, 1982, 294 pages, by Lynn B. Squires and Marjorie Dick Rombauer, Professor of Law, University of Washington.

Legislative Law and Process, 2nd Ed., 1986, 346 pages, by Jack Davies, Professor of Law, William Mitchell College of Law.

Local Government Law, 2nd Ed., 1983, 404 pages, by David J. McCarthy, Jr., Professor of Law, Georgetown University.

Mass Communications Law, 3rd Ed., 1988, 538 pages, by Harvey L. Zuckman, Professor of Law, Catholic University, Martin J. Gaynes, Lecturer in Law, Temple University, T. Barton Carter, Professor of Public Communications, Boston University, and Juliet Lushbough Dee, Professor of Communications, University of Delaware.

Medical Malpractice—The Law of, 2nd Ed., 1986, 342 pages, by Joseph H. King, Professor of Law, University of Tennessee.

Military Law, 1980, 378 pages, by Charles A. Shanor, Professor of Law, Emory University and Timothy P. Terrell, Professor of Law, Emory University.

Oil and Gas Law, 1983, 443 pages, by John S. Lowe, Professor of Law, Southern Methodist University.

Personal Property, 1983, 322 pages, by Barlow Burke, Jr., Professor of Law, American University.

Post-Conviction Remedies, 1978, 360 pages, by Robert Popper, Dean and Professor of Law, University of Missouri, Kansas City.

Presidential Power, 1977, 328 pages, by Arthur Selwyn Miller, Professor of Law Emeritus, George Washington University.

Products Liability, 3rd Ed., 1988, about 350 pages, by Jerry J. Phillips, Professor of Law, University of Tennessee.

Professional Responsibility, 1980, 399 pages, by Robert H. Aronson, Professor of Law, University of Washington, and Donald T. Weckstein, Professor of Law, University of San Diego.

Real Estate Finance, 2nd Ed., 1985, 262 pages, by Jon W. Bruce, Professor of Law, Vanderbilt University.

Real Property, 2nd Ed., 1981, 448 pages, by Roger H. Bernhardt, Professor of Law, Golden Gate University.

Regulated Industries, 2nd Ed., 1987, 389 pages, by Ernest Gellhorn, Former Dean and Professor of Law, Case Western Reserve University, and Richard J. Pierce, Professor of Law, Southern Methodist University.

Remedies, 2nd Ed., 1985, 320 pages, by John F. O'Connell, Dean and Professor of Law, Southern California College of Law.

Res Judicata, 1976, 310 pages, by Robert C. Casad, Professor of Law, University of Kansas.

Sales, 2nd Ed., 1981, 370 pages, by John M. Stockton, Professor of Business Law, Wharton School of Finance and Commerce, University of Pennsylvania.

Schools, Students and Teachers—Law of, 1984, 409 pages, by Kern Alexander, President, Western Kentucky University and M. David Alexander, Professor, Virginia Tech University.

Sea—Law of, 1984, 264 pages, by Louis B. Sohn, Professor of Law, University of Georgia and Kristen Gustafson.

Secured Transactions, 2nd Ed., 1981, 391 pages, by Henry J. Bailey, Professor of Law Emeritus, Willamette University.

Securities Regulation, 3rd Ed., 1988, about 350 pages, by David L. Ratner, Dean and Professor of Law, University of San Francisco.

Sex Discrimination, 1982, 399 pages, by Claire Sherman Thomas, Lecturer, University of Washington, Women's Studies Department.

Taxation and Finance, State and Local, 1986, 309 pages, by M. David Gelfand, Professor of Law, Tulane University and Peter W. Salsich, Professor of Law, St. Louis University.

Taxation of Individuals, Federal Income, 3rd Ed., 1983, 487 pages, by John K. McNulty, Professor of Law, University of California, Berkeley.

Torts—Injuries to Persons and Property, 1977, 434 pages, by Edward J. Kionka, Professor of Law, Southern Illinois University.

Torts—Injuries to Family, Social and Trade Relations, 1979, 358 pages, by Wex S. Malone, Professor of Law Emeritus, Louisiana State University.

Trial Advocacy, 1979, 402 pages, by Paul B. Bergman, Adjunct Professor of Law, University of California, Los Angeles.

Trial and Practice Skills, 1978, 346 pages, by Kenney F. Hegland, Professor of Law, University of Arizona.

Trial, The First—Where Do I Sit? What Do I Say?, 1982, 396 pages, by Steven H. Goldberg, Professor of Law, University of Minnesota.

Unfair Trade Practices, 1982, 445 pages, by Charles R. McManis, Professor of Law, Washington University.

Uniform Commercial Code, 2nd Ed., 1984, 516 pages, by Bradford Stone, Professor of Law, Stetson University.

Uniform Probate Code, 2nd Ed., 1987, 454 pages, by Lawrence H. Averill, Jr., Dean and Professor of Law, University of Arkansas, Little Rock.

Water Law, 1984, 439 pages, by David H. Getches, Professor of Law, University of Colorado.

Welfare Law—Structure and Entitlement, 1979, 455 pages, by Arthur B. LaFrance, Professor of Law, Lewis and Clark College, Northwestern School of Law.

Wills and Trusts, 1979, 392 pages, by Robert L. Mennell, Former Professor of Law, Hamline University.

Workers' Compensation and Employee Protection Laws, 1984, 274 pages, by Jack B. Hood, Former Professor of Law, Cumberland School of Law, Samford University and Benjamin A. Hardy, Former Professor of Law, Cumberland School of Law, Samford University.

Hornbook Series

and

Basic Legal Texts

of

WEST PUBLISHING COMPANY

P.O. Box 64526

St. Paul, Minnesota 55164–0526

Admiralty and Maritime Law, Schoenbaum's Hornbook on, 1987, 692 pages, by Thomas J. Schoenbaum, Professor of Law, University of Georgia.

Agency and Partnership, Reuschlein & Gregory's Hornbook on the Law of, 1979 with 1981 Pocket Part, 625 pages, by Harold Gill Reuschlein, Professor of Law Emeritus, Villanova University and William A. Gregory, Professor of Law, Georgia State University.

Antitrust, Sullivan's Hornbook on the Law of, 1977, 886 pages, by Lawrence A. Sullivan, Professor of Law, University of California, Berkeley.

Civil Procedure, Friedenthal, Kane and Miller's Hornbook on, 1985, 876 pages, by Jack H. Friedental, Professor of Law, Stanford University, Mary Kay Kane, Professor of Law, University of California, Hastings College of the Law and Arthur R. Miller, Professor of Law, Harvard University.

Common Law Pleading, Koffler and Reppy's Hornbook on, 1969, 663 pages, by Joseph H. Koffler, Professor of Law, New York Law School and Alison Reppy, Late Dean and Professor of Law, New York Law School.

Conflict of Laws, Scoles and Hay's Hornbook on, 1982, with 1986 Pocket Part, 1085 pages, by Eugene F. Scoles, Professor of Law, University of Illinois and Peter Hay, Dean and Professor of Law, University of Illinois.

Constitutional Law, Nowak, Rotunda and Young's Hornbook on, 3rd Ed., 1986, 1191 pages, by John E. Nowak, Professor of Law, University of Illinois, Ronald D. Rotunda, Professor of Law, University of Illinois, and J. Nelson Young, Late Professor of Law, University of North Carolina.

Contracts, Calamari and Perillo's Hornbook on, 3rd Ed., 1987, 1049 pages, by John D. Calamari, Professor of Law, Fordham University and Joseph M. Perillo, Professor of Law, Fordham University.

Contracts, Corbin's One Volume Student Ed., 1952, 1224 pages, by Arthur L. Corbin, Late Professor of Law, Yale University.

Corporations, Henn and Alexander's Hornbook on, 3rd Ed., 1983, with 1986 Pocket Part, 1371 pages, by Harry G. Henn, Professor of Law Emeritus, Cornell University and John R. Alexander.

Criminal Law, LaFave and Scott's Hornbook on, 2nd Ed., 1986, 918 pages, by Wayne R. LaFave, Professor of Law, University of Illinois, and Austin Scott, Jr., Late Professor of Law, University of Colorado.

Criminal Procedure, LaFave and Israel's Hornbook on, 1985 with 1986 pocket part, 1142 pages, by Wayne R. LaFave, Professor of Law, University of Illinois and Jerold H. Israel, Professor of Law University of Michigan.

Damages, McCormick's Hornbook on, 1935, 811 pages, by Charles T. McCormick, Late Dean and Professor of Law, University of Texas.

Domestic Relations, Clark's Hornbook on, 2nd Ed., 1988, about 1100 pages, by Homer H. Clark, Jr., Professor of Law, University of Colorado.

Economics and Federal Antitrust Law, Hovenkamp's Hornbook on, 1985, 414 pages, by Herbert Hovenkamp, Professor of Law, University of Iowa.

Employment Discrimination Law, Player's Hornbook on, about 650 pages, 1988, by Mack A. Player, Professor of Law, University of Georgia.

Environmental Law, Rodgers' Hornbook on, 1977 with 1984 Pocket Part, 956 pages, by William H. Rodgers, Jr., Professor of Law, University of Washington.

Evidence, Lilly's Introduction to, 2nd Ed., 1987, 585 pages, by Graham C. Lilly, Professor of Law, University of Virginia.

Evidence, McCormick's Hornbook on, 3rd Ed., 1984 with 1987 Pocket Part, 1156 pages, General Editor, Edward W. Cleary, Professor of Law Emeritus, Arizona State University.

Federal Courts, Wright's Hornbook on, 4th Ed., 1983, 870 pages, by Charles Alan Wright, Professor of Law, University of Texas.

Federal Income Taxation, Rose and Chommie's Hornbook on, 3rd Ed., 1988, about 875 pages, by Michael D. Rose, Professor of Law, Ohio State University and John C. Chommie, Late Professor of Law, University of Miami.

Federal Income Taxation of Individuals, Posin's Hornbook on, 1983 with 1987 Pocket Part, 491 pages, by Daniel Q. Posin, Jr., Professor of Law, Catholic University.

Future Interest, Simes' Hornbook on, 2nd Ed., 1966, 355 pages, by Lewis M. Simes, Late Professor of Law, University of Michigan.

Insurance, Keeton and Widiss' Basic Text on, 1988, about 1000 pages, by Robert E. Keeton, Professor of Law Emeritus, Harvard University and Alan I. Widiss, Professor of Law, University of Iowa.

Labor Law, Gorman's Basic Text on, 1976, 914 pages, by Robert A. Gorman, Professor of Law, University of Pennsylvania.

Law Problems, Ballentine's, 5th Ed., 1975, 767 pages, General Editor, William E. Burby, Late Professor of Law, University of Southern California.

Legal Ethics, Wolfram's Hornbook on, 1986, 1120 pages, by Charles W. Wolfram, Professor of Law, Cornell University.

Legal Writing Style, Weihofen's, 2nd Ed., 1980, 332 pages, by Henry Weihofen, Professor of Law Emeritus, University of New Mexico.

Local Government Law, Reynolds' Hornbook on, 1982 with 1987 Pocket Part, 860 pages, by Osborne M. Reynolds, Professor of Law, University of Oklahoma.

New York Estate Administration, Turano and Radigan's Hornbook on, 1986, 676 pages, by Margaret V. Turano, Professor of Law, St. John's University and Raymond Radigan.

New York Practice, Siegel's Hornbook on, 1978 with 1987 Pocket Part, 1011 pages, by David D. Siegel, Professor of Law, St. John's University.

Oil and Gas Law, Hemingway's Hornbook on, 2nd Ed., 1983, with 1986 Pocket Part, 543 pages, by Richard W. Hemingway, Professor of Law, University of Oklahoma.

Property, Boyer's Survey of, 3rd Ed., 1981, 766 pages, by Ralph E. Boyer, Professor of Law Emeritus, University of Miami.

Property, Law of, Cunningham, Whitman and Stoebuck's Hornbook on, 1984, with 1987 Pocket Part, 916 pages, by Roger A. Cunningham, Professor of Law, University of Michigan, Dale A. Whitman, Dean and Professor of Law, University of Missouri, Columbia and William B. Stoebuck, Professor of Law, University of Washington.

Real Estate Finance Law, Nelson and Whitman's Hornbook on, 2nd Ed., 1985, 941 pages, by Grant S. Nelson, Professor of Law, University of Missouri, Columbia and Dale A. Whitman, Dean and Professor of Law, University of Missouri, Columbia.

Real Property, Moynihan's Introduction to, 2nd Ed., 1987, 239 pages, by Cornelius J. Moynihan, Late Professor of Law, Suffolk University.

Remedies, Dobbs' Hornbook on, 1973, 1067 pages, by Dan B. Dobbs, Professor of Law, University of Arizona.

Secured Transactions under the U.C.C., Henson's Hornbook on, 2nd Ed., 1979 with 1979 Pocket Part, 504 pages, by Ray D. Henson, Professor of Law, University of California, Hastings College of the Law.

Securities Regulation, Hazen's Hornbook on the Law of, 1985, with 1988 Pocket Part, 739 pages, by Thomas Lee Hazen, Professor of Law, University of North Carolina.

Sports Law, Schubert, Smith and Trentadue's, 1986, 395 pages, by George W. Schubert, Dean of University College, University of North Dakota, Rodney K. Smith, Professor of Law, Delaware Law School, Widener University, and Jesse C. Trentadue, Former Professor of Law, University of North Dakota.

Torts, Prosser and Keeton's Hornbook on, 5th Ed., 1984 with 1988 Pocket Part, 1286 pages, by William L. Prosser, Late Dean and Professor of Law, University of California, Berkeley, Page Keeton, Professor of Law Emeritus, University of Texas, Dan B. Dobbs, Professor of Law, University of Arizona, Robert E. Keeton, Professor of Law Emeritus, Harvard University and David G. Owen, Professor of Law, University of South Carolina.

Trial Advocacy, Jeans' Handbook on, Soft cover, 1975, 473 pages, by James W. Jeans, Professor of Law, University of Missouri, Kansas City.

Trusts, Bogert's Hornbook on, 6th Ed., 1987, 794 pages, by George T. Bogert.

Uniform Commercial Code, White and Summers' Hornbook on, 3rd Ed., 1988, about 1250 pages, by James J. White, Professor of Law, University of Michigan and Robert S. Summers, Professor of Law, Cornell University.

Urban Planning and Land Development Control Law, Hagman and Juergensmeyer's Hornbook on, 2nd Ed., 1986, 680 pages, by Donald G. Hagman, Late Professor of Law, University of California, Los Angeles and Julian C. Juergensmeyer, Professor of Law, University of Florida.

Wills, Atkinson's Hornbook on, 2nd Ed., 1953, 975 pages, by Thomas E. Atkinson, Late Professor of Law, New York University.

Wills, Trusts and Estates, McGovern, Rein and Kurtz' Hornbook on, 1988, by William M. McGovern, Professor of Law, University of California, Los Angeles, Jan Ellen Rein, Professor of Law, Gonzaga University, and Sheldon F. Kurtz, Professor of Law, University of Iowa.

Advisory Board

EVIDENCE

IN A NUTSHELL:
STATE AND FEDERAL RULES

By
PAUL F. ROTHSTEIN
Professor of Law
Georgetown University Law Center

SECOND EDITION

ST. PAUL, MINN.
WEST PUBLISHING CO.
1981

Printed in the United States of America

Library of Congress Cataloging in Publication Data

Rothstein, Paul F   1938–
  Evidence in a nutshell.

  (Nutshell series)
  Bibliography: p.
  Includes index.
  1. Evidence (Law—United States.   I. Title.
KF8935.Z9R6   1981   347.73'6   80-28713

ISBN 0-8299-2131-1

      Rothstein-Evid. 2nd Ed.
        4th Reprint—1988

To
Thelma, Lillian and Alexander

*

PREFACE

This Nutshell is designed to be a convenience for the student and an aid to understanding and remembering. Hopefully it will also impart some of the fascination I find inherent in the subject of Evidence.

The litigating attorney will meet Evidence law not only during the trial itself, but during discovery and in connection with fact finding for motions at all stages. Regarding depositions, objections other than those based on privilege or the mechanics of proceeding ordinarily are proper only if and when the transcript is offered at trial. Motion practice may vary from strict trial practice, e. g., by freely receiving affidavits. Trial evidence, however, furnishes the basic pattern, and is the main concern of this book.

A detailed bibliography is out of place in a Nutshell. I will say only that Evidence law is susceptible of the same kinds of research as other areas of the law. One must of course mention specially the giants in the field, Wigmore, Morgan, McCormick, Ladd, and Prince; California's Evidence Code; the Federal Rules of Evidence ("F.R.E."); the 1953 and 1974 Uniform Rules of Evidence; and the Model Code of Evidence of the American Law Institute. (Drafter's comments, where available, are often more valuable than the text.) A particularly useful one volume work is McCormick, Evidence (West Publ. Co., 2d ed., 1972, supplemented). On the Federal Rules, see Rothstein, The Federal Rules of Evidence (Clark Boardman Co., Ltd., 2d ed., 1980, annually revised and supplemented).

PREFACE

The Federal Rules of Evidence, and state rules and rulings, whether common law or codified, are treated in this Nutshell. In addition, citations to the California Evidence Code appear from time to time in text, particularly under presumptions.

Some special aids to help the student have been incorporated in this book. A system of black-letter summaries of main principles has been used. These appear at the beginning of most sections. Indeed, if the headings and the black-letter summaries were copied out on paper, they would make a fairly comprehensive outline of Evidence. In addition, the Federal Rules of Evidence are fully treated, and can be readily located in the text by reference to the Table of Rules provided herein. The rule numbers are the same in most of the modern state codes. And there is also a Table of Cases, index, and detailed Table of Contents.

One final note. Be careful, in reading cases on evidence, to distinguish between what the trial judge *may*, and *must*, do.

P.F.R.

Washington, D.C.
May, 1981

TOPIC OUTLINE OR TABLE OF CONTENTS

A more comprehensive sentence outline may be obtained, if the student wishes, by copying out, under each heading here, the black-letter summaries of law that appear in the main text in connection with each of these headings.

OUTLINE

*

TABLE OF CASES

C

TABLE OF CASES

D

E

F

G

H

TABLE OF CASES

L

M

TABLE OF CASES

TABLE OF CASES

TABLE OF RULES

The following rules are the Federal Rules of Evidence and the 1974 Uniform Rules of Evidence. In most cases the rule numbers are the same. In some instances earlier drafts of the F.R.E. are included. Rules mentioned but not substantially discussed do not appear in this table. Citations to the California Evidence Code are not in this table but appear from time to time in text, particularly under presumptions.

TABLE OF RULES

TABLE OF RULES

TABLE OF RULES

TABLE OF RULES

TABLE OF RULES

L

TABLE OF RULES

TABLE OF RULES

EVIDENCE
IN A NUTSHELL

CHAPTER I

BASIC PRINCIPLES

What is Evidence Law?

The study of Evidence law is the study of the legal regulation of the proof used to persuade on fact questions at the trial of a lawsuit.

The precise contours of the legal regulation spoken of in the above definition is the concern of the remainder of this book. It is worth noting that in many cases, Evidence law makes no distinction between civil and criminal lawsuits.

In your study of Evidence law you are asked to master a body of legal prohibitions; but such mastery should yield, as an incidental benefit, some useful insights into how minds come to accept propositions of fact as true.

While Evidence law was originally almost entirely decisional law, it is becoming increasingly codified in statutes and rules of court. The discussion hereinafter will not identify which of these sources is at work in any particular area, except where it is essential to understanding, or where some provision of the major codifications—i.e., the Federal Rules of Evidence or the 1974 Uniform Rules—is involved. But remember, no generalized "nutshell" can substitute for careful consultation of the various pertinent sources during the preparation and trial of a specific case in a specific jurisdiction. On the other hand, even authoritative law often leaves room for argument.

The most influential codification of Evidence law in recent years has been the Federal Rules of Evidence ("F.R.E."), 28 U.S.C.A. Rules Appendix, enacted by Congress to govern proceedings in federal courts, effective July 1, 1975. The enacted rules were based largely though not entirely on a draft prepared by a distinguished panel of lawyers, judges, and Evidence scholars, which draft had been approved and transmitted to Congress by the Supreme Court. On the Congressional changing of this draft, and enactment of the final product, see the following articles by the present author: The Proposed Amendments to the F.R.E., 62 Geo.L.J. 125 (1973), updated in 24 Federation of Ins. Couns. Q. 54 (1974), and Some Themes in the Proposed F.R.E., 33 Fed. Bar J. 21 (1974). The Federal Rules draw heavily on the earlier California Evidence Code, and also on the Uniform Rules of Evidence (1953) of the National Conference of Commissioners on Uniform State Laws, promulgated as a model for state adoption. Although influential, the Uniform Rules were not widely adopted. In 1974 they were amended to substantially conform to the Federal Rules of Evidence. A growing number of states are now codifying along the lines of the Federal and Uniform Rules.

The Federal and Uniform Rules do not depart greatly from what was regarded as the better reasoned rulings found previously under the common law system.

In addition to strictly evidentiary sources, it should be recognized that state and federal constitutions exert some constraint on evidence rules and rulings, particularly in criminal cases.

Relevancy

The first requisite for evidence to be admissible is that it must be relevant. Evidence is relevant if a reasonable fact-finder could feel that, assuming

the evidence is true, it renders some fact that is properly in issue under the applicable substantive law more probable or less probable in any degree than it appeared before the introduction of the evidence.

Relevancy does not require that the fact be made to appear more probable *than not.* We are not, under the relevancy standard, testing the sufficiency of the party's total proof in the case as a whole, but rather only a particular building block. See F.R.E. 401.

Notice that the standard of relevancy implies that the judge and jury must have resort (to a limited extent) to matters not in the record in order to determine whether a piece of evidence renders a proposition more probable than before. Thus, love letters between the accused and the victim's wife would be admissible in a homicide prosecution, without any formal proof of the notion that a person writing such letters is more likely to have committed the crime than one who did not so write. The love letters would not be *sufficient to convict,* but they are relevant. Similarly, an accused thief's pecuniary position before and/ or after the alleged theft, his efforts to borrow, and/or the outcome thereof, will often be relevant. And the state of intoxication or sobriety of one of a group of companions at a given time will often be indicative of the state of one of the others at the same time. In each case the evidence relies on an assumption concerning human behavior that is not required to be proved. (To say that this evidence is relevant is not to say that it is admissible. It may be objectionable on other scores. These will be reserved for future discussion.)

"Immateriality" is the term used by some authorities and lawyers to indicate that a particular piece of evidence is relevant to a proposition of fact, but that the proposition itself is not relevant under the substantive law. Instead of requiring evidence to be "material," the Federal Rules of Evidence require that the proposition of fact to which the evidence is addressed be a proposition that is "of consequence to the determination of the action," which amounts to the same thing. F.R.E. 401.

"Relevancy" as used in this book and in common legal parlance subsumes "materiality." Thus, we will say that evidence is irrelevant if it either does not conduce to the fact proposition it is meant to conduce to, or if the fact proposition itself is not "relevant" ("material;" "of consequence").

Sometimes evidence is relevant only if certain other facts are also put in evidence. If those facts are not yet in evidence, a conditional ruling of admissibility may result, based upon the offering counsel's representations as to what he expects to put in evidence later. If he later defaults on the promise, and the proper motion is made, the evidence may be "stricken" or a mistrial declared, depending on the degree and remediable nature of the prejudice. Conditional admissibility may also be ordered when the objection is other than lack of relevancy (although, unfortunately, F.R.E. 104 mentions this power only in connection with relevancy). Other ways of handling a situation where admissibility depends on facts not yet introduced are apparent, as are methods of dealing with a situation where, after admission, facts appear rendering the evidence inadmissible.

As already indicated, relevancy is a *sine qua non* of admissibility, but is not itself alone sufficient to produce admissibility. The evidence must pass other tests or hurdles as well (which is the subject of much of the remainder of this book and most of the exclusionary rules). The Federal Rules suggest that at least there is a kind of *overcomeable presumption* of admissibility that attaches to evidence found to be relevant: F.R.E. 402 provides that relevant evidence is admissible unless rendered inadmissible by some other provision or principle of law.[1] Thus relevant evidence should be assumed to overcome the other tests or hurdles until it is shown otherwise.

---

[1] The provision or principle must be found in the F.R.E., other rules authorized by Congress, a statute, or the Constitution. What does this do to the old "supervisory power" of courts to exclude evidence (say, for police illegality or other irregularity in its obtention) that does not violate a rule, statute, or the Constitution? See United States v. Payner, 447 U.S. 727, 100 S.Ct. 2439 (1980); United States v. Jacobs, 547 F.2d 772 (2d Cir. 1976); United States v. Grajeda, 570 F.2d 872 (9th Cir. 1978); fourth paragraph Advisory Committee Note to F.R.E. 402 (reference to *Mallory*, a supervisory power case). Is such power encompassed by the word "prejudice" within the meaning of F.R.E. 403 which allows exclusion for undue prejudice and other factors? And what of other common law or evolving common-law-process exclusionary principles, such as regulation of impeachment by bias, etc., not specifically encompassed by the F.R.E.; after all, the F.R.E. cannot be and do not purport to be all inclusive. Are these encompassed by 403? Cf. F.R.E. 102 (F.R.E. to be interpreted liberally), and 501 (privileges to be determined from state and evolving common law), 803(24) and 804(b)(5) (these two allow the creation of new exceptions to the hearsay rule), which are specific rules allowing for common law development in particular cases. What authority there is on this whole problem is inconclusive. Would the Constitution countenance such a legislative restriction of the judicial power? Perhaps the answer lies in F.R.E. 501 which allows the court some latitude with respect to privileges. Can the exclusionary principle addressed in this note be considered a privilege? If so, has Congress' attempt in Rule 402 to confine evidence rule making power, been in vain?

The "presumption" of admissibility attaching to relevant evidence mentioned in text above is confirmed by F.R.E. 403, which codifies the ad hoc, largely discretionary common law power of the judge to exclude relevant evidence in a particular case, but only if he finds that *"unfair"* prejudice or other similar factor *"substantially"* outweighs" the relevance (probative value). The italicized words seem to confirm that relevant evidence is ordinarily admissible unless substantial reason can be found to keep it out.

Distrust of the Jury as the Basis of Much of Evidence Law: Prejudice as a Counterweight to Relevancy

Relevant evidence may be excluded pursuant to a specific "rule," or a less specific "guideline" (that is, a "standard") or may be left by some provision of law broadly to "judicial discretion" subject to review for abuse. Most often the policy concern behind each of these is avoidance of "prejudice," i. e., undue influence on the fact-finder. Frequently what purports to be a "rule" is a mixture of the three.

Many (if not most) of the exclusionary rules, guidelines, or standards of evidence, and exclusionary acts of discretion of judges where permitted, exclude relevant evidence on the rationale that juries would be inclined to give the particular piece or class of evidence more effect than they ought. That is, the evidence is "prejudicial," and by that is meant that juries could not be trusted to give it its logical, rational weight, or to perceive that it had none, but instead would, perhaps because of the emotional impact of the evidence, allow it to be more persuasive or influential than they should. This can happen where the evidence has some warranted weight as well as where it has none, so long as there is the danger that the jury will not evaluate it properly, but will over-inflate its role *to an extent that renders the trial better off without the evidence.*

Let us say a word about what a difficult computation this last would be if scrupulously made.

Two kinds of "prejudice" may be distinguished: (1) exaggeration and (2) disregard of the issues.

The first category ("exaggeration") embraces cases where evidence is excluded because of concern with its over-persuasiveness before the jury on the issue for which the evidence is offered. If a judge or rulemaker were to scrupulously make the computation called for in italics in the text just above, in this kind of case he would be required to estimate what probability (that the fact sought to be proved by the piece of evidence is true) the jury would ascribe (a) having the benefit of the piece of evidence, and (b) without it. He would then have to decide what probability a wholly rational trier-of-fact (who without the evidence ascribes the same probability as the real jury) would ascribe if given the piece of evidence. Only when exclusion rather than admission would cause the real jury to come closer to the probability ascribed by the wholly rational trier in receipt of the evidence, should the evidence be excluded. For example, suppose a piece of evidence is offered at trial and objected to along the lines described. The judge estimates that the real jurors would find the probability of the fact sought to be proved to be 95%, if they have the disputed evidence before them together with everything likely to be marshalled to deflate it. He feels the jury will assign a 70% probability at this point in trial without the evidence. He feels a rational trier estimating 70% without the piece of evidence, would move the figure up to 80% with the evidence. The evidence should be excluded. For the jury will be "off" only ten percentage points (from the true 80%) without the evidence, but fifteen with it. On the other hand, suppose the judge estimates that the jury and the rational trier will assign a 55% probability without the evidence, that a rational trier with the piece of evidence would move that figure up to 80%, but that the jury with the piece of evidence would move it up to 95%. The evidence should be admitted. For the jury would be twenty-five points "off" (from the true 80%) without the evidence, compared with fifteen with it.[2]

[2] Suppose the judge's estimates in a civil case (where 50% probability is the dividing line between winning and losing) are as follows:

Of course, numbers cannot be affixed in this fashion; nor do judges engage in such a mathematical computation. Nevertheless, the mathematics illustrate (albeit with unattainable precision) the sort of judgment the law seems to be calling for. The judge or law-maker is supposed to be able to (a) estimate probability better than the jury, and (b) predict what the jury will do with and without the evidence.

It is apparent that the numbers in the computation become vastly different depending upon what other proof for and against the fact there is in the case. Yet often the law will have made the judgment for a class of evidence as a whole. It is also apparent that some consideration must be given to the fact that exclusion of evidence may cause the offering party to offer other evidence he might not otherwise have offered, changing the probabilities. This has not been included in our computations.

The above "formula" for admission and exclusion comprehends only some of the kinds of cases in which evidence has been excluded on grounds that it would be unduly influential on the jury. Those are the cases embraced by item (1) in our black-letters just above, "exag-

---

Real jury and rational trier without the piece of evidence—40%; real jury with the evidence—90%; rational trier with the evidence —60%. Suppose further that the piece of evidence is the last to be offered in the case. The formula would seem to dictate exclusion, which would mean the proponent would lose the issue; whereas the rational trier would award him the victory. Must we make an adjustment in our formula? Suppose another situation: At one point during trial the proponent offers successive pieces of evidence, which are excluded because the numbers (as to each piece considered separately) are precisely those set forth above in the text where we said the evidence would be excluded (i. e., in the middle of the paragraph to which this footnote is appended). Suppose further that if a perfectly rational trier had received all of the excluded evidence he would have placed the probability figure at 95%—the place it was feared the jury might put it for each piece of evidence. What should be done? Should prospective evidence be considered?

geration." There are, however, instances of the exclusion of evidence, also on grounds of prejudice, where one cannot say the piece of evidence tends to establish unduly the factual proposition for which it is offered, or even any other mediate factual proposition in the case; and thus it is not a case of feared "exaggeration." Rather the piece of evidence tends to make the jury unduly prone to awarding the ultimate decision one way or the other. For example, it is clear that, in the absence of special circumstances, no court in the land would permit the fact of death in a criminal homicide case to be proved by introducing the battered body, even where the "rational" appraisal of such evidence would be that death is at least 99% probable, the jury could not greatly exaggerate that probability, and excluding the body might leave them only 90% convinced of death. The body might cause the jury to be overzealous to convict somebody. This kind of prejudice may be called "disregard of the issues," which is item (2) in our breakdown of types of prejudice, above. The ban on introducing prior convictions of a criminal defendant is in part based on this rationale (along with the exaggeration rationale, and certain other policy considerations related to rehabilitation and the like). The example of the battered body also highlights the question of the extent to which the availability of alternative sources of proof ought to be considered in our calculus. To use the language of F.R.E. 403, particular evidence that may have some prejudice associated with it may be considered "unfairly" prejudicial if (or sometimes only if) other less prejudicial means are reasonably available to prove the matter sought to be proved.

It is easy to see from all of the foregoing, that one question recurring throughout any study of Evidence law is this: When can we trust the jurors to properly confine the effect of evidence, observe its proper limits, and spot its infirmities, perhaps with the aid of other evidence, argument by counsel, and advice by the judge; and when should we exclude the evidence because the jury will be inclined to give it too much weight? When can something said by the judge or counsel, or introduced into evidence, forestall or cure a tendency to overemphasize on the part of the jury, sufficiently so that the evidence may safely be admitted, or sufficiently so that a new trial is not necessary where inadmissible evidence has already improperly gotten in? How should the instruction be put? When do the aids that would be needed to neutralize undue effect consume too much time, effort, or expense?

When relevant evidence is excluded on the basis of the two kinds of distrust of jurors discussed in this section, it is usually said to be excluded because it is "prejudicial." In a sense all evidence is "prejudicial" insofar as it helps one side and hinders the other, no matter how legitimately and logically. But the term "prejudicial" is normally used to mean "unduly" or "unwarrantedly" prejudicial. Query: are there more than two types of undue prejudice which Evidence law will or should recognize? What about, for example, prejudice to the victim in a rape case, from allowing exploration of her sexual history, a much debated current topic? Are there others?

Evidence rules, standards, and exercises of discretion are often based on (or call for the judge to make) a balancing of probativity (i. e., relevance or logical tendency to prove) against prejudice and other factors phrased in various ways but frequently including protraction, surprise, confusion, misleadingness and cumulativeness.

"Prejudice" is but one of the factors which courts and commentators say must be "balanced against" relevancy (or probativity) in the fashion outlined in the last several paragraphs. Other factors include "protraction [i. e., consumption of time]," "unfair surprise," and "confusion of the fact-finder." (The others in the heading, frequently also listed, are probably redundant.) The balancing of these factors, including "prejudice," will be illuminated as the present work proceeds. In certain areas the balance has been struck as a matter of law for a class of evidence as a whole. Thus, for example, F.R.E. 404 prohibits evidence of character used to prove an act in conformity with the character (subject to certain exceptions); and Rule 411 prohibits proof of liability insurance offered for certain purposes. In other areas (usually those of a less recurrent nature) the law permits the judge (subject to review for abuse of discretion) to do an *ad hoc* balancing of these factors on the facts of the particular case. Thus, F.R.E. 403 allows the judge to exclude evidence in a particular case (though there is no specific rule concerning the evidence; or frequently even if there is a specific rule if the rule is a ban from which this evidence is specifically excepted) based on his conclusion that the probative value (relevance) of the evidence is substantially outweighed by the other factors. "Surprise" is omitted as a factor presumably unless one can argue that evidence for which the opponent could not prepare adequately is likely to be "misleading," "confusing," or "prejudicial" (all factors which do appear) since weaknesses may go unexplored. The rationale of the omission was that modern discovery, coupled with the possibility of a continuance of the trial, makes surprise less of a problem. Perhaps this assumes full discovery in every case, which is not always the fact, or even desirable, from the standpoint of economics. (Surprise at the introduction of evidence the offeror was under obligation to surrender-up in discovery and didn't, can be grounds for exclusion under Federal Rule of Civil Procedure 37.)

Frequently, in the areas where the *ad hoc* balancing is done, a considerable amount of discretion on the part of the trial judge is allowed. By "considerable discretion" is meant that only a blatantly egregious ruling will be over-turned by the appellate court.

The terms "rule," "standard" (or "guideline"), and "dis-cretion" may be used to show three gradations according to how much discretion the trial judge has. A rule like "evi-dence of [certain specified other wrongdoing] shall not be admissible against the accused in a criminal case" would, in this terminology, be a "rule." If it added "except for im-peachment [or for certain other specified purposes] pro-vided that probativity is found to outweigh prejudice in the particular case," the prohibitive part would be a rule, the exception part would be a standard. A more pure "stan-dard" would be a provision stating that expert or lay opin-ion testimony is admissible only when it is "of assistance" and "rationally based on perception" or based on "grounds reasonably relied on in the field." These provisions would be neither rule nor standard if they left admissibility more unguidedly to the judge—for example, left to a naked con-sideration of the factors of probativity and its counterweights discussed in the last several pages. Grey areas between these classifications are frequent. The classifications are not intended to be airtight or absolutely precise, but merely to show a general direction or framework for thinking. Nor are we in this particular regard necessarily using the lan-guage used by courts and rules, although "discretion" is a word frequently found.

With respect to the element of "time consumption" men-tioned above as a factor in the balance, there may be evidence whose legitimate persuasive power or relevance is so minor (or nonexistent) that it is not worth the time to receive it, even if the fact-finder can be counted on to give it only the weight it deserves (i. e., it cannot be said to be prejudicial). Indeed, "time" seems to be the only reason for excluding irrelevant evidence where the jury can be counted on to spot its total lack of value (i. e., evidence that is irrelevant but not "prejudicial"). Including "time" as a consideration implies that we are willing to compromise accuracy of result in the interests of handling more cases more quickly. While the other considerations seem primarily to be related to accuracy of fact-finding, some of their applications and certain other regulations of evidence appear to be designed on notions of fairness that may at times diverge from the goal of fact-finding accuracy. Of course, the effectiveness of law depends in part on promulgating a feeling of fair treatment and subserving litigants' and the community's notion of fairness, however misguided. On the other hand, the law can guide it, too.

At this point it is well to note that a number of exclusionary rules of evidence have little to do with relevancy, prejudice, surprise, confusion, or protraction; with the accuracy, economy, or speed of the dispute-resolving mechanism; or with standards of fairness. Insofar as privileges are designed to stimulate socially desirable communications (e. g., between doctor and patient), they seem to fall into this class, being concerned primarily with conduct outside the courthouse. They may, however, be part of our concept of fairness, too.

The study of Evidence law will teach not only something about the admission and exclusion of evidence, its main function, but incidentally it will also teach something about what kinds of argument should be made as a matter of tactics to triers-of-fact in connection with inflating or deflating the weight they ascribe to evidence. Oftentimes in a jury trial, arguments made to the judge in an effort to show that the legitimate probativeness of a piece of evidence is below the point where it is desirable to admit the evidence (under the balancing mentioned above), may fail because lack of probativeness has not been shown in sufficient degree to be more than a matter of weight for the jury. The same arguments may then be repeated to the jury, to induce them to discount the weight of the evidence in some measure. Similarly, arguments for admissibility can be made again to the jury, to bolster and emphasize the weight of the evidence. Thus, a study of arguments concerning admission and exclusion is also a study of argument to the fact-finder. The lesson is also adaptable to argument directed at avoiding or obtaining peremptory rulings (such as directed verdicts, judgments notwithstanding the verdict, etc.) which often turn on the probative force of the evidence (see infra).

Several areas where the balancing process described earlier is quite evident will be indicated in the immediately succeeding sections (in addition to areas that are treated elsewhere in the present work).

Some Illustrations of the Balancing Process: Insurance; Financial Standing

In most jurisdictions evidence revealing liability insurance is inadmissible save in exceptional situations. Similar authority exists with respect to showing financial strength or weakness of the parties.

Evidence or mention or suggestion that the defendant is insured against the kind of liability being pressed in the lawsuit is regarded as highly prejudicial because (a) the jury is believed likely to overemphasize the tendency of insurance to render the holder careless (does insurance in fact suggest carelessness to any degree, or rather, foresight and prudence?) and/or (b) the jury is believed prone to "pin the bill on the deepest pocket." Frequently, however, it is found that the balancing spoken of above swings in favor of admission (perhaps only if there are cautionary instructions to the jury exhorting against the evils) where (1) there are circumstances rendering inference (a) above extremely reliable (e. g., defendant says immediately prior to the collision, "I have insurance, so I don't care if I hit anything"); or (2) the evidence is regarded as having some direct impeachment or contradicting value (e. g., defendant *says* he is *not* insured); or (3) there is some substantial admission or other important piece of evidence relatively unseverable from the evidence of insurance; or (4) there is a difficult issue of ownership of a vehicle or other item that can be most expeditiously and accurately resolved by reference to the insurance policy covering the vehicle or item; or (5) the insurance company is the real party in interest and a witness for that side is to be impeached by a showing of his connection with that company or a similar company; or (6) jurors are sought to be disqualified on the same basis. To minimize prejudice in this last situation, many jurisdictions inquire into insurance affiliation as a matter of routine in every case, on a form or in a general session, directed at the entire panel of prospective jurors before any jury is selected or assigned to a particular case. In certain other jurisdictions, inquiry will not be permitted unless there is evidence of affiliation on the part of the prospective juror to be questioned. Consider the propriety of inquiry into insurance affiliation of a juror or his family where none of the parties is insured, on grounds that such affiliation might make the juror "defense minded".

Before the "exceptions to the ban on insurance evidence" outlined above will be applied, and the evidence admitted, the judge will have to be convinced that probativity is not outweighed by the other factors (prejudice, etc.) discussed earlier herein, on the particular facts. Limiting and cautionary instructions to the jury, guarding against the "bad" effects—e. g., telling the jury that the insurance may not be considered as evidence of negligence or ability to bear the burden, or cautioning against over-valuation of the evidence —may help and are frequently given.

Some jurisdictions have taken the view that insurance may be inquired into upon discovery, even though it may not be used in evidence. (It is interesting to consider what reasons may be behind such a rule. Is it a desire to increase the likelihood of settlement?)

The subject of defendant's ability to pay is particularly in issue where punitive damages are requested, because such damages should have sting. Should the presence of a claim for punitive damages increase the chances of his insurance being considered discoverable and/or admissible? If so, wouldn't litigants be tempted to add perhaps unsupportable claims for punitive damages? Courts are in disagreement as to what to do in this area. One solution might be to preliminarily screen such claims to see if they are totally unfounded.

In the absence of something suggesting to the jury that the defendant is insured against the liability being pressed in the case, he may not introduce evidence that he is not so insured. How much is required before he can so show varies, but the fact that juries in general assume defendants are insured, or the fact that defendant's counsel is a well-known insurance company lawyer, will not normally be sufficient. It is otherwise, however, if plaintiff inquires, on jury *voir dire*, into connection with insurance companies. (Such inquiry by plaintiff on *voir dire* might be permitted by some courts even though the defendant is uninsured, e. g., where a co-defendant is insured or where the court believes insurance affiliation results in general defense-mindedness.) Consider how it affects these problems that there may be doubts about coverage or the extent of coverage.[3]

[3] Doubts concerning the extent to which a policy may cover a certain event is another reason why courts are reluctant to get into the

F.R.E. 411 codifies many of the above principles concerning insurance. It is a good example of the general approach of many of the Federal Rules. It provides that the evidence is inadmissible to prove certain things (negligence or wrongful conduct) but may be admissible for other purposes. It does not say that the evidence is *admissible* for those other purposes; merely that such evidence is then relieved of the automatic ban expressed by this rule. Admissibility then is to be controlled by the *ad hoc* balancing process (on the facts of the particular case) described above preceding this section, codified by Rule 403, assuming, as is ordinarily the case, that the particular piece of evidence is not in an area controlled by some other specific rule.

Evidence of a plaintiff's or defendant's wealth or lack thereof bears certain resemblances to insurance evidence, but has not been sufficiently manifest in recurring pattern situations to result in a relatively definite rule like insurance. But the reader should not be surprised to find the evidence frequently excluded for reasons similar to those operable in the insurance area, except where roughly similar exceptional circumstances can be shown swinging the balancing factors toward admissibility. For example, if there is a dispute as to whether A bought an expensive item for his own account, or as agent for B, the relative strengths and weaknesses of their wealth might be received to illuminate the likelihoods. Similarly, a legitimate claim for punitive damages might change the balance.

insurance question at all in a case not directly concerned with that issue.

Some Illustrations of the Balancing Process: Offering Results of Experiments (Done in or Out of Court) that Attempt to Re-create a Litigated Event or Some Portion Thereof, and Offering Models, Photos, Graphic Representations, etc.

In most jurisdictions the test for this kind of evidence is that the replication must be substantially similar to the thing replicated.

The inquiry the court makes here is into whether there is any dissimilarity in the experiment, model, etc., from the actual conditions, of a kind that is likely to make a significant difference that would be difficult for the jury to detect or assess (or difficult to detect or assess without excessive time being spent in the essentially collateral matter of ascertaining, clarifying, and describing the effect of the variances). A prima facie case of acceptability on these scores must be shown, or appear from the other evidence or the thing itself, before the opponent has the burden to show anything in order to bar the evidence. This is the "foundation" that must be laid. Some courts have said that if the prima facie case is made, the evidence is admissible and contrary showings are merely matters of weight unless they reveal a very severe deficiency.

In the case of experiments, the more technical the area, the more the court suspects there may be differences of some consequence, and will need to be convinced otherwise. In a non-technical area, the court may be willing to assume, without much of a showing, that there are no significant differences. In the case of explanatory aids such as charts, the court considers, in addition to the factors mentioned earlier, the need for this kind of explanation, and the effect of giving the jury double information on one selected aspect of the case (if the chart summarizes other evidence). Similar selective overemphasis may occur if the exhibit is allowed to go to the jury room.

The Federal Rules drafters apparently felt the fact situations that come up in these areas are so diverse that no rule could be fashioned. They left the matter to the general balancing process described herein in earlier sections and codified in Rule 403. Under that standard, the "significant difference" test and other factors described in this section continue to be the test.

Opportunity *vel non* for the other side to participate in an experiment is usually considered only a matter of weight, as is the factor of whether the test was conducted by an impartial (court-appointed or bilaterally agreed upon) expert.

Some Illustrations of the Balancing Process: Scientific Evidence (Evidence of the Results of Blood-type Comparisons; Intoxication Tests; Radar Speed Clocking; Lie Detector Tests; Fingerprinting; Ballistics Examinations; Handwriting Analyses; Voiceprinting; etc.)

More traditional varieties of this evidence have been freely received with little difficulty, and the rule seems to be that they are admissible if proper procedures were employed. Newer varieties have been tested by three different standards: (1) the predominant or so-called "Frye" test requiring general acceptance of the principle by the relevant scientific community; (2) whatever test the particular jurisdiction applies to expert testimony generally (see page 58 infra); or (3) a "substantial similarity" test like that of the last section herein, requiring the experiments establishing the validity of the technique to conform to the actual conditions under which the technique was used in the case at bar.

It would seem that the central problem under the balancing process, in the area of the kinds of scientific evidence described in the main heading above, is one of insuring that the real reliability of the evidence approaches that with which the jurors endow it, considering their susceptibility to being "snowed" by science. Thus the principal questions are whether (1) the theory, (2) the apparatus, (3) the manner of conducting the test, (4) the operator, and (5) the report, are reliable, (a) in general and (b) in this particular instance; and whether the extent of unreliability is readily assessable by a lay jury. The various "tests" for admissibility of scientific evidence are probably merely ways to predetermine or enable the judge to determine one or more of these questions.

Sometimes a judgment of unacceptability will have been made by the decisional (or occasionally statutory) law of the jurisdiction, for a class of evidence as a whole. Most jurisdictions have taken this approach to lie detector (polygraph) evidence, and somewhat more than half have with respect to "voiceprint" (sound spectrograph) evidence. In the case of the polygraph, the unreliability of interpreting the data recorded is the principal concern.

Sometimes the reliability of the general theory and type of machinery or apparatus will have been accepted as a matter of law, and no showing thereof will be required, as in the case of the standard theories of fingerprint, handwriting, and ballistics evidence in most jurisdictions. Where this has been done, a prima facie showing ("foundation") that the particular machinery, mode of conducting, operator, and report were proper is required upon offer of the evidence. This foundation will usually be furnished by the testing expert himself.

Sometimes the middle position is taken: the reliability of the theory and type of machinery or apparatus must be established as part of the foundation (along with the other foundational matters just described) by the evidence in each particular case. Under this position, different forums may reach different results, even within the same state or jurisdiction. Indeed, even the same judge may reach different results on the general acceptability of the same technique in different cases, depending upon what is put into each record concerning the technique.

Which of these three positions (blanket inadmissibility; narrow foundation; or broad foundation) is taken usually is related to the state of maturity or development of the scientific technique—in its infancy, it is more suspect.

With respect to the ever increasing array of new scientific forms of evidence, courts have tried to articulate various "tests" for when the probative-prejudice-protraction-etc. balance swings to make the theory and type of machinery acceptable. These are the "tests" enumerated in the subheading above. The most prevalent one, articulated in Frye v. United States, 293 F. 1013 (D.C.Cir. 1923), a case rejecting lie detector evidence, requires that "[t]he [theory] from which the deduction is made [must] be sufficiently established to have gained general acceptance in the field in which it belongs." This has had wide currency even beyond lie detector cases (e. g., in cases involving voice identification by spectrography or "voiceprints," on the admissibility of which courts are badly split), despite questions about how broadly to construe the relevant "field" (e. g., in the case of voiceprints: voiceprint practitioners? sound physicists? physicists generally? acoustical engineers? engineers generally?) and what "general acceptance" means (how large a slice of the "field" must accept? what must they accept? that it has X% reliability, or that the percent reliability is sufficient for certain purposes? what purposes—scientific or legal?). This test, requiring a rather high degree of reliability, has tended to be applied to scientific evidence having a "black box" mystique or great potential for "snowing" the jury or for concluding a very central issue or one deemed peculiarly within the jury's province, such as credibility—i. e., evidence that is very prejudicial because of an illusion of scientific infallibility on a "heartland" issue. It is to be wondered whether the test in such cases is exactly the opposite of what it should be. It would seem that the more accepted a technique, the fewer experts there are to point out the shortcomings of the evidence to the jury. Additionally, the relevant "field," if construed narrowly, may consist of the very people who have an interest in the use of the technique in litigation. And why should the "field," and not the courts, determine acceptable levels of reliability (once the scientific community supplies the reliability figure the technique possesses), especially if the "field's" primary occupation is law enforcement or litigation (as with polygraphs and voiceprints) as opposed to a field that has other incentives to accuracy (e. g., medicine). A mechanism for effective self-certification should also be required. Courts generally state, in applying this test, that if the test is failed, the evidence is inadmissible whatever showings of reliability may be made to the court. It has been suggested that this ought not to be the case—that the *Frye* test should merely control whether judicial notice of reliability of the theory will be taken without evidence thereof.

Another "test" courts have applied for identifying when the balance swings in favor of admissibility has been the "substantial similarity" test originally intended for evidence that attempts to re-create a litigated event. See the section immediately previous to this section hereinabove. This test requires that it be shown that the studies establishing the reliability of a process such as voiceprint identification, actually involved experiments having conditions substantially similar to the real forensic conditions surrounding the evidence used at trial. For example, the real voiceprint at trial may have been taken through a poorer set of equipment; or there may be a difference in the examiner's foreknowledge of what the results should be; or there may have been an attempt to disguise the voice; or the voice may have used a dialect or had a foreign accent.

Other "tests" applied have been those noted at No. (3) on p. 58 governing expert testimony generally. The line between when the "tests" of the present section should apply and when only the "tests" described there should be applied has never been satisfactorily delineated—usually medicine, the social sciences, economics, psychiatry, and the like have been treated according to the latter only. As will be noted, there are at least two alternative tests there: Permissive jurisdictions ask "Will the testimony be of any assistance to the trier-of-fact?" Others ask "Is the [ultimate] matter [totally] beyond lay ken?", which tends more to exclude here. Conceptually, the "tests" of the *present* section may be viewed as an attempt to define when the "of-assistance-to-the-trier-of-fact" test (codified by F.R.E. 702) is satisfied as to certain scientific evidence, and both may be viewed as particularizations of the probative-prejudice-time-etc. balance codified by F.R.E. 403. For a somewhat contrary view, see State v. Williams, 388 A.2d 500 (Me.1978) (Maine Rules, similar to Federal Rules, meant to overturn *Frye* test; voiceprint evidence admitted pursuant to "of assistance" test); United States v. Williams, 583 F.2d 1194 (2d Cir. 1978) (similar ruling under F.R.E.). See also National Academy of Sciences, "On the Theory and Practice of Voice Identification" (1979), reviewed 17 Amer.Crim.L.Rev. 153 (1979).

A small number of courts in the area of scientific evidence have attempted a naked balancing of factors, without a "test," an approach which in practice often results in concentration on the reliability factor; or have tried to hinge admissibility on such factors as whether the case is civil or criminal; which party is offering the evidence; what issue is it offered upon (a substantive or a credibility issue, and what particular substantive or credibility issue); is it a judge or jury trial; the availability of scientific rebuttal testimony; what other evidence there is; how needed the scientific evidence is; how determinative the scientific evidence will be; is it corroborated; was the result of the scientific procedure positive or negative; the degree of certainty or uncertainty of the finding; the precision with which only the warranted degree of certainty is expressed to the jury by the expert, and the balanced nature of his presentation; the availability and effectiveness of cautionary instructions or even more extensive impartial comment or material stemming from the judge or his appointee; is the witness a court appointed impartial expert; the nature of any agreements or stipulations between the parties respecting the employment of the technique or use of the evidence; were certain safeguards taken when the technique was administered (e. g., presence of counsel; safeguards against suggestibility; court-appointment or impartiality of the expert; the training of the expert); etc. Of course we are always assuming the procedure was properly conducted, with proper equipment in proper repair.

A number of courts hold that even stipulation of the parties cannot make certain scientific evidence admissible.

The federal courts have not been any more unified than other courts in their approach to scientific evidence. The Federal Rules of Evidence have not directly addressed the problem, leaving it to the general probativity-prejudice balancing provisions of Rule 403 and the general requirement that expert testimony be of a kind that will "assist" the trier-of-fact (Rule 702—probably a particularization of the 403 factors). As the tests discussed in the present section of our text are generally viewed merely as efforts to define when factors like those in 403 are satisfied or when the evidence is "of assistance," the prevalent attitude seems to be that tests such as the *Frye* test, etc. persist even after adoption of the Federal Rules. See, e. g., United States v. Kilgus, 571 F.2d 508 (9th Cir. 1978) ("forward looking infrared system" for distinguishing among night flying planes of same model; evidence rejected); United States v. Brown, 557 F.2d 541 (6th Cir. 1977) ("ion microprobic analysis" for comparison and identification of hair samples; evidence rejected). On the other hand, the drafters' comments to F.R.E. Rules 702–706 relating to expert testimony generally, evince an intent to increase receptivity to expert testimony and to widen the kinds of things experts may rely on and report. This has been seized upon by a few courts to broaden admissibility of the kind of scientific evidence discussed here. See, e. g., the two *Williams* cases, supra. In addition, the broadening, under F.R.E. 405 and 608, of the reception of "opinion" on the issue of character offered for substantive or credibility purposes, could be argued to broaden receptivity to the opinion of lie detector experts, psychologists and psychiatrists, etc. See discussion in Ch. 8. Nevertheless, these problems were not addressed directly in the Federal Rules.

If any of the tests discussed in the present section are viewed as more than merely a particularization of the probative-prejudice-time-etc. balance codified in F.R.E. 403 (or of the similar principle found in F.R.E. 702 that expert testimony must be of *of assistance* to the trier-of-fact), then a good argument may be made that the test does not survive passage of the Federal Rules (or the state equivalent of the Federal Rules) because F.R.E. 402 provides that all relevant evidence (which this evidence almost always is) is admissible unless excluded pursuant to other of the Rules, other statutorily authorized rules of the Supreme Court, or the Constitution or a statute—none of which embrace these tests, which are usually a matter of decisional law. In other words, there may be no common-law evidence power surviving with which to impose these tests. Will the Constitution permit such infringement of the judicial power? Does this bring the test within the reference to the Constitution in Rule 402? Could Rule 501 be invoked?

Respecting particular kinds of scientific evidence (in state and federal courts), the more recognized forms of blood type comparisons (at least where offered in their conclusive aspect[4]), are not excluded per se and do get to the stage where a foundation showing (jurisdictions vary as to how extensive) will get them received.

The more standard varieties of blood, breath, or urine tests for intoxication by alcohol or drugs are meeting with increasing favor, as are radar and "vascar" speed detection

---

[4] A blood typing expert will say (for example in a paternity case) that fathers having certain blood types, when mated with mothers having certain blood types, can produce children of only certain blood types and not others. Thus, while the expert may be able to say this man could not be the father by this mother of this child (where all their blood types are known), the expert could never say this man *is* the father, but at most only that a man of *the same blood-type as this man* is the father. Nevertheless, this latter testimony would seem to be at least *relevant* as tested by the standard of relevancy at the opening of this chapter, and probative in an amount inversely proportional to the size of the class having this man's blood-type.

Similarly, there is a conclusive and an inconclusive side to blood-type comparisons used to establish whose blood stains were found at a particular scene or on a suspect's clothes.

Courts have been more reluctant to let in the evidence in its inconclusive aspect. Why? Isn't it relevant to narrow the field? Cf. People v. Sturdivant, 91 Mich.App. 128, 283 N.W.2d 669 (1979) (similar problem in sperm identification).

Courts have split on the question of when a jury must find in accord with the obvious conclusions from blood-type comparisons offered in their conclusive aspect, where there is little evidence pointing to a contrary conclusion, no contrary blood comparison evidence, and no evidence directed at impugning the reliability of the theory or the procedure in the particular case. Many courts have allowed the jury almost complete freedom in this regard. On what theory might a jury disregard such apparently conclusive evidence?

techniques, although radar has recently been experiencing set-backs that threaten to turn the tide. E. g., State v. Aquilera, 25 Crim.L.Rptr. 2189 (Dade County, Fla.1979). On hypnotizing a witness for greater recall, see State v. Mack, 292 N.W.2d 764 (Minn.1980). Frequently a jurisdiction will have a statute prescribing the conditions under which scientific speed or intoxication evidence will be received and its legal effect under various circumstances. Indeed, the law (particularly the case law) of the particular jurisdiction on the particular technique must be closely checked as respects *all* scientific evidence. The field is fast changing. Techniques mature. Or new ones or new variations are invented. In addition, your legal research should be directed not at, for example, "radar speed detection" or "blood typing," but rather at the specific *variety* involved in your case, since there are many competing methods of each, some more accepted than others. Newer techniques tend to be less accepted than older ones, but as time passes they often achieve more acceptability.

It must be noted that in the absence of proper consent to certain of the scientific or medical procedures discussed in this section, conducted on certain parties or witnesses, a problem of compelled self-incrimination conceivably could arise. The Supreme Court has held, however, that the *federal* constitutional privilege against self-incrimination protects only against *testimonial* self-incrimination. Schmerber v. California, 384 U.S. 757, 86 S.Ct. 1826 (1966) (extraction of blood did not violate privilege); United States v. Dionisio, 410 U.S. 1, 93 S.Ct. 764 (1973) (requiring voice exemplars for comparison and identification did not violate privilege). This would seem to exclude from the federal privilege many of these procedures. Extremely barbaric or offensive practices (for example stomach pumping to obtain evidence as in Rochin v. California, 342 U.S. 165, 72 S.Ct. 205 (1952)), may violate general due process. Consider also the constitutional right to counsel (infra, p. 310) and right to be free of unreasonable searches and seizures (infra, pp. 474–5). *Schmerber* and *Dionisio* also discuss a number of these other constitutional rights, finding no violation on the facts. Violation of a constitutional right may result in inadmissibility.

Some Illustrations of the Balancing Process: Miscellaneous Areas of Broad Judicial Discretion

Where fact patterns tend to be highly individual, where experience has been insufficient to enable the law to decree in advance what is and is not desirable, and where close reference to the particular facts of the case is felt to be needed, the law has made little or no prescription as to how the balancing should come out, and leaves the matter to the discretion of the trial judge, often with little practical review because of the breadth allowed before abuse of discretion will be found.

One such area is the permissibility of exhibiting a child in a paternity suit, in order to establish resemblance. In practice, where the child is very young, such evidence of resemblance or non-resemblance is considered by most judges to be less reliable than the jury would suppose. It is frequently said that the conflicting inferences of resemblance and non-resemblance are so equally likely that it would not be reasonable for a juror to draw either inference. The jury is not trusted to appreciate this; or it is felt that the jury will appreciate it and the evidence will be a waste of time. Sometimes the interests of the child and the convenience of the mother play a role.

Another such area is the permissibility of exhibiting one's bodily condition or a picture thereof, or demonstrating in court bodily ability or inability to move or feel pain, or the like, say in a personal injury lawsuit. Again, as a practical matter, judges are wary of the inflammatory nature of such evidence and the ease with which it can be "faked." They feel that juries are not so wary. While courtroom ploys such as suddenly knocking away the crutches of, or passing amongst the jury the glass eye of, or sticking pins in the paralyzed limbs of, a personal injury plaintiff have been sanctioned (see, e. g., cases in Note, 14 Brooklyn L.Rev. 261 (1948)), judges generally view such histrionics with disfavor. The trial judge is allowed considerable latitude either way, however, by the appellate courts.

One sometimes puzzling phenomenon has been the relatively free admission by courts of evidence offered on a theory that it shows "background" enabling the jury to "picture" the case more readily. This has included such matters as the witnesses' or parties' occupations and addresses, weapons in assault and homicide cases, photos of the body, etc. While frequently this is valuable, frequently it is not. In a large number of cases the legitimate increment such evidence makes over what is already known or can be known by other means, is very small; and therefore one would suppose that any prejudice or time consumption would play a great role in the determination of admissibility. For example, if in a murder case there is no issue of self-defense or the like that would make the exact positioning of the stab wounds important, or if their position could be established as well orally or by stipulation, there would seem to be little reason to allow a picture of the body showing the stab wounds, which might only serve to incite the jury to convict *somebody*. Similarly, in a tort case where personal injuries or bodily or motion impairment could be described as satisfactorily orally or by stipulation, why allow a picture or demonstration? It might be otherwise if the disfigurement had healed or been cured by plastic surgery by the time of trial and words could not dispel the impression that very little had happened to the plaintiff.

Curative and Cautionary Instructions to the Jury

> **Throughout the study of Evidence, you will find the judge ordering the jurors to disregard certain evidence (or argument or other matter) that has erroneously gotten before them. (Mistrials, as an additional or alternative remedy, are seldom granted and occur only where an instruction to disregard is deemed insufficient to cure the prejudice, a rare finding. In addition, mistrials for the government in criminal cases may in certain circumstances present double jeopardy problems which judges are anxious to avoid.)**

Where jurors are ordered to disregard a piece of evidence they think is of some probative value, they are going to be influenced by that piece of evidence anyway, to a greater extent than if it had never gotten before them. This is so despite the usual judicial reluctance, for pragmatic reasons, to recognize that it is so. Consider a case where the evidence to be disregarded is very relevant and probative and not at all prejudicial (as we use that term), but is impermissible for policy reasons wholly extrinsic to trial. For example, very logically persuasive (indeed, even determinative) evidence having no impact beyond what is rationally warranted, may be inadmissible because of the doctor-patient privilege, designed to encourage persons to make full disclosure to their doctors, confident in the knowledge that nothing they say can ever be used against them. Will the jury be able to disregard?

Or suppose the jury is instructed to disregard a confession because it is involuntary. Suppose in addition they know the gun has been found where the confession relates the confessor buried it. The effect of the instruction will be minimal.

It is questionable whether and to what extent a jury heeds an instruction not to consider the fact that the accused invoked his privilege against self-incrimination and did not testify; an instruction that evidence of defendant's insurance should not be considered in a personal injury case; an instruction that prior crimes and other evidence of the bad character of the accused should not be considered; or an instruction that hearsay should be disregarded. Indeed, such instructions may be like telling someone not to think of elephants. It invites the very thing it purports to prohibit. Counsel may want to think twice before asking for such an instruction. (Could it be given anyway?)

An instruction to disregard may in some instances alert the jurors that the law regards the evidence as suspect, and may cause them to devaluate its force somewhat more than they are inclined to—in short, to utilize the evidence with caution. Perhaps such devaluation is all that should happen and all that should be asked, rather than complete nullification, where the evidence deserves some weight and the only concern of the law is a fear of over-valuation. The instruction, then, should be more particularly explanatory about what is wrong with the evidence. Only if the jury understands can it cooperate.

> **Sometimes evidence is admissible for only one of several possible purposes, or for or against only one of several joined parties. The jury, by means of instruction, is supposedly confined to considering the evidence for that use only.**

The problems here are much the same as described above in connection with the instruction to completely disregard. The following instructions are typical of instructions that are given in this connection. Consider what efficacy they will have beyond alerting the jury, in a not too precise way, to possible weight-devaluing considerations concerning the evidence. Will they invite the prohibited inference? Will they be given if not requested? (a) "John's confession [stating 'George and I did it' and narrating details of the planning and execution of the crime] can be taken against John but not against George, his co-defendant." (b) "The evidence of past criminal acts of the accused introduced in this case, other than the crime charged, can be considered only insofar as they impeach his truth-telling ability on the stand, impeach his good character witnesses by showing they do not know all about the defendant, or establish his intent or motive with respect to the crime charged. Although they are very similar to the crime charged, they may not be considered to render it more likely that the defendant is the sort who would commit the crime charged, or who should be punished regardless of what he did in this case." (c) "The defendant's testimony that he is qualified to give an opinion of what is a safe speed on a certain road may be impeached by evidence of his prior collisions, but those collisions may not be considered with respect to the likelihood he was responsible for the present collision." (d) "A previous statement made by a witness that is wholly inconsistent with his present testimony may not be taken as evidence of the facts stated, since it was made out of court. But it may be deemed to raise a doubt of the witness' credibility on either occasion." (e) "Similar injuries on the same premises are not evidence of negligence or the happening of the injury in controversy, but they may be considered on the issues of the existence of, and notice of, a dangerous condition." (f) "Safety measures taken to remedy a condition that allegedly produced injury are not evidence of negligence, are not admissions, but they may be taken as evidence of the existence of a dangerous condition." Such instructions may be given when the evidence is introduced, or at the close of all the evidence and argument, or both.

[*32*]

One area in which jurors are frequently requested to "compartmentalize" their minds in the fashion discussed just above, is the hearsay area, where quite often a piece of evidence is excludable hearsay if used for one purpose, but permissible if used for another purpose, both possible in the same case. As in most cases of "multiple admissibility" (i. e., cases where there is a permitted and a prohibited potential use of the evidence), the evidence is usually admitted for the permitted purpose (with cautionary instructions given at the opponent's option) notwithstanding the danger of an improper use. Only in an aggravated case is this not so.

Two not atypical examples will suffice to illustrate:

In a suit for alienation of his wife's affections plaintiff had to prove (1) a change in the wife's state of mind toward him (2) induced by the defendant. Evidence was offered that the wife had recently said to the husband that she had received various attentions from the defendant which she welcomed and would continue to welcome and that the husband was distasteful to her. This was admissible on issue (1) under an exception to the hearsay rule for state of mind, but inadmissible hearsay on issue (2). The court held the evidence would be admitted under proper limiting instructions. (Why not sever the wife's statement in two and admit only the part about the husband being distasteful? This is an option available to the judge, which will often be utilized unless it is felt that the omission would unduly mislead or distort.)

In a suit for defamation plaintiff offered testimony of his foreman that workers had, in quitting plaintiff's employ, given as a reason therefor that defendant had said plaintiff's materials with which they had to work, were unsafe. This statement of defendant was the defamation alleged, and the exodus of the workers constituted the claimed damages. The court held that the foreman's report of what the workers said could be offered to prove the damage was attributable to the defamation, but not to prove the defamation had been uttered or uttered by the defendant. The former purpose came within an exception to the hearsay rule for state of mind, but the latter did not. The court held that since there was other evidence of the utterance of the defamation by defendant, the exclusion of the evidence was reversible error.

The court seems to be saying, in multiple admissibility cases of these and other kinds where the evidence is admitted for the permitted purpose, that the legitimate probative value of the evidence is so increased by the presence of the additional issue (i. e., the issue on which the evidence would be permitted), that the probative-prejudice balance swings in favor of admission if proper safeguards are observed.

When a court must decide whether to admit evidence capable in the same case of one permissible and one impermissible use, or exclude it, in theory the court goes through the same percentage-of-probability calculus we discussed earlier under the "probativity-prejudice-etc." balancing (*including consideration of whether a limiting instruction would change the balance*). In practice the evidence is usually admitted with a cautionary instruction given at the option of the objecting party.

A similar balancing process would apply whenever a court must decide whether erroneously received evidence can be cured to the extent necessary to avoid the need for a new trial, by an instruction (e. g. an instruction to strike from all consideration).

It is often suggested in decisions that the judge in a non-jury trial is more able to disregard or regard only for certain purposes, than a jury would be in a jury trial.

[*34*]

It is difficult to verify this proposition, and courts are uneven about applying it. It would seem that much would depend on the particular evidence.

The United States Supreme Court has increasingly recognized the inefficacy of instructions to prevent prejudicial uses that the Constitution protects against.

The Supreme Court has held (in different decisions) that an instruction to the jury to disregard an involuntary confession will not cure error in its admission; that at least in certain circumstances a co-defendant's confession implicating the defendant cannot be introduced in a joint trial without opportunity of the latter to effectively cross examine the confessor (which would in all likelihood be barred by the privilege against self incrimination), despite instructions to the jury that the confession cannot be used against the non-confessor; and that a jury instruction to disregard evidence of former convictions that were obtained without counsel was inadequate to prevent a holding that consequences flowed from the counsel-less proceedings in the present proceeding, in violation of the constitutional right to counsel. These results must obtain now in both federal and state proceedings, it would seem.

Judicial Comment on Weight of Evidence

Many jurisdictions have a rule against the judge commenting to the jury on the weight to be ascribed to evidence. In others, the judge may give balanced and fair comment concerning what weight he believes should be ascribed to evidence in the case, so long as the jurors are given to understand that they are free to decide the weight for themselves.

In federal courts, judges are allowed to (but seldom do) give their views as to weight, so long as their comments do

not surpass the bounds of the judicious. The express deletion of the power to comment from the Federal Rules of
Evidence (see draft Rule 105, 56 F.R.D. 183, 1972, ultimately
deleted) was not intended to abridge this power. Rather
the subject was deemed to be a matter of "procedure," not
"evidence." The thought also seems to have been, however, that codifying the power would over-encourage its use.
Dubbed "controversial," the power was left with the judge,
subject to future Congressional re-consideration.

Sometimes the power to comment is expressed more
cautiously as a power to "marshal" or "summarize" the
evidence.

Insofar as they in effect caution against exaggeration and
possible probative infirmities in the evidence, the instructions discussed in the last sections above (i. e., instructions
to disregard or only regard in certain connections) could
seem to violate a ban on judicial comment on weight.
Similarly, as we shall see, instructions given a jury about the
existence of a *presumption* (a presumption of the sort that
has a common sense basis) are in fact instructions that a
certain inference may or must be drawn from proved facts
to unproved under certain conditions; and as such they
could seem also to be judicial comment on the weight of
the evidence. Nevertheless, neither of these categories of
instruction is considered to come within the ban on comment.

It is axiomatic that even in jurisdictions allowing the
judge to comment on the weight of evidence, the jury is
the final arbiter on matters of weight of evidence, and may
reject the advice (comment) altogether. But unless the
judge is careful in his phrasing, it may be difficult for the
jury to tell what is a mandatory legal *direction* and what
merely advice. Some of the judge's directions—those on
matters of law—are indeed binding, and may be difficult to
distinguish from comment on weight, which is advisory

only. In both "comment" and "no comment" jurisdictions, there may in addition be certain standard instructions that are given describing just what factual inferences are warranted and unwarranted from various kinds of admissible evidence. Not every admissible piece of evidence carries with it such an instruction. Sometimes a party is *entitled* of right to the instruction, sometimes it is purely discretionary, and sometimes it would be error to give such an instruction. The law, practice, and permissible forms of these and other jury instructions, in the particular jurisdiction, must be studied. Bar associations and others in particular jurisdictions often put together books of "pattern" jury instructions (both substantive and evidentiary) which frequently achieve official or quasi-official status through use and approval by the courts there.

While law makers and courts have not often realized it, liberalization of the law of evidence, to increase admissibility and judicial discretion, may be more acceptable where a power to comment (warn against pitfalls) is also incorporated. For example, the liberalized reception of hearsay evidence and of expert testimony on ultimate issues found under the Federal Rules of Evidence and some of the state codes following suit makes more sense if the jury can be judicially cautioned about the evidence's weight.

A judge has the prerogative in most jurisdictions to examine, and even call, witnesses himself if he deems it necessary. Obviously exercise of this power can, depending on how it is done, imply a view regarding the weight of evidence. He must be careful not to do by indirection what the jurisdiction's view on commenting would not permit directly.

Legal Argument

While largely unregulated, trial argument is subject to some limits growing out of the rules of

**admissibility of evidence, the Code of Professional
Responsibility, and local practice.**

The limitations on legal argumentation concerning evidence are implicit in the rules respecting the evidence itself, as will become increasingly apparent. In addition to this, opening and closing arguments and summations are limited by "balancing" considerations similar to those discussed above, administered with a large measure of discretion. The American Bar Association's Code of Professional Responsibility and judicial and other interpretations thereof also directly or indirectly impose some limits. For example, banned are statements in which the attorney in opening or closing argument refers to his own personal knowledge or own personal belief in the truth or falsity of the evidence or of his own or his opponent's case or clients. See the Code, DR 7–106; A.B.A. Defense Function Standards, § 7.6; A.B.A. Prosecution Function Standards, § 5.8; Melinkoff, Lawyers and the System of Justice (West, 1976) pp. 608 et seq. (Incidentally, a lawyer becoming a witness in a case he is handling, presents very similar problems.)   On lawyers weeping during argument, see Ferguson v. Moore, 98 Tenn. 342, 39 S.W. 341 (1897); People v. McGrane, 12 A.D.2d 465, 207 N.Y.S.2d 88 (1960); People v. Dukes, 12 Ill.2d 334, 146 N.E.2d 14 (1957).

Local practice of particular courts, sometimes embodied in rulings or appellate decisions, also operates. Thus, we frequently find a ban on the so-called "per diem" argument whereby counsel for a personal injury plaintiff, in closing argument asks the jurors to imagine what pay they themselves would want in order for them to voluntarily undergo for one day (or hour or minute) pain, suffering or disability like the plaintiff's; and asks them to multiply that figure by the duration or expected duration (perhaps a lifetime) of the plaintiff's pain, suffering, or disability. This argument has many variations.

Also banned, of course, are opening or closing arguments going beyond inferences the evidence in the case will bear, or going beyond the applicable law. (Thus it may be a good idea to find out what the judge will instruct on the law, before closing argument.) See DR 7–106; Defense Function Standards, §§ 7.4, 7.8, 7.9; Prosecution Function Standards, §§ 5.5, 5.8, 5.9. Along these lines, juries are frequently instructed that statements of the attorneys are not evidence. Lawyers are fond of telling the juries this about the statements of their opponents, or, more subtly, about their own statements (in order to curry favor as fair-minded persons).

The purpose of an opening statement is to tell what the evidence will be and what it will show in the light of the issues in the case. Closing statements perform a similar function looking back at the trial retrospectively, but with somewhat more latitude. See Defense Function Standards, § 7.4; Prosecution Function Standards, § 5.5; cf. DR 7–106.

Many lawyers and judges follow a practice of extreme reluctance to interrupt an opening or closing argument of a lawyer except for very good cause.

Attorneys sometimes use evidentiary objections and associated or responsive statements or arguments to communicate certain matters to the witness, or to the jury (rather than waiting for final argument), or to fluster or break the dramatic impact of the opponent. These practices are highly questionable. Evidentiary matters that are likely to influence the jury unduly are more properly taken up at the bench ("may we approach the bench, your honor"), or in chambers, or before the trial. Good practice in these respects, however, is very frequently allowed to be breached: Evidentiary matters are often raised aloud in open court in the jury's hearing, apparently in the interests of expedition.

For an interesting, practical, and colorful book on legal argument, see Stein, Closing Argument—The Art and the Law (Callaghan & Co., 1976).

Order of Presentation of Evidence at Trial

The basic pattern of trial is that each party puts his case on in turn, subjecting each of his witnesses to the hammer of cross examination by the other side immediately after the party's own direct examination of the witness.

The usual order of presentation at a civil trial is (1) plaintiff's main case in chief (witnesses, documents, and other evidence); (2) the defendant's main case in defense (witnesses, documents, and other evidence, not only those denying facts asserted in plaintiff's main case in chief, but also those tending to establish affirmative defenses, if any); (3) plaintiff's rebuttal case (witnesses [possibly some of the same as appeared earlier], documents, and other evidence, supposedly confined to rebutting the defendant's main case in defense, absent an exercise of the judge's discretion); and (4) defendant's rejoinder evidence, in theory confined to new matter introduced by plaintiff in the last numbered stage. This stage will normally be omitted if there is no such new matter. Then follows argument of counsel (usually opened and closed by plaintiff) and the judge's instructions to the jury (there may also have been some instructions during the presentation of evidence). (Some courts give the end-of-the-case jury instructions *before* closing argument so that the arguments will be presented and received in the light of the instructions.) At each of the above numbered stages, a witness presented at that stage will normally be, in uninterrupted sequence, (1) examined directly by the counsel presenting him; (2) cross examined by opposing counsel; (3) perhaps subjected to a re-direct examination by the counsel who presented him, to repair the damage of cross examination; and (4) perhaps subjected to a re-cross examination by opposing counsel, to repair the damage of the re-direct. In the absence of an exercise of the judge's discretion, repair is the only acceptable purpose of the last two. Furthermore, they may be severely limited or even disallowed completely by the judge in the interests of time or avoidance of redundancy where he feels the contribution would be minimal.

If the defendant admits the plaintiff's main case in chief before it is presented, and relies on affirmative defenses, he opens the proof, and may open and close argument to the jury, a much coveted right.

The order of presentation in a criminal trial is basically the same.

Method of Examination of Witnesses

Material is generally elicited from witnesses through a series of narrow, specific questions capable of short (yes-no) type answers.

In many jurisdictions the trial judge's discretion to permit a different format than the preferred specific "yes or no" questions and answers—i. e., to permit an extended narrative presentation by the witness—is being increasingly upheld on the theory that getting the witness' own words and story may sometimes be more important than requiring that the examining attorney have precise control over the exact order of points, or than the need to forewarn the opponent as to when objectionable material is about to come out.

Scope of Cross Examination

There are two views as to the permissible scope of cross examination where the cross examination is not directed at impeachment (i. e., where the cross examination is "substantive;" see p. 320, infra). The "restrictive" rule confines the cross examiner to matters "opened up" by the direct

[41]

**examination. The "wide open" rule does not, but
rather allows any material issue in the case to be
explored. (What has and has not been "opened
up" will frequently be subject to debate, and more
and less restrictive views are possible.)**

Cross examination directed at impeachment is not subject
to these rules.

Uncertainty as to what will develop from a line of cross
examination makes judges reluctant to limit on any ground
a line of questioning during cross examination, especially
since cross examination is regarded as a very important
guarantee. This reluctance is respected on appeal. One
consequence is that the restrictive rule is difficult to enforce
rigidly, since a line of questioning on cross examination
may be leading to impeachment or to something opened
up on direct. The cross examiner therefore is given more
latitude than we might expect.

The two rules ("restrictive" and "wide open") express a
difference of view as to the time at trial at which a party
ought to be able to present new substantive points favoring
his own case out of the mouth of a witness who has been
put on originally against him: i. e., at the time of cross
examination, or by calling the witness when it is the party's
own turn to call witnesses. The latter may entail some of
the legal limitations that apply to examining one's own
witnesses, but it should not, if the judge is allowed under
the law to have reference to the policy underlying those
limitations. The principal limitations would be limitations
on leading and impeaching. See pp. 321–3, infra. Also, if
properly handled, calling and examining such a witness
should not result in the jury identifying the calling party
with the witness.

F.R.E. 611(b) adopts the restrictive rule, but allows the
judge to make exceptions, in which event the witness dur-

ing that time is treated as the cross-examiner's own witness in that, apparently, leading questions will only be allowed if necessary.

> **In criminal cases, because of the privilege against self-incrimination, the accused cannot be called to the stand by the prosecution if he does not wish to be, even if he has already taken the stand in his own behalf. But most cases hold that the privilege permits, upon cross examination of an accused who has voluntarily taken the stand in his own behalf, inquiry into any substantive matter, regardless of whether it was opened up on direct.[5] If inquiry into substantive matters not opened up on direct is barred, it will be because of a rule regarding the proper scope of cross examination (the "restrictive rule" addressed above).**

It follows from this black-letter proposition, that in jurisdictions having the "restrictive" cross examination rule, a prosecutor may be totally foreclosed from bringing out certain matters he could bring out in "wide open" jurisdictions. For, where the accused takes the stand, the "restrictive rule" bars cross examination as to substantive matters not previously opened up on direct, and the privilege against self-

---

[5] By the prevalent view, an accused waives, by taking the stand, the privilege to turn away substantive questions, but not to turn away impeachment questions that might open up other crimes for which there is still a danger of conviction. Cf. F.R.E. 608(b), final paragraph. Nor does he waive his right to refuse to take the stand again later. Some holdings have implied that he waives as to substantive questions asked on cross examination, only insofar as his only fear from the question is *incrimination in the present case*. Some holdings have implied that he waives only as to substantive matters opened up on direct examination.

It has become the law that the privilege is guaranteed by the federal constitution even in state proceedings. Does this mean that there should not be differences among jurisdictions on the question of waiver?

incrimination bars calling the accused to the stand to testify as to such matters. In the absence of the restrictive rule of cross examination, there would be no bar to asking the question on cross examination, though the privilege would still bar calling the accused to the stand.

It is submitted that this makes little sense. Where the accused testifies for himself, then to the extent the privilege against self-incrimination is waived for purposes of cross examination, it should permit the same questions whether they are asked by the prosecution upon cross examination or upon calling the accused to the stand. Or, if the privilege prevents the prosecutor from calling him to the stand, it ought to prevent asking the same questions on cross examination. In other words, the prosecution's right to get information should not depend upon whether the jurisdiction follows the "restrictive" or the "wide open" rule —rules designed merely to regulate *order* of proof.

Refreshing a Witness' Recollection: Consultation with the Attorney; Attendance at Trial; Referring to Documents; and Form of Questions

There are almost no formal limits on bona fide efforts to refresh recollection before trial. Documents used for this purpose at trial are regulated, in some jurisdictions, as respects author, time written, and similar matters. Ordinarily a document when sought to be so used at trial must be necessary for recollection and disclosed to the other side. Some jurisdictions extend the obligation to disclose to documents that were used before trial to refresh for trial notwithstanding work-product and other privileges. Leading questions (also arguably employed to stimulate memory) ordinarily are (1) improper on direct examination, at least of friendly witnesses who do not need special directing because of age or other factor and (2) proper on cross examination, at least of non-friendly witnesses.

[44]

Access of a witness to other testimony in the case (which can also affect his recollection) may also be regulated.

A witness may consult practically anything he chooses *prior to taking* the stand, in preparation for his testimony. This includes documents, reminders of all sorts, etc. He may be rehearsed by attorneys (short of prompting to tell an untruth). In many jurisdictions, however, there is a procedure ("sequestration"—often termed "being under The Rule") whereby he may be prevented from listening to the other testimony in the case. Questions have arisen regarding whether this bars the reading of transcripts, attendance at depositions, and listening to oral reports of what transpired at the hearings. F.R.E. 615 exempts from sequestration witnesses who are (1) parties, (2) the designated representative of an organization that is a party, or (3) essential persons, such as an expert needed at counsel table to aid the attorney.

What may a witness consult *on the stand* to refresh his recollection? If a document is truly going to be confined to this purpose of stimulating memory—that is, the attorney presenting the witness does not intend to read the document aloud or present it or the statements in it as evidence of facts, but rather intends (and the judge believes) that the witness's statement, springing from active, current (though revived) recollection, will be the evidence—then the matter is governed by the rules for Refreshing Recollection (rather than the stricter rules for Past Recollection Recorded), to be discussed below. Opposing counsel will ordinarily be granted the right to examine a document proposed to be so used, though in *most* jurisdictions he would not have the right if the document were presented to the witness not on the stand but rather before trial only (though the purpose in both cases be to refresh recollection for trial). F.R.E. 612 entrusts the question of disclosure of a document so used before trial, to the discretion of the judge, and cases like

Berkey Photo, Inc. v. Eastman Kodak Co., 74 F.R.D. 613 (S.D.N.Y.1977) serve as notice to attorneys that (1) work product and other privileges (e. g. attorney-client privilege) surrounding a document so used may be held waived; (2) *any* documents used to prepare expert or lay witnesses, not just those employed to refresh memory, may be subjected to disclosure; and (3) preparation of witnesses for depositions is within the rule.

It would seem to follow that marking for identification, authenticating, entering into evidence, and reading the document aloud, will not be done, and the Best Evidence Rule will not be applied, to documents used to refresh recollection on or before taking the stand. (See pp. 72–88.) However, for tactical reasons, one side or the other may do certain of these steps. For example, the opponent may read the document or introduce it into evidence (the proponent is not allowed to) in order to call attention to a disparity between the document and the supposedly memory-refreshed testimony (technically this is to cast doubt on credibility and is not an offer of the document as proof of the facts stated), or either side may mark it for identification in order to have an identification number on the document to refer to, for the record. Unless the refresher is attacked, the side initially using it to refresh cannot *enter it into evidence* or read it aloud, even if marked for identification.

If the document is not used as a memory refresher in the above fashion, but instead is put forth or read *as evidence of the facts it relates*, it will usually be hearsay and must come within an exception to the hearsay rule. One exception to the hearsay rule that frequently becomes confused with Refreshing Recollection on the stand, is the exception for the witness' *Past Recollection Recorded.*

In some jurisdictions the prerequisites to use of the document during trial under both doctrines will be the same: (1) The witness must have had firsthand knowledge of the facts recorded. (2) The document must have been made by the witness (or if made by someone else, must have been recognized as correct by the witness) at a time very near the occurrence of the matter recorded (or while it was fresh in his memory). (3) The witness must express present confidence that the document correctly recorded the facts (either because he presently remembers being certain at one time that it did, or because he remembers it was made pursuant to a regular practice to record accurately, or because his signature or writing means to him that the facts related in the document must have been true). (4) He must no longer remember the recorded facts (without consultation of the document in the case of Refreshing Recollection; regardless of consultation, in the case of Past Recollection Recorded). Should imperfect or less perfect present memory be sufficient?

In most jurisdictions the requirements apply only where the document is used as Past Recollection Recorded, and the *refreshing of recollection* on the stand is left largely unregulated (except for the obligation to disclose and the requirement that there must be no memory without the document). Intermediate positions are also found. (Refreshing Recollection before taking the stand is never subject to any of the requirements except sometimes the obligation to disclose as described earlier.)

The difference between Refreshing Recollection and Past Recollection Recorded is really a difference in what is to be the evidence: the witness' current recollection (current testimony), or the contents of the document (read, or introduced physically). Assume the Refreshing of Recollection is to take place on the stand (which is what usually engenders the confusion of the two doctrines). The difference between the doctrines may be illustrated by the following question-and-answer series from two separate trial occasions. In each the attorney establishes the requisite elements (foundation) for one of the doctrines. Under the Refreshing Recollection example, whether or not the jurisdiction requires some connection between the witness and the making of the document, requires that the memo be made from firsthand knowledge, and/or requires a voucher for the memo's accuracy, you will note that the attorney nevertheless finds it wise to establish these things as a matter of weight and credibility. This course of prudence would also aid him if through some unforseen change since case preparation, the witness' memory should fail to be refreshed and the attorney should have to introduce the document itself as Past Recollection Recorded, which does require those elements:

Refreshing Recollection:

Q. [by plaintiff's attorney]: State whether or not anything else was damaged by the fire?

A. [by plaintiff as witness]: There were some other items.

Q. What were they?

A. I cannot remember.

Q. Do you know of anything that might help refresh your memory?

A. Yes, I have a list of items damaged.

Q. Where is that list?

A. I have it here.

Q. May I have it? [Witness has taken it out of pocket and hands it over, all without looking at it. Attorney says to court reporter]: Please mark this document purporting to be a list, "Plaintiff's Exhibit No. 10 For Identification." [Done] [Plaintiff's attorney hands it to opposing counsel, for his perusal, who examines it and hands it back to plaintiff's attorney.] [Then, without returning the list to the witness, plaintiff's attorney continues questioning witness.] Who wrote this Plaintiff's Exhibit No. 10?

A. I did.

Q. When?

A. The evening of the day of the fire.

Q. Did you write it from firsthand, personal knowledge by you of what was damaged or did you get your information secondhand?

A. Firsthand, personal. I visited the scene and examined the items as I wrote.

Q. State whether the list was true and correct at the time you wrote it?

A. It was true and correct.

Q. Would a reference to it now help you to recall what was damaged in the fire, or not?

A. It would.

Q. I show you what has been marked "Plaintiff's Exhibit No. 10 For Identification" and ask you to state again whether or not that is the list you are referring to?

A. It is.

Q. Examine it, please.

A. Yes. [Witness does]

Q. Please return it to me.

A. [Witness does]

Q. Do you remember now—do you now have an *independent recollection*—of what other items were damaged in the fire?

A. Yes. A winter coat, an oak dining room table, four upholstered chairs . . .. [If, as this sentence continues, a point is reached where memory again fails on some items, the process of handing the list over briefly to refresh and returning it to the lawyer before continuing to itemize, is again repeated.]

Past Recollection Recorded:

[The progress of the question-and-answer is the same as in the example above except for the last answer. Also, the material concerning who made the document, when it was made, its accuracy, and its firsthand nature, here becomes a *necessary* part of the foundation, not just desirable. Picking up from just before the last question-and-answer, the script goes on as follows:]

Q.   Do you remember now—do you have an independent recollection—of what other items were damaged in the fire?

A.   No I do not. [This is the required answer in order to license the use of the document as Past Recollection Recorded.][6]

Q.   May it please the court, I offer "Plaintiff's Exhibit No. 10 For Identification" into evidence as "Plaintiff's Exhibit No. 10."

The Court: Any objections?

Opposing Counsel: None, Your Honor.

The Court: It may be received and so marked.

[At this point under Past Recollection Recorded the options include the attorney or witness reading the document aloud and/or passing it to the jury. Sometimes the witness is simply asked to look at the document and tell what items were damaged in the fire according to the list. The exhibit

---

[6] Some jurisdictions would allow such use if the witness' answer indicates not total lack of memory, but somewhat weak memory (e. g., he answers "I do recollect, but not very well"). See F.R.E. 803(5). Of course, in the context here weak memory is perhaps equivalent to total lack of memory as to some items, and full memory as to others. On this theory, a jurisdiction requiring total lack of memory would allow the list into evidence only to prove the items that could not be recalled even after consultation of the list and would probably block off or excise the other entries.

may or may not be allowed to be taken to the jury room during the final deliberations. F.R.E. 803(5), to prevent undue emphasis, allows the document to be read to the jury but not to be introduced physically as an exhibit by the proponent, perhaps unless it is attacked.]

Turning now to another (but related) subject, the law recognizes that leading questions (questions that in some way suggest the desired answer), like documents, can sometimes serve a valid function in refreshing memory or directing the witness' attention. For example, hostile, forgetful, aged, and juvenile witnesses, may be questioned in a leading manner, within limits; and judges may employ a leading manner of questioning witnesses so long as it does not evidence improper bias. In the case of hostile witnesses, (or, in the normal course of things, witnesses being cross examined), the danger that leading questions present—that the witness will consciously or unconsciously "play ball" with the attorney—is minimal, and leading questions are thus allowed.

It should be noted that there are restrictions not only on leading questions, but upon those deemed "argumentative," "misleading," or "compound" (multi-faceted), as well.

Ordinary Witnesses: Opinion; First-Hand Knowledge

Ordinary lay witnesses (1) must speak only of what they know first-hand, and (2) may testify only as to facts (i. e. they may not give opinions, inferences, or conclusions) (but cf. F.R.E., infra p. 57).

The meaning of these terms is not always free from doubt. The first rule is designed to minimize error and keep sources, relevant to evaluation, clear. The second is designed to put the tribunal as close to the witness' primary component perceptions as practicable in order to minimize error and maximize the jury's role in fact-finding. Where articulation of more primary perceptions would be highly difficult, protracted or otherwise impractical; or where insistence on strict application of the rule would result in more loss than gain in terms of valuable evidence; or where the danger is small or obvious;—in all these cases, the rule against opinions (inferences, conclusions) has been held by at least the more modern courts, to be satisfied, since what is fact and what opinion, inference, or conclusion is relative and determined by practicality. Thus, for example, speed is commonly allowed to be estimated, even sometimes in such terms as "fast" or "slow;" and witnesses have been allowed to say that a person was or appeared to be "angry," "kidding," "dying," "strong," "sober," or, less often, "drunk." The theory is, however, that it must somehow be "necessary" to have the shorthand rendition. Other examples would be that "it was a sturdy fence," or "the produce was rotten," etc. (See relaxation in F.R.E., infra.)

Once primary perceptions are recounted, articulation of less primary ones ("conclusions," "inferences," or "opinions," by comparison) is superfluous, time consuming, and may even be misleading or dangerous. In theory it is forbidden; but this is strayed from where little prejudice ensues.

Lay testimony in terms of "sanity" or "mental competence," and, less often, "insanity" or "lack of mental competence," may be permitted, and sometimes, especially in the case of sanity and mental competence, it is permitted even though no supporting data is given by the witness. This can be so even where an ultimate issue in the case may be phrased in closely similar terms—sanity or insanity, mental competence or incompetence. We normally find great reluctance to allow a witness, lay or expert, to use a term that could appear to have direct legal significance (e. g., "negligent" or "careless;" although experts are often allowed to testify in terms of "cause" and "adequacy"). This is known as the rule against "ultimate opinions or conclusions" but again there is no bright line demarking the ultimate from the non-ultimate and the rule seems to be administered with considerable "flexibility." (See infra for relaxation of this rule under the F.R.E. and similar codes.)

The requirement of first-hand knowledge should not be confused with the hearsay rule. If a witness states "Jack shot Mary" but knows this only from others, he violates the first-hand knowledge rule because he seems to imply that he has first-hand knowledge which he does not have. If the same witness in the same circumstances testifies instead that "Joe told me Jack shot Mary," he does not violate the first-hand knowledge rule (because he does not appear to have first-hand knowledge of other than Joe's statement, which statement he presumably does know first-hand), but he violates the hearsay rule.

There is considerable dispute over whether the first-hand knowledge and the opinion rules should apply to declarants whose out-of-court statements may be recounted by someone (or by a document) in court pursuant to an exception to or exemption from the hearsay rule. Sometimes the answer depends upon which exception or exemption is involved, with out-of-court admissions of a party often being excused from compliance on the grounds that, unlike the case of in-court testimony, this valuable "testimony" cannot be rephrased and would be lost if the rules were applied; and anyway how can a party say that an adverse statement of his was not founded on thorough, careful grounds? (Would this apply to admissions via an agent? Are there other exceptions or exemptions to which such rationale(s) would apply? Similar reasoning is on occasion applied to other exceptions or exemptions.) Of course, lack of first-hand knowledge, and presence of opinion, would affect the weight of such evidence.

Expert Witnesses

> Where it is felt by courts that conclusions, inferences, or opinions are needed that require special expertise and that are not within the competence of a lay jury to draw accurately and economically, a party or the court may call an "expert witness" to give the expert's opinion, inference, or conclusion, usually together with some exposition of the basis thereof, and he need not have the kind of firsthand knowledge required of lay witnesses.

As an example of the principle in the heading, see Ibn-Tamas v. United States, 368 A.2d 520 (D.C.App.1977) (expert psychological testimony that battered wives seldom leave their husbands, and why, allowed to lend credence to defendant-wife's homicide defense that she killed husband because she was a battered wife, since without it jury would be skeptical and ask themselves "why would she stay with him if he were a batterer?"). The principle can be invoked to prove a wide range of issues at trial, if the judge is convinced the conditions are satisfied. Common applications are medical opinions on cause, extensiveness, and duration of personal injuries; economists' opinions on issues in antitrust cases; etc. On expert testimony on the unreliability of eye-witness testimony, see Note, 29 Stan.L.Rev. 969 (1977).

Not only does an expert enjoy a dispensation from the rule against opinions, inferences, and conclusions, he also enjoys a dispensation from the first-hand knowledge rule, in a sense. His opinion testimony may be elicited in the form of (a) an opinion expressly based on his examination and observation of the person or matter in controversy, or (b) an opinion on a "hypothetical" state of facts put to him by counsel, if the hypothetical is based on facts the jury could find on the evidence presented or to be presented in the case. Where he testifies in the latter fashion, he need not have made an examination or observation; theoretically the jury is competent to decide ultimately how far the real facts differ from the hypothetical, and what effect this should have on the value and applicability of the opinion. In some jurisdictions, experts or some experts may be confined to (a) or to (b). Otherwise, counsel will have the choice, subject to the trial judge's discretion. A mixed approach on the part of counsel is also possible on occasion; as is an approach that puts the hypothetical in terms of testimony or evidence in the case, e. g., "Do you have an opinion based on the evidence of plaintiff in the case [or the testimony of W, etc.]?", assuming it is first established that the expert has heard the evidence referred to.

Who is an "expert", and what particular matters are appropriate for, require, or admit only of, expert testimony, is an area in which the trial judge is accorded much leeway and discretion, although some law will have crystallized, if the situation recurs enough. A police officer may be an expert in examining auto tracks and deducing speed or force or angle of impact. A ranch-hand may be expert on the adequacy of a fence for containing cattle. Medical doctors are the most frequent experts.

If the minimum qualifications to be regarded as "expert" by the court are met, shortcomings in qualifications are matters of weight and not admissibility.

On some issues, such as mental competency, both expert and lay testimony may be received.

When an expert is not testifying in an expert capacity, but only as an ordinary witness to lay facts within his knowledge, he is to that extent a lay witness and subject to the rules binding on ordinary witnesses.

An expert witness's testimony giving the basis of his opinion will often involve hearsay—things the expert has read or heard in his education, in his experience, and in consultation with others. A doctor (and in particular, a psychiatrist) will in addition rely on much the patient has told him (rely in a way which frequently will involve giving credence to what was said). A hearsay objection might be raised to the giving of the opinion itself, as well as to the giving of the basis. To suppress the opinion on hearsay grounds in every case where the opinion involved some hearsay would put an end to the whole institution of expert testimony; and to suppress the recounting of hearsay constituents of the basis could deprive the jury of a valuable source for evaluation of the testimony. A decision has to be made as to whether the hearsay aspects of the testimony are too prevalent or render the evidence too unreliable. Might expert testimony utilizing hearsay run afoul of the constitutional confrontation clause (especially under the liberalized position on such utilization under the new codes: see Opinions and Experts Under the F.R.E., infra)? See Reardon v. Manson, 491 F.Supp. 982 (D.Conn.1980) (toxicologist's testimony that substance possessed by criminal defendant was a narcotic, based on tests done and reported to him by others in the lab).

Both sides of a case will be accorded equal opportunity to produce experts if there is an issue for experts. The judge has discretion to limit the number and duration. He also has power at common law, and under some formalized impartial expert testimony provisions adopted in some jurisdictions, to appoint his own expert or experts, who can be expected to carry great weight with juries that are told, as they often are, of the special judicial appointment. Normally judges' experts will not impact on the parties' right to also adduce experts of their own choosing, except where there would be redundancy.

When a record or report that is hearsay, or other hearsay evidence, comes in through an exception to the hearsay rule, it often contains expert opinion, such as in a medical record. Is there more, or less, reason to tolerate such opinion? Is the opiner present at trial to explain? Are there other considerations? Should the result be different according to type of opinion?

Opinions and Experts Under the F.R.E. as Compared With the Common Law (Still Found in a Number of States): A Good Example of How the F.R.E. Operate[7]

The F.R.E. (Art. VII) contain seven liberalizations in this area: (1) a "helpfulness" test for lay opinions; (2) expansion of the class of experts; (3) expansion of subjects appropriate for expert testimony; (4) reform of the hypothetical question; (5) licensing of certain inadmissible evidence in the basis for an expert's opinion; (6) optional omission of the opinion's basis from the direct exam; and (7) abolition of the "rule" against ultimate opinions.

F.R.E. Article VII accomplishes seven liberalizations over at least the stricter of the views that prevailed under traditional evidence law (which still applies in a number of states) in the area of opinions and experts. (Of course there were always a number of decisions that foreshadowed the positions of the F.R.E.—the F.R.E. never make a position up out of whole cloth.) By liberalization is meant a broadening, an increase in admissibility.

(1) The first liberalization has to do with lay opinions. Lay opinions under the F.R.E. are allowed whenever they would be "helpful", provided that they are "rationally based" in the witness's perception. All the latter requirement

---

[7] As noted earlier, discussion in terms of the Federal Rules of Evidence ("F.R.E."), is also largely applicable to the newer state codifications and the 1974 Uniform Rules, all patterned on the Federal Rules. A few exceptions will be noted.

means is that the witness must have first-hand (personal) knowledge of the matter that he is speaking about. The "helpfulness" test abolishes the restrictive so-called "collective facts rule," under which a lay person could only express an opinion on the stand if it was impossible or terribly impractical to express what he has observed in any other fashion. Whether in actual day-to-day administration the two rules produce different results remains to be seen, but there is some evidence that decisions under the F.R.E. are taking a liberalized approach.

(2) The second liberalization expands who will be considered "experts." Under F.R.E. 702 the category includes not just professionals, scientists and people with specialized university degrees as some restrictive decisions seemed to require (and still do require in a number of states), but includes also "skilled" witnesses, such as bankers, farmers, police patrolmen, and home owners, testifying in their particular area of experience. All that is required is "specialized knowledge" of a kind that will "assist" the fact-finder, acquired in any fashion—that is, by "experience, training, or education."

(3) The third liberalization (implicit in the last) expands what subjects are proper subjects for expert testimony. Under one strict common law view, the only proper subjects for expert testimony are matters that are "totally beyond lay ken." If a lay person knows anything about the area, has any knowledge in the area, then an expert cannot testify in that area, under that view. Such testimony would be considered an invasion of the province of the jury. Thus, under a strict application, a fire chief might be prevented from testifying as to likely causes of a house or grass fire. The test under F.R.E. 702 is that an expert may testify in any area where his specialized knowledge would "assist" the trier-of-fact—a very broad, liberal, highly discretionary test.

(4) The fourth liberalization has to do with the much maligned and much touted hypothetical question. F.R.E. 703 and 705 make it clear that expert testimony need not be presented in the stilted format of the in-court hypothetical question. The in-court hypothetical question in the past usually has taken something like the following form: "Now, assuming, doctor, that a patient comes to you with such-and-such and so-and-so, and has a history of such-and-such and so-and-so, do you have an opinion, doctor, as to whether the condition would be permanent?" "Yes, I do." "What is that opinion?" Hypothetical questions can run for a half-hour or more—sometimes days! Lawyers are fond of building into the hypothetical every conceivable favorable fact in the case, using this as early argumentation and propaganda.

Under F.R.E. 703 and 705 there are five alternative formats to the traditional, open-court hypothetical question (which is not prohibited), although they are not expressly enumerated: (a) a set of facts given to the expert before trial, perhaps in the privacy of the lawyer's office, the expert then testifying on the stand based on that; (b) the familiar "personal observation" method—testimony based upon personal knowledge (for example, a medical-doctor-expert who has made a personal examination of the patient); (c) testimony based upon reading the transcript in the case; (d) testimony based on the expert's attendance at the trial, sitting in the audience and listening to the fact witnesses; and (e) testimony based upon a mixture of any of the above (including the in-court hypo). These methods were not unknown at the common law, but the in-court hypothetical or personal observation methods were so frequent that they were often believed mandatory.

(5) The fifth liberalization is that an expert on the stand may rely on unadmitted and inadmissible material in giving

his opinion, if they are of the kind that are reasonably relied upon by experts in the field. F.R.E. 703. Thus he may base his opinion on oral or written hearsay, documents that are not in evidence, documents that violate the best evidence or the authentication rules—any kind of inadmissible evidence—provided that it is the kind that is "reasonably relied upon by experts in the particular field in forming inferences or opinions on the subject." Thus, a judgment of reasonableness has to be made here by the judge. A question could be raised: "Reasonable for whom? —the court or these experts?" "Reasonableness" has usually been held synonymous with "customary in the field," although a good argument can be made that more judicial independence is required by the rule's phrase.

You will notice that this fifth liberalization is an end run around the hearsay rule. If an attorney has a piece of hearsay and has trouble getting it into evidence under the hearsay rule, being unable to find an exception to or exemption from the hearsay rule for it, then he might endeavor to find an expert who will base his opinion on the inadmissible hearsay. The attorney might then put the expert on the stand to recount not only his opinion but (and this is unclear under the Rules) perhaps also the hearsay basis of his opinion. (Regardless of how the unclear point is resolved, this has tremendous implications for getting into evidence at least the gist of such things as government, university, or industry studies; polls; surveys; second-hand statements, say, by patients; consultations with other doctors; books; articles; and other items of a sort that might otherwise be inadmissible hearsay.) As a simple example of this principle in operation, in one case a police officer from the Drug Enforcement Administration was allowed to testify as to the selling price of heroin in various cities of the world. He had found out the prices from other agents. United States v. Golden, 532 F.2d 1244 (9th Cir. 1976), cert.

denied 429 U.S. 842, 97 S.Ct. 118. Other, more complex cases, are readily imaginable. The idea is not new, but the new rules button it down and reject those cases (still prevalent in a number of states) that seem to suggest that opinions must be based on admissible or admitted evidence, or which take an extremely narrow view of when and how much inadmissible evidence will be tolerated in the basis.

(6) The sixth liberalization has to do with *disclosure* of the facts and material upon which the expert witness bases his opinion. Traditional practice, still applicable in most states, requires that the expert give the basis for his opinion in the direct examination, so that the cross-examiner has some advance warning and can decide whether or not to cross-examine, and if he decides to cross-examine, what tack to take. (Sometimes it is the better part of discretion not to cross-examine an articulate, well qualified, and soundly based expert.)

F.R.E. 705 states that this is no longer required; that the direct examination does not need to include the basis of the expert's opinion. The expert can give a bare opinion with the scantiest glimpse of his reasons.[8] Admittedly, in

---

[8] The Rule states in relevant part, that "the expert may testify in terms of opinion or inference and give his reasons therefor without prior disclosure of the underlying facts or data [i. e., without disclosing his basis, that is, the assumed facts about the case, any observations or examinations he has made, books or studies or consultations he has relied upon, etc.] . . . ." Thus, after parading the doctor's credentials, a personal-injury plaintiff's lawyer could go directly into the following direct examination of his medical expert, without establishing where the expert got his facts about the plaintiff's injury and condition, what facts he assumes to be present or absent, and what, if any, materials, examinations, consultations, studies, books, propositions, tests, or statements of the plaintiff he relied on:

Q. Are you familiar with the facts of the case?

A. Yes.

Q. Do you have an opinion as to the cause of plaintiff's pain and disability?

[Footnote continued next page.]

many cases the direct examiner will not proceed this way because such a bare opinion is not very persuasive. But on occasion, for tactical reasons, the direct examiner will not put a basis in on the direct examination, either because there is no very good basis or because there is a substantial basis and he would like the cross-examiner to trigger it. He may know from past experience with this cross-examiner that he can depend upon the cross-examiner to do just that; that the cross-examiner cannot keep his mouth shut. If the cross-examiner triggers the basis, it is more effective for the side putting on the expert than if the basis had been included in the direct examination. Some of the state codes patterned on the F.R.E. provide for the parties to

A.   Yes. It is caused by the auto collision he suffered on Jan. 24.

Q.   What will be their duration?

A.   His condition will remain unchanged for his whole life.

Q.   Dr., will you tell the jury why you conclude as you do?

A.   My reasons are that plaintiff's symptoms are typical in cases of this kind of injury and can be expected to follow the normal course.

Q.   Thank you, Dr. No further questions.

At this point the cross examiner is in a considerable dilemma about whether and how to cross examine, because a good cross examiner likes to know something of what the answer may be before he asks a question. Discovery of the expert is likely to have been quite restricted under Rule of Civil Procedure 26, unless the lawyer was able to bring home to the judge a foreshadowing of this dilemma situation at trial. At any rate, the Perry Mason syndrome of relying on getting enough information at trial to fashion a cross examination on your feet, is dangerous. Indeed, forgoing vigorous pre-trial investigation and discovery for *any* reason, be it economics, laziness, or undue confidence, bears a heavy cost under F.R.E. 705.

Rule 705 goes on, after the quotation above, to provide "unless the court requires otherwise." Restricted discovery could perhaps be attempted to be argued to be a reason for a court "requir[ing] otherwise." The rule further continues: "The expert may in any event be required to disclose the underlying facts or data on cross-examination." But this is the very unknown potential trap the cross examiner does not wish to walk into blind.

exhange in advance written summaries of expert testimony and its grounds, to make up for the combined effect of no basis appearing in the direct, and none having been revealed during discovery either because of restricted discovery mechanisms (e. g. restrictions respecting experts in civil cases in many jurisdictions and respecting discovery generally in criminal cases) or because of failure to take full advantage of discovery for economic or other reasons. A similar provision for exchange of written summaries in Federal Rule of Civil Procedures 26 has often met with no more than perfunctory compliance, except where an unusual trial judge has amplified and enforced what is required by issuing a more detailed pretrial order and threatening in advance to strike testimony at trial.

(7) The seventh liberalization has to do with the so-called ultimate issue rule. This rule provided that an opinion, be it an expert opinion or a lay opinion, could not be given in terms that smacked of, that sounded of, an ultimate issue in the case. It is still the law in a number of states. It has been abolished by F.R.E. 704. There is no longer in federal courts (and states following the F.R.E. pattern) a ban on expert or lay opinions that are expressed in terms of the ultimate issue in the case. If there is any objection to such opinions, it will have to be placed on the more general ground that the opinion is not "helpful" or does not "assist" as is required by F.R.E. 701 and 702 (see supra), or violates F.R.E. 403 (the probative-prejudice-etc. balancing provision) or some other provision of the Rules. It is no longer sufficient in such jurisdictions to merely state that the opinion is on an ultimate issue.

Let us see how these seven liberalizations interrelate with each other to produce results in particular cases. Let us take an automobile accident reconstruction expert or "accidentologist." Accident reconstruction experts are found recently in many different areas, including industrial mishaps and auto collisions. Some may be qualified, some not. Let us suppose that he proposes to testify about who caused an automobile accident. He wishes to say "the Ford was at fault and wasn't keeping a proper lookout," based not upon any personal observation that he had made of the automobile accident, but based primarily upon bystanders' statements he obtained in interviews and has put together to deduce what happened. Are there any impediments to this sort of testimony coming in? It seems to be hearsay; and he may be an expert of somewhat specious qualifications. Nevertheless with an appropriate judge he could overcome all the hurdles and get his evidence in under the Federal Rules. He could convince the judge that he possesses "specialized knowledge" that has something "of assistance" to offer the trier of fact. (Rule 702). In addition, we have learned that he is allowed to base his testimony on hearsay, provided that he convinces the judge that experts in this field reasonably (customarily) rely upon this kind of hearsay (bystanders' statements). (Rule 703). Let us say that he does so convince the judge by testifying that "All us accidentologists rely all the time on this kind of bystanders' statements." (This assumes the opponent knows enough to even raise the question—remember, under Rule 705 the direct exam may not have alerted him that there is a possibly faulty basis; see liberalization (6), supra.) The final impediment seems to be that the expert is expressing his conclusion in terms of the ultimate issue in the case ("The Ford was at fault; the Ford didn't keep a proper lookout"). But we saw that there is no longer a ban on opinions on the ultimate issue in the case. (Rule 704). So he overcomes that hurdle as well. One additional hurdle might be mentioned. Rule 403 (which may be termed "the great override") states that, notwithstanding anything else the Rules provide, the judge can bar evidence in a particular case if in his discretion he finds that the probativity is substantially outweighed by the prejudice, the time consumption, the confusion, the misleadingness, or similar factors. It would seem, however, that a judge might well decide—having made all these determinations that Article VII (in particular Rules 702 to 705), relating to experts, is complied with in the case of this accidentologist—that Rule 403 is also complied with.

It can easily be seen that there is some risk that a judge would be motivated to admit the evidence and that the Rules provide little guarantee against it. While the Advisory Committee comments try to assure us that it is not contemplated that such evidence should be admitted, there are no assurances in the text of the rules. And the risk is not confined to accidentologists.

Let us take another case. Suppose a financial investigator from the Internal Revenue Service takes the stand to testify that Mr. So-and-so (the defendant) "is guilty of tax fraud," or "owns" certain funds (the taxable funds) ostensibly held in the name of an independent corporation the government contends is a dummy or front for Mr. So-and-so. The investigator's conclusion, let us further assume, is based upon his examination of bank records, i. e., documents that are not at trial, have not been admitted, may not even be admissible, are not authenticated, and do not comply with the best evidence rule. They may be hearsay and may not really meet the requirements of any exception, for all we know. And he works for the government—a party in interest. The rules are broad enough to permit this testimony. Indeed, the expert may never specify any facts underlying his conclusion.

Hopefully judges will not allow what we have been discussing, but there is a risk some will, and the Rules can be interpreted to give them power to do so, as well as power not to.

Article VII (opinions and experts) which we are addressing will be one of the most important articles in all the Rules in future 20th and 21st Century litigation. In today's world of increasing expertise and specialization, increased demands for rapid resolution rather than painstaking exegesis of underlying fact, and increasingly complex technical issues that are beyond the ability of lay juries to resolve or to resolve expeditiously without expert help, expert testimony will be relied upon more and more as time goes on. At one and the same time Article VII has the greatest potential for good and also the greatest potential for harm and abuse in all the Rules.

On the good side, Article VII opens the door to all sorts of valuable modern expertise which the courts have been barring by applying 18th Century precedents to today's vastly more complex problems. Article VII thus laudably brings courts into the 20th Century. But in opening the door wider to expertise, more charlatans are also going to get in. There will be an avalanche of sociologists, economists, safety experts, employment discrimination experts, psychologists, etc.—some of them good and some of them bad. These Rules give the court no concrete guidance in distinguishing the charlatans from the savants. Of course, a first-rate judge usually can distinguish between them under the standards provided in the Rules. But in any system of law, not all the judges are going to be first-rate. (These Rules bind federal judges. They are being adopted at an increasing rate by the states. Many states that have not adopted them are using them in an advisory fashion. There are many levels of judges, from lay J.P.s and magistrates to high courts. In addition, administrative agencies are using them in an advisory capacity. Eventually many administrative agencies will probably adopt them.) The F.R.E. ask us to trust the judge, trust the jury and trust the lawyers. Trust the judge to keep out unworthy evidence. Trust the jury to spot weaknesses in formerly inadmissible evidence that is admitted and to assess its weight correctly. Most importantly, trust the lawyers to point out the weaknesses in the evidence so that the judge and jury can spot them. There is thus a heavy onus on the lawyers under these rules. It is obvious that the quality of the bench and bar is critical. It is up to the reader to decide whether these provisions can be administered properly. While these rules may seem to give the judge too much flexibility, the reader should be cautioned against the opposite extreme—a rigid specification that unduly hems the judge in. Do these provisions draw the right balance between too much rigid specificity (which would unduly tie the hands of the judge) and uncontrolled discretion? Do they draw the line between the two in the proper place?

What is true of Article VII is also true thoughout the entire body of the Rules. There are two themes in the F.R.E. that are strongly illustrated by Article VII. These two themes are *admissibility* and *discretion.* Throughout their length and breadth the F.R.E. favor admissibility and grant strong doses of discretion.

Admissibility is manifest in the fundamental, easily satisfied definition of relevance (Rule 401), and in the way the balancing of the counterweights to relevancy are weighted against exclusion (Rule 403). See pp. 4–5 supra. The admissibility theme is further illustrated by the fact that the F.R.E. severely limit witness incompetencies (Article VI). And they allow you freely to impeach your own witness, contrary to former law (Rule 607). The hearsay rule is considerably eroded (Article VIII). The authentication of documents requirement is whittled down (Article IX). There is an expanded list of self-authenticating documents,

i. e., documents that on their face are authenticated (Rule 902). The best evidence rule is radically altered—xeroxes and photocopies are freely admitted on a par with originals in most cases (Article X). (These matters are all discussed elsewhere herein.) Further examples could be cited.

What about the theme of discretion? The knell of discretion is sounded in the "great override," Rule 403, which conditions nearly all the rules by granting the judge wide discretion to exclude on a balancing of relatively subjective factors. See pp. 10–12 supra. In addition, the judge is given discretion over the order and manner of presentation of evidence and the examination of witnesses. (Rule 611). This means he has considerable discretion concerning the scope of cross-examination (Rule 611(b); see pp. 42–43 supra), the scope and permissibility of rebuttal and surrebuttal, the number of witnesses, and things of that nature. And he has discretion over whether or not and when to allow leading questions, with certain guidelines (Rule 611 (c)).

Discretion and breadth of phrasing engendering discretion appear at every turn, not merely in the sections on experts and opinions and the other sections we have referred to. Indeed, some people have called the Federal Rules of Evidence the "Federal Non-Rules of Evidence." This is an exaggeration. But it is true that most of the rules are actually not rules but guidelines only. Nevertheless, discretion is not unlimited; there are standards that must be learned; failure to do so can spell disaster in the trial of cases (all the more so where there is discretion, because he who is familiar with the standards guiding discretion can motivate that discretion).

These twin themes of admissibility and discretion have certain implications in addition to those already mentioned. Broad discretion means that even under the codification there will still be considerable diversity from circuit to circuit, district to district, judge to judge, which rules and codes are meant to eliminate. Discretion and broad phrases engender differences of opinion as to meaning and as to how discretion should be exercised.

Discretion also means that all of evidence law will not be between the two covers of the codification. Old cases and new cases will still play a tremendous role, despite some exaggerated promises for a code. It is fatuous to say that the common law is abolished. It cannot be abolished where you have broad provisions and discretion like this. You have got to give such rules content by reference to the old cases and the new cases.

In addition, discretion means that dissatisfied litigants will be able to focus some of their dissatisfaction on the judge personally. He cannot say that the result was entirely compelled by law. While discretion gives the trial judge much more latitude than he formerly had, it also gives some new license to appellate judges. They can reverse distasteful decisions for nothing more precise than abuse of discretion, in many instances.

The ability of lawyers to plan, predict and advise—to proportion expenses to a case in advance, to give a reading of what it will cost and of the probabilities of outcome—is impaired under a code that gives broad discretion, because discretion means uncertainty. Can one precisely plan a case or give intelligent estimates of probability of outcome when he doesn't know what evidence is going to be admissible because admissibility hinges on the discretion of the judge? Can the attorney advise the client as to whether or not to go into litigation, how much to spend, how much it will cost, and the likelihood of success?

Finally, there are going to be more appeals, at least in the short run. You must get appellate courts to tell you what are the limits of the discretion, what is an abuse of discretion, what the broad phrases mean. Codes use new words. Nobody knows for sure what the new words mean. So they say, "Let's ask the appellate court." Furthermore, whenever a new code is enacted (and despite the period of time that the F.R.E. have been in effect, they are "new" as legal history and developments go; and the state codes patterned on them are even newer), lawyers have a heightened sense of the subject. Lawyers are reading, attending continuing legal education seminars, conferences, and lectures, and studying up on Evidence, like never before. It makes them more appeal-minded.

The discussion thus far seems to be saying that the Rules are and will be a failure; that they will not accomplish what codification is intended to accomplish. But that is *not* my message. Instead, it is a plea for a realistic rather than an exaggerated expectation as to what rules of this kind can accomplish. They may not accomplish the goals of codification 100 per cent. They may only accomplish them 50 or 70 per cent. They have been amended and will need further amending as problems are revealed. But, nevertheless, codified rules of evidence of some kind are, on the whole, desirable and salutary. Codified rules at the very least cause all the judges to shoot toward the same target, something they had not been doing, even within a given jurisdiction. Authority will all be gathered together in convenient annotations to rules by the glossators. Law students can conveniently study a code. It will be uniform law they will be learning and subsequently spreading. A code is a convenient and appealing focus for the continuing legal education of practitioners as well. Interest in learning the law of evidence with precision is stimulated. The system will tend toward simplification, uniformity, professionalism and expedition, though the goals will never be accomplished 100 per cent.

Adoption of an evidence code does not mean that lawyers should give up arguing the fine points of interpretation for their clients and engaging in the sophisticated use and distinguishing of case decisions. How else will they give content to generalized words like "helpful," "of assistance" and the other broad words that constantly recur throughout the code. Lawyers should continue to do this so that the courts may ultimately decide what is the best interpretation of each provision in the code, and drafters may make amendments when needed. It is a lawyer's duty, not only to his client but to society. Only then can we be confident that the courts have been presented with all the alternative interpretations of a word or phrase and that they have been adequately argued. Only then can we feel assured that the court has selected the right alternative and that we have the best interpretation possible.

Even under a code, lawyers argue the pros and cons of past resolutions from the old cases and from the common law. And there are conflicting cases coming down under the code which lawyers also argue from, because ambiguity, broad phrases, and discretion engender conflicting differences of opinion by different judges. This is unavoidable unless the code is so detailed as to answer every question in advance. Such specificity is impossible and undesirable for a number of reasons, not the least of which is that the drafters cannot possibly foresee every contingency or be alerted to all the pros and cons of every interpretation in advance.

It is worth also noting, in connection with the F.R.E., that not all evidence subjects are covered by the F.R.E. There are large gaps (impeachment by bias, for just one example). Many of the gaps are intentional, it would seem, the drafters wishing, for reasons like those above, to provide only a skeleton. Thus, there is a large role for the common law and for case development. Whatever may be the technical permissibility of filling gaps this way under the grammar of the Rules (which may seem to some to have thrown up an unintentional road block to this approach—see n. 1, p. 5, supra), this is the approach the courts seem by-and-large to be taking. Unregulated subjects will generally fall within Rule 403, which can be a handle for continuing, or developing, the common law.

Dead Man Rule

Many jurisdictions have a statute or rule prohibiting certain parties to certain transactions from testifying concerning the transaction if the other party to the transaction is deceased and therefore cannot give his version.

The scope of this prohibition or witness-incompetency varies widely from jurisdiction to jurisdiction, and must be studied locally. (Indeed, in some jurisdictions, it is not a prohibition or incompetency at all, but merely a provision that the survivor's testimony must be corroborated and/or that hearsay statements of the deceased are admissible to rebut it.) Its purpose is said to be to squelch a tendency to falsification for gain that exists where the surviving party knows that he who could say nay to the falsification and at whose expense the gain will be gotten, is deceased. F.R.E. 601 abolishes this and most other witness incompetencies except in certain cases where state law provides the rule of decision, in which event state witness-competency law may govern.

Writings: (a) Authentication

Documents which depend for their relevance on a certain authorship, to be admissible must be accompanied by evidence (of the genuineness of their authorship) in a quantum over and above the quantum of evidence one would require in daily life; unless the document is one of a small group

viewed as "self-authenticating," i. e., rebuttably presumed authentic from its mere appearance.

In general, wherever the probative value of a piece of evidence depends upon some fact, at least enough evidence of that fact to warrant a trier to find that fact, is prerequisite to admissibility unless such a finding would be warranted on the face of things as they stand. Where the relevance of a document depends upon its authorship, the law has evolved rules concerning what will be a satisfactory quantum of evidence of that authorship. This is the subject of *authentication of a writing*, and it has its obvious parallels wherever, for example, a weapon (purporting to be the weapon used in a crime), or a photograph, movie film, videotape, or sound recording (each purporting to reproduce some event), or a blood or other specimen (purporting to come from a certain person or thing), or a scientific test result (purporting to have been conducted on a certain person or thing), or a witness (purporting to be an eyewitness to relevant facts), or other similar piece of evidence is offered: there must be certain minimum assurances that the evidence is (or depicts or records) what it purports to be (or depict or record)—i. e., that the evidence is what it is offered as being, and is what its value depends upon. (In the case of some of the physical items other than documents, photos, films, and sound and video recordings, it is customary to speak of "identifying" rather than "authenticating" the item.) Even if the jury could be depended upon to spot evidence not meeting this standard, it would be a waste of time to receive it. In the case of documents, the quantum required seems to be more than just the amount that would warrant a reasonable person in the affairs of daily life to assume authenticity, and this is probably justifiable because falsification is more likely in connection with trials. The F.R.E. are somewhat schizophrenic on whether a quantum which merely would warrant a reasonable person to find authenticity is sufficient. Compare

[73]

F.R.E. 901(a) and (b). Courts under the F.R.E. by and large are continuing the earlier, higher, requirement.

It has been held innumerable times that it is not sufficient evidence of authorship by Mr. X that a signature purporting to be his appears on the document, without some proof of the authenticity of the signature. This may take the form of testimony (by the signatory, one who witnessed the signature, a handwriting expert, or anyone knowing the signature), other proof (including circumstantial evidence such as peculiar penmanship characteristics or knowledge, on the part of the writer; display of handwriting samples to the jurors for their own comparison; certain government certificates of authenticity; proper governmental or business custody; etc.), stipulation, or judicial admission. Extreme age (generally over 30 years—20 under F.R.E. 901(b)(8)) has been held to authenticate, if there are other factors such as regularity on the document's face, proper custody, and (in some places under some circumstances) possession taken under the document. (The theory is that it is unlikely that a fraud was laid so many years ago to bear fruit so many years later.) Authenticity has been found where a letter on its face directly responds to another letter sent to the purported signatory; or where he or others in a position to know acted in some fashion indicating authenticity, as, e. g., engaging in prolonged business relations apparently based on the document. Authentication does not require that the persons in the chain of custody of the document before its appearance in court be produced, although such may be desirable as a tactical matter (and, in a severe case, as a matter of admissibility) where there is evidence of alteration, substitution, etc.

As to authentication of the "authorship" of statements made over the telephone, it is not enough that the voice identified itself as so-and-so. It is otherwise if the voice was, in addition, recognized by the witness or if the telephone number was that of Mr. So-and-so and there was no other person by that name at that number. See F.R.E. 901 (b)(5) and (6).

We must not confuse evidence offered to authenticate a document with evidence offered to prove the contents of a document (e. g., testimony as to the contents, a copy of the document itself, etc.). Furthermore, we must assume that the contemplated use of the writing or conversation is not violative of the hearsay rule. Finally, the principle of authentication by age must not be confused with the Ancient Records exception to the hearsay rule, which relates not to the genuineness of the document, but to the truth of the recitals therein.

Authentication is required of documents whether they are offered as legal instruments themselves having legal consequences (as, e. g., a contract), or as evidence of (recital of) facts that are in issue (often hearsay but coming within an exception to the rule against hearsay). It is also important to realize that a document that has satisfied the authentication requirement is only rebuttably presumed authentic. In addition, even an authentic document may violate, and be attacked under, other evidence rules.

A small group of documents have been held to be self-authenticating on their face, which means a rebuttable presumption of authenticity arises from their mere appearance. F.R.E. 902 is one of the most expansive provisions in this regard, listing as self-authenticating certain sealed and certain unsealed official domestic and foreign public documents and publications; newspapers; periodicals; trade inscriptions, signs, tags, and labels; acknowledged (notarized) documents; commercial paper and related documents; and items specifically so provided by statute. Thus, it will usually be sufficient that the document *appears* to be one of these enumerated kinds of document.

Writings: (b) The Best Evidence Rule

To prove the contents of a writing, the law requires the original document where available rather than a copy or other evidence of contents such as an oral report.

The term "Best Evidence Rule" (sometimes known as the "Original Documents Rule") is a term confined to the following principles about writings (or items such as sound or video recordings, movie films, photos, computer printouts, etc., that can be analogized to writings). Writings (whether offered as legal instruments or as recitals of facts in issue) may be proved only by introduction of the original, unless the original has become "unavailable" without serious fault on the part of the offering party. If there is such unavailability without fault, secondary evidence of the contents will be admissible. In this situation, some jurisdictions are indifferent as to what form of secondary evidence, so long as it is reliable. See F.R.E. 1004. Others require the *best available* form of secondary evidence. Only if a better form is unavailable (through no serious fault of the offeror) will a less desirable form be permitted. Under this view, a copy is generally regarded as preferable to testimony as to the contents. Some copies are regarded as better than others. The order of preference is usually certified copies, carbons, photostats, hand-written copies, etc. Under all views, some copies are regarded as worthy of being considered originals. Copies actually signed (with an original, not copied, signature) come within this category and are often called "duplicate originals" (not to be confused with the term "duplicate" used in the F.R.E., discussed just below). Business transactions often involve signatures put to many copies along with the original, resulting in "duplicate originals," all treated as originals by evidence law. Many courts accord the same treatment to carbon copies that are not duplicate signed originals, and a growing body of law (principally statutory) is according similar treatment to photostatic copies, at least where such are kept in the ordinary course of business. Officially certified copies of official documents are also often so treated. Under F.R.E. 1001(4) and 1003, carbons and photostatic copies, whether bearing an original signature or not, and usually whether kept in the ordinary course of business or not, are accepted as originals, unless, in the case of the ones not bearing an original signature (called "duplicates;" the ones with original signatures would be called *duplicate-originals* or just *originals*), a genuine issue of authenticity is raised. (In all the above, I mean the term "photostat" to include photographic, xerographic, etc. copies.)

An oral statement precisely like another written statement is not necessarily a "copy" of the written and may qualify as primary evidence even if it comes later; just as the same can be true of two independently written but identical writings. Both these situations may be illustrated by the example of an eye-witness to an occurrence who tells his story once in a writing, then tells it again shortly thereafter in a second writing or orally. The later statement is not "evidence of the contents of the [earlier] writing" but is an account from perception and memory, and thus the Best Evidence Rule would not exclude the later statement even if the earlier were available. So, too, where a witness tells a story at an informal interview, and someone overhears it, as well as a transcript being taken. Assume we want to prove at trial what was said at the hearing and both the transcript and the overhearer are available. *Insofar as the Best Evidence Rule is concerned,* either the transcript or the overhearer may be used; they are both independent evidence of *what was said at the hearing.* The overhearer is not testifying to what the transcript said, and therefore his testimony is not secondary evidence of the contents of a writing.

Thus, we re-emphasize: testimony about an occurrence (e. g., an auto collision) by one with first-hand knowledge thereof, is not regarded as "secondary evidence of a writing" even where the facts of the occurrence are also related in writing, whether by him or someone else, regardless of whether the writing came earlier or later than the testimony. Hence, such testimony is beyond the reach of the present rule. It is otherwise if the testimony is that the writing states such-and-such (assuming no hearsay problem).

There is no general rule that only the best available evidence of a fact sought to be proved is admissible—no universal Best Evidence Rule. The Best Evidence Rule requires only the best of available alternative proofs of the contents of a *writing*. Most other facts may be proved by the best evidence available to the party, or by the worst, or anything in between, at his option, so long as the other rules of evidence are complied with. To make this crystal clear, the tendency is growing to refer to the Best Evidence Rule as the "Original Documents Rule" and to drop the phrase "Best Evidence." See F.R.E. Article X and the Advisory Committee's Notes thereto.

Writings: (c) The Parol Evidence Rule

Evidence of prior oral statements (known as "parol evidence") is inadmissible to vary, contradict, or add to the terms of a written instrument, subject to some exceptions.

Certain oral and written expressions are given legal effect by law in a fashion that cannot be described as evidentiary. Into this class fall contracts, deeds, wills, etc. (Outside the class would be expressions offered to prove the facts they recount where it is those facts themselves that have the legal consequences—as, for example, a statement detailing an automobile collision in a personal injury case.) As to expressions within the class, oftentimes there will be an earlier and a later expression (either or both oral or written) and a question arises whether and to what extent the later super-

[78]

sedes the earlier, not only as to matters expressly inconsistent between the two, but as to matters that can logically coexist and matters covered by the earlier one but not mentioned in the later one (in which case arguably the silence or absence in the later expression may mean the earlier undertaking is negated). This would seem to be a problem of substantive contract law (or will or deed law) to be decided on the basis of the intent of the parties. While this is in fact the way it is handled, we must note that where the later expression is written and the former oral the law does not permit the jury to decide the issue, as would normally be the case, but gives it to the judge. And, more importantly, the judge decides it, not frankly as a matter of intent, but as a matter of whether the former (oral) expression comes within the Parol Evidence Rule (in which case it is *inadmissible in evidence*) or within an exception to the Parol Evidence Rule (many of the exceptions in practice turning on whether the parties intended the later expression to supersede or preempt the former). In theory the earlier parol expression, which would seem to be evidence of that intent, is not to be considered by the judge in deciding whether an exception applies, but only the face of the instrument and, sometimes, surrounding circumstances.

The same rules apply to oral expressions made contemporaneously with the writing, as apply to oral expressions preceding the writing.

Evidence of such prior or contemporaneous oral expressions is known as "parol evidence."

The Parol Evidence Rule is that "parol evidence is inadmissible to vary, contradict, or add to the terms of a written instrument." The rule does not apply (or there are exceptions) where the writing is "incomplete" or is but a "partial memorandum" or not a "full integration of the terms."

The oral expression may then supply the lacks. (Indeed, some jurisdictions even hold that the oral terms might be added if they are such as might reasonably have been left out.) This is also the result insofar as the earlier or contemporaneous oral expression can be said to form a separate or collateral agreement. Oral expressions *subsequent* to the writing are beyond the pale of the rule and can constitute agreed changes in the terms of the undertaking. Where there is an ambiguity in a term of the writing, earlier and contemporaneous as well as later oral expressions are admissible to determine what the parties meant. Matters affecting the basic validity of the instrument or written undertaking, such as fraud, compulsion, lack of consideration, conditions precedent, mistake to which the law attaches effect, grounds for reformation, and their opposites, may be shown by otherwise impermissible parol evidence, as may factors bearing on the propriety of specific performance. There may be other "exceptions" in various jurisdictions.

Phrasing the problem (of whether to consider the oral expression) in terms of the Parol Evidence Rule and its exceptions rather than frankly in terms of intent (1) takes the issue from the jury, as described, on the theory that the judge is better able to decide it, and (2) tends to limit the range of materials the judge feels able to look at in deciding the issue, also as described above. The latter may be justified on the basis that looking only at the completeness of and other features of the face of the instrument generally results in a decision in accord with the previous intent of the parties, and the additional accuracy to be gained from a more thorough investigation is not worth the time, effort, and expense. With respect to both (1) and (2), why should the case where the earlier and later expressions are both oral or both written be treated differently than a case where the later expression is written and the earlier oral?

There are certain other policy considerations which also may be partly responsible for the Parol Evidence Rule and may influence the shape or application of the exceptions. One is a fear that juries will accept the existence of or terms of an oral expression with too much gullibility; another is that, for commercial functioning, one must be able to rely on the face of writings; and another is that parties should be encouraged to include as much of the bargain as possible in the writing. The jury, of course, would not be mindful of these considerations.

The fact that the rule is relaxed in Equity, where there is a judge trial, confirms the notion that distrust of the jury plays a considerable role in the Parol Evidence Rule.

Where it is determined that parol evidence comes in under one of the exceptions to the rule, the jury should (and usually will) be allowed to decide to what extent the writing was meant to supersede (if there is doubt) even if the judge has impliedly made some kind of determination on this already. Of course, the jury will not be told he has.

Writings and Other Exhibits: Manner of Introduction

"Exhibit" is a term that refers to items (tangible "things," as opposed to testimony) which are used at trial to persuade the trier-of-fact. They must comply with the rules of evidence like any other evidence, and, like other evidence, such compliance must be shown (usually in some sort of "foundation" testimony) or must otherwise appear, at least if objection is made. Certain additional mechanical steps (marking) are also required for clarity of presentation in the record.

An exhibit can be a document, chart, photograph, x-ray film, motion picture, videotape, sound recording, specimen, model, weapon, or other thing. An exhibit may be merely an explanatory aid, as a chart or blackboard drawing, or something probative and relevant in a more direct sense, as for example, a writing offered as evidence of the truth of the statements therein, a written contract offered in a suit upon the contract, the murder weapon offered in a homicide prosecution, a piece of clothing offered to aid identification, the exhibiting of a child to establish paternity by resemblance, the exhibiting of a person to establish nationality, or even documents used to impeach or refresh recollection.   The terms "demonstrative," "real," "tangible," or "autoptic" are often applied to these or some of these kinds of items.   Exhibits are, of course, subject to all the ordinary rules of evidence.   In the case of explanatory aids, and photographs and motion pictures purporting to depict a scene or event in issue, the most frequently invoked principle of Evidence is the one embodied in F.R.E. 403, the probative-prejudice-misleadingness-time balancing rule of discretion.   The question under that principle as applied here is usually whether the item *fairly* represents or depicts the thing it purports to represent or depict, and whether it is needed.

Exhibits also require some additional mechanical steps for their introduction.   These are known as "marking," described as follows:

Unless the attorneys and court officials have done it in advance of the hearing, just prior to referring to an exhibit for the first time at trial, the offering attorney requests aloud the court reporter or other official provided therefor, to "mark [the item, which counsel briefly describes in general terms, i. e., what it appears or purports to be] '[Plaintiff's] Exhibit No. [1] for Identification'."   This legend (including the words "for identification") is then actually inscribed upon the exhibit, and thereafter the exhibit can be referred to by that name ("Plaintiff's Exhibit No. 1 for Identification") without confusion and in a fashion that will be clear in the written transcript of the words spoken at the trial.   (The trial lawyer must always remember that cases are reviewed on the written record. He must be certain that everything he may want to be reviewed appears therein. To give one example, nods and facial expressions do not.) If the attorney later wishes to "introduce the exhibit into evidence" (after laying whatever legal predicate or "foundation" is necessary for admissibility) and the exhibit is held admissible, he then, again by simple request spoken aloud, "offers in evidence Plaintiff's Exhibit No. 1 for Identification," and if it is admitted by the judge, it becomes merely "Plaintiff's Exhibit No. 1," or "Plaintiff's Exhibit No. 1 in evidence," the court reporter striking off that part of the notation on the exhibit that says "for Identification." A wise attorney will request the latter, to be certain no misunderstanding arises later. In a multi-exhibit case, he will also keep a running list of all his exhibits to be used at trial, with two separate columns opposite each, one column to check off as he marks the exhibit for identification, and the other to check off as he introduces the exhibit into evidence. Too often an attorney realizes only at the end of the case that he has fatally forgotten to introduce into evidence a critical document he has only marked for identification. The consequences of "introducing an exhibit into evidence" are that for purposes of instructions to the jury, for purposes of burdens of proof (both the production burden and persuasion burden, including directed verdicts and findings), and for purposes of arguments and comments, etc., the exhibit is considered to be in evidence and usable in the case; it becomes a part of the record for purposes of judicial review; and the jurors usually may take it with them when they retire to consider the case, at least (in some courts) if they specially request.[9] (Under the

---

[9] Exhibits (including such things as deposition transcripts or transcripts of other hearings, introduced in the present trial) must be distinguished from transcripts or portions of transcripts of the arguments made or testimony given in the current trial itself. These normally may not be given to or "re-played" for the jury. Selective

F.R.E., certain exhibits may not be physically given to the jury, because of feared emphasis or misuse by the jury, or use of the wrong portions. Treatises, and documents introduced as past recollection recorded, are so treated. Query, does the judge have discretion to keep other exhibits from the jury in a particular case on similar grounds?) It must be pointed out that the jury may not perform "experiments" with exhibits taken to the jury room because this is evidence outside the presence of the parties and their counsel. What is an "experiment", and what mere examination, should be, as usual, determined with reference to the purposes of the rule.

In a number of jurisdictions, exhibits may not be offered during cross examination, subject to some discretion on the judge's part. In some, such introduction by defendant during the plaintiff's or prosecutor's case may result in a forfeiture of defendant's right to move for a directed verdict at the close of that case.

Generally, before an exhibit is admitted in evidence (and this is especially true of a writing), opposing counsel must have an opportunity to examine it. Many jurisdictions will not permit a document that has been admitted into evidence to be used in the case unless it has been read to the jury. It is good practice to read it immediately upon admission. The reading may be done by the witness (if one having something to do with the document is on the stand, as is usually the case) or by the attorney. The judge may also allow the document to be circulated to the jury at that

emphasis is feared. A similar concern is felt with respect to juror note-taking, which may or may not be allowed. A related problem is the occasional jury desire to have instructions repeated or explained after the jury has retired to deliberate. Repetition of particular instructions is frowned upon, because of similar concerns, although occasionally it is done. Instructions may be explained by the judge on request or even given in writing, perhaps initially.

time. If the document is a transcript of another proceeding or a deposition (this is a common form of impeachment or establishing facts via an exception to the hearsay rule), an alternative and dramatically effective method of reading it aloud is to have the attorney read the questions and the witness read the answers.

After a case is closed, exhibits normally remain part of the record. Methods are available for securing their return to the parties.

With respect to all the exhibits procedures above and in the next section, it should be borne in mind that it is often desirable to get the marking for identification and even the question of the admissibility (a quite distinct question) of your exhibits taken care of in sessions prior to the trial. Marking, rulings, and stipulations can be requested then as well as at the trial. Remember, stipulations or rulings as to authenticity or best evidence have nothing to do with whether the evidence is acceptable under other rules.

Closely allied to the subject of tangible evidence is the subject of jury views: in certain situations the judge in his discretion may be receptive to the suggestion that it is appropriate for a jury to go to view particular premises or things that cannot be satisfactorily described in, brought to, or reproduced in, the courtroom. The same is also possible in a non-jury trial, where the suggestion may be more favorably received because more convenient.

Example of Specific Questions and Answers ("Foundation") for Identifying, Authenticating and Otherwise Rendering Admissible, and Introducing, a Simple Documentary Exhibit; Also, Example of Objection Technique

Q. (By counsel): What did you then do, if anything?

A. (By witness): I wrote a letter to him.

Q. Mr. Reporter, will you please mark this written instrument—appearing to be a letter from Mrs. Jane Brown to Mr. Fred Smith dated April 4, 1980—"Plaintiff's Exhibit No. 1 for Identification?"

[Instrument marked "Pl. Ex. 1 for Id."]

Q. (To witness): Mrs. Brown, I show you Plaintiff's Exhibit No. 1 for Identification and ask you whether or not it is the letter to which you have referred?

A. Yes, it is.

Q. If the Court please, at this time I wish to offer Plaintiff's Exhibit No. 1 for Identification, being the letter spoken of by Mrs. Brown, in evidence as Plaintiff's Exhibit No. 1; and I offer both the face and the reverse sides. I hand it to opposing counsel for examination.[10]   [The

---

[10] Alternative authenticating foundation:

Q. Mrs. Brown, I show you Plaintiff's Exhibit No. 1 for Identification, purporting to be a letter from you to Mr. Fred Smith dated April 4, 1980 and ask you if your name and signature appear thereon. [or, "and ask you if you have ever seen it before"].

A. Yes, it does.

Q. Was it signed by you on or about the date it bears?

A. Yes, it was.

Q. I offer .   . ., etc.

Laying the foundation for (authenticating) a photograph usually involves merely producing a witness to say that the scene depicted is known to him and is accurately portrayed. The witness need not be the photographer, just someone familiar with the scene. (In some jurisdictions or in some circumstances the testimony may have to be that it accurately portrays the scene as it was at the relevant time. Sometimes this will be an issue of admissibility only if raised by the opponent and there seems to be a danger of misleading. In others, it would not be an issue of admissibility at all, but only weight.) The chain of custody of the photo ordinarily need not be shown, but such showing vel non can affect weight. Showing chain of custody may in some instances be an alternative foundation. As in the case of documents, a showing of inaccuracy, inauthenticity, or "doctoring," after the foundation is once properly laid, will frequently be left for the jury to consider.

In the example in text, some lawyers prefer to mark each sithe of the document with a separate number.

document could have been handed to him at the time it was marked for identification, instead.]

Opposing Counsel: [Optional preface to the objection: "May we approach the bench, your Honor?"] I object to the introduction of Plaintiff's Exhibit No. 1 for the reason that [here follow specific reasons].

or

If the Court please, we would like your Honor to reserve decision on the admissibility of this exhibit until we have had an opportunity to cross examine Mrs. Brown respecting it. [The judge could even be requested to allow early cross examination at this point, known as "voir dire," directed at admissibility, either in or out of the jury's hearing.]

or

May it please the Court, I object that only the second paragraph of the exhibit is admissible, for the reason that . . ., and I therefore move that other portions of the exhibit be covered or excised, or that the admissible portion be copied off on to other paper. [The admissibility of only a part, by blocking out part, is known as "redaction" and can apply to oral as well as written evidence.] [Counsel may content himself with a ruling that portions are inadmissible, taking up the manner of keeping unacceptable portions from the eyes of the jury later when the document is presented physically to the jury if it is not to be done now. He must be careful to bring the matter up then. Be wary that the document may be handed to the jury for a preliminary examination before the close of the evidence —e. g., when it is admitted.]

I further ask that the Court rule that the document is received only for the purpose of . . . and not for the purpose of . . ..

The Court: The document may be received [or, the document may be received for the limited purpose of . . . and not . . . or may be received under the following conditions; etc. Counsel should always be certain that a clear ruling on each of his requests appears on the record, and that limitations of purpose are judicially announced to, and understood by, the jury. A limitation of purpose frequently may also be requested again at the close of all the evidence before submission to the jury, in the form of an instruction.]

Offering Counsel: I will ask that the identification mark be stricken and that the instrument be marked "Plaintiff's Exhibit No. 1 in Evidence."

The Court: The identification mark may be stricken.

[Reporter strikes off last part of his former marking, so the mark now reads "Pl. Ex. 1."]

Offering Counsel: If it please the Court, I would like to read Plaintiff's Exhibit No. 1 to the jury [or read such part as has been admitted]. [Near this point the document might be given the jury for preliminary examination.]

Necessity for Requesting Action by the Trial Judge

As a general rule, action by the trial judge of any sort (e. g., exclusion of evidence, instruction, etc.) must be solicited, and will be waived if the solicitation is not timely made.

Notwithstanding the above black-letter rule, it is usually held not to be error for the trial judge to issue a correct ruling or instruction where he need not have owing to failure of counsel to request it. Furthermore, occasionally a trial court will be required to act of its own motion: so-called "plain error" committed at trial is not waived by failure to object and may be rectified even if it is noticed for the first time only on appeal. The appellate court may, but need not, notice plain error of its own motion. "Plain error" exists where it is felt that the error is so fundamental that justice would be egregiously denied were it considered waived; or so palpable that it should have come to the judge's attention without solicitation. See F.R.E. 103(d). Objections to evidence must, as a general matter, specify their grounds, and the correct grounds, in a particular enough way to pinpoint the issue, unless the grounds are self-evident. See F.R.E. 103(a)(1). Otherwise the trial court will be sustained whatever it does, provided there is some conceivable rationale. In jurisdictions with enacted evidence codes or rules, it might be wise to add rule numbers and subdivisions to your objections, to be absolutely specific; and someday this may even be required. Concerning offers of evidence, in order to secure a proper trial ruling and to preserve the right to appeal an improper one, a formal offer of proof (or "proffer" as it is sometimes called) stating the proposed purpose and expected substance of an offered piece of evidence must always be made by the offering attorney if an objection is raised and the purpose and substance of the evidence is not self-evident. Otherwise the appellate court will ordinarily sustain even an erroneous exclusion of the evidence. See F.R.E. 103(a)(2). "Plain error" is an exception to all these rules.

The requirement of making the substance of the evidence known may be difficult where it is *cross* examination that is being blocked by the objection. Usually the best that can be done is to explain what is hoped to be developed.

In direct examination situations, there are several ways to make a proffer, that is, make the substance of the evidence known: (1) Q. and A. of the witness before the judge and counsel alone; (2) oral summary by counsel; or (3) written submission. Which one is employed depends on the discretion of the judge. The jury generally would not be privy to any of them, but both counsel would be.

Forcing an offer of proof can be a method of finding out about the opponent's case, and the tactics of this are often considered by both attorneys.

In most jurisdictions there are procedures for making objections in advance of trial to evidence it is known will be sought to be introduced. This is sometimes called a "motion in limine." Certain objections may be waived if anticipatable and not made through this procedure.

Harmless Error

Errors committed by the trial court, even if promptly and properly noted there by the attorney, may be regarded by the appellate court as "harmless," though errors.

The standard for determining what constitutes "prejudicial" (reversible) as opposed to "harmless" (non-reversible) error varies from jurisdiction to jurisdiction, and may also vary according to whether a criminal, civil, or criminal-constitutional issue is involved, and what particular constitutional issue it is. The variance will be in the degree of probability with which it must appear that the error affected the verdict, from "may have" through "probably did." One articulation regards error (in the admission of evidence) as harmless if there was sufficient other evidence independent of the erroneously admitted evidence, upon which a reasonable juror could have based the verdict that was handed down, even if the erroneously admitted piece of evidence probably was the decisive one in the jury's mind. Federal courts (in particular the Supreme Court) have restricted state and federal courts' and legislatures' freedom to choose among these tests in cases of certain constitutional rights in criminal proceedings. E.g., error in admitting a constitutionally inadmissible confession or in denying the constitutional right to confrontation probably cannot be dismissed as harmless on any test, although in the latter case the prejudiciality of what was done may play a role in the determination of whether a constitutional right has been violated. Furthermore, it becomes increasingly clear that the "sufficient independent evidence" test, and the test requiring, for a finding of prejudicial error, that the error "probably affected" the verdict (as opposed to "may have affected"), are unacceptable respecting most of the constitutional evidentiary rights of criminal accuseds. Several Supreme Court cases suggest that the error must be found to be "harmless beyond a reasonable doubt." (As used herein, "constitutional" refers to the U.S. Constitution.)

Preliminary Questions of Fact

    Particular evidence rules and standards may call for a determination of fact in order to decide whether evidence is admissible or not. The law is mixed as to how this function is to be allocated between judge and jury and what rules and standards govern such determinations of fact. For most practical purposes it is useful to assume the judge normally makes the determination.

In many instances, admissibility of evidence is said to be contingent on the finding of certain preliminary facts or conditions germane to the relevance or acceptability of the evidence or to the "balancing" calculus discussed earlier in this chapter, but not directly germane to the legal issues in the case. For example, the husband-wife privilege applies to bar evidence only if the relevant persons were married. Their marriage vel non is a preliminary issue of fact as we are presently using the term. Sometimes there is a coincidence of a preliminary issue and an ultimate substantive issue in the same case. Thus, in a suit for non-support, the issue of marriage vel non between plaintiff and defendant may govern not only the admissibility of a piece of evidence but also the plaintiff's right to support. It is not absolutely certain that "marriage" in the evidentiary context means the same as "marriage" in other areas of the law, but even if it does, the determination for each purpose in the case would be done independently, and inconsistency between them would be permitted. Usually the judge would determine the question for evidentiary purposes, and the jury would for purposes of the case at large. The same problem arises under the co-conspirator exception to or exemption from the hearsay rule, under which out-of-court statements of a co-conspirator are admissible against a fellow conspirator. When this co-conspirator rule comes into issue in a prosecution charging criminal conspiracy and the statement is sought to be used against the defendant, courts have become very confused as to who is to make the determination as to whether there *was* a conspiracy, what is the burden of proof, what evidence is needed, what is to be the role of the statement itself, and how can the issue be kept separate from the substantive issue of conspiracy in the case at large. See Rothstein, Federal Rules of Evidence (Clark Boardman Co., Ltd., 2d Ed.) at Rules 104 and 801(d)(2)(E).

There are many other examples of preliminary facts or conditions that could be cited. Testimonial privilege may turn upon the existence of a doctor-patient or lawyer-client relationship. The privilege against self-incrimination turns upon the incriminating nature of the information sought. The admissibility of copies may depend upon whether the original document is available. The admissibility of an offer to settle may turn upon whether suit was filed. Silence in the face of an accusation is admissible as an admission only if the circumstances reasonably called for a reply. A confession must be voluntary and made in the presence of certain safeguards, to be admissible against the confessor in a criminal case. Evidence is inadmissible against an accused if it is the product of an illegal search or seizure perpetrated against him. A witness may give testimony only if he is competent and has first-hand knowledge. An expert opinion is admissible only if the witness is indeed an expert. A document is admissible only if certain authenticating facts are submitted. Factual foundations must be laid for experiments, photographs, so-called scientific evidence, and certain other forms of evidence. (As we shall see, not all of these are precisely the same kind of animal.)

Where there is a genuine dispute over the existence of a preliminary fact or condition which must be *affirmatively found* before the evidence may be used, usually (but not everywhere, or in every kind of case) the judge is to make this finding before the evidence is admissible, and that is the end of the matter except insofar as the jury is permitted to consider showings like those made to the judge, in assessing weight if the judge admits the evidence. But notice that not all such showings will have relevance to weight;[11] refer back, for example, to the mention of privileges (marital, doctor-patient, lawyer-client) just above. F.R.E. 104(a) adopts the approach of this paragraph for the decision of *most* preliminary fact questions.

Under another approach (again where the preliminary fact must be affirmatively found), once the judge finds the prerequisite to admissibility to exist, the jury is given the evidence, is requested to make the determination over again on their own (generally without guidance as to what the judge has found), and is told to disregard the evidence if they do not find the prerequisite to exist. It is unrealistic to expect the jury to do this last, in cases where the lack of the prerequisite fact or condition would not to the ordinary lay mind deprive the evidence of all weight. For example,

---

[11] Where they *are* relevant to weight as well as to admissibility, judges often find it economical to have the showings made at one and the same time for both judge and jury, rather than made out of the jury's hearing for purposes of the preliminary fact and then made again before the jury for purposes of weight. The judge thus holds the preliminary fact hearing (that is, the showings portion of it) before the jury rather than at the bench or in chambers; or he waits altogether before entertaining the question, until the showings have naturally come before the jury in the course of the trial (which will happen if the showings have some other independent significance in the case as well as their significance on the preliminary fact and weight). If he follows the latter procedure, he can conditionally admit or conditionally exclude, pending the later resolution.

while a totally coerced confession might have no weight to a lay mind, a confession that is "involuntary" under the legal standard often does not rise to this degree of involuntariness. It should also be noted that double preliminary fact finding (judge first, then jury) may lead a judge to be less than scrupulous in his finding, and to favor admissibility, in reliance on the jury to make a more careful finding and to obey the instructions. This may offset the advantage the double fact finding method would give, say, to an objector to a criminal confession, even though that method accords him two chances to prove involuntariness.

Sometimes the jury alone is allowed to make the determination of whether a prerequisite fact or condition exists (without any initial screening by the judge), and is instructed to disregard the evidence if the fact or condition does not exist (again something they may not be able to do). This mode of preliminary fact determination is clearly impermissible in the constitutional area of involuntary criminal confessions, as is the variation thereof whereunder the judge must first find "some substantial evidence" of the prerequisite fact or condition or that a reasonable person might find that it exists.

Another position sometimes taken with respect to preliminary facts or conditions is that the fact or condition need not be established by any *finding* on anyone's part, but rather the evidence will be admissible upon *some showing* or a *substantial showing* to the judge that the fact or condition exists. This is the position F.R.E. 104(b) takes with respect to preliminary questions of fact upon which "relevancy" depends. If this minimum showing is made (and, under some versions, if it survives attempts to reduce it below the minimum), the jury receives the evidence and considers similar showings and counter-showings in assessing weight. This is usually intended to insure at least some probability that the evidence is worthwhile and reliable before it is received. Thus, e. g., in the case of authentication, first-hand knowledge, and competence and qualifications of witnesses, once the prima facie showing is made, attempts to defeat it are generally regarded as purely matters of weight for the jury. Some commentators would not classify genuineness and these other matters as preliminary facts where handled in this fashion. Not content with the provisions of Rule 104, which may or may not produce the desired result, F.R.E. 602 (first-hand personal knowledge rule), 901(a) (authentication) and 1008 (certain questions under Best Evidence Rule) provide that preliminary fact questions under those rules will be handled pursuant to the view set forth in this paragraph.

Where a so-called preliminary fact or condition has significance *solely* as a matter for the jury to consider in assessing weight of the evidence, and is not a prerequisite to admissibility or use in any of the above fashions, the fact or condition is not a preliminary fact or condition in the sense used here.

A preliminary issue of fact should have its own law of burdens, proof, and pleading, like any issue in the case, but courts often leave the matter in great obscurity. F.R.E. 104 provides no guidance. Practice varies. Preliminary facts may be assumed as a matter of law to exist, or not exist, unless and until evidence to the contrary appears. Several of the modes of fact-determination above presuppose that the proponent of the evidence has the burden to show the existence of the preliminary fact; but they have analogies where the burden is on the other party. Also perhaps not reflected in some of the modes above, is the notion that the judge can foreclose the issue from jury consideration, even when the jury would be the usual finder of the preliminary fact, if he feels there is no issue, that is, that the evidence is overwhelmingly clear one way or the other.

The rules of evidence are less stringently applied to proof of a preliminary fact, at least where the judge is to make the decision.   F.R.E. 104(a), concerning preliminary fact determinations that do not relate to relevancy, provides that the rules of evidence, other than privilege, do not apply.

Respecting both preliminary facts and other matters such as objections and offers of proof, evidence and argument that is presented for the benefit of the judge should be presented out of the jury's hearing or presence, if potentially prejudicial.   The mechanisms are requests for bench and chambers conferences, temporary excusal of the jury, etc. The judge, however, has discretion.   See footnote 11, supra; F.R.E. 103(c), 104(c) (providing for the hearing of certain preliminary matters outside the hearing of the jury).

Occasionally a matter bearing on a preliminary fact issue, which matter would have changed the determination of that issue, will come out only after the preliminary issue has been resolved and the evidence has been admitted or excluded.   If the failure to bring the matter out is regarded as excusable, the judge will attempt to remedy the situation in some appropriate way with the tools we have seen are at his command.   Sometimes the new material will be left to the jury as a matter of weight (if the evidence has been admitted).

The standard of review of judge and/or jury determinations of preliminary fact is probably the same as where substantive findings of the fact-finder are reviewed by the trial judge (on motion for a judgment notwithstanding the verdict) or by an appellate judge: They will be overturned only if *unreasonable* (not supported by any reasonable quantum of evidence ["some evidence" is the rubric in some jurisdictions]).   This is the degree of deference except as respects certain constitutional evidentiary preliminary fact findings that are deemed to require *de novo* consideration.

Non-Jury Trials

We have seen that Evidence law seems in large measure to be designed with a view to regulating the jury, and that underlying it at many points is a tacit assumption that judges are less fallible than jurors. To what extent, then, should Evidence law be modified where the judge is the trier of fact? This question can be asked with respect to each and every Evidence precept in this book. Commentators have suggested that exclusionary rules whose only concern is with prejudice, be done away with in non-jury cases except in areas where judges are deemed to be susceptible to the same sort of undue influence as juries. As an example of such area, we should note that these commentators usually do not suggest that the rule against involuntary confessions be lifted in judge trials. Some writers have questioned the feasibility of excluding evidence in judge trials where the judge must hear the evidence in order to determine admissibility vel non.

But courts adhere to the rubric that the law of Evidence applies to jury and non-jury cases alike. The F.R.E. make no express distinction. But of course the rules under which prejudice, misleadingness, and protraction are factors will and should produce some results that are different in jury and non-jury cases. For what is likely to be misconstrued or exaggerated (i. e., rendered "prejudicial" and "misleading") by a jury is not necessarily going to be by a judge, at least not to the same extent. Nor will as much time be needed to put it in perspective. Cf. Gulf States Utilities Co. v. Ecodyne Corp., 635 F.2d 517 (5th Cir. 1981) (most of F.R.E. 403 "has no application to bench trials": holding is broader than necessary for the case and arguably dictum to that extent). Of perhaps more impact, however, is the appellate practice (apparently left untouched by the F.R.E.) of treating erroneous exclusion of evidence in a non-jury trial precisely as in a jury trial; while, with respect to erroneously *admitted* evidence, expressing a presumption that, if there was sufficient competent evidence to support the findings, the trial judge relied on competent evidence only. This presumption sometimes prevails even in the face of an expression by the judge of an erroneous view of which evidence was admissible, not merely where the judge allows the evidence without ruling either way on its admissibility. The presumption would thus be overcome only when there is a clear indication that he *relied* on inadmissible evidence. In consequence of all this, trial judges in non-jury cases tend to admit, reserving ruling on admissibility and then hold ruling unnecessary on the grounds that their decision is reached on the basis of the *unquestioned* evidence; or, if they have ruled to admit, they find the facts expressly on the basis of evidence that has not been questioned. As a result of these several factors, rules of evidence have a somewhat muffled though still important impact in judge trials. Privileges, however, are generally fully applicable.

For obvious reasons, mistrials are granted less liberally, too.

Exclusionary rules of evidence may or may not be enforced in administrative proceedings, depending upon the administrative tribunal's particular adjective law. Privilege, however, is usually recognized. The law or regulations of a number of federal agencies have apparently incorporated the Federal Rules of Evidence, at least to some extent, by reference to "the rules that govern evidence in non-jury trials in Federal District Courts" or similar language, often with certain exceptions. Some language of the Administrative Procedure Act may cut in a different direction, more receptive to evidence, but it is not absolutely clear. As a practical matter a large number of agencies (both those subject to the Act, and those not) find the Federal Rules of Evidence quite influential. Some authority is developing in various jurisdictions that administrative agency rulings on evidence may not be *more* restrictive than the rules drafted for or applicable in courts.

CHAPTER II

PRESUMPTIONS

Burdens of Pleading and Proof: Prerequisite to Understanding Presumptions

There is a pleading burden, a production-of-evidence burden (or burden of going forward with the evidence), and a persuasion burden, for each issue in a case. The latter two are the so-called "burdens of proof": discharge or preventing the discharge of them is the goal of introducing evidence. An understanding of how these two burdens operate in the absence of evidentiary presumptions is essential to an understanding of evidentiary presumptions (our next subject) since evidentiary presumptions affect or aid in the discharge of (or preventing discharge of) these burdens. Hence we first examine these burdens as they operate in ordinary cases without presumptions.

Considering the burdens mentioned above, it is well to note at the outset that a particular burden may be on one party as to some issues, and on the other party as to other issues, in the same case. Even as to one particular given issue, all three burdens may not be on the same party.[1]

[1] It is not clear what has dictated the allocation of the burdens in cases. Considerations of convenience; of relative accessibility of proof to the two parties; of who is disturbing the status quo; of what is likely to be the truth in the absence of pleading, proof, or persuasion on the factual issue; of the unusualness of the claim relied upon by the one party or the other; of whether the proposition is negatively or affirmatively stated; of whether the matter raises an exception to a statute or general rule; of public policies such as deterrence; etc., have all been suggested.

Furthermore, the production burden on an issue may shift from one party to the other several times during the course of the trial. What this means is that as evidence is introduced, first one party, then the other, may run the risk of a directed verdict or equivalent ruling if he allows the state of the evidence to remain as it is without going forward with the evidence. The party on whom this risk rests is said to have the burden of "going forward with the evidence," i. e., producing additional evidence.

That which a party must put in his pleading (e. g., in his complaint, indictment, answer, plea) in order for it to be in issue in the case, constitutes his *pleading* burden. Thus, in a murder case, the prosecution must plead that the defendant killed the victim, or the case can be dismissed before it ever gets to trial. In other words, the prosecution has the burden of pleading on the issue of whether the defendant killed the victim. I. e., the risk of not pleading on that issue is on the prosecution. We will not have much more to say about the pleading burden but will go on to the other burdens.

(a) *Production Burden.*

A party has the *production* burden when, if he allows the evidence to stay as it is, the issue will be concluded against him as a matter of law. For example, the prosecutor in the above murder case has something more to worry about than his pleading burden. This is the production burden which initially and at various other times will be on him. By this we mean as follows. At the close of the prosecution's evidence, and again at the end of all of the evidence, the state of the evidence must be such that the judge can say some reasonable juror could find beyond a reasonable doubt that the defendant killed the victim,[2] or else the

---

[2] If this were a civil wrongful death case, all the judge need be able to say is that some reasonable juror could find by a preponderance of the evidence that D killed V. In other words, the degree of the

prosecution will be liable to suffer an adverse judicial ruling establishing that fact against the prosecution without the aid of or despite the jury. Thus, whenever during the course of the trial the evidence does not permit the judge to feel a reasonable juror could find for the prosecution on that issue, the risk of a peremptory ruling on that issue is on the prosecution unless and until additional evidence favorable to the prosecution is adduced. (Of course, it does not matter which side adduces it.) If the evidence lines up in this unfavorable way for the prosecutor at any time when he can still introduce more evidence, he had better not rest; he had better go forward and adduce more evidence. He has the burden, in other words, to *produce more evidence.* (Of course, one side cannot move for a peremptory ruling so long as the other indicates it has more evidence to introduce and the time for introducing it has not passed.)

Sometimes the problem is talked about in terms of whether or not the prosecutor's (or plaintiff's) evidence (or, more properly, the evidence that cuts in his favor) is sufficient to get the issue to the jury (or sufficient to sustain a verdict in his favor on the issue).

It is obvious that as to most issues, the plaintiff and the prosecution bear the production burden initially, in that if no evidence on the issue is adduced, they will suffer a peremptory ruling. The adduction of sufficient evidence to get to the jury (i. e., the overcoming of the production

---

persuasion burden influences the production burden. Some cases hold it is drawing too fine a line to require the judge to distinguish in this fashion between criminal and civil cases as respects the ruling spoken of here. Such cases may articulate the standard in both instances simply as "whether a reasonable juror could find D killed V." This may imply the distinction, however. Some decisions seem to apply the civil standard in both kinds of cases.

Notice that, whatever the test, the question is *not* whether the *judge himself* can say D killed V (beyond a reasonable doubt or by a preponderance of the evidence or under any other standard).

burden) does not shift the production burden to the other side. Only when the evidence is so overwhelming as to subject the other side to the specter of a peremptory ruling if the evidence remains in that state, do we say the production burden has shifted. As we shall see, this shifting ordinarily cannot be accomplished by the prosecution on the issue whether D killed V. It can be accomplished by a plaintiff on the same issue in a corresponding civil context. A production burden once shifted may, of course, be shifted back again by a change in the state of the evidence that once again renders the original party liable to a peremptory ruling.

We have a bunch of unnecessarily fancy names for the judicial decree or order requested or motion that is made to call to the attention of the judge that one has failed to discharge a pleading or production burden. Depending upon the time when made and the name used in the particular jurisdiction, these may be called judgment on the pleadings, summary judgment, dismissal, non-suit, a directed verdict, judgment notwithstanding the verdict, etc. But they all assert merely the essentially simple fact that one of these burdens (pleading or production burden) has not been met, on some issue. The failure to meet the burden, and hence the request or order (called generically a "peremptory" ruling or order), may pertain to only one issue, foreclosing only it from further debate; or, if that issue is determinative, as in the example, the ruling will determine the entire case. The ruling generally must be solicited of the court.

Suppose the murder example above were a *civil* wrongful death action, with a similar allocation of burdens on the issue of whether the defendant killed the victim. (Assume the pleading burden is discharged.) In addition to the peremptory judicial rulings possible in the criminal analogue, the plaintiff can move for one in *his* favor at the close of all the evidence on grounds that on the state of the evidence, all reasonable jurors must agree that the issue whether D killed V must be resolved in his favor. In other words, he argues that the evidence has not only discharged plaintiff's production burden (i. e., allowed him to avoid the specter of an adverse peremptory ruling), but has shifted that burden (the burden to go forward and produce additional evidence, or else suffer an adverse peremptory ruling) to the defendant on that issue. He is saying that the risk of an adverse peremptory ruling upon no further production of evidence has shifted, or should now be shifted, to the defendant; and that the defendant has closed his case and indicated he has no more to present. If the issue of whether the defendant killed the victim is the only issue in the case, success of the plaintiff's motion will mean success in the case at large. However, there may be other closely contested issues in the case, e. g., a defense that plaintiff instigated the killing and thus cannot recover, or an argument that plaintiff has no real damages or is not related in the proper way to the deceased. If so, and the plaintiff's motion is successful, the jury will be instructed that they are to find on the remaining issues only, it being established that the defendant killed the victim.

Owing to a special dispensation to criminal defendants, the prosecutor in the analogous criminal case cannot obtain the analogous peremptory ruling (that D killed V). Is this in fact a special dispensation? Or is it because we can never say reasonable men must agree that the evidence that D killed V is credible beyond a reasonable doubt?

A peremptory ruling might, in both the civil and the criminal example, take the form of an instruction to the jury, "If you believe [to the requisite degree] that defendant was seen dismembering the body of V at such and such time under such and such circumstances, then you must find defendant killed V." This would be appropriate where the judge could not direct the jury to find that defendant was seen dismembering the body at such and such time under such and such circumstances (because in a criminal case the "special dispensation" would not permit such a direction, or because in the civil or criminal case reasonable people could differ over whether to so find on the particular state of the evidence in that case), but he could direct as to what must follow if that fact is so found, because all reasonable people must agree that it follows [beyond a reasonable doubt, in the criminal case]. Some authorities would dispute the propriety of this ruling in a criminal case. A similar conditional ruling might be granted in favor of the *defendant* in either the civil or the criminal case. An instruction might also begin, "If you do not believe . . . then you may not find . . ." or "Only if you believe . . . may you find . . .".

Notice that in deciding whether a production burden is discharged, the judge is to consider *everything* that is properly to be considered in the case at large, not merely evidence proceeding from the side with the production burden. This includes evidence from the other side, experience, and common-sense notions, to the extent permitted to the jury.

"Summary judgment" is the term used where a peremptory judicial ruling of the kind discussed here is granted in advance of trial because it is made apparent by affidavits that the evidence that will be adduced at trial will entitle the movant to such a peremptory judicial ruling at trial. "Judgment notwithstanding the verdict" is the term usually used where the peremptory judicial ruling is granted after a jury verdict and overturns the verdict. The ruling is in essence a ruling that the verdict was unreasonable—that no reasonable juror could have rendered it. That is indeed the standard for such a ruling. The standard is the same as before verdict (at which time the ruling would normally be called a "directed verdict"), but often the judge will wait until after a verdict in case the ruling is rendered unnecessary by a consonant verdict, or in case the judge's ruling is reversed on appeal, in which event there would be a verdict on record to reinstate to avoid the necessity of a new trial.

The judgment notwithstanding the verdict spoken of here should not be confused with a granting of a new trial on grounds that the verdict is contrary to what the judge feels was the greater weight of the evidence. Such a ruling does not say the jury was unreasonable. It comes closer to saying that the judge, acting as a kind of thirteenth juror, would not have found the way the jury did, although he concedes that a reasonable juror could find as they did. Probably, however, the disagreement must be more than mild—the judge must not feel merely that he disagrees in a close case. He must feel the jury went against the "manifest" weight of the evidence, although they were not acting unreasonably. This granting of a new trial does not *conclude* the case or issue, but merely results in a new trial. As such, it is not the kind of peremptory ruling about which we are speaking.

Why don't these powers of the judge infringe the right to trial by jury? We cannot pause to examine that important question in this short work.

Putting aside any special criminal dispensation, it is established above that the standard for a peremptory judicial ruling on a matter of fact is whether a reasonable person could find in favor of the non-moving party on the issue. If some reasonable person could, the motion must be denied—the jury must be allowed the chance to find for the non-moving party. If *no* reasonable person could, then all reasonable people must agree that the issue must be resolved in the movant's favor, and the motion should be granted, to prevent an irrational finding by the jury. It must be added, however, that the law holds that reasonable people nearly always may disagree over whether witnesses can be believed or not, except in extraordinary situations. In some jurisdictions, direct testimony of an uncontradicted and unimpeached witness may constitute such an extraordinary situation, at least where he is not an interested witness and no other facts appear to cast any doubt on his credibility. In this situation it may be that the law will permit the judge to hold that all reasonable people must agree he is to be believed.[3] It will be a very rare situation indeed, however, where a judge will be permitted to say reasonable people must agree a witness is *not* to be believed. The mere fact that an overwhelming number tell one story, and a single witness tells the opposite, is not ordinarily grounds for saying reasonable people must agree that the majority's story is true, the other false.

The consequence of all this is that one in the position of our plaintiff above will seldom be entitled to a favorable peremptory ruling on an issue like whether D killed V unless the defendant concedes the credibility of a story told by plaintiff's side, which story is such that the inference to be drawn therefrom, while in dispute, seems to the judge to be such that all reasonable people must draw it in favor of the plaintiff regardless of the credibility of anyone else. A further consequence is that one in the position of our civil defendant can seldom procure a peremptory ruling in his favor on an issue like whether D killed V unless the inference that D killed V cannot be drawn even if all testimony favorable to the plaintiff is accepted as true. The test (for granting a peremptory ruling) that is sometimes

---

[3] Another such situation may be where a question is exclusively within the ken of experts and all the expert testimony is one way. Consider also that where a matter is said to require (not just to be appropriate for) expert testimony, the trier-of-fact will not be permitted to draw the inference in question unless an expert testifies it can be drawn.

articulated to take account of these matters is that all issues of credibility must be assumed to be resolved in favor of the non-moving party; and then, if a reasonable person still could not find for him, the motion is granted.

(b) *Persuasion Burden.*

In effect (though not in so many words) the fact-finders in a case are instructed by the law as to each fact issue in the case, that they are to assume it one way, unless convinced to a certain degree (preponderance of the probabilities or of the evidence; or beyond a reasonable doubt) that it is the other way. In other words, the electric switch (if a fact issue may be viewed as such) starts out in one of its two positions, and rests there with some degree of stickiness unless and until sufficient force (proof by a "preponderance of the evidence [or of the probabilities]" or "beyond a reasonable doubt") is mustered (or otherwise appears) to dislodge it to the other position. The party who loses the issue if it is not dislodged, has the "persuasion burden," and the degree of force (preponderance; or beyond a reasonable doubt) needed (i. e., the degree of stickiness) is the degree of that burden. In other words, the switch starts out lodged in the position (from among its two possible positions) that is against the position of the party with the burden.

Let us return to our example of a murder prosecution for illustration. Assume that liability to an adverse peremptory judicial ruling based on failure to plead that D killed V or to adduce sufficient evidence of that fact, is overcome by the prosecution. I. e., the prosecution has discharged its pleading and production burden, and the case "gets to the jury" on the issue. The prosecution will still suffer an adverse verdict if the jury is not persuaded beyond a reasonable doubt that the defendant killed the victim. Thus, as respects this issue, the risk of non-persuasion, or the so-called "persuasion burden," is on the prosecution, as were the pleading and production burdens. (As in the case of the other burdens, the language of "burden," as opposed to "risk [of non-persuasion]", is the less preferred. It suggests that only evidence proceeding from the side with the burden is considered in deciding whether the burden is discharged, which is not so. On another point, it should be noted that with *this* burden, it is the *jury* who decides whether it is discharged; whereas the judge decides in the cases of the pleading and production burdens.)

To what degree must the prosecution convince the minds of the jurors? I. e., how "heavy" is the persuasion burden? The jurors must be convinced "beyond a reasonable doubt" that D killed V, and they are so instructed. Belief that it is slightly more probable that the defendant killed the victim than that he didn't, would be insufficient to convict. The probability must appear to the jurors to be much higher —perhaps upwards of 90%, if we must affix a figure. Thus a criminal defendant might be acquitted though the jury thinks he did it. While a 51% probability would be insufficient in a criminal case, it might be sufficient for a plaintiff's verdict in an analogous civil wrongful death action. For as to most civil issues, the persuasion burden is to "prove by a preponderance of the evidence"—a standard which we may take to mean "establish by a preponderance of the probabilities." It would seem that the merest preponderance will do. Some cases seem to insist that the standard means something other than this.

Notice that contrary to the language of the criminal standard, the language of the civil standard addresses itself to the state of the evidence rather than to the degree of "convincedness" or "conviction" that must be felt or produced in the minds of the jurors. This, it is submitted, is not the intendment of the civil standard, and the selection of language is unfortunate and misleading to both judges and jurors. The language is further unfortunate and misleading insofar as it suggests, quite erroneously, (a) that only evidence, not common sense and experience, may be considered;[4] (b) that the quantity and not the quality of the evidence counts;[5] (c) that only evidence adduced by his

[4] But there are and must be limits to the use of matters brought by the jurors with them in their minds to the courtroom. The law has never been able to satisfactorily delineate this area. Perhaps the line ought to be drawn at the point where it is no longer fair to assume the parties are apprised of what is influencing the jurors.

One use of the terms "judicial notice" and "common knowledge" in the opinions has been to relieve a party of the necessity of proving something which is regarded as properly taken account of by the judge or jury from their own knowledge and experience. (This may affect either or both the production and persuasion burden.)

Other uses of these terms are (1) where a peremptory ruling as discussed above would be in order on some isolated fact; (2) where facts are taken account of by a court in fashioning a policy or rule of law, even if the facts are not beyond dispute; (3) where a court accepts "facts" concerning relevant domestic or foreign law or procedure; and (4) a miscellany of other situations.

[5] Suppose one plaintiff must prove someone to be right-handed and another in another case must prove someone left-handed. It is obvious that the same quantum of evidence (e. g., an instance of eating with the hand sought to be proved) will go farther in persuading a jury (and, incidentally, in discharging the production burden and avoiding a peremptory ruling by the judge) depending upon whether it is introduced to prove right-handedness or left-handedness. For in the former case, it works together with the common sense notion that most people are right-handed; and works against it in the latter. Occasionally this common sense notion will be enshrined in a *legal (evidentiary) presumption*, which is an instruction to the judge or the jury, or both, to take it into account. Query whether the presumption (whether enshrined in law or left as a common sense notion) would be sufficient to discharge either burden where the plaintiff who must prove right-handedness adduces no evidence of right-handedness at all. Would it be sufficient evidence of right-handedness merely to show the person was a human being (since this would supply the inference that humans are generally right-handed)? Do we need *evidence* to

own side may be considered in favor of a party ("he must show by a preponderance of evidence"); (d) that there can be only *belief* or *disbelief* in the truth of a proposition, with nothing in between, such as belief that a proposition is probable ("you may find for plaintiff if you *believe*, upon a preponderance of evidence, that . . ."); and (e) that *probability* of truth is an insufficient basis for awarding a verdict to the party having the persuasion burden.

A standard somewhere between the civil and the criminal standard is frequently applied to proof of certain special issues in certain civil cases. These are often issues of an equitable nature, such as "mistake" in a suit for reformation of a deed or contract. This standard is most often phrased as "clear and convincing evidence." See Addington v. Texas, 441 U.S. 418, 99 S.Ct. 1804 (1979) (this is the constitutionally required burden for civil commitment).

It has been suggested that the three standards (civil, civil-equitable, and criminal) be described, respectively, as requiring belief that the proposition is "probably so" (i. e.,

show he is human? Would you expect that the burdens of pleading and proof would be on the plaintiff to prove right-handedness, in view of the common sense of the matter? Suppose the judge and/or the jury is instructed (for certain policy reasons) in a legal presumption that does not have a basis in common sense—e. g., that there is a presumption of left-handedness. How will they be able to decide when such a presumption is offset by the evidence? Is it offset by the merest evidence—say, that the person in issue is a human being? If so, can we dispense with such obvious proof? Would precisely the same effect as this non-common-sense presumption be accomplished by placing the burden of pleading and persuasion on the party seeking to prove right-handedness? Which way would his job be easier? Under the latter approach, could he have his case submitted to the jury without adducing evidence? If not, would it be sufficient to allege that the person in issue is a human being? If the answer is yes, why should proof of such an obvious fact (that he is human) be required?

more probably true than false); "very probably so" (i. e., considerably more probable than not); and "almost certainly so" (i. e., very highly probable).

Are three standards enough? In daily life persons require different degrees of convincedness depending upon what "rides" on their decision—i. e., upon the stakes. Civil cases are not all alike as respects stakes. Nor are criminal cases. Indeed, the stakes in some civil cases are greater than in some criminal cases. How is the jury likely to get around this? Will there be some correlation between the degree of convincedness felt by the jury on the issue of liability, and the degree of punishment or amount of damages they mete out? Are we forgetting, in this analysis, that a decision either way by the jury helps the one side as much as it hurts the other?

In closing it should be noted that at least conceptually, there is a light persuasion burden on the party who is conventionally thought not to have the burden. For example, in the case of the typical criminal issue, we might say that the defendant, though *favored* by the persuasion burden, has a burden to raise or preserve a reasonable doubt.

It should also be noted that in a civil case, the only time it makes a practical difference who has the persuasion burden is when the state of the evidence leaves the trier-of-fact's mind in perfect 50–50 equipoise. In such a case, if the burden instruction is obeyed, the issue must be resolved against the party with the burden, because he has failed to show even the merest preponderence (51%), as he must do under the standard. On the other hand, in a criminal case, whom the persuasion burden is upon should make a great deal of difference in most instances. A scrupulous jury may be quite convinced the defendant "did it," and yet feel compelled to acquit because not convinced to the requisite degree (beyond a reasonable doubt).

(c) *Visualization, Summary, and Some Other Applications.*

The above material concerning burdens (in particular the production burden) may be graphically represented as in figure 1 below:

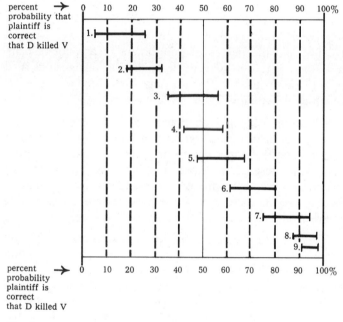

Fig. 1

The first heavy black bar represents what hypothetical Judge Jones estimates to be the range over which reasonable people could differ in assessing the probability that plaintiff is correct that D killed V, given the state of the

[*112*]

evidence at the time he is asked to make a peremptory ruling in a civil wrongful death action (where all the burdens initially are on the plaintiff). No reasonable person, he feels, could possibly believe (while remaining reasonable) the probability to be less than 5%. Similarly, Judge Jones feels, no reasonable person could possibly believe (while remaining reasonable) that the probability is more than 25%. In other words, he feels any assessment placing the figure anywhere between 5% and 25% is reasonable; all others are unreasonable. What the judge himself feels to be the probability is irrelevant. The judge, if properly presented with a request for the proper motion at this particular time, would have to grant a peremptory ruling on the issue, in defendant's favor.

The bars numbered 2 through 9 represent exactly the same thing, but on different states of evidence.

As to all bars that intersect the center (50%) line—that is, all bars that *at any point* cross or are crossed by the center line—the judge must allow the case to go to the jury. These are bars 3, 4, and 5. As to all bars that lie wholly to the left of the center line (i. e., the top two bars, numbered 1 and 2), a peremptory ruling should issue against plaintiff, in defendant's favor. As to bars 6, 7, 8, and 9, which lie wholly beyond the 50% line, a peremptory ruling should issue in plaintiff's favor.

If this were a criminal prosecution for murder, a peremptory ruling against the prosecution would be in order for all bars except those that intersect, or lie wholly beyond, the 90% line. Thus, the prosecution would survive a motion for a peremptory ruling only with respect to bars 7, 8, and 9. Since bar 9 lies wholly beyond the 90% mark (90% or more being assumed to be what is meant by "beyond a reasonable doubt"), on that particular state of the evidence no reasonable person could find less than 90% probability that D killed V—in other words, all reasonable people must agree D killed V beyond a reasonable doubt. A peremptory ruling would seem to be in order in favor of the prosecution on that issue; but owing to a special dispensation to criminal defendants, none is allowed.

See McNaughton, Burden of Production of Evidence: A Function of the Burden of Persuasion, 68 Harv.L.Rev. 1382 (1955).

Turning now to some other points not directly connected with our chart, in the example in this chapter concerning a murder prosecution, we have seen that, on the issue of whether D killed V, the prosecution will have had all three burdens (pleading, production, and persuasion). On the other hand, if the defendant wishes to be excused on grounds of insanity, he must plead it. The law perhaps feels that it is safe to assume sanity in the absence of a plea to the contrary by the person who is closest to the matter. If insanity is *pleaded* but no *evidence* of it appears that could justify a reasonable juror in acquitting on that ground, either the jury will not be informed by the judge of the possibility of acquittal on grounds of insanity, or the jury will be affirmatively instructed that they cannot acquit on such grounds; and, of course, legal argument will not be permitted that would suggest that they can so acquit. (Suppose they do anyway? Will we know why they have acquitted?) Again, perhaps the law feels it is safe to assume sanity in the absence of *evidence* to the contrary. Thus, at least initially, both the pleading and production burdens are on the defendant.

If by the end of the trial there appears some evidence of insanity which could justify a reasonable doubt concerning his sanity, the jury is usually instructed that before they may convict, they must be convinced of sanity beyond a reasonable doubt—i. e., the *persuasion burden is on the prose-*

cution as respects this issue to the same extent as it is on the issue of whether D killed V. (Of course, a common-sense presumption that people are normally sane, perhaps reinforced by mention of such a presumption by the judge, may play a role in bringing the jury to this state of convinc-edness.) The defendant wins the issue if he (or the prosecution, or the common sense or experience of the jury based on some evidence in the case) succeeds in creating and maintaining a reasonable doubt. (If on the evidence there *must* be a reasonable doubt, he is, of course, entitled to a directed acquittal.)

Some jurisdictions place the persuasion burden (as well as the other burdens) on defendant on the sanity-insanity issue. The burden may be to prove "by a preponderance of the evidence" or even "beyond a reasonable doubt."

Can we say that whatever the allocation of the burdens and whatever their weight, it is still true as a philosophical matter, that sanity is an element of the crime? Is this merely a question of the use of language?

Presumptions

> **A presumption (as that term is used in Evidence and Procedure) is a legal mechanism that helps a party meet or prevent another party meeting, or on occasion shifts, a burden or burdens of proof.**

As used in the law of evidence and procedure, a "pre-sumption" generally is nothing more than a direction of law to a judge (to be heeded in considering whether a produc-tion burden is overcome) and/or to the jury (to be heeded in considering whether the persuasion burden is over-come), that if fact A is believed by the jury to be establish-ed (to the degree required by the persuasion burden) or is otherwise established, then fact B *must be* (in the case of a mandatory presumption) or *may be* (in the case of a per-

missive presumption) taken by the jury as similarly established, where there is no evidence directed at fact B itself.[6]
The presumption may or may not accord with what a reasonable person would have to or could believe. (In other
words, presumptions may be expressions of common sense
rational connections, or of extrinsic policy concerning which
way it is desirable to "tilt" the case to achieve certain social
objectives.) If the proof of fact A is such that a peremptory
ruling establishing it is in order, then if the presumption is
mandatory, a peremptory ruling would have to issue establishing fact B (absent evidence of non-B). It is as though
reasonable people could not differ as to whether fact B
exists. If the presumption is permissive, a peremptory ruling establishing fact A would mean the jury must be *allowed*
to find fact B, but also must be allowed to find against fact
B. It is as though reasonable minds can differ on whether
fact B exists, and we cannot say they must agree the one
way or the other. No peremptory ruling either way on fact
B would be in order. (Incidentally, it should be noted that
some authorities do not call permissive presumptions "presumptions" at all, but have some other term for them.
This raises questions as to whether presumptions which
under traditional law have been treated as permissive are
within a provision like F.R.E. 301 purporting to prescribe
the effect of "presumptions" which are found in existing
law, without listing or creating particular presumptions.)
(Query: To what extent do presumptions of either variety
seem to impinge on the spirit of the civil or criminal right
to [or policy to accord] jury trial?)

---

[6] Even in those jurisdictions that hold simply that a presumption
(or at least some presumptions) is an expression by the law that the
burden of persuasion should rest on the party presumed against
(which view obviously also affects production burden), this is the effect of
a presumption in this situation. Such a presumption is given the
mandatory (as opposed to permissive) effect. See 1974 Uniform Rule 301.

Thus far we have assumed that there is no evidence in the case directed at B itself. If there is such evidence and it tends to rebut B, what should be the role of the presumption, with judge and jury? All authorities agree that presumptions of the kind we are speaking about—whether they are "mandatory" or "permissive"—are not "conclusive." [7] That is, they are rebuttable. They can be overcome not only by evidence of non-A, but of non-B as well. Thus, when there is evidence of non-B, no matter how conclusively established A is (even to the extent that there must be a peremptory ruling that A exists), if the evidence of non-B is such that a reasonable person could find non-B, B may not be established by a peremptory ruling, nor may the presumption command that B follows if A is found. This is so whether we have a mandatory or a permissive

---

[7] A conclusive presumption is not a presumption at all, but a rule of substantive law. E. g., the conclusive (i. e., irrebuttable) presumption that "every man is presumed to know the law" really means that it is irrelevant whether the defendant knew the law or not—ignorance of the law is no defense, even if proved, and therefore cannot be the subject of proof. In other words, the "presumption" really renders the fact presumed of no relevance or importance to the case. It would be better, then, to state the matter in just that way: that ignorance of the law makes no difference, legally; and abandon the bogus "presumption" language. In terms of "fact A" and "fact B," an irrebuttable presumption of B from A renders A the only important fact and B irrelevant. Is there an A and B in the presumption of knowledge of law?

The California Evidence Code (§§ 621–624) lists some conclusive presumptions, even though in reality such presumptions should not be considered matters of evidence. These include, among others, the following provisions:

". . . [T]he . . . [offspring] of a wife cohabiting with her husband who is not impotent, is conclusively presumed to be legitimate . . . ."

"The facts recited in a written instrument are conclusively presumed to be true as between the parties thereto, or their successors in interest; but this rule does not apply to the recital of a consideration. . . ."

presumption.   Indeed, the evidence of non-B may be such that a reasonable person *must* find non-B, so that a peremptory ruling of non-B would be in order.   But then, in these situations (where there is evidence of non-B), isn't the case treated just as though there were no *legal* presumption at all?   What is added or changed by telling the judge or jury there is a legal presumption?   Perhaps it would to some inarticulable extent make it more difficult to prove non-B than would otherwise be the case.   But if the presumption of B is not to be overcome (by the production of evidence of non-B) at the point where common sense would say it is, when is it to be overcome?   To give an example, suppose there is a presumption from wearing a watch on the right hand that the wearer is left-handed. The judge or jury feels the additional fact that the wearer used a baseball bat right-handedly would just barely overcome this presumption if it were merely a matter of common sense.   How much more is required to overcome the presumption if it is a legal presumption?

Suppose a non-common-sense presumption: that men with two apparently normal arms and hands are left-handed. How much (and what sort of) evidence would overcome this?   (Does it make sense to give this kind of presumption any effect in a situation where there is evidence of non-B?) (Why might the law have a non-common-sense presumption?)

So again we ask the question: if there is evidence directed at fact B itself, that tends to rebut fact B, what, if anything should be the special role of a presumption (either kind of evidentiary presumption) with judge and/or jury? (We are assuming the evidence is not so insubstantial that it is tantamount to no evidence.)   Should the "presumption" be ignored by the judge (insofar as it is anything beyond what his common sense would require without any legal presumption) and not told to the jury?   If that would not be the correct course, what role *should* the presumption play in "beating back" the force of or inferences arising from the other evidence in the judge's and/or jury's deliberations? What force should the judge give the presumption in changing what he would otherwise be inclined to do on a motion for a directed verdict or similar peremptory ruling? Could a presumption be confined to only having an effect on the trier-of-law and not the trier-of-fact? Or vice-versa? Assuming the presumption is to have effect on the jury, what should they be told? That the law presumes B from A? That if they find A, they may but need not find B? That the law holds that proof of A can be [sufficient?] evidence of B? (Do these give any guidance concerning *how much* is needed to overcome the presumption?) To consider the presumption as evidence on the question of the existence of B? Strong evidence? (How strong? How much stronger than if there was no presumption? In other words, how much force should it have in countering what they would otherwise feel is the force of the contrary evidence? How can such a degree be articulated or obeyed?) That the burden of persuasion is that the party asserting non-B must convince the jury of non-B?[8] To find in accord with the presumption if they don't believe the evidence of non-B (at least if the presumption is mandatory)? Should an extrinsic-policy-based presumption be treated differently (respecting the questions raised here) from one based on common sense connection? Should a distinction be drawn, as respects all these questions, between mandatory and permissive presumptions, as is done where there is no evidence of non-B? Should each particular presumption have its own rule concerning the questions raised here? These are all matters concerning which judges,

---

[8] The view treated in footnote 6 supra obviously takes this position, and thus rather neatly solves not only the problem of what is to be done in the absence of evidence of non-B, but also the problems treated here, of what is to be done if there is evidence of non-B.

as well as code drafters, have differed. Are any of these approaches unacceptable in criminal cases?

The questions raised in this section concerning the effect to be given a presumption in the presence of evidence of non-B have usually been left to be treated (and treated rather obscurely and inconsistently even within the same jurisdiction concerning the same presumption) by judicial decision. The decisions, needless to say, show no clear cut answers. Occasionally attempts have been made to codify particular answers. (Until the section entitled "Criminal Cases," we discuss only civil presumptions, to illustrate the principles.)

In order to examine some of the possible answers, let us consider the common presumption that delivery of a letter (fact B, or the "presumed fact") is presumed from proper mailing (fact A, or the "basic fact"). Let us assume that (at least in the absence of a presumption) the normal burden of proof is that the plaintiff must prove delivery by a preponderance. Let us further assume that he relies solely on establishing proper mailing (which we are assuming he can establish) and on the presumption, to prove delivery. If it is a mandatory presumption, then once proper mailing is established (to the satisfaction of the jury; or as a matter of law by overwhelming evidence, concessions in the pleadings, stipulations, or judicial notice), then delivery *must* be taken as established by the judge and jury, if there is no evidence of non-delivery. If it were merely a *permissive* presumption, we would merely have a jury issue as to whether or not there was delivery, and there would be a question as to what, if anything, to tell the jury over and above what is told them in an ordinary case where there is a jury question of fact ("you are to decide whether there was delivery . . . .") Are they to be told to give any special weight to the fact of proper mailing in this determination? If so, what weight? How much more, if any, than the weight common sense tells them to give in the absence of a presumption? Answers have varied.

Suppose, however, that some not-insubstantial evidence of non-delivery (non-B) *had* been introduced—for example, testimony of the addressee's mailroom clerk that he does not remember receiving the letter, and the circumstances are such that one could feel that he would remember if he had received it. In this situation courts have seldom distinguished between mandatory and permissive presumptions (although a distinction could well be made), and have given the presumption one of the following effects or some variant thereof:

View (1): The presumption and any common-sense notion underlying the presumption disappear from the case and play no further role upon the introduction of the defendant's evidence of non-B. The case is to be determined exactly as if they never existed. Under this view, in our hypothetical case above, there would be a directed verdict or directed finding of non-delivery against the plaintiff. To the extent this view removes common sense notions from the case, it is unwise and frequently unworkable.

View (2): The presumption, but not the common-sense notion underlying it (if any), disappears. The case is to be determined exactly as if there were no presumption. But the common-sense notion (that proper mailing may bear some weight in establishing receipt) continues. It may be taken into account by the judge in deciding a motion for a directed finding or verdict. The jury is allowed to take it into account in deciding the issue of delivery, and may even be instructed on the possibility of so taking it into account, if the jurisdiction is in the habit of advising the jury on such common-sense notions concerning the weight of evidence in non-presumption cases. Thus, the issue of delivery vel non in our hypothetical case (where plaintiff has at least something of some substance to establish proper mailing) would go to the jury (no matter how strongly proper mailing was established—even if established as a matter of law), perhaps with the indicated advisory instruction. The jury is still told the plaintiff has the burden of proving delivery by a preponderance. (On our facts, then, the finding would be more in doubt than under View (1).) A variant of this View (2) holds that the presumption disappears for purposes of the jury's deliberations (as distinct from the judge's deliberations over directed verdicts and findings) *only if the jury believes the mailroom clerk.* (A variant like this is also possible to View (1) above.) The jury is thus instructed that *if they do not believe the clerk*, the presumption remains, and is entitled to some weight, or in some jurisdictions is compulsory, i. e., receipt *must* be found if mailing is established. (This may depend upon whether the presumption is viewed as permissive or mandatory.)

Except for the presumption of legitimacy of a child born in wedlock (under which the drafters provide there is a burden to prove the illegitimacy beyond a reasonable doubt), View (2) has been adopted by Rule 704 of the American Law Institute's Model Code of Evidence:

"(1) . . . [W]hen the basic fact of a presumption has been established [9] in an action, the existence of the presumed fact must be assumed unless and until evidence has been introduced which would support a finding of its non-existence . . . ..

"(2) . . . [W]hen the basic fact of a presumption has been established in an action and evidence has been introduced which would support a finding of the

[9] "Established" means established "by the pleadings, or by stipulation of the parties, or by judicial notice, or by evidence which compels a finding of the basic fact, or by a finding of the basic fact from the evidence." Model Code, Rule 702.

non-existence of the presumed fact . . . the existence or non-existence of the presumed fact is to be determined exactly as if no presumption had ever been applicable in the action."

(You will note from subdivision (1) of the rule, the mandatory effect of the presumption where there is no substantial evidence of non-B.)

View (3): The presumption continues in the case (for both the trier-of-law and trier-of-fact) and thus creates or lends strength to a connection of A and B (or to the analogous common-sense inference, if any). Just what strength or how much strength is lent or created is undetermined. Perhaps the judge is to take more account of the connection or inference in deciding motions for directed verdicts and findings. Perhaps the jury is instructed that proper mailing can mean delivery, though the jurisdiction does not ordinarily so intruct in the absence of a legal presumption; or, if an instruction is ordinarily given, perhaps it is somehow "beefed up" (i. e., "A strong inference of delivery arises from proper mailing, unless that inference is rebutted . . .", or "The law presumes —though not irrebuttably—from proper mailing that . . ."). The burden of persuasion on delivery is still as above (that is, the jury must find it by a preponderance, for plaintiff to win). Under this view (View (3)), in our hypothetical case, where there is at least something of some substance indicating proper mailing, there would be a jury issue on delivery even if proper mailing were so overwhelmingly indisputably established as to be established as a matter of law. (Remember, there is the mailroom clerk's testimony suggesting non-delivery; even with the presumption operating at the directed finding stage, this would still probably be enough to make a jury issue.) But the jury would be impelled a bit more toward finding delivery (from the mailing) than under the other views above. Being notified of the presumption may also play a role (as would the common-sense notion in this and the last view), in the jury's deliberations over whether to believe the word of the mailroom clerk.

View (4): The mailroom clerk's testimony of non-delivery causes the presumption to disappear for purposes of the judge's deliberations concerning directed verdicts and findings (which, *on the facts of our particular case* probably makes no difference since in either event the clerk's testimony is probably sufficient to make a jury issue), but can not do so for purposes of the jury's deliberations (whether the testimony is believed or not). The converse—disappearance for purposes of the jury's but not the judge's deliberations—is also found.

View (5): The presumption continues in the case, by shifting the burden of persuasion on the issue of delivery, to the defendant, if proper mailing is believed by the jury or otherwise established as a matter of law. In our hypothetical, since proper mailing might be believed, or even *must* be believed, no directed verdict or directed finding could be awarded either way on the issue of delivery. Assuming the evidence of proper mailing to be strong enough to satisfy the jury or to establish proper mailing as a matter of law, the defendant would, under this view, have the burden of proving non-delivery by a preponderance of the evidence. His evidence on this score is, in our hypothetical case, not terribly strong, although it probably would raise a jury issue. Under the instruction that would be given, that the burden is on him to prove non-delivery (if the jury finds proper mailing or if proper mailing is established as a matter of law, which we are assuming is the case), it is unlikely that the jury would find in his favor on the issue.

View (5) above was the one adopted by Rule 301 of the *Supreme Court Draft* of the F.R.E., codifying the effect of presumptions in those civil cases where federal presumption law was to govern. The 1974 Uniform Rules of Evidence, and several states, have copied this provision. It automatically (though not expressly) answers, in what is possibly the only feasible way (as unsatisfactory as it might be), the many important questions relating to the weight of presumptions, raised above, which the other views seem necessarily to leave in limbo. The provision is as follows:

> "In all cases not otherwise provided for by Act of Congress or by these rules a presumption imposes on the party against whom it is directed the burden of proving that the nonexistence of the presumed fact is more probable than its existence."

An earlier draft of the F.R.E. (March, 1969) had an additional, very enlightening (though turgid) section explaining what the above language means in terms of the production and persuasion burdens:

> "(1) DETERMINATION ON EVIDENCE OF BASIC FACTS. When no evidence is introduced contrary to the existence of the presumed fact, the question of its existence depends upon the existence of the basic facts and is determined as follows:

> "(A) If reasonable minds would necessarily agree that the evidence renders the existence of the basic facts more probable than not, the judge shall direct the jury to find in favor of the existence of the presumed fact; or

> "(B) If reasonable minds would necessarily agree that the evidence does not render the existence of the basic facts more probable than not, the judge shall direct the jury to find against the existence of the presumed fact; or

> "(C) If reasonable minds would not necessarily agree as to whether the evidence renders the existence of the

basic facts more probable than not, the judge shall submit the matter to the jury with an instruction to find in favor of the existence of the presumed fact if they find from the evidence that the existence of the basic facts is more probable than not, but otherwise to find against the existence of the presumed fact.

"(2) DETERMINATION ON EVIDENCE OF PRESUMED FACT. When reasonable minds would necessarily agree that the evidence renders the existence of the basic facts more probable than not, the question of the existence of the presumed fact is determined as follows:

"(A) If reasonable minds would necessarily agree that the evidence renders the nonexistence of the presumed fact more probable than not, the judge shall direct the jury to find against the existence of the presumed fact; or

"(B) If reasonable minds would necessarily agree that the evidence does not render the nonexistence of the presumed fact more probable than not, the judge shall direct the jury to find in favor of the presumed fact; or

"(C) If reasonable minds would not necessarily agree as to whether the evidence renders the nonexistence of the presumed fact more probable than not, the judge shall submit the matter to the jury with an instruction to find in favor of the existence of the presumed fact unless they find from the evidence that its nonexistence is more probable than its existence, in which event they should find against its existence.

"(3) DETERMINATION ON EVIDENCE OF BOTH BASIC AND PRESUMED FACTS. When evidence as to the existence of the basic facts is such that reasonable minds would not necessarily agree whether their existence is more probable than not and evidence as to the nonexistence of the presumed fact is such that they would not necessarily agree that its nonexistence is more probable than not, the judge shall submit the matter to the jury with an instruction to find in favor of the existence of the presumed fact if they find from the evidence that the existence of the basic facts is more probable than not and unless they find the nonexistence of the presumed fact more probable than not, otherwise to find against the existence of the presumed fact."

A preliminary draft of the A.L.I. Model Code of Evidence, and the final draft of the 1954 Uniform Rules, took a mixed approach, applying two of the above views, depending upon the kind of presumption involved, which required the courts to make a difficult distinction:

Model Code, Preliminary Draft Rule 904:

"(2) . . . [W]hen the basic fact of a presumption has been established in an action and evidence has been introduced which would support a finding of the non-existence of the presumed fact

"(a) if the basic fact has no probative value as evidence of the existence of the presumed fact, the existence or non-existence of the presumed fact is to be determined exactly as if the presumption had never been applicable in the action;

"(b) if the basic fact has any probative value as evidence of the existence of the presumed fact, whether or not sufficient to support a finding of the presumed fact, the party asserting the non-existence of the presumed fact has the burden of persuading the trier of fact that its non-existence is more probable than its existence."

1954 Uniform Rule 14:

> ". . . (a) if the facts from which the presumption is derived have any probative value as evidence of the existence of the presumed fact, the presumption continues to exist and the burden of establishing the non-existence of the presumed fact is upon the party against whom the presumption operates; (b) if the facts from which the presumption arises have no probative value as evidence of the presumed fact the presumption does not exist when evidence is introduced which would support a finding of the non-existence of the presumed fact, and the fact which would otherwise be presumed shall be determined from the evidence exactly as if no presumption was or had ever been involved."

Among the jurisdictions picking up this mixed approach was California, but with important differences:

> ". . . Every rebuttable presumption is either (a) a presumption affecting the burden of producing evidence or (b) a presumption affecting the burden of proof [i. e., the burden of persuasion] . . .

> ". . . A presumption affecting the burden of producing evidence is a presumption established to implement no public policy other than to facilitate the determination of the particular action in which the presumption is applied. . . .

> ". . . The effect of a presumption affecting the burden of producing evidence is to require the trier of fact to assume the existence of the presumed fact unless and until evidence is introduced which would support a finding of its nonexistence, in which case the trier of fact shall determine the existence or nonexistence of the presumed fact from the evidence and without regard to the presumption. Nothing in this

section shall be construed to prevent the drawing of any inference that may be appropriate. . . .

". . . A presumption affecting the burden of proof is a presumption established to implement some public policy other than to facilitate the determination of the particular action in which the presumption is applied, such as the policy in favor of the legitimacy of children, the validity of marriage, the stability of titles to property, or the security of those who entrust themselves or their property to the administration of others.
. . .

". . . The effect of a presumption affecting the burden of proof is to impose upon the party against whom it operates the burden of proof as to the nonexistence of the presumed fact. . . ."

(Cal.Evid.Code §§ 601, 603–606).

In addition, California attempts to give some further guidance as to which particular presumptions are in which category. Examples of these provisions appear in the margin. They express some fairly typical presumptions, although the effects of these presumptions vary around the country, and they are not always classified as here.[10]

---

[10] Cal.Evid.Code, §§ 630 et seq. state that the following, among others, are presumptions affecting production burden:

". . . Money delivered by one to another is presumed to have been due to the latter. . . . A thing delivered by one to another is presumed to have belonged to the latter. . . . An obligation delivered up to the debtor is presumed to have been paid. . . . A person in possession of an order on himself for the payment of money, or delivery of a thing, is presumed to have paid the money or delivered the thing accordingly. . . . An obligation possessed by the creditor is presumed not to have been paid. . . . The payment of earlier rent or installments is presumed from a receipt for later rent or installments. . . . The things which a person possesses are presumed to be owned by him. . . . A person who exercises acts of ownership over property is presumed to be the owner of it. . . . A judgment, when not conclusive, is presumed to correctly determine or set forth the rights of the parties, but there is no presumption that the facts essential to the judgment have been correctly determined. . . . A writing is presumed to have been truly dated. . . . A letter correctly addressed and properly mailed is presumed to have been received in the ordinary course of mail. . . . A trustee or other person, whose duty it was to convey real property to a particular person, is presumed to have actually conveyed to him when such presumption is necessary to perfect title of such person or his successor in interest. . . . A book, purporting to be printed or published by public authority is presumed to have been so printed or published."

Sections 660 et seq. state that the following among others, are presumptions affecting "burden of proof":

". . . A child of a woman who is or has been married, born during the marriage or within 300 days after the dissolution thereof, is presumed to be a legitimate child of that marriage. This presumption may be disputed only by the people of the State of California in a criminal action brought under Section 270 of the Penal Code or by the husband or wife, or the descendant of one or both of them. In a civil action, this presumption may be rebutted only by clear and convincing proof. . . . The owner of the legal title to property is presumed to be the owner of the full beneficial title. This presumption may be rebutted only by clear and convincing proof. . . . A ceremonial marriage is presumed to be valid. . . . It is presumed that official duty has been regularly performed. This presumption does not apply on an issue as to the lawfulness of an arrest if it is found or otherwise established that the arrest was made without a warrant. . . . A person is presumed to intend the ordinary consequences of his voluntary act. This presumption is inapplicable in a criminal action to establish the specific intent of the defendant where specific intent is an element of the crime charged. . . . Any court of this state or the United States, or any court of general jurisdiction in any other state or nation, or any judge of such a court, acting as such, is presumed to have acted in the lawful exercise of its jurisdiction. This presumption applies only when the act of the court or judge is under collateral attack. . . . A person not heard from in seven years is presumed to be dead. . . . An unlawful intent is presumed from the doing of an unlawful act. This presumption is inapplicable in a criminal action to establish the specific intent of the defendant where specific intent is an element of the crime charged. . . ."

The statutory list in each category is not meant to be exhaustive. Any presumption from other case or statutory law that fits the general definition for the category (see supra) will be in that category.

F.R.E. 301

The Federal Rules of Evidence do not codify particular presumptions. They deal only with the *effect* of presumptions, once a presumption is found in other sources of law. Thus, the question of whether or not there is a presumption is left to other decisional and statutory law and other rules, in which particular presumptions may be found. The effect of presumptions is prescribed in F.R.E. 301. Excepted from 301 are presumptions for which some different effect has been provided by a rule or statute (does this mean expressly provided, or is interpretation enough?); criminal cases (see next section, infra); and presumptions that presume elements of a claim or defense that is governed by state substantive law (i. e., state rules of decision) in the federal court. As to this last category, the state law of the effect of presumptions is to govern (presumably also, the state law would have to be the source for the existence of the presumption).[11] See F.R.E. 302. What this normally

Other commonly found presumptions are the *res ipsa loquitur* presumption which presumes negligence where the injuring instrumentality was in the exclusive control of the defendant and injury does not ordinarily occur when due care is exercised; a presumption of authority granted to a driver by the owner of an automobile under certain circumstances; a presumption of negligence from statutory violations; and the presumptions of innocence, sanity, and competency. (Are these last three of a special character? What is the basic fact and what is the presumed fact in these?)

Other commonly found and helpful statutory or rule provisions are illustrated by § 602 of the Cal.Evid.Code and Rule 301(b) of the 1974 Uniform Rules, respectively (they do not appear in the F.R.E.):

"A statute providing that a fact or group of facts is prima facie evidence of another fact establishes a rebuttable presumption."

"If presumptions are inconsistent, the presumption applies that is founded upon weightier considerations of policy. If considerations of policy are of equal weight neither presumption applies."

[11] The F.R.E. defer to state evidence law only in three areas: presumptions (Rule 302), privileges (Rule 501), and witness competency (Rule 601). In each area, the deference is on the same basis as here: state evidence law applies where a state issue is involved in the federal-court lawsuit. But see discussion under privileges.

means is that state presumption law governs in diversity cases in federal court, and federal presumption law (including Rule 301) governs in federal question cases in federal courts. (The state law of effect of presumptions is apt to be different from F.R.E. 301, especially since the 1974 Uniform Rules position on the effect of presumptions is different from F.R.E. 301. The Uniform Rules' position is being adopted by the states. For this position, see supra.) But this statement as to when the state evidence law will govern on the effect of presumptions in federal courts is an overgeneralization. Diversity cases often contain questions upon which federal rather than state substantive law governs. And federal question cases often contain questions upon which state substantive law governs. Mixed or joined state and federal claims and defenses, or issues, are possible, as are mixed jurisdictional bases, in federal lawsuits. What evidence law governs—state or federal—on the effect of presumptions, is linked under the rule to the particular issue attempting to be proved, not to the general nature of the case. The matter is further complicated by the fact that under the rule state evidence law governs only if the state issue being proved is an *element* (i. e., an ultimate fact, as opposed to a mediate or subordinate fact or step along the way). The rule presents the confusing specter of two different laws of presumption having to be applied in the same case—even on an identical factual issue (the same factual issue could come up under both the state claim count and the federal claim count), and even as to the selfsame piece of evidence.

But perhaps the most confusing question of coverage not answered by Rule 301 is whether the rule applies to what were formerly permissive presumptions, as well as to those that were formerly mandatory (the rule would give them both mandatory effect). The rule expressly covers "presumptions," but we have seen above that there was some difference of view as to whether or not to call permissive presumptions "presumptions," or merely inferences.

Questions of coverage aside, we may ask which of the five views, above, as to the effect of presumptions, is prescribed by F.R.E. 301? F.R.E. 301 provides:

> ". . . [A] presumption imposes on the party against whom it is directed the burden of going forward with evidence [i. e. the production burden] to rebut or meet the presumption, but does not shift to such party the burden of proof in the sense of the risk of non-persuasion [i. e. does not shift to him the burden of persuasion], which remains throughout the trial upon the party on whom it was originally cast."

It can be seen immediately that this provision does very little. It (1) prescribes (by virtue of the "burden of going forward" language) the *mandatory* (as opposed to the *permissive*) variety of effect (for the situation where there is no evidence of non-B); and (2), in the situation where there is some evidence of non-B (i. e., where the party against whom the presumption is directed meets his burden of going forward with the evidence to rebut or meet the presumption), the provision merely provides that our View (5) (shifting the persuasion burden), supra, shall not apply; *but does not say which of the other four views shall apply* (all of them being consistent with what is said in the provision). The provision says nothing about what, if any, effect the presumption is to be given by the fact-finder (as opposed to the trier-of-law), and what, if anything, is to be told the fact-finders (other than providing they are *not* to be told the persuasion burden has shifted). Is the presumption to have *any* effect on the fact-finder? Is it to have any reach beyond the role it plays with the *trier-of-law* in deciding motions for directed verdicts and findings and similar peremptory rulings (to which role the "burden of going forward" language is addressed)?   If it is to have an effect on the trier-of-fact, *what* effect?   These questions are un-answered.

In addition, the provision has nothing to say about *how much* weight or force (if *any*, once evidence of non-B is introduced) the presumption is to have (over and above any common sense inference he would otherwise indulge) in the trier-of-law's mind in deciding *whether* the production burden (burden of going forward), which the rule casts on the party opposing the presumption, has been met by a *sufficient amount* of evidence to overcome (meet, dis-charge) it.   If the presumption is supposed to make it more difficult to satisfy the production burden than the judge would require without a presumption, *how much* more dif-ficult?   (Production-burden questions, that is, burden-of-going-forward questions, are always for the judge, not the jury.)   Similar questions can be raised about *how much* (if any) weight or force the jury is to give it (in comparison to the contrary evidence and what they would do in the absence of a presumption) in deciding whether the per-suasion burden (which has not shifted) has been met. (The question of the satisfaction of the persuasion burden is always for the trier-of-fact.)

Criminal Cases.

F.R.E. 301 leaves presumptions in criminal cases for later, as yet unformulated, special treatment, in some future codification.   Thus, criminal presumptions is a subject cur-rently governed by the common law and constitutional law. Neither is particularly clear in this area.

Because of the criminal defendant's constitutional right to jury trial (probably of greater dimension than a civil party's) and right to require the prosecution to prove its case beyond a reasonable doubt, and because of policies akin to these constitutional rights, the freedom of courts and legislators to prescribe rules of presumption and of effect of presumptions is generally considered somewhat more circumscribed in criminal than in civil cases, at least insofar as presumptions against the accused are concerned. For example, can we have mandatory presumptions against him? Can we have presumptions against him that shift or affect the burden of persuasion? The burden of production? The *defendant's* burden of production? Does it depend upon whether the matter is an element of the crime in some sense, or could be made the subject of an affirmative defense? Can we have ones that affect both the trier-of-law and trier-of-fact? Must we be especially cautious to be sure the jury understands that the presumption weighs lightly compared with their own independent judgment and assessment? More fundamentally, can we have presumptions against the accused at all? Does this depend upon whether the particular presumption follows common sense? Common sense operating on what record—the one compiled at trial, on appeal, or in the legislature? Does the test of validity of a presumption vary with what effects the presumption is to be given?

Not all these questions can be answered with assurance, but some materials follow that can help. The first group are some proposed codifications of the subject of criminal presumptions, that show how some competent draftsmen —scholars, lawyers, judges, legislators—would answer these questions based upon their reading of the current state of the law or what the current state of the law will bear. Then we will examine two Supreme Court cases dealing with certain aspects of the problem:

1974 Uniform Rule 303

"Presumptions in Criminal Cases":

[Adopted by a number of states. Modelled on Supreme Court Draft (unenacted) Rule 303 of

[135]

F.R.E. Brackets below indicate significant different language in the latter.]:

"(a) SCOPE—Except as otherwise provided by statute, in criminal cases, presumptions against an accused, recognized at common law or created by statute, including statutory provisions that certain facts are prima facie evidence of other facts or of guilt, are governed by this rule.

"(b) SUBMISSION TO JURY—The court is not authorized to direct the jury to find a presumed fact against the accused. If a presumed fact establishes guilt or is an element of the offense or negatives a defense, the court may submit the question of guilt or of the existence of the presumed fact to the jury, but only if a reasonable juror on the evidence as a whole, including the evidence of the basic facts, could find guilt or the presumed fact beyond a reasonable doubt. If the presumed fact has a lesser effect, the question of its existence may be submitted to the jury provided the basic facts are supported by substantial evidence or are otherwise established, unless the court determines that a reasonable juror on the evidence as a whole could not find the existence of the presumed fact. [The final "unless" clause reads, in the F.R.E. draft: "unless the evidence as a whole negatives the existence of the presumed fact."]

"(c) INSTRUCTING THE JURY—Whenever the existence of a presumed fact against the accused is submitted to the jury, the court shall instruct the jury that [the law declares] the jury may regard the basic facts as sufficient evidence of the presumed fact but is not required to do so. In addition, if the presumed fact establishes guilt or is an element of the offense or

[*136*]

negatives a defense, the court shall instruct the jury that its existence, on all the evidence, must be proved beyond a reasonable doubt."

Draft New Rule 25.1, Sections 5 and 6, Federal Rules of Criminal Procedure, as Proposed in Draft Recodification of the Federal Criminal Laws (See Senate Bill S. 1722, 96th Cong., 1st Sess.) (Unenacted) (1979–80):

"(5) PRESUMPTIONS.—If a statute provides that a given fact gives rise to a presumption, the statute has the following consequences:

"(A) TRIAL BY JURY.—In a case tried before a jury:

"(i) if there is sufficient evidence of the fact that gives rise to the presumption to support a reasonable belief as to the fact's existence beyond a reasonable doubt, the court shall submit the issue to the jury unless the evidence as a whole clearly precludes a reasonable juror from finding the presumed fact beyond a reasonable doubt; and

"(ii) in submitting to the jury the issue of the existence of the presumed fact, the court shall, upon request of the Government, charge that, although the evidence as a whole must establish the presumed fact beyond a reasonable doubt, the jury may arrive at that judgment on the basis of the presumption alone, since the law regards the fact giving rise to the presumption as strong evidence of the fact presumed.

"(B) TRIAL BY COURT.—In a case tried before the court sitting without a jury, although the evidence as a whole must establish the presumed fact beyond a reasonable doubt, the court may arrive at that judgment on the basis of the presumption alone.

"(6) PRIMA FACIE EVIDENCE.—If a statute provides that a given fact constitutes prima facie evidence, the statute has the following consequences:

"(A) TRIAL BY JURY.—In a case before a jury:

"(i) if there is sufficient evidence of the fact that constitutes prima facie evidence to support a reasonable belief as to fact's existence beyond a reasonable doubt, the court shall submit the issue to the jury unless the evidence as a whole clearly precludes a reasonable juror from finding the inferred fact beyond a reasonable doubt; and

"(ii) in submitting to the jury the issue of the inferred fact concerning which the given fact is prima facie evidence, the court, upon the request of the Government or the defendant, shall charge that, although the evidence as a whole must establish the inferred fact beyond a reasonable doubt, the jury may consider that the given fact is ordinarily a circumstance from which the existence of the inferred fact may be drawn.

"(B) TRIAL BY COURT.—In a case before the court sitting without a jury, although the evidence as a whole must establish the inferred fact beyond a reasonable doubt, the court may consider that the given fact is ordinarily a circumstance from which the existence of the inferred fact may be drawn."

American Law Institute, Model Penal Code,
Proposed Official Draft (1962), Section
1.12, Subsections 5 and 6:

"(5) When the Code establishes a presumption with respect to any fact which is an element of an offense, it has the following consequences:

"(a) when there is evidence of the facts which give rise to the presumption, the issue of the existence of the presumed fact must be submitted to the jury, unless the Court is satisfied that the evidence as a whole clearly negatives the presumed fact; and

"(b) when the issue of the existence of the presumed fact is submitted to the jury, the Court shall charge that while the presumed fact must, on all the evidence, be proved beyond a reasonable doubt, the law declares that the jury may regard the facts giving rise to the presumption as sufficient evidence of the presumed fact.

"(6) A presumption not established by the Code or inconsistent with it has the consequences otherwise accorded it by law."

Notice that some of the provisions above provide stronger effect than others; and that some give stronger effect to "presumptions" than to "prima facie inferences" while others draw no distinction between these. Also note the prohibition of a directed finding at the outset of Rule 303(b). Does it appear in the others? Should it? Should there be a distinction drawn with respect to this, between matters that could be made the subject of an affirmative defense, and matters that could not be? What is the position of each of the quoted provisions with respect to non-statutory presumptions 'or non-statutory prima facie inferences? Do some of the provisions leave a gap here? Should they? Do they all make clear whether they mean to cover presumptions and prima facie inferences *in favor* of the accused? Should such presumptions and inferences be treated according to the same standards (for example, the beyond-a-reasonable-doubt standard and other prescriptions in these provisions) as presumptions and prima facie inferences *against* the accused? Do any of the above provisions seem to do so?

Assuming we have a presumption or prima facie inference against the accused, do any of the provisions do anything to either party's production burden? Or are they confined to affecting the jury's consideration of whether the persuasion burden is overcome? Why would drafters want to prescribe minimal effect on production burden of defendant? Of prosecution? Do the drafters ever tell the jury that the jury *must* find? Why?

Which of the provisions draw a distinction between presumptions (or prima facie inferences) that would establish guilt (or affect an ultimate element of a charge or defense), on the one hand, and, on the other, presumptions (or prima facie inferences) affecting lesser links in the circumstantial chain against defendant? Should they all? Does it make sense to impose a "beyond a reasonable doubt" standard with respect to both kinds? Do any of the quoted provisions appear to do that? Is submission to the jury mandatory if the conditions for submission are met, under any of the above provisions; or does the judge still have the choice to not submit? Is there a difference among the above provisions on this matter? Which is the better position?

These questions will help you to appreciate the similarities and differences of the above formulations and views.

We now turn to two U.S. Supreme Court decisions in the area of criminal presumptions.

The first deals with the matter of the test to be applied to determine whether particular presumptions (or prima facie inferences) against the accused are constitutional under the due process clause of the federal constitution. This area has not been a model of clarity. Usually the matter comes up in connection with particular *statutory* presumptions (or prima facie inferences) that provide, in varying language, that proof of fact A (for example, proof of defendant's presence at an unlicensed distillery; or his possession of narcotics; or his presence at a place where an unlawful gun is found) gives rise (with varying degrees of strength) to an inference of the existence of fact B (for example, the fact that he had a part in the ownership or operation of the distillery; or knew the narcotics were imported; or had possession of—i. e., a right to dominion or control over—the gun). The latter fact (fact B) is usually the one essential for conviction. Conceptually, the provision could play a role at either or both of two stages of the trial: the directed acquittal stage or the stage of the instructions to and deliberations of the jury. By-and-large the constitutional cases have involved only the latter stage. And they have generally lumped prima facie and presumption provisions together under the term "presumption."

Owing to a long line of decisions including, among others, Tot v. United States, 319 U.S. 463, 63 S.Ct. 1241 (1943), United States v. Gainey, 380 U.S. 63, 85 S.Ct. 754 (1965), United States v. Romano, 382 U.S. 136, 86 S.Ct. 279 (1965), Leary v. United States, 395 U.S. 6, 89 S.Ct. 1532 (1969), Turner v. United States, 396 U.S. 398, 90 S.Ct. 642 (1970), and Barnes v. United States, 412 U.S. 837, 93 S.Ct. 2357 (1973), it had generally been thought that the test of the constitutional validity of these provisions (be they state or federal) under the federal due process clause, is whether there is a "rational connection" (common-sense connection) between fact A and fact B. There was some suggestion in the cases that even if no factual background showing a rational connection appeared in the case itself, it would be sufficient if a factual background justifying the linking of fact A to fact B appeared in the legislative history of findings or in research on the part of the appellate judges. What is and is not a "rational connection" seemed to depend upon some instinctual feel of the Supreme Court—"I know it when I see it."

The court in such cases repeatedly avoided deciding whether "rational connection" meant that a reasonable person must be able to find fact B to exist *beyond a reasonable doubt* from fact A, or merely *by a preponderance of the probabilities* (i. e., more probable than not). This avoidance was accomplished by holding, when a particular presumption was believed to pass constitutional muster, that the presumption would pass *whichever* test was applied. When one did *not* pass constitutional muster, it was said that it did not pass either test. In addition, the court seemed to indicate that if a presumption *viewed in the abstract divorced of the facts in the particular case* did not meet the test, it could not be saved by facts making the presumption sensible and sound in the particular case. Thus, for example, in the *Leary* case, the facts that Timothy Leary was a learned professor who studied marijuana, and who had recently traveled in a country that was the world's major exporter of marijuana, and who thus would have known that his marijuana was probably of foreign origin and imported, could not be considered. They could not save the presumption that people who possess marijuana are presumed to know it is imported, since that presumption or proposition must be viewed in the abstract. So viewed, even taking into account facts outside the record that were found or studied by Congress or uncovered by the Supreme Court's own research (which facts were argued to support the presumption), the Court concluded that a majority of people possessing marijuana are generally *not* so aware. Thus, the presumption was held constitutionally invalid. The reason for viewing the proposition in the abstract, divorced of the particular facts about Leary himself, is that the jury possibly may not find that Leary is a learned professor who ought to know. Yet they might still use the presumption. So the presumption must be supportable independent of those facts.

Thus, the court had *apparently* delineated a relatively tidy theory testing all these statutory provisions by a single test, without drawing nice distinctions based upon what the jury was actually *told* about the presumption and their freedom to depart from it.

Then along came the Supreme Court case to be discussed here, Ulster County Court of New York v. Allen, 442 U.S. 140, 99 S.Ct. 2213 (1979), not only addressing some of the questions left ambiguous by the previous decisions; but also holding that much of the previous law applies only where the presumption is a "mandatory," rather than a "permissive," presumption. By these quoted terms, the court means something quite different from what evidence scholars have traditionally meant by the terms "mandatory" and "permissive" presumptions, and thus different from what we have meant by those terms in our discussion of presumptions in this book. (We will discuss later what the court means by those terms.) The court also makes clear that, as to its so-called mandatory presumptions, the "rational connection" that must be lived up to is the "beyond a reasonable doubt" rational connection. In such cases the presumption must be tested independently of the facts in the particular case—that is, it must be considered in the general or abstract, as described above in connection with *Leary.*

As respects what the *Ulster County* decision calls *permissive* presumptions (i. e., the kind of presumption actually involved in *Ulster County*), the rational connection that must be lived up to is merely a "preponderance of probabilities." In addition, with respect to permissive presumptions, the *facts of the particular case* are to be taken into account in deciding whether this standard is met. Thus, in *Ulster County* itself, the defendants were passengers in a car where a gun was found. The applicable N. Y. State presumption was that, from their presence on the premises (i. e., in the car), possession (a right to dominion and control) of the weapon on the part of each passenger could be inferred. Viewed in general, it does not follow that guns found on premises or in cars are possessed by (subject to the dominion and control of) all persons on the premises or all passengers. What about hitch-hikers? Or guns hidden in trunks, glove compartments, under seats, in drawers, or otherwise concealed? Nevertheless, in *this* particular case, the gun was very large, and sticking out of the bag of the only minor passenger, a 16-year-old girl; the bag was in the front seat; and the gun looked as though it was stashed there at the last minute. On such facts, it would be reasonable to assume possession on the part of the other adult passengers, unless shown otherwise (of course, in all cases, the presumed fact is always rebuttable, whether we class the presumption as mandatory or permissive in either our terminology or the court's). Thus, the presumption was constitutional. The problem, of course, is this: What if the jury disbelieves that the gun was in open view? They may still feel the presumption may be used—yet on such facts it makes no sense. Much depends upon what freedom the words of the instructions convey to the jury to disregard the presumption, and perhaps also on whether there is any genuine dispute as to where within the car the gun was found (i. e., as to whether it was in open view). One of the bones of contention between majority and dissent in *Ulster* seems to be that the dissent feels that this freedom to disregard was *not* sufficiently conveyed in the instructions. It is interesting to note, however, that as to another gun, hidden in the trunk, the jury did not bring in a conviction of the passengers.

What the decision in *Ulster* means by "mandatory" and "permissive" seems to be this:

The presumption is "permissive" if the jury is instructed clearly that the presumption is advisory, not very strong, and dependent upon what facts the jury finds. The jury must understand, for example, that if the jury believes the gun was hidden and believes that therefore no common sense inference of passenger possession arises, they should disregard the presumption concerning the passengers. The decision in some of its language seems to phrase the test of "permissive" or "mandatory" in terms of whether the jury is given to understand that the law declares that proof of fact A (presence in car with the gun) can be *sufficient*, standing *alone*, by itself, regardless of anything else or of anything the jury might believe about the other facts, to bring in a finding of possession (dominion and control) on the part of the passengers. This comes to the same thing.

Most of the cases, including this one, avoid any discussion of the kind of presumption that might more properly be called "mandatory": a presumption where the jurors are told that fact B (possession) *must* be found if fact A (presence in car with weapon) is found and they credit no evidence of non-B (e. g., that the weapon was hidden). In the presumptions *Ulster* calls "mandatory," the jury is still given to understand that while they *can* find proof of A sufficient alone to establish B in such a situation, they do not necessarily have to so find. (Presumptions that might more properly be called mandatory and presumptions this court calls mandatory are to be distinguished from "irrebuttable" presumptions—ones that could not be rebutted once A is proven, even by powerful evidence of non-B. It is questionable whether mandatory presumptions in the more proper senses, and irrebuttable presumptions, are constitutionally permissible in criminal cases. Another kind of presumption—one that shifts a burden to persuade beyond a reasonable doubt or by a preponderance of evidence, to the defendant, is also not involved in the cases, and may not be constitutional—at least not if they affect certain protected "elements" of the crime. See discussion of the *Mullaney* and *Patterson* cases, infra. Perhaps the "elements" distinction needs to be drawn for these other presumptions as well.)

The approach of the court in *Ulster County* is basically sound. After all, the really important thing to look at is what the jury was told—how far were the jurors constrained from their natural evaluation of the facts? Only to this extent does the defendant have any complaint that jury consideration of his case was infringed. It makes sense, then, to say there is a stricter test or standard for instructions that constrain more. The important questions are: What was the jury told? Is there justification for it? Could it be harmful on *any* picture of the facts the jury may piece together by selectively believing and disbelieving certain facts? It makes no sense to apply the same test to whatever the jury is told. It is important to determine whether they are told, in effect, that they practically *must* find; or that it is up to them, with some advice that certain inferences sometimes follow. Putting aside the role of presumptions at the directed acquittal stage (not involved in these cases), the constitutional question of presumptions is merely, was the jury told something misleading or unsupportable that could be harmful. Suppose the judge had told the jury about a possible inference of B from A, in his power to comment on the weight of evidence, allowed in many jurisdictions. The constitutional question would be the same: how strongly did he phrase it; did the jurors understand they had freedom to disregard it and appraise it on the facts as they have found them; was the advice supportable and justified. Indeed, this case amounts to nothing more than a comment case. (What I would quarrel with, however, is the continued vitality of the doctrine that facts uncovered by Congress or the Supreme Court and not in the record before the trier-of-fact, can sustain an otherwise invalid presumption. That does seem to me to deprive the defendant of full jury consideration of factual inferences. It is least objectionable [and perhaps no worse than putting before them an expert conclusion to choose to believe or not believe] where the jury is plainly given to understand that they may reject the inference [although an expert's basis for his conclusion or inference is usually revealed].)

There are no required forms of jury instructions to give under particular statutory presumptions. Yet the question of whether a particular presumption is "mandatory" or "permissive" and thus what test of validity applies, depends, under the court's analysis, upon exactly what the judge told the jury. Thus, the selfsame statutory presumption will be mandatory or permissive, valid or invalid, depending upon what form of words the judge accidentally chooses (and it usually is somewhat accidental). This is as it should be. The Supreme Court is ruling not on the statutory presumption, but on particular instructions. And that is a very practical approach. For we should be concerned with whether there was a harmful influence on a particular jury, not with some abstraction called a "presumption." The court has shifted the emphasis to practical reality rather than the reification.

The court, to support its decision, and to be consistent with earlier law, declares that some previous Supreme Court authority that applied the test now applicable to "mandatory" presumptions, actually did involve "mandatory" rather than "permissive" presumptions. Very little of what the jury was told appears in that authority; nor, it would seem, does the present court go back to the record there to find out. Yet what the jury was told is all important, under this court's analysis, in determining whether a presumption is "mandatory." How does the court know that such a presumption was "mandatory" without the instructions? The court seems to assume, at least at one point, that the precise language of the particular statute was used, without any amplification or qualification, by the trial judge in his instructions. But since the practice of trial judges varies in this respect, this is not necessarily a valid assumption, except in the few instances where the particular decision tells us this was done. Nor can the determination be made from looking at a part of the instructions without scrutinizing the whole.

The decision has certain implications for proposed Rule 25.1 of the Federal Rules of Criminal Procedure, reproduced above. (This draft rule has been continually re-proposed over the years.) The proposed rule, you will remember, provides a uniform effect for all criminal presumptions found in statutes, and a uniform effect for all criminal statutory provisions purporting to set up "prima facie inferences" (some attempted codifications you will remember have lumped these two together). The effect given is somewhat more forceful than in some of the other efforts (reproduced above) to prescribe effects. Since statutory prima facie provisions and presumptions are usually against the accused, proposed Rule 25.1 may be said to have issued out of pro-law-enforcement sentiments. But, in the light of *Ulster*, that pro-law-enforcement effort may have backfired. For, in providing a quite forceful effect (in the form of an instruction that fact A is "strong evidence" and "sufficient evidence" of fact B) for all statutory presumptions, proposed Rule 25.1 probably insures that all statutory presumptions will be considered "mandatory" under *Ulster*, with the result that the stricter test for constitutional validity will apply to them and more of them will fail to pass muster. Previously at least some judges were giving at least some of them the "permissive" effect. The same seems also to be true under proposed Rule 25.1 for prima facie inferences, since they are given only slightly less forceful effect under that rule.

Proposed Rule 25.1 cannot be said to be either constitutional or unconstitutional—it depends upon what particular statutory presumption or inference it is applied to, and whether that presumption or inference can meet the strict version of the rational connection test that applies to "mandatory" provisions.

The other Supreme Court decision we will discuss in connection with criminal presumptions is Mullaney v. Wilbur, 421 U.S. 684, 95 S.Ct. 1881 (1975). Unlike *Ulster County*, it involved a presumption that *shifted the persuasion burden onto the accused* (in the jury instruction), on a matter (malice aforethought) arguably as central or more central than that in *Ulster*. Thus, the jury-effect of this presumption was stronger than any of those just discussed. The court struck the presumption down without regard to whether any "rational connection" test could be met.

The inter-relationship of the subject of burdens and the subject of presumptions (an inter-relationship raised more by *Mullaney* than *Ulster*, though both deal with, and only with, the persuasion burden) presents some interesting questions. For example, it is quite clear that all three burdens may be directly placed on the accused on the issue of insanity (by making insanity an affirmative defense); and/or there may be a presumption of sanity. Is the same effect achieved by the presumption as by placing the burdens on the accused? (Consider, among others, the effect if no evidence of insanity is introduced.) Can we do both in the same case? (On the other side of the coin, cf. Taylor v. Kentucky, 436 U.S. 478, 98 S.Ct. 1930 (1978) and Kentucky v. Whorton, 441 U.S. 786, 99 S.Ct. 2088 (1979), dealing in part with when an instruction on the presumption of innocence is unnecessary in view of the instruction that it is the state's burden to prove beyond a reasonable doubt.) The burdens on the issue of killing by the accused may not be constitutionally placed on the accused in an ordinary homicide prosecution. But the cases discussed just above may indicate that there may be a presumption of such killing where the presumption is very strongly based on common sense ("rational connection"), assuming it is not understood as being "conclusive" or as changing the burden of persuasion. Cf. Sandstrom v. Montana, 442 U.S. 510, 99 S.Ct. 2450 (1979) (presumption of intent from acts suggesting intent). A number of cases have come up concerning illegal distilleries ("stills"). Assume (as is in fact the case), under any version of the rational connection test, that a presumption, whether "mandatory" or "permissive" under *Ulster*, of ownership of a "still" (a crime where the "still" is unlicensed) might constitutionally arise from the accused's unexplained presence at the still *plus* certain specified circumstances suggesting that he was an owner; but not merely from the unexplained presence alone. It is usually assumed that the state could make mere presence at the unlicensed "still" a crime, without the additional circumstances, if it chose to. So why should the presumption based on mere presence alone, without the circumstances, be forbidden?

Could the state make it a crime to be present at an unlicensed still under the specified circumstances? And make it an affirmative defense that defendant was not an owner? Could the state make a crime of merely being present at such a still, without the additional circumstances, with or without the defense mentioned? If it can be done without the defense, isn't the defense just a matter of added grace, or would that be just another way of creating the impermissible presumption? If it is just a matter of added grace and therefore permissible, why can't the law presume ownership from mere unexplained presence? Can the jury *infer* ownership from mere unexplained presence?

Is the presumption route (crime is ownership; ownership is rebuttably presumed from mere presence) for achieving the same result that would be achieved by rephrasing the crime and providing a defense (crime is presence; affirmative defense is "defendant was not owner") inferior as respects confusion of the jury and as respects advance notice to citizens of exactly what behavior is criminal? Does a statutory presumption usurp a judicial or jury role? Assuming you answered yes to these questions in this case, do these same problems (confusion of jury; lack of notice; usurpation) inhere in presumptions the Supreme Court clearly upholds (particularly where the rational connection appears only on the evidence before Congress and not the trial court)? Would they inhere, for example, in the presumption mentioned above, of ownership of a "still" from presence *plus* specified circumstances, where the significance of the circumstances in indicating ownership was known only to Congress?

Mullaney v. Wilbur attempts to answer only some of our questions. It raises others.

Wilbur was convicted of murder by a Maine jury. He claimed he struck deceased in the heat of passion provoked by an indecent homosexual overture. The jury was instructed that "malice aforethought" (necessary for a murder conviction) is presumed and that the defendant must prove *absence* of "malice aforethought" by a preponderance of the evidence, in order not to be guilty of murder but to be guilty of manslaughter instead, a lower and less severely punished offense that did not require malice aforethought. Wilbur appealed on the grounds that this instruction violated his right to due process, including the presumption of innocence until the state proves guilt (every element of the crime) beyond a reasonable doubt; and cited in support the case that most clearly elevated the "beyond a reasonable doubt" notion into a constitutional requirement, *In re Winship,* 397 U.S. 358, 90 S.Ct. 1068 (1970) (holding that, under the constitution, the burden of proof on the state in a juvenile proceeding must be to prove the elements of the offense "beyond a reasonable doubt" as in a criminal proceeding, and not a lesser standard such as preponderance of the evidence or clear and convincing evidence). The Maine Supreme Court affirmed Wilbur's conviction on the grounds that under Maine judicial law, murder and manslaughter were but degrees of one crime, felonious homicide, notwithstanding they are two separate statutory provisions; and that *Winship* did not apply to a factor such as "malice aforethought" that merely reduced the degree of the crime. Wilbur then petitioned the U.S. District Court (habeas corpus). The District Court overturned the conviction on the grounds that Maine law was *not* to the effect that there was but one crime. Maine appealed to the U.S. Court of Appeals which affirmed the District Court on the same grounds. Maine petitioned the U.S. Supreme Court for a Writ of Certiorari which was granted, and the U.S. Supreme Court remanded the case to the Court of Appeals for reconsideration in the light of an intervening Maine decision in another case seemingly confirming Maine's view that murder and manslaughter are one crime under Maine law. The Court of Appeals this time accepted Maine's view of its own law, but persisted in overturning Wilbur's conviction, saying that whether there is one or two crimes, in substance the burden imposed on the defendant by the state judge's instruction is the same and flouts the reasons for the requirement of proof beyond a reasonable doubt.

Maine thereupon petitioned the U.S. Supreme Court again for a Writ of Certiorari, which was granted and which ultimately led to the U.S. Supreme Court decision on the merits that we are reporting here.

Under the trial judge's instructions to the jury in *Mullaney*, a killing (not justified by war, police powers, etc.) that was intentional, had to be shown by the state before the presumption of "malice aforethought" and the defendant's burden to disprove it arose. ("Malice aforethought" and intention may be distinguished in that a person may have intention, in the sense that it is known or obvious death will result; yet "malice aforethought" is absent because the intention arose suddenly in the heat of passion upon adequate provocation. Thus, the burden cast on defendant by the trial judge's instructions in the present case was to prove sudden heat of passion on adequate provocation).

It was argued by the state that, under the trial judge's instructions, the state was required to prove beyond a reasonable doubt every element necessary to make the defendant a *criminal*—the only thing left to the defendant to show was whether he was a murderer or a manslaughterer ("malice aforethought" being the dividing line between the two). Maine law in essence views the two (murder and manslaughter) as one crime, felonious homicide, with the difference being one of degree—degree of punishment (sentence). Proof beyond a reasonable doubt by the state had never been required in sentence-setting. Against this it was argued that if the state could do this, it could also consider *involuntary* manslaughter (which does not require intent—just criminal negligence) to be an even lower degree of the same crime, felonious homicide, and make the defendant guilty of murder unless he proves lack of intention by a preponderance of the evidence. (There was some grounds for reading Maine law in such a fashion.) If this could be done, a state could phrase a whole variety of separate crimes as degrees of one (e. g., assault with intent to kill, assault with intent to rob, and simple assault), and make all assaulters guilty of the highest unless they proved the lack of the requisite intent. To be guilty of the lowest they would have to disprove the requisite intent for the two higher.

It was argued by defendant that *Winship* itself had required proof beyond a reasonable doubt by the state where all that was at stake was a relatively short sentence (as a juvenile offender). Here much more was at stake—the difference between murder and manslaughter could in Maine be the difference between a life sentence and a very minor or no sentence, not to mention the difference in stigma. Furthermore, in *Winship* the state had not tried to impose the persuasion burden on defendant—merely to reduce its own burden to a showing by a preponderance of the evidence. But even that was held bad.

Could the state make an intentional killing punishable as murder regardless of malice aforethought and heat of passion? If so, isn't it doing the defense a *favor* to allow a defense of lack of malice aforethought or a defense of heat of passion, even if defendant has to prove it by a preponderance of the evidence? If so, were defendant's rights violated here?

The problem in *Mullaney* arose, in a sense, out of the need to harmonize a number of rules, previously sanctioned by the U.S. Supreme Court, that seemed, at least in spirit, to conflict with the requirement that the state must prove the facts of the crime beyond a reasonable doubt. The Supreme Court had relieved the state of some or all of that burden a number of times. It had held (see our earlier discussion) that certain facts against the accused may be *presumed*—even, it might be added, if the presumed facts were the ultimate constituents of the crime. (But in such cases the jurors were always given to understand that if a reasonable doubt existed in their minds as to whether the presumed fact exists, the presumption is overcome and they must acquit; thus this principle casts a lighter burden on defendant—to raise a reasonable doubt—than the presumption in *Mullaney*). More importantly, the Supreme Court had always made it clear that a state can impose (by means of the device of creating "affirmative defenses") on criminal defendants the burden of proving certain facts like lack of sanity, lack of capacity, or self defense, in order to be excused, or can create other such "affirmative defenses." On at least one of these, the burden had been that defendant must prove "beyond a reasonable doubt." Leland v. Oregon, 343 U.S. 790, 72 S.Ct. 1002 (1952) (insanity). On most others, it was "preponderance of the evidence." The Court also seemed in a number of previous decisions to sanction the common practice that juries are not instructed about certain legal excuses unless defendant meets a burden of producing some evidence on them. (If that is met, the jury is instructed that the prosecution has the burden to negate the excuse "beyond a reasonable doubt," except for the above "affirmative defenses.") If one thinks about it, it becomes apparent that under this last principle, the issue becomes conclusively resolved against defendant if he produces no evidence on it. For example, if the issue of sanity is treated this way, as it is in some jurisdictions, and the defendant has no evidence of insanity, the jury would not be told that they can acquit on grounds of insanity, and indeed, may even be instructed that he cannot be acquitted on grounds of insanity (i. e., that he must be taken to be sane—is this the same thing as a directed finding of fact against accused, or even a mandatory presumption of sanity?).

Thus, apparently the constitution allowed some burdens, of some kind, on some factual issues, to be placed on the accused. What were to be the limits? Apparently, when a burden on defendant was considered by the Court to be *too* onerous, central, important, or counter to widespread national practice or current tradition, it would be considered to run afoul of the notion that it is up to the state to prove guilt, not the defendant to prove innocence—and up to the state to prove it beyond a reasonable doubt.

The question, then, in *Mullaney*, seems to have come down to the question of whether making the defendant negate "malice aforethought" by a preponderance of the evidence, is too onerous, central, important, or counter to widespread national practice or current tradition, to comport with the constitution.

While placing this burden on the defendant on this issue was originally the rule at common law in both England and the U.S., in the 50 years preceding *Mullaney* the tradition in both England and the large majority of American states had reversed itself.

The Supreme Court's decision on the merits in *Mullaney* is that malice aforethought must be proved by the state beyond a reasonable doubt, because of the importance of malice aforethought (in terms of the consequences, among other things) and because modern tradition places that burden on that issue on the state (notwithstanding the relative difficulty to the state of proving such a subjective factor—indeed, proving a negative—and notwithstanding the fact that the defense is likely to have more information on it). Such an important, now traditionally prosecution-allocated issue like malice-aforethought might be called an "element" of the crime (be wary of different uses of the word "element").

The holding would seem to apply *however* the burden of persuading by a preponderance [12] is placed on the defendant as respects such an element—whether via a presumption, as in this case (thus, our "View (5)," supra, of the effect of a presumption, that is, the view that imposes the burden of persuasion, would be illegal if applied in a criminal case against the accused as respects such an element, although other of the views, that do not affect persuasion burden, may be all right, and even "View (5)" may be all

---

[12] *A fortiori*, the placing of the burden to persuade *beyond a reasonable doubt* on the defendant as respects an important, traditionally prosecution-allocated element such as malice aforethought or heat of passion, would be bad. Query: How do you distinguish (if at all), the issue of sanity in *Leland v. Oregon*, several paragraphs above?

right as respects things that are not "elements" in the sense used here [13]); or via the mechanism of making "lack of malice aforethought" ("presence of heat of passion on sudden and adequate provocation") an affirmative defense in the statute itself. The decision thus has implications for the recodification-of-criminal-law efforts that have been going on in the states and in Congress for the last several decades. Under these efforts, great use is made of the device of affirmative defenses that place on the defendant the burden to persuade by a preponderance as respects the facts that make out the defense.[14]

[13] Among the non-elements, is there a distinction to be drawn between, on the one hand, those that are *almost* elements, and, on the other hand, those that are not like elements at all? As to the former, we could allow only a *preponderance* burden to be placed on the defendant, rather than a *beyond a reasonable doubt* burden.

[14] For example, under Senate Bill S. 1722 (cited at page 137, above), it is an affirmative defense (sometimes called a "bar to prosecution" rather than "affirmative defense," for reasons that need not now concern us) to sexual abuse of a minor, that the actor reasonably believed the other person to be over age 16; to arson and property destruction, that the act was consented to or was reasonably so believed; to receiving stolen property, that it was with intent to return or report it; to theft, that the property was intangible government property obtained to disseminate it to the public and not obtained by means of eavesdropping, interception, burglary, or criminal entry or trespass; to obscenity, that the material was disseminated only to someone engaged in teaching at an educational institution or authorized by a licensed physician or psychologist or psychiatrist; to restraint of a child by an unauthorized parent, that the child was returned unharmed within 30 days; to certain crimes of inflicting, risking, or threatening bodily harm (such as assault, menacing, reckless endangerment, and terrorizing), that the conduct was consented to or the hazard was a reasonably foreseeable hazard of a joint undertaking, medical treatment, or an occupation; to murder in consequence of a felony, that death was not a reasonably foreseeable consequence; to pressuring a public servant in various ways, that it was done to compel legal action or compliance with duty and the means used was lawful; to certain false statement offenses, that the false statement was timely retracted; to offenses of failure to obey judicial or other process, that the process was invalid or unconstitutional, that reasonably available, timely means were taken to challenge it, that the process or order constituted a prior restraint on news, that there

[157]

was a privilege, and/or that the failure was due to circumstances beyond the actor's control; to attempt, conspiracy, and solicitation, that there was abandonment, renunciation, and prevention of the crime; etc. In each case, it would have been possible, instead, to include the issue that is the subject of the affirmative defense, in the definition of the crime itself (i. e., the reverse of the fact that constitutes the defense would become part of the definition of the crime —that is, part of the facts necessary to constitute the crime), with the usual (though not inevitable) result that the prosecution would have had the burden to persuade beyond a reasonable doubt, on it. However, the fact that conceptually it *could have been* made part of the definition does not necessarily make it an "element" in the *Mullaney* sense—that is, an element that may not be allocated to the defendant to prove by a preponderance. (If it *is* made part of the definition of the crime in the statute, rather than an affirmative defense, is it *necessarily* an "element" in the *Mullaney* sense?) To be such an element, the opinion seems to suggest that the issue must be considered to be at least as important and traditionally allocated to the prosecution, as the malice aforethought issue. The Supreme Court has not said, in *Mullaney*, that there are *no* issues upon which the burden to persuade by a preponderance, may be placed upon the accused. The court appears to have merely prohibited it as to *some* issues—those that are so important and so frequently prosecution-allocated in the states in this country in recent history, that to go against this trend would be unconscionable. A decision has to be made concerning the *particular factual issue* that has been assigned to the accused. (In *Mullaney* itself, the recent history and the importance of the issue both pointed in the same direction. A more difficult case may arise in the future where they do not.) See also Sandstrom v. Montana, 442 U.S. 510, 99 S.Ct. 2450 (1979) (intent is such an element).

Do you think *Mullaney* has implications for "affirmative defenses" such as self-defense, insanity, intoxication, immaturity, defense of property, defense of others, or necessity?

Although we will not mention them, it should be noted that the bill (S.1722) also provides "defenses" that are not *"affirmative* defenses." As to these, it is provided that the prosecution still has the burden of persuasion beyond a reasonable doubt. But that burden arises—that is, an instruction will be given that the state must prove it beyond a reasonable doubt—only if *some evidence* to substantiate the defense is introduced. Such defenses (and possibly presumptions having a similar effect, although such criminal presumptions—"mandatory," in the parlance of evidence scholars—may or may not be valid) are known in traditional law, as well. *Mullaney* probably would not affect them. What may be novel under the bill, however, and possibly subject to constitutional challenge, is the quantum of evidence that will qualify

Such would seem to be what the Supreme Court was saying in *Mullaney*—until we read Patterson v. New York, 432 U.S. 197, 97 S.Ct. 2319 (1977), which came along two years later. In *Patterson,* the state imposed on the accused the identical burden (to persuade the jury by a preponderance) on an issue ("extreme emotional disturbance") that is hard to distinguish from (and served essentially the same mitigating function as) the "provocation-heat-of-passion" issue in *Mullaney.* But this time the state did it by means of making the issue an *affirmative defense,* rather than using the device of a presumption. The Supreme Court this time upheld the state. Can this be squared with *Mullaney?* Is the Supreme Court elevating form over substance, by holding that it matters whether the result is accomplished by use of an affirmative defense or a presumption? The court does indicate in *Patterson* that there are some matters related to culpability that could not be assigned to the defendant (to persuade the jury by a preponderance) *regardless* of which of the two devices is used. What are they? Are we going to have a heirarchy—i. e., matters which cannot be assigned to the defendant (to persuade by a preponderance) by either device; matters which can be so assigned to him by means of an affirmative defense but not by means of a presumption (i. e., the matter in *Mullaney* and *Patterson*); and matters which can be so assigned to him by either device? (What will be the scheme with respect to assigning him the burden to persuade beyond a reasonable doubt?) We have seen that presumptions against the accused like those involved and

as *some evidence* for these purposes. It is defined as *such evidence as will justify a reasonable belief* in the *existence* of the fact, rather than such evidence as would justify a reasonable doubt about its existence. The constitutional challenge might be most serious where the defense consisted of a fact that is in some sense considered central to the concept of culpability or an "element" as we have been using that term.

discussed in *Ulster*, that have some lesser effect on the jury than putting the persuasion burden on the defendant, must meet one version or another of the rational connection test (depending upon the strength of that effect) in order to be valid. What test must a presumption that imposes the burden to persuade by a preponderance on defendant meet, where the heirarchy indicates such a presumption could be allowed? If there are issues which can be assigned (by means of a presumption) to the defendant to prove beyond a reasonable doubt (cf. Leland v. Oregon, supra), what test of validity must such a presumption meet?[15]

It must be borne in mind, that any device that imposes the persuasion burden on the criminal defendant allows a conviction even when the jury has a reasonable doubt on that particular issue, for the jury may feel the defendant has succeeded in raising a reasonable doubt but not in showing that the fact is *most probably* as he contends. Consider the issues of killing, of duress, of insanity, of intention, etc. Upon which (if any) should the jury be allowed to have a reasonable doubt and yet convict?

---

[15] In reading *Patterson* one cannot help but get the feeling that the real distinction from *Mullaney* the court had in mind (perhaps only hinted at in the decision), was that in *Patterson* the imposing of the burden on the defendant was done by the *legislature* rather than by *common-law-process court decision.* Aside from implying some conception of the relative roles of the judicial and political processes, the Supreme Court was mindful that the legislature might choose to punish the crime as murder without regard to extreme emotional disturbance (or heat of passion) if the Supreme Court made it too difficult for the state to recognize liberalizing or mitigating factors such as extreme emotional disturbance or heat of passion. The Supreme Court was worried about the effect on the codification movement generally, of a rule that mitigating or excusing factors can only be enacted if the legislature is willing to put the burden on the state. In addition, legislative imposing of the burden in an affirmative defense communicates in advance much more clearly. Would you say after *Patterson* that if the legislature has constitutional power to make acts criminal, it may provide for conviction based on those acts alone and relegate all mitigating facts to the status of affirmative defenses to be proved by a preponderance?

CHAPTER III

HEARSAY: THE BASIC THEORY AND RATIONALE

What Is This Thing Called Hearsay?

W (witness) reports on the stand that he heard D (declarant, not defendant) state out of court that he (D) saw X shoot Y. Perhaps W relates D's story in relevant detail. D does not testify. W's testimony as to what D said is hearsay if offered to establish that the shooting took place, that X did it, or that it was in any other respect as stated by D. Hearsay is inadmissible in civil and criminal cases unless an exception can be applied.

What is wrong with W's testimony in the above situation (which is the basic hearsay situation)?

W may be lying, mistaken, joking, misremembering, or reporting ineptly. He may be speaking loosely, carelessly, incompletely, or misleadingly. He may not be entirely credible, accurate, or sincere. There may be some consciously or unconsciously produced disparity between the picture he gives the fact-finder of what was said and what was actually said. His veracity is in issue. But don't these dangers accompany all testimony given in court? Normally we rely on certain courtroom adjuncts to incline a witness toward faithful reporting and to alert the fact-finder to some of the otherwise hidden pitfalls involved in accepting the testimony. We rely on courtroom confrontation, the threat or actuality of cross examination, the open display of the witness, the oath, the possibility of penalties for perjury and contempt, the solemnity and seriousness of the situation, and the witness' contemplation of the stakes involved in the litigation.   Our apprehensions concerning W in our hypothetical case seem to be taken care of at least as well as in any other case. W is on the stand.

But what about D? *He* may have been lying or mistaken (or any of the other things we said of W). There may be a variance between the picture D gives of what happened and what actually happened. His veracity, like W's, is in issue. But D has not been subjected to the courtroom. Therefore, W's testimony as to what D said outside of the courtroom is hearsay.

On the facts of the case as we have given them, D is, albeit indirectly, acting as a witness (although we do not term him such), and ought to be subjected to the courtroom processes designed for witnesses. As we shall see, the question "is the declarant acting as an absent witness," as opposed to acting as a verbally contracting party or acting in some other capacity, is a good shorthand test of whether his words are being offered in a hearsay capacity.

In justification of the rule that the evidence of what D said in the above example is hearsay because D has been untested by the courtroom processes, consider the following parade of potential horribles, which are by no means exhaustive. D may have been suffering from myopia or some other defect of physical perceptual capacity. He may have been under the influence of a drug or intoxicant. He may have been deficient in mind, memory, or linguistic ability. He may be a careless person, or may have been careless on that occasion. Weather conditions may have interfered with his observation.   He may not have had his glasses on. There may have been characteristics about the shooter, perhaps noticed but not understood by D, which would mean the shooter could not have been X. D may have been unfamiliar with X.   D may have made contradictory statements about who killed Y. D may harbor a long-standing grudge against X. D may have said on some occasion, "I'd lie to see X burn." The prosecutor may have made a "deal" with D. D himself might be the killer or related to the killer. D may have been speaking of a different Mr. X, repeating a rumor, or deducing that X shot Y from clues rather than first-hand eye-witness observation. The gun may have been filled with blanks or not loaded. The whole scene may have been done for a film. Or D may have been making an accusation he scarcely believed in, to discover, by X's response, whether there was any truth to it. Or D may have been joking. (While a similar parade of horribles could be made concerning the reliability of W's perception and report, it is not his, but D's we are concerned with.)

These things would affect the weight, and perhaps the admissibility, of the evidence. There are many ways they might be revealed in court with D on the stand, including close scrutiny of and pressure on his demeanor and manner, deeper inquiry into the facts, etc.

One should consider that there may be other ways to protect the opponent of the evidence with respect to some of these "horribles" than requiring the proponent to put D on the stand as the price of using his statement. For example, it has been suggested that we allow the hearsay in and leave it up to X (i. e., the opponent of the evidence, whom we assume is X) to produce D if X wants to test the hearsay. Some have said that this might be sound when D is sitting in the visitors' gallery or is testifying in some capacity in the cause, or is a party, but otherwise the burden of producing him would be unfairly great. Others have pointed out restrictions on cross-examining and impeaching one's own witness, as an argument against this suggestion. Another suggestion has been that X can bring out at least some of the potential "horribles" just mentioned through independent evidence or by examining W, without examining D.   It should be realized, however, that W may not be familiar with D, D's capacities and vantage point, the weather conditions at the shooting, etc.   W did not neces- sarily hear D's declaration at the same time and place as the shooting.   Another suggestion has been that, as to some of the potential horribles, it might be sufficient to call to the jury's attention the *possibility* they exist, by argumentation of counsel and/or instruction from the judge.   The jury often weighs evidence in the light of possibilities or likelihoods that are not specifically evidenced in the case at bar. (Conceivably the jury might even take account of the possi- bilities without any mention of them by judge or counsel.) But these suggestions by and large are ill-received by courts.

A question that has troubled courts and commen- tators, and about which a conflict of authority re- mains, is this: Would it cure the defect if D, rather than W, reported on the stand D's prior statement?

There are several reasons why D might do what is described in the black-letters.   D might remember only that he *said* so-and- so, and not remember the facts any longer;   or the earlier statement might be offered to buttress the present testimony as to the facts, being closer to them in point of time.   The commonest example is the station-house line-up identification recounted on the stand by the identifier himself.[1]

---

[1] There might be no hearsay problem if the earlier (station-house) statement were used merely to refresh the witness' memory for an on-the-stand present-memory statement that the criminal was the accused, if it could be confined to that.   What about using the earlier (station-house) statement to bolster the credibility of the witness and of the later (in court) testimony that the witness remembers the criminal and he is the accused, on a theory of prior consistent state- ment analogous to prior inconsistent statement?   See p. 170, infra. Even though the evidence may not be hearsay, courtroom economies usually forbid prior *consistent* statements to *support* credibility, even when consistency is attacked, except in certain narrow situations.

The controversy amongst authorities on how to treat this situation centers around whether it is the lack of courtroom safeguards, or the lack of courtroom safeguards *at the time of making the statement* that is significant. Do you think there is any reason to make a distinction between statements of identification (on the street or at the station-house) and other out-of-court statements?

See pp. 348–49 and n. 4 there. *Inconsistent* ones to *attack* credibility are freely allowed. Why the difference?

If the earlier (station-house) identification was conducted under circumstances violative of the defendant's rights (e. g., the right to counsel or to "fundamental fairness" under general due process) and if that station-house identification played a significant though perhaps subconscious role in bringing about the later (in court) identification, the in-court testimony might be inadmissible as well as the declaration of identity made at the line-up, being "fruit of the poisonous tree." See United States v. Wade, 388 U.S. 218, 87 S.Ct. 1926 (1967), Gilbert v. California, 388 U.S. 263, 87 S.Ct. 1951 (1967), and Stovall v. Denno, 388 U.S. 293, 87 S.Ct. 1967 (1967). See also Biggers v. Tennessee, 390 U.S. 404, 88 S.Ct. 979 (1968); Palmer v. Peyton, 359 F.2d 199 (4th Cir. 1966). But see Section 701(a) of the 1968 Omnibus Crime Control Act, 18 U.S.C.A. § 3502 (which seems to say nothing shall bar an eye-witness from identifying from the stand the accused; can this override a constitutional defect in the way the evidence was obtained?).

In the situation in the black-letters and text above, should distinctions be made (concerning the adequacy of the opportunity to cross examine) among a case where the witness remembers the facts stated in his former statement and vouches that they are true; a case where the witness says he said it and, though he doesn't remember the facts now, he remembers making a true statement; a case where he remembers making the statement and feels it "must have been true;" a case where he says "if I said it, it was true;" a case where he says "I said it; it wasn't true;" and a case where he says "I didn't say it, and it wasn't true?" What about a case where he doesn't remember whether he made the statement; and denies, affirms, or doesn't remember the underlying facts reported in it, or tells a different story now? How might the statement be evidenced where the witness doesn't say he made it? Is cross examination equally effective in all the cases mentioned? Is the first case really not an offer of a former statement at all, but rather a current recollection of facts?

**If D's statement in our prototype situation open-
ing this chapter, though reported by W at the present trial, was itself originally made at another trial
in D's capacity as a witness there (rather than
made on the street), we may have a candidate for
special treatment.**

It would seem that the dangers of hearsay would be
obviated in the situation in the black-letters immediately above,
provided that the stimuli to accuracy and the incentives to test
D's statement are substantially the same at the two trials, which
gives rise to a requirement of identity of parties, issues, and
stakes, insofar as necessary in view of these objectives.
Similarity of opportunity to cross-examine is regarded as more
important than what the party did with that opportunity.
Unavailability of the declarant at the later proceeding is also a
requirement for admission of the prior statement in this
situation. (The commonest example of this situation is where
testimony has been given at an earlier trial, preliminary hearing,
or deposition, in the same case.) The matter is usually treated,
however, as an exception to the hearsay rule, rather than as not
being hearsay. If the declarant also appears as a witness at the
present trial, might there be good reason to dispense with the
requirement that there have been an opportunity at the earlier
proceeding to cross examine, and that the parties and issues
there have been similar to those here (a requirement intended
to insure that, both in degree and kind, the attention, care, and
incentives of both witness and cross-examiner would be
focused on the same facts as having the same significance,
consequences, importance, and stakes, as in the present case)?
If you feel this should be admissible, would you call it an
exception to the hearsay rule, or non-hearsay?

**In general, in the determination of hearsay vel
non, official traditional doctrine takes little account of the reliability and necessities in the particular case.**

Suppose D in the original hypothetical opening this chapter
was the only eyewitness and he is now dead; and there is no

determinative evidence (civil; criminal). Assume also that there appears to be nothing suggesting that D is lying or unreliable. It would seem that the jury is more likely to reach a correct result if the evidence is admitted than if it is excluded. This becomes highlighted if we further suppose that his statement is the only thing that can clear Mr. Q of a charge of murder. Remember that all that is needed to acquit is a reasonable doubt. But considerations such as these seem to have no part in the traditional doctrine, except to the formalistic extent that need and reliability are recognized in the exceptions to the hearsay rule, *infra*. If it is hearsay, and it does not come within one of the recognized exceptions (which this probably would not), it is inadmissible. And yet, citizens, in making important decisions in their daily lives, commonly rely on their ability to correctly evaluate hearsay. Even attempts under some of the newer codes to add a broad new exception, sometimes dubbed the "catch-all" exception, to the traditional exceptions, do not go all the way toward embracing such evidence. As we shall see when we come to them, these "catch-all" provisions do not indeed catch *all*, nor even *most.*

It should also be noted that there are times when an out-of-court declaration, nearer the time of the occurrence, and *ante litem motam*, might be more accurate than the declarant's present testimony would be, and should be preferred. But again, this seldom plays an official role, except as mentioned hereinafter in connection with specific exceptions.

An Outmoded Rationale of the Hearsay Rule

The hearsay rule may originally have been based on the notion that there are peculiar dangers involved in perceiving, remembering, and recounting a statement (probably only an oral statement), as opposed to perceiving, remembering, and recounting some other fact.

For example, in the familiar party game of "telephone," a secret message whispered from one person to the next person, on down a long line of people, comes out remarkably distorted at the end.

On the rationale expressed by the black letters, it is W's inaccuracy, rather than D's, with which we are concerned. Under this rationale, testimony as to the terms of oral contracts and other oral statements would be hearsay whatever the purpose of their offer, which, as we shall see, is not the law. Furthermore, conduct could not be hearsay even in the clearest case of an implied declaration; and written statements could not be hearsay. Again, such is not the law.

Written Declarations

In the original hypothetical opening this chapter, if D's out-of-court declaration had been in writing, and the writing were attempted to be introduced into evidence, rather than W's testimony, we still have hearsay (the same is so for audio records.)

Had it been the worry that courtroom safeguards would be inadequate against the possibility of W's inaccuracy that led us to pin the label "hearsay" on the evidence in our original hypothetical, then the writing we are speaking of in the heading here would not be hearsay, for we have eliminated W as a reporter of the contents of the statement, and have not really substituted analogous worries concerning inauthenticity or alteration of the writing. As to those worries, the writing is no different than any writing customarily offered in court, for which we rely on the courtroom machinery.

But it was not W's inaccuracy that worried us. It was D's. And that remains the same. An argument could be made that this worry is attenuated, at least in the case of some writings that people make with great seriousness. But even a sworn affidavit, which bears a penalty if falsely sworn, is not considered to have safeguards sufficient to substitute for the courtroom.   Nevertheless, the argument plays a role when we come to consider specific exceptions to the hearsay rule embracing certain textbooks, transcripts, and written records.

Prior Inconsistent Statements

There are special considerations where a witness tells one story on the stand, and the opposing attorney wishes to adduce that the witness told a contrary story, or made an apparently contrary statement, on some previous occasion, out of court.

Suppose D, after saying on some earlier out-of-court occasion, that the Ford went through the red light, turns coat and on the stand denies that the Ford went through a red light, or denies seeing anything.   Firstly, it is clear the reference by the attorney to the prior story to stimulate the witness' memory or to secure present assent to its accuracy based on current memory of the facts presents no hearsay problem if it can be satisfactorily confined to that.   The former statement would become current testimony.   Similarly, if the witness will say the statement was probably true although he doesn't remember the facts, we may have no problem (if the previous statement is written), for it will usually comply with the requirements for the exception to the hearsay rule for "past recollection recorded."   But suppose it is regarded as futile to attempt to use the previous statement in these ways.   Assume, however, that the witness will admit, or the attorney is prepared to prove, that the witness at least *made* the statement.   Assume also that the attorney is prepared to prove the contents of the statement, either through the witness' admission that he *made* the statement as quoted by the attorney, or via another witness or document.   Can the statement be offered on the theory that it is evidence of the fact that the Ford did go through the red light? D is on the stand and available for questioning about the prior statement. However, unlike the situation mentioned earlier where D testifies to his own prior out-of-court statement (p. 164 supra), here the witness does not stand behind his earlier statement at all, even if he acknowledges he made it. This might render it difficult for the opponent of the earlier statement to conduct a searching, cross-examining type of examination concerning the earlier statement. On the other hand, can he really complain, since the witness has already fulfilled the dream of anyone conducting such a cross-examination or challenge to any statement: the witness has repudiated the statement. At least until some of the newer codes, and even under some of them, and in most non-code states, the evidence offered for these purposes is usually regarded as hearsay. (A few authorities treat this situation, and the situation of the prior consistent statement spoken of at p. 164, as being the same; and also do not make any of the distinctions at the end of footnote 1 supra. They take an essentially mechanical view, splitting over whether to consider prior statements of witnesses *as a category* hearsay or not.)

Suppose the theory of the attorney offering the prior inconsistent statement in the case opening the last paragraph is confined to *impeachment,* i. e., to demonstrating that this is the sort of witness who cannot be trusted on *either* occasion because he "blows hot and cold." Today he says the Ford stopped for the full duration of the light. Previously he said the Ford went through the red light. He can't be believed. It is usually held in these circumstances that the earlier statement is offered not as true, but to cast doubt on both statements; that the offeror does not depend upon the veracity or testimonial qualities of the witness on the earlier occasion, and that he is not offering the out-of-court statement as an accurate reflection of the facts it reports (that the Ford went through the red light). It is said not to detract from the aim of the evidence, that on the former occasion the witness may have been mistaken, lying, etc. The offeror is supposedly attempting to bring out just such possibilities with respect to both occasions. Courts therefore conclude that the lack of courtroom safeguards respecting the earlier statement is not important, and there is no hearsay, when offered for and confined to this purpose.

Conduct: Assertive and Non-Assertive; Declarations Implied from Conduct and from Other Statements

So-called "assertive" behavior of declarants, such as pointing or nodding, is frequently considered to be hearsay. So-called "non-assertive" behavior is more controversial; as are declarant's words offered as meaning something other than they purport to say.

Let us return to the original hypothetical involving an oral declaration by D that X shot Y, reported on the stand by W as substantive evidence of X's guilt. D does not testify. Suppose instead of making a declaration, D, after being in the position of an eye-witness, *behaved* in some non-verbal fashion as though he believed X shot Y, and this out-of-court behavior is reported on the stand by W (who observed D's behavior) for the same purposes as the declaration was. Clearly, if the behavior were intended by D to be a substitute for the declaration, as for example where D points to X in response to an inquiry as to who is the killer, it should be treated no differently from the declaration, for the policy considerations are the same. Where behavior is intended by D in this fashion to be a substitute for words, we call it "assertive." He intends it to be a communication.

But suppose the behavior by D that is supposed to indicate X's guilt, is *non*-assertive—not intended by D as a substitute for words. More concretely, let us suppose that it is conclusively established that the victim was the beloved brother of D and D directly observed the shooting that killed him. W testifies that immediately after the victim fell, W observed D chasing X. (Perhaps W himself was not positioned so as to be able to see the actual killing, but only the aftermath.) Of course, such evidence is offered at the trial as a kind of implied statement of or implied assertion of the other's guilt, but probably not as something *intended by D at the time as a communication to the watchers or a substitute for the words "he did it."* This intention of D at the time is what is responsible for the short-hand term, "non-assertive," used to characterize this kind of behavior. Let's examine this behavior.

You will note that the evidence is offered on the theory that D's apparent belief in X's guilt was translated into action rather than words. The chain of reasoning urged here by the offeror is that because D *behaved* in this way, he probably believed X killed Y; the belief was probably well founded in direct observation of facts corresponding to and giving rise to the belief; therefore, X probably did kill Y. The chain of reasoning in the original hypothetical involving an express declaration, "X killed Y," was identical except that the word "declared" should be substituted for the word "behaved." And a similar chain is present in the case of "pointing" just above, too. In each case a belief is sought to be implied from an outward manifestation (words or conduct); and a fact is sought to be implied from the belief in it. It would seem that there are many of the same possibilities of unreliability (mistake, dishonesty, attempt to divert suspicion, etc.) in each case. The reader should review them, ascribing each to a link in the reasoning chain just set out.

In some ways, however, the evidence is more reliable in the case involving chasing than in the case of the express declaration. Persons generally require more certainty before taking action than before speaking. Further, it is less likely that a person will act out (to the extent of chasing) a lie or joke than speak one. And the jury is more "on guard" in drawing the offered inference from the chasing than they are in believing a direct verbal declaration. For these reasons, there is perhaps less need to insist on the courtroom safeguards in the chasing example than in the case of the express declaration. On the other hand, the chasing of X by D may have been due to something like, say, a desire to secure a scared X as a witness to the slaying committed by someone else, or an unkind word by X about the just deceased brother, or, less likely, an old money debt owed by X to D of which D happened to be reminded at the moment, which possibilities have no analogue in the case of the express declaration. In this sense, the "chasing" evidence is *less* reliable than the declaration, and there may be *more* need for safeguards. But perhaps these new dangers are not comparable to those involved in accepting statements as true, and are therefore not in the peculiar province of the courtroom processes (cross-exam, etc.) discussed. Perhaps they are provable other ways than by having D on the stand. Perhaps the jury will make allowance for them regardless of whether they are shown, at least if prodded.

The problem would be much the same if D, rather than declaring X's guilt or manifesting it by pointing or chasing, called X a "filthy swine," and this were later reported in court to indicate that D saw X shoot Y. In this case, we are implying one statement from another, rather than from conduct, but the problem is much the same: conduct or statement offered as meaning something else—i. e., as amounting to an *implied* statement.

These problems are usually subsumed under the heading "implied declarations." The authorities are in considerable disagreement over whether to regard these kinds of things as "declarations" for purposes of the hearsay rule, with the result that they would be hearsay. Where they do regard them as declarations and hence hearsay, the theory is confined to cases like the above, where there are weaknesses in the inference the offeror seeks to draw which are analogous to the weaknesses inherent in ordinary witness testimony and which the courtroom processes discussed are deemed peculiarly adept at minimizing or exposing. Thus, the credibility, accuracy, or sincerity of the actor must be drawn into issue. His words or conduct must be offered as a reflection of a belief which is itself offered as an accurate representation of some other fact. In other words, the person whose conduct is being testified to must be being offered as in effect an absent *witness.* W's testimony in a murder case that he had seen the conduct of the defendant in killing the victim, would not present a hearsay problem (even though it is a report of out-of-court conduct) because it does not meet this criterion. This example has its analogue where an out-of-court *express declaration* is offered for itself and not as a representation of any further fact; as, for example, where a slander or oral contract which is the subject of suit is proven by one who overheard it. In each case the out-of-court person is not in effect acting as an absent *witness.*

Conduct: The Element of Human Voluntariness

A series of hypotheticals can help elucidate whether and what role human voluntariness plays.

Consider the following pieces of evidence. In each case, you are to assume that the effort is to prove the direction of the wind, and whether or not it was raining, at the time of the occurrence in controversy.

(1) Testimony as to the behavior of weather vanes, sails on the lake, and rain detection equipment at the time.

(2) Testimony as to the behavior of cows in a nearby field. (Assume it is proven that it is the habit of cows to lie down in the rain, and face into the wind.) (In one case it was sought to be proved that certain chickens held by X belonged to Y, by showing they flocked to Y's premises and bedded down there upon being released by X.)

(3) Testimony by a witness (who was not himself in a position to tell whether it was raining or to sense the wind, being, say, at a sheltered window, covered by an over-hang, high up in a tall building) that the passersby had their umbrellas up and were hunched as though walking into the wind (when proceeding in one direction).

(4) The witness in (3) reports that, rather than seeing umbrellas, he shouted down "is it raining?" and the passers-by replied that it was.

(5) The same cases as (3) and (4) except that only one passerby is involved, rather than many.

Consider also the following:

(6) An observation that a person or persons turned up his collar and wrapped his coat around himself, offered to prove it was cold on that occasion, (a) where the evidence shows this action was done to express to another (say someone in a window) that it was cold, or (b) where there is no evidence it was done for such purpose.

(7) Police use of tear gas is sought to be proved by showing that people staggered from the building coughing and wiping their eyes (a) where tears were also seen, (b) where tears were not seen but would not have been susceptible of being seen if present, or (c) where there is disputed evidence that a delivery boy dropped and broke a keg of chemical nearby that would have a similar effect.

Of course there are differences in weight among these pieces of evidence, and the differences would manifest themselves not only in the jury's evaluation of the evidence, but probably also in the balancing process effecting admissibility described in Chapter I.   But what about the hearsay rule?   Most courts would agree that (1) and (2) are not hearsay.   Inaccuracies that might inhere in machinery or in an animal's perception and reaction are not regarded as peculiar subjects of the courtroom safeguards we have been speaking about.   Most would agree that (4) is hearsay; and that the application of the hearsay rule, like the requirement of cross examination in court in ordinary cases, cannot turn upon how many people say the same thing (see (5)), although where a witness has become unavoidably unavailable for cross examination after giving his direct testimony—e. g., has become sick or has died—this factor may influence the decision as to what is to be done.   Most courts would also agree that 6(a) is hearsay.   As to the others, there is bound to be substantial disagreement. What can be said about them is that courts agree in principle that the application of the hearsay rule should not turn on distinctions regarding the probativity of the evidence; and yet it is difficult to escape the conclusion that degree of involuntariness of the declaration or conduct, and opportunity for premeditation and fabrication, play a role in the rule's applicability, being within the traditional provinces of the courtroom safeguards and perhaps outside the jury's competence to evaluate without those safeguards.   Thus, a startled physical flinching, offered to prove an explosion, would generally be admissible and might even be likened to evidence that a person was seen hurtling through the air, offered for the same purpose.   It should be noted in this connection, that there is a specific exception to the hearsay rule, discussed infra, for certain kinds of spontaneous utterances, stimulated by excitement over a shocking contemporaneous occurrence.   It is to be wondered whether it is true that such reports are likely to be superior to other

[*176*]

forms of hearsay, or whether, on the other hand, persons are less careful in such circumstances. Perhaps the feeling is that the jury is equipped to evaluate that kind of possibility of inaccuracy and is not greatly in need of the courtroom aids.

Conduct: Omission

A number of cases involving the *absence* of statements or conduct by "declarants" have presented a problem which has split authorities.

Seller delivers corn to Buyer, pursuant to a purchase contract between them calling for Grade One corn. Grades of corn are clearly ascertainable. Buyer complains that he received Grade Two corn, which is inferior. Buyer therefore sues Seller for breach of contract. It is stipulated that the corn delivered came from a certain bulk lot; and that all corn in a bulk lot is of uniform grade (fungible). Seller introduces in defense evidence that Seller had sold to others, as Grade One corn, corn from precisely the same bulk lot as that from which the corn delivered to Buyer was drawn; *and that none of these other customers ever complained.* (An agent of Seller's company having personal knowledge of this testifies. The other customers do not.) The inference Seller hopes will be drawn from this evidence is that the corn was Grade One. Is this hearsay? The problem is essentially the same as that involved in the hypothetical about D chasing X, above, except that some might find it more difficult to imply a statement from silence than from affirmative conduct. The customers whose non-complaint (conduct) is offered are in the out-of-court position of D. W is the testifying agent of Seller's company. The evidence is offered on the theory that the non-complaining customers believed they received Grade One corn, or at least did not believe otherwise, as manifest by their out-of-court silence, and this state of belief was probably founded on the corresponding fact in the real world that it *was* Grade One corn they received. As in the case of the express declaration, the pointing, and the chasing, the chain of inference sought to be drawn involves two distinct links or deductions: (1) that the persons held the belief (or lacked a contrary one), and (2) that they did so because the facts were in accord therewith. These same two are also involved in accepting as true any statement made on or off the stand. Both are fallible.

Some possible unreliabilities in the first link are, of course, that the customers may have believed it was Grade *Two*, but may have foregone complaint because complaint was too much trouble, or because of a bribe, a wish not to jeopardize good and generally advantageous business relations, a selling price such that it was not worth complaining, a minor disparity between the value of Grade One and Grade Two corn, a contemplated usage for which the two grades were equally adequate (such as feeding pigs), or some other factor giving rise to a reluctance to complain. Of course, the likelihood of these varies with the facts, e. g., the number of non-complaining customers, the prices paid, and the difference in value between the two grades.

Coming to weaknesses in the second link, even if the customers believed the corn they received was Grade One, their belief may have been incorrect. They may have failed to inspect or to inspect properly, their inspection facilities may have been poor, someone may have been careless, information as to the criteria for determining grades may have been deficient, etc. Again, the particular facts, such as the number of customers, would be important to the strength of the inference. An additional unreliability is that perhaps they didn't believe either way, would not necessarily have noticed if it were Grade Two, and didn't care.

Requiring the customers to be subjected to courtroom processes would certainly help to some extent, but not entirely in the customary manner. Clearly there are certain other ways for the opponent of the evidence to at least somewhat help himself. He could bring in other evidence illuminating these possibilities. Or, indeed, *he* might be able to subject the customers to courtroom processes. Or (to some extent) he could rely on the sophistication of the jury, at least with instruction and argument. Courts are in disagreement over what the result should be.

A similar case is presented where an out-of-court silence in the face of an accusation is offered as implied acquiescence—an admission of the guilt charged by the accuser—or where lack of response to a letter or bill is offered as an implied admission of the correctness of the facts stated. Notice that the accusation, letter, or bill itself is not offered in a hearsay capacity, but as a predicate for the lack of response, which lack would itself on one theory, be hearsay (but perhaps within the exception for admissions discussed infra). Other considerations, however, might dictate exclusion of this line of proof. E. g., particular facts might render it slim in probativity and inadmissible under the balancing noted in Ch. 1. See Ch. 6, too.

Conduct: Mistake and Insincerity
The possibility of mistake and insincerity (lying, joking) on the part of the person who is not presented seems to be the touchstone of hearsay.

In the foregoing examples involving committive and omittive non-assertive conduct, the weaknesses in what we have called the second link or inference (i. e., that the belief and the objective fact correspond) seem to be analogous to those that infect the same link or inference wherever a statement is propounded as true; except that perhaps some kinds of conduct suggest that greater care was taken in fashioning the generating belief than do some kinds of statements. If the weaknesses are precisely analogous in the two kinds of cases, they demand equally the courtroom safeguards we have been discussing. Without exactitude, we may summarize weaknesses in this link (the link between belief and fact) as "the possibility of mistake."

[*179*]

Weaknesses in the *first* link (the link or inference that the words or conduct evidence the propounded state of belief) may be summarized (again without exactitude) as "the possibility of insincerity" (lying, joking), when we are dealing with any express statement (made on or off the stand) offered as true; and as "the possibility of insincerity or other explanation for the conduct" in the case of conduct offered in the fashion described in preceding sections. An example of "other explanation" would be the money debt, unkind word, or desire to secure a witness which we said might have motivated D to chase X, rather than any belief in X's having done the killing. While the possibility of insincerity may be attenuated in the case of certain conduct as compared with certain declarations (owing to the fact that more energy is expended or more "put on the line" by D in the former), there is usually the addition of the possibility of "other explanation" for the conduct. But questions may be raised as to (1) whether the possibility of "other explanation" is something peculiarly within the province of the pertinent courtroom safeguards, since it generally does not arise in connection with statements; and (2) whether the jury will ignore or significantly mis-evaluate the possibility of other explanation without the specific courtroom safeguards that are the concern of the hearsay rule.

We will come to cases involving out-of-court declarations in which one or more of the possible unreliabilities in one or other of these links is of no concern. This may come about because the link is not involved in the theory upon which the evidence is offered. E. g., in a suit for misrepresentation that land is 500 acres, statements of plaintiff about the "250 acre tract" offered to prove knowledge of the true facts and lack of reliance, would not involve the second link (the link between belief and objective fact). Or it may come about because the unreliability is practically eliminated. This is the case, at least in theory, where a person knowingly makes a self-damaging declaration. The fact that the possibility of unreliability is only present to minor degree ordinarily will not mean the evidence is not hearsay; if it has any effect, it will normally be by way of playing a role in the shape of an exception to the hearsay rule. The question faced by courts in each of the cases mentioned at the opening of this paragraph will be, will the remaining possibilities of unreliability necessitate subjection to the courtroom safeguards and render the evidence inadmissible hearsay?

Special Guarantees of Trustworthiness

In the determination of hearsay vel non, as opposed to the creation of the exceptions, special trustworthiness of the evidence has traditionally played little role.

In drawing a possible distinction between the case where D declares X's guilt and the case where D acts as though X is guilty by chasing him, we said that because talk is cheaper than action, the conduct evidence was the more trustworthy in certain respects, namely D's sincerity and his care in ascertaining the facts. Different kinds of action can be distinguished along the same lines. It would seem that in the corn hypothetical just given, if the customers held the propounded belief, they may be staking more on its accuracy than D would be in chasing X, at least if the chasing were for some minor crime rather than murder. This of course would depend upon particular undisclosed facts in the two cases, such as the price paid for the corn, the disparity in value between the two grades, the vigor, length, and difficulty of the chase, etc.

Cases of extraordinary reliability can be imagined. A sea captain inspects a ship and then embarks on it with his wife and children. This is offered as evidence of the seaworthiness of the ship. He has staked quite a lot on the correctness of his judgment of seaworthiness, which speaks loudly for his care, sincerity, and accuracy, and for the trustworthiness and reliability of the offered inference. Of course, there is a chance that he was mistaken or planning a suicide and multiple killing. Suppose instead of a captain we have just an ordinary seaman of lower competence and qualifications. This reduces the likelihood of accuracy and increases the need for safeguards. Suppose someone bets a large sum of money that a fact is true. He pays off, out of court. Would he have paid off if the fact were true? The pay-off would seem to be some evidence that the fact is untrue, its reliability in some measure depending on the amount bet or perhaps on how that amount compares with his wealth or with the courtroom stakes in the case in which it is offered as evidence. The same situation is presented where payment by an indemnitor or insurer is attempted to be offered as evidence of the happening of the event indemnified or insured against. Or suppose someone entrusts important business to a testator during his life, around the time the testator is executing his will. This would seem to be somewhat reliable evidence of the soundness of mind with which the testator executed the will, although there are other explanations for the entruster's conduct than that he carefully determined the testator was of sound mind. Perhaps he *had* to deal with the testator, or was mistaken in his assessment of the testator.

Are we saying anything peculiar about conduct as hearsay? Express declarations similarly differ among themselves respecting reliability. In their case, the merest presence, in however minor a degree, of a risk of untrustworthiness of the sort traditionally in the province of the courtroom safeguards, will mean the evidence is hearsay. Special circumstances reducing that risk may play a limited role in the exceptions to the hearsay rule, and of course affect weight

[*182*]

and the probative-prejudice balancing outlined in Chapter I, but they do not normally affect the determination of hearsay vel non.[2] (Some deviations from this will be noted, infra.) It is submitted that conduct should not be treated any differently.

Evidence of State of Belief for Its Own Sake

Evidence of the declarant's belief, offered to establish nothing beyond the belief, if the belief is relevant for itself alone, has frequently, but not uniformly, been admissible as non-hearsay.

Suppose the government prosecutes Orange-O Co., a leading orange *drink* manufacturer, for promulgating the misleading impression that their product is orange *juice*. To prove that people generally are under the impression that Orange-O is orange juice, the government introduces the answers to questionnaires distributed in the population in which people said they believed Orange-O was orange *juice* (i. e., that it contained whatever is required to legally constitute it a "juice" rather than a "drink"). (The problem would be the same if the government attempted to introduce, via testimony of those conducting the survey, the out-of-court oral answers given in an orally conducted survey.) Notice that the government is not trying to prove that the belief was correct—that Orange-O is orange juice (i. e., that it does in fact contain what the people believed it

---

[2] While special circumstances reducing the risk of untrustworthiness would not obviate the necessity for the oath and for the opportunity to cross examine in the case of ordinary in-court non-hearsay testimony, the analogy is not entirely apposite. For in hearsay cases we are often faced with the choice of either having the evidence without oath and cross examination, or not having it (or not having it conveniently). The analogy would be better if we consider as our non-hearsay situation a case where the witness has become unavailable after direct but before cross examination. Then, in certain circumstances, cross examination might be dispensed with. (Of course, as to him at least some of the courtroom safeguards, such as the oath, have been applied.)

contained). This would be against the government's interests in the litigation. The government is merely attempting to prove by this evidence that persons (in the position of Ds) *held* such a belief. The accuracy of these Ds' perception of and assessment of the liquid is not relied upon by the offeror. In fact, the offeror is ultimately alleging that they were mistaken. But he is pressing for acceptance of the fact that these people, in these answers, were truly reporting, not a phenomenon in the outside world, but their own conscious belief. They may be lying, joking, or speaking carelessly about this belief, but hardly mistaken. It thus seems that the offeror's offered inference involves only one of the links (inferences) and its attendant sources of unreliability we spoke of in the cases in the last several sections: that is, it involves the inference of belief from outward manifestation (which outward manifestation is a statement in this case), attended by the possibility of insincerity (and perhaps misstatement); but it does not involve the inference that the belief correctly records external fact, which would be attended by the possibility of mistaken perception.

Thus, only some of the testimonial qualities that are ordinarily in question when a trier-of-fact is asked to accept reports of external fact made on or off the stand, are in question here with respect to the out-of-court declarant.[3] Are they sufficient to result in the barring of the evidence as hearsay because of the absence of the courtroom safeguards?[4] A decision on these facts held that the evidence

[3] The same would be true if, instead of a survey being taken, these declarants were called to the stand to say they presently believe Orange-O is orange juice (i. e., made of such-and-such). In such a case they would not be exempt from cross examination, etc.

[4] How might it help to have the declarants on the stand? A bribe might be revealed. They might change their story because of greater care, fear, or consideration of the consequences to the parties. Suggestive or misleading questioning and susceptibility to it could be

was not hearsay and was admissible. (Even if the evidence clears the hearsay rule, the court will have to be satisfied, from the method of conducting the survey, etc., that the evidence is reliable enough to pass the probative-prejudice balance addressed in Chapter I, supra.) Similar evidence has at times been rejected as hearsay, presumably because sincerity is in issue. Evidence that persons *behaved* as though they believed Orange-O consisted of what is legally required for an orange juice, would probably be safer, if the court rejects the arguments noted above that suggest that such conduct may be functionally equivalent to the statement for purposes of the hearsay rule.

It should make no difference whether the out-of-court statement was "*I believe* Orange-O is made of such-and-such" or "Orange-O *is* made of such-and-such". Both would be offered to show that the declarant believed it to be made of such-and-such, not that it *was* made of such-and-such. But the former statement is offered to prove the truth of the matter stated; whereas the latter is not. The matter stated in the former is that the declarant held a certain belief. That is exactly what the government wants to prove—that he held the belief he said he held. The matter stated in the second statement is simply that *Orange-O is made of such-and-such.* The government is not trying to

revealed, or prevented. It might be revealed that the particular persons questioned gained their impressions of Orange-O under atypical circumstances. Misconduct in the survey might be revealed, such as the elimination of unfavorable answers or the screening of "questionees" beforehand in order to select only those who indicated they would give a favorable answer. Is having the declarants on the stand the only way of protecting the opponent against these things? Are they within the traditional province of cross examination? Are they the sort of thing for which cross examination was designed? In answering these questions, consider the typical case of a witness on the stand reporting a fact like an auto accident or stabbing, for which cross examination was designed and by analogy to which the notion that a declarant ought to be cross examined (i. e., the notion underlying the hearsay rule) arose.

prove that Orange-O is so constituted. Thus, the latter statement, as distinguished from the former, is not offered to prove the truth of the matter stated. Because most statements on the stand in non-hearsay situations are offered to prove the truth of the matter stated (e. g., a witness on the stand in a murder case or auto accident case reports seeing a stabbing or crash), and because in hearsay cases it is *generally* only when the declaration is offered for its truth that questions of D's credibility arise (e. g., D has declared X stabbed Y or went through a red light, in a murder or auto collision case; as opposed to D's declaration "yes" offered as constituting agreement in an oral contract case), some definitions of hearsay state that we have hearsay whenever, and only when, the out-of-court declaration is offered *for the truth of the matter declared.* Adhering strictly to that definition in the present case, "*I believe* Orange-O is made of such-and-such" would be hearsay, whereas "Orange-O is made of such-and-such" would not be. However, it would seem that whichever statement was made, the issue of credibility is precisely the same and equally in need of or not in need of elucidation by the application of courtroom processes to the declarant. The result should not turn on the declarant's fortuitous selection of words. The declarant *means* the same thing, whichever formulation he chooses. Analysts who follow the "truth of the matter declared" definition just described and also allow "implied declarations" would be in a quandary in the present case, because either of the two declarations ("I believe Orange-O is made of such-and-such" and "Orange-O is made of such-and-such") may be implied from the other. Such analysts would have to resort to something other than the "truth of the matter declared" definition and the doctrine of implied declarations, for a solution.

Evidence of State of Belief for Its Own Sake: Principle Analyzed and Extended to Other States of Mind than Belief: Intent, Knowledge, Feelings; Requirement of Concurrency

Under certain conditions, evidence of the state of mind or feelings of declarant will be received as non-hearsay or as an exception to the hearsay rule.

When a declarant expresses a certain conscious state of mind (e. g., a conscious intent, belief, or knowledge) which he holds contemporaneously with the expression, we can hardly suspect that he is mistaken about, misperceiving, or misremembering his own state of mind, because of his peculiar privity with it and its contemporaneity with the expression. He may, however, be insincere (lying or joking) about it, or misreporting it. There is perhaps some slight possibility that he is not aware of the true nature of his state of mind, but when it is a conscious state of mind this danger is minimal. It is fair to say that at least where the declarant *expressly* declares his *present, conscious* state of mind to be so-and-so, and this state of mind is offered *for itself* (assuming we have a case where such would be relevant) and not on a theory that it accurately reproduces an external fact, some of the fears responsible for the courtroom guarantees are removed. We have a rather reliable kind of evidence. The declarant is declaring or reporting an *internal* fact of consciousness, and the fact and the declaration are contemporaneous. There is not the same possibility of inaccuracy as where a witness on the stand (or a declarant off the stand) reports an *external* fact (in the real world) from which he was removed in space (when he observed it) and time (when he reports it), with all the attendant possibilities of misperception and failure of memory. But if the state of mind is *past* rather than contemporaneous with the declaration, the opportunities for falsification and failure of memory are much greater and the special reliability is not present. Nor would it be present where the state of mind (e. g., belief) is contemporaneous with the declaration but offered to prove that it truly records (reproduces) some external fact.[5] Thus, in our original hypothetical involving Declarant's oral declaration "X shot Y", it adds nothing to the offeror's case to characterize Declarant's declaration as an expression of Declarant's belief that X shot Y, if the offeror is offering the belief in order to prove X shot Y. Nor would it seem to change matters if Declarant had said "*I believe* X shot Y". (Assume that it is made clear that "believe" is not used as an expression of doubt or lack of first-hand knowledge.) Though both are evidence of belief, the belief in both cases is offered as true.

Courts are undecided as to whether evidence that meets the reliability criteria of the last paragraph should be regarded as an exception to the hearsay rule, or not hearsay at all. Compare the discussion of mistake and insincerity and special guarantees of trustworthiness, supra, pp. 179–183.

It is obvious that the principles espoused thus far in this section would also seem to apply to declarations of presently felt pain or lack of pain, or other feelings. Such declarations would be relatively unobjectionable in terms of the concerns of this chapter if the conditions of concurrency with the declaration, etc., are met. A distinction is sometimes drawn between spontaneous exclamations of pain, and those made in response to a question or delivered in narrative form, the former being considered less subject to

---

[5] Does it make any difference whether or not the fact or occurrence itself is also contemporaneous with the declaration about it? What if they are contemporaneous and the occurrence is a very exciting one (e. g., a collision or shooting)? See infra, pp. 217–20. Assume at the present juncture that they are not contemporaneous at all, although it would make no difference for purposes of the points made in text, but only for purposes of the applicability of the "excited utterances" exception (and a modern expansion thereof) not presently under discussion.

the kind of infirmity the hearsay rule is meant to protect against. Should such a distinction be drawn respecting the expressions of states of mind discussed previously? It should be noted here that a narrative, unspontaneous statement of pain or bodily feeling (including lack of certain feeling or pain) made to a doctor whose treatment is sought is deemed to have a guarantee of accuracy that substitutes both for spontaneity and contemporaneity, under a recognized exception to the hearsay rule. Statements to doctors of objective fact rather than subjective feelings may also qualify, if motivated by a similar desire for treatment.

The principles of this section would be applicable to out-of-court manifestations (of contemporaneous state of mind or feelings) *other than express declarations,* such as conduct (flinching, failure to flinch, behavior as though one believed, intended, or knew a certain thing) and words not directly expressing a state of mind or feeling but perhaps doing so by implication (e. g., "You are a brute," offered to show a change of affection in a suit for alienation of affections).

It is often said that there is a greater need to admit expressions of subjective state of mind or feelings than in the case of the ordinary hearsay declaration.

Some applications of the above principles follow:

(1) D (declarant) declares as he takes a bus load of people on a scenic ride: "[I know] the brakes are bad. But don't worry." (The presence or absence of the bracketed words should make no difference. See supra, p. 185). The bus has a collision and the company is sued for the negligence of its driver, D, the declarant. D's negligence is alleged to consist in the fact that he took a bus out, knowing the brakes to be bad, something a reasonable man would not have done. Assuming all appropriate rulings are requested and the law is followed, the plaintiff probably

will be permitted to offer D's statement via occupants of the bus who overheard it; but only for purposes of establishing D's notice of the faulty brakes, not to establish that the brakes were in fact bad.[6] The jury will be instructed that, on this latter issue, they are not to consider this evidence, but only such other evidence as may be adduced. The judge similarly will not consider this to be evidence on that issue, and will make peremptory rulings on that issue on the basis of whatever other evidence there is concerning it. (You may well wonder whether judge and jury can and will so confine themselves.) Offering counsel will not be permitted to argue any but the permissible usage of the evidence. If there is no other evidence on the issue of the faultiness of the brakes or if such other evidence is obviously insufficient for the plaintiff to get to the jury, a verdict would have to be directed. (One might well ask whether, at least where the evidence is before the tribunal on one issue, it ought not to be allowed whatever probativeness it rationally has on the other issue, at least with a judge.) If the issue of notice were not in the case, but only the issue of the soundness of the brakes, the evidence could not be received.

If the driver had made the statement *after* the accident, saying to someone out of court, "I *knew* the brakes were bad when I went out earlier," the statement would not come within the above principles, because it is a statement of past state of mind, although the statement may coin-

---

[6] We put aside the possibility this might come within exceptions to the hearsay rule for *declarations against interest* (the statement may be incriminating, e. g., it may expose him to or increase his risk of being held criminally or civilly liable), *admissions of a party opponent* (if he becomes a party or is viewed for these purposes as an agent of a party), or, less conceivably, *excited utterances* (if uttered in the heat of the moment going into or immediately after collision) or *present sense impressions* (where recognized). These would render the declaration admissible to prove the brakes were bad, as well as to show knowledge.

cidentally come within some other exception to the hearsay rule such as declarations against interest, infra.

(2) Wealthy Mrs. Q says to her neighbor, "My husband John is a brute" (or "I believe my husband John is a brute"). The neighbor reports this on the stand for the defendant bus company in a suit by the husband (Mr. Q) against the bus company for the wrongful death of his wife (Mrs. Q). The bus company's reason for introducing such evidence is to reduce damages—i. e., to show that Mr. Q could not have expected much of value from Mrs. Q had she lived. Let us assume the damages in a wrongful death action are loss of monetary expectancy and support. The evidence is offered to show that, regardless of what may be the truth about John, Mrs. Q thought he was a brute, and probably would not be inclined to do more for him than she had to. It would seem that this evidence is offered not to show the accuracy of Mrs. Q's belief (that John is indeed a brute), but to show that she held the belief, or felt a certain way toward John. Thus far, it fits the reliability criteria set out above. But there is an additional link in the offered chain of inference: that because she had this belief, she probably would have acted in a certain way in the future. It would seem, however, that this is the kind of inference the jury customarily is deemed quite competent to assess and is not the special subject of the courtroom safeguards we have been discussing, at least insofar as they would be addressed to Mrs. Q and the need to have her on the stand. Having her on the stand would, of course, enable the jury to more accurately guess what she might be expected to give him during life. Her feeling of hatred might have been fleeting and temporary, inspired by a very recent spat and evaporating again. She might not be the sort to carry these things out into action. She might be the kind of person who would have felt duty bound to give him considerable amounts of money, despite her feelings toward

him.   She might have been ashamed to have him go
without luxuries and money. She might have been able to
testify that what she said has no bearing on what she
intends to do in the future.   In speaking to her neighbor,
she might have been attempting to create a certain impression, or speaking for a very limited purpose. She might
be the sort of person who is given to overly extreme
expressions or to making contradictory statements.   She may
have indeed contradicted herself on this matter many times.
All this would be relevant to weight, if not admissibility, and
would be elucidated more clearly if she were on the stand.

Is Mrs. Q available to be put on the stand? She is no
longer alive.   Is there need for this evidence also on
grounds that there is little other evidence on the matter of
as definitive a nature?

A decision on similar facts held that the evidence was
admissible and probably would not have drawn a distinction
based on the facts in the paragraph immediately above.
Consider whether the evidence would be even more likely
to be admissible if she had said, instead, "I do not intend
to give him any money"; or had made many statements like
the one in the first version of the hypothetical; or the
evidence was of violent fights or of throwing a rolling pin at
him; or the statement was in her will rather than to her
neighbor.

(3) Suppose D (declarant) says he is going to Frank's
house tomorrow at 8:00 p. m. The day after D was supposed to go to Frank's house, D is found murdered in a
field, not having been seen by anyone since the time he
was supposed to go to Frank's. Can D's out-of-court statement ("I am going to Frank's house tomorrow at 8:00") be
offered by the prosecution to show that he probably went
to Frank's, and to increase the likelihood that Frank had
something to do with his demise? This out-of-court declara-

[*192*]

tion is not offered to show D's intent *simpliciter,* but to suggest that the intent was probably carried out (as intents of this sort often are). Should that make a difference? Notice that the statement (or the underlying state of mind) is not offered as a report or reflection of some external pre-existing or contemporaneous fact, but embodies a future intention. Could the courtroom processes have revealed anything helpful? Is the possibility that they could such that you would hesitate to admit the evidence without them? This sort of evidence has been held admissible. Justice Cardozo has said, "Declarations of intention, casting light upon the future, have been sharply distinguished from declarations of memory, pointing backwards to the past. There would be an end, or nearly that, to the rule against hearsay, if the distinction were ignored."

(4) Suppose a small girl is taken to a man's house and sexually molested by him. She cannot identify him, but at the police station she is able to recount the details of the furnishings of the house. At trial she can no longer even do this. At trial, her earlier description is introduced, and it is shown to tally spectacularly with the furnishings of defendant's house. Is her statement "There were green chairs, blue curtains [etc.]" offered for its truth? But isn't her statement really or impliedly "The house where I was molested had green chairs [etc.]"? Is this offered for its truth? What if she were really recounting a place (his place) she saw only on another occasion—say, in selling girl-scout cookies the week before—rather than the scene of the crime? Or suppose the details of the furnishings were learned from her mother or the police? Do you feel there are things that might be brought out if the statement could be subject to cross examination? Are you uneasy enough about them to exclude the evidence? This evidence was admitted to "show her state of mind." But cf. pp. 187–88, supra.

(5) A train runs over a little boy, the engineer's excuse being he thought it was a chicken until it was too late to stop. Out-of-court experiments are done by placing a child on the track and persons in train cabins at varying points on the track to ascertain at what distance they can identify a child. Assume the conditions, knowledge of participants, etc., fairly approximate those of the accident; and that the experiment is not objectionable on grounds of the balancing discussed in Chapter I or on grounds of lack of opportunity for the opponents to participate. Can the results be introduced? Would that be offering an out-of-court statement, "That is a child."? To prove that was indeed a child? This kind of evidence has been held admissible.

(6) In a suit for negligent entrustment of an automobile to a color-blind driver, testimony is offered reporting an out-of-court test of the driver in which he responded correctly every time in identifying colors. Assume the experiment is not objectionable as differing too much from the conditions, colors, etc., involved in the accident, or on grounds that the opponent was not present. Is this essentially a report of a series of out-of-court statements, "That's green," "That's red," etc., offered for their truth? It has been held not to be.

(7) Can a patient's flinching, exclamation, or declaration "That hurts," or his complete impassivity, upon being jabbed with a pin by a doctor prior to trial, be introduced to show numbness or lack thereof in a personal injury action? It has often been admitted.

Out-of-Court Statements Offered to Show They Were Made, Regardless of the Belief of the Stater, and Regardless of Whether They Reflect Fact: (1) Proving a Slander

Evidence of the out-of-court slander in a slander action is not hearsay evidence.

Plaintiff charges defendant with slander. The slander allegedly uttered by the defendant is "He [plaintiff] stole a watch." Plaintiff introduces witnesses who testify that they heard the defendant say this, in order to prove the utterance of the slander. While this is evidence of an out-of-court statement, it is not offered to prove the truth of the matter stated by defendant—that plaintiff stole a watch. Indeed, plaintiff must avoid establishing its truth, or the defendant will have a valid substantive defense (the defense of truth). The evidence is offered to show that the statement was made, not that it was true. The veracity, credibility, accuracy, sincerity, etc., of the defendant in reporting plaintiff's thievery is not at all relied upon by the plaintiff in offering this evidence. Indeed, plaintiff would like to show just the reverse of these, and to make defendant and his statement look as untrustworthy, unfounded, and malicious as possible. Nor is the evidence offered to show that defendant believed in its truth, like in the Orange-O case, supra. Once again, it might be in plaintiff's interests to show the opposite.

Such evidence would not be considered hearsay. The out-of-court utterer is not being used as a kind of absent witness to objective fact. But it is instructive to note that something could perhaps be illuminated by having defendant on the stand. Suppose it had been apparent at the time of the utterance, that he was joking. Or lying. Or mistaken. Would that not affect plaintiff's case? But are there other ways to bring this out? Is defendant himself likely to be accurate on this matter? Can W enlighten just as well or better? Is the defendant actually present and able to be called if needed or wished? (This last would make no difference to the hearsay analysis here; but cf. the exception for party admissions.)

Out-of-Court Statements Offered to Show They Were Made, Regardless of the Belief of the Stater, and Regardless of Whether They Reflect Fact: (2) Statements Constituting a Contract or Gift

Evidence of out-of-court statements offered as themselves creating contract or property rights is not hearsay evidence.

Professor D places a book in front of him on a table, stating to student Jones, "This is your book, Jones." Student W overhears this and testifies to it later in court. If the purpose is to establish a gift or transfer of the property in the book from Professor D to student Jones, under a body of substantive law that holds that such a statement constitutes a gift or transfer, then the evidence is not hearsay. The out-of-court utterer is not being used as an absent witness to objective fact. However, if the purpose is to establish that the book was Jones' all along, then the statement of Professor D is hearsay. For in the latter case he *is* being used an an absent witness to objective fact—the statement is offered as an accurate reflection of an external, objective fact pre-existing the statement and existing independently of it, about which fact Professor D may have been mistaken, lying, joking, etc. In the former case, however, the words themselves create the rights whereof they speak, and Professor D's credibility and accuracy as a reporter of fact is irrelevant. (How might the latter case arise? —perhaps as a theft prosecution.)

Suppose that, under the substantive law in the non-hearsay example, a gift or transfer is not made merely by utterance of the statement, but there must also be intent to make a gift or transfer; and/or the circumstances must be such that a reasonable man or ordinary persons in the situation would regard the statement as reasonably appearing to be an intentional transfer. Would it then be useful to have Professor D on the stand? Necessary? This probably would not be regarded as hearsay, either.

In the above examples, it makes no difference whether the statement was oral or written. And, just as the Professor's statement may be proved to show a gift or transfer, so too may the terms of an oral or written contract be proved in a suit upon the contract, by introducing the contract or testimony by one who overheard it, even though it is an out-of-court statement. Out-of-court statements that are offered on the theory that they themselves have legal effect in this fashion, and not because they reflect the truth, are known as "verbal acts" or "operative facts." This appellation also covers the slander example in the last section, and might also be applied to the agency example in the next section.

Out-of-Court Statements Offered to Show They Were Made, Regardless of the Belief of the Stater, and Regardless of Whether They Reflect Fact: (3) Apparent Authority

Evidence of out-of-court statements offered on a theory that they contribute to establishing apparent authority is not hearsay.

Mr. D presents himself to Mr. Palmer at the latter's gasoline station where Mr. Palmer has reported leakage to the Gasco gasoline company that supplies him and maintains his premises. Mr. D drives a company car and wears a company uniform. He says to Mr. Palmer, "I am the agent of the Gasco gasoline company, and am authorized to investigate your leak. Show it to me." Mr. Palmer does so, whereupon Mr. D lights a match to get a closer look, blowing the place up.   Injured Mr. Palmer sues the Gasco gasoline company on a theory of respondeat superior (vicarious responsibility) for the putative agent's negligence. The company disputes only that Mr. D was the company's agent for purposes of investigating leakage.   They assert that his investigation of the leak was outside the scope of his employment;   that he was authorized only to take orders for gasoline;   and that he was expressly forbidden to investigate leaks.   Thus, they maintain, his actions were wholly unauthorized by the company.   If liability depended upon express authorization of Mr. D by the company, to investigate leaks or the leak, the only bearing Mr. D's statement to Mr. Palmer would have on the issue would be as evidence that the company did in fact expressly so authorize him.   The offeror would hope the jury would ask themselves, "Why would Mr. D say he was authorized to investigate the leak if it weren't true—if he weren't expressly so authorized?"   Mr. D would be being used as an absent witness to an objective fact: an act or statement of actual conferral of authorization done by the company back at the shop, for example, which he had perceived.   As such, the evidence would be hearsay.

But suppose the liability of the company can be maintained on a theory of *apparent* authority to investigate the leak—that is, there would be liability not only if there were *express* authority, but also if it *reasonably appeared* to Palmer that D had such authority and the company was in part responsible for those appearances, regardless of actual authority.   The reasonableness of Palmer's belief that D had such authority (i. e., the reasonableness of the appearance of authority) would be in issue.   The facts that D (1) drove a company car, (2) wore a company uniform, (3) was the man with whom P customarily dealt in his relations with the company, and (4) said "I have authority to investigate the leak," are all relevant to a determination of whether it rea-

sonably appeared that D had the authority, i. e., to a determination of whether it was reasonable and justified to
suppose that D was authorized to investigate the leak.[7]
Offered on this theory, the evidence would not be hearsay.
The actual credibility of the statement would not be in issue.
Mr. D would not be being used as an absent witness to
objective fact. (Understanding might be facilitated if you
suppose that as a matter of law the presence or absence of
factor (4) is determinative on these facts. Then it becomes
apparent that the case is analogous to the verbal act or operative
fact cases.) Can the jury be effectively confined to using the
statement along these lines?

Out-of-Court Statements Offered to Show the State of Mind of the Hearer

Evidence of these statements is frequently not considered to be hearsay evidence.

Suppose in the hypothetical in the last section concerning
the gasoline leak, the company pleads that Mr. Palmer was
contributorily negligent in allowing Mr. D to approach and
light a match near the leak. Mr. Palmer offers Mr. D's
statement, "I am the agent of Gasco gasoline company and
am authorized to investigate your leak; show it to me," as a
circumstance tending to render reasonable, Palmer's reliance
on D's knowing the right thing to do. The actual credibility of
the statement of D is not in issue. His statement is as
much the basis for a claim of justified reliance if it was false
as it is if it was true—so long as nothing "fishy" about it
appeared to one in Palmer's shoes. On this theory of the
offer of the evidence, D is not being used as an absent

---

[7] They are also relevant to the issue of whether Palmer actually
believed Mr. D was Gasco's agent for examining the leak, which issue,
too, is raised by a theory of apparent authority. Offered in this
capacity, the evidence would come within the principle of the next
section infra.

witness to objective fact. The evidence is not hearsay. Can the jury be effectively confined to this usage?

Mrs. Smith slips and falls on a wet patch on the floor of a grocery store. W testifies for her that he (or someone he overheard) had told the manager about the wet spot earlier that same day. This is offered to show that the store management had notice of a dangerous condition, and therefore acted unreasonably in failing to remedy it. The actual credibility of the out-of-court statement is not in issue under this theory. The fact that the statement was made, and not its truth, is important (do you agree?). It would be otherwise if the evidence were offered to substantiate the fact that there was a wet spot there. Can the two uses be effectively separated? Is the actual credibility of the statement in issue, then, whatever the avowed purpose of the offer?

Mrs. Jones sues a doctor who gave her X-ray treatments, which she alleges resulted in an inflamed and ulcerated condition of the area X-rayed. She offers the out-of-court statement of another doctor, who told her the inflamed and ulcerated condition would develop into cancer. If offered on the issue of damages to help prove that the inflamed and ulcerated condition may develop into cancer, the evidence would plainly be hearsay. The actual credibility of the statement would be in issue. It is otherwise if she offers the evidence to help show her own mental anguish and suffering (which is also on the issue of damages)—i. e., she offers it to show that because of the statement, she had grounds to feel considerable anxiety over the X-ray treatments given her by the first doctor. A court may feel anxiety over allowing this, however, because the primary use of the evidence will probably be the hearsay use, whatever is said.

It should be noted that in the hearsay area, if the evidence is offered and argued, etc., on a theory that does not involve excludable hearsay, a danger of misuse along impermissible hearsay lines will very seldom result in exclusion of the evidence. Cautionary instructions and regulation of argument, etc., are considered sufficient. Indeed, as an illustration of how far at least some courts will go in implementing this principle, it should be noted that the court in the X-ray case just above did allow the evidence with a cautionary instruction.

Reputation

Testimony as to the reputation of a person can have a strong hearsay aspect.

If a witness (W) were to take the stand and testify "Q's reputation is such-and-such," the witness essentially would be saying that he (the witness) has heard a number of Ds (Declarants) on the street say either one or both of two things: "Q is a such-and-such" or "I have heard [from other Ds] that Q is such-and-such".

Let us see when such testimony by W (witness) would be hearsay.

Suppose Mr. Black, the defendant in a libel action, attempts, via the above quoted testimony of W, to prove the truth of his (Black's) alleged defamatory statement that "Q is reputed to be a thief." His purpose is to establish a defense of truth. If W is saying, in effect, "I have heard a number of Ds say Q is a thief," the evidence would not seem to be hearsay, since it is immaterial whether the reputation (the statements by the Ds that Q is a thief) are correct or not. The issue is simply whether there was such a reputation (i. e., whether Ds said Q is a thief), not its accuracy. But does this rationale apply insofar as W is saying he heard Ds say *they* heard Q is a thief? What if the Ds W heard are lying or mistaken about what *they* heard? This distinction is largely ignored in the cases.

Suppose that the alleged libel is "Q is a thief." Mr. Black attempts, with W's testimony that Q has always had a reputation for thievery, to prove that the libel did not significantly damage Q's already poor reputation. It would seem that exactly the same reasoning would apply: the accuracy of the reputation is not at all in issue—its mere nature and existence are. But again there is the element that W is also reporting what the Ds said *they* heard. The situation would be the same as respects Q's (plaintiff's) proof of *good* reputation on the same issue. The evidence is generally admitted, whichever party introduces it.

Where reputation of a testator for soundness of judgment is offered to establish his mental capacity to make a will, the evidence is plainly hearsay, however viewed, because it is hoped the reputation will be credited. The same is true of reputation introduced on the other side of the same issue. Where such evidence is admitted, it is through an exception to the hearsay rule—either one of the standard ones or one specially tailored for this situation.

Similarly, reputation introduced for purposes of the propensity (or character) reasoning discussed in Chapter 8 is hearsay, however viewed, because it is hoped that the reputation will be credited. Where it is admissible, a special exception to the hearsay rule is tacitly manufactured for it. (The cited chapter should be referred to, since reputation offered for those purposes is an important area covering both impeachment and substantive proof.)

Hearsay and the Constitution

Like the hearsay rule, the constitutional confrontation clause exerts constraints on the admissibility of evidence of statements made outside the trial. Thus, new and unwarranted extensions of the traditional exceptions to and exemptions from the hearsay rule, or new and unwarranted contractions to the scope of the hearsay rule, may run into

constitutional trouble. However, it would seem from the recent cases, that the Supreme Court will make exceptions to the requirement of confrontation of the declarant wherever there is a traditional exception to or exemption from the hearsay rule, and even will do so where the jurisdiction has a new or untraditional one, so long as the exception or exemption is not wholly without basis in precedent, reason, or experience.

Considerations very similar to those behind the hearsay rule seem to be behind constitutional confrontation requirements. Consequently there is some constitutional restraint on curtailment of the hearsay ban and on expansion of its exceptions. And many of the same controversies over the same unclarities rage in both areas.

The Fifth, Sixth, and Fourteenth Amendments to the federal constitution provide some kind of right to confrontation in federal and state civil and criminal actions (although the guarantee in criminal cases is the one that is most often addressed in constitutional terms). Several cases illustrate the connection with the hearsay rule. In Pointer v. Texas, 380 U.S. 400, 85 S.Ct. 1065 (1965), use in a state criminal prosecution of a transcript of a witness' testimony given at the preliminary hearing in the same case was held unconstitutional owing to the lack of opportunity to cross examine at the preliminary hearing (the defendant was without counsel then). The witness was, at the time of trial, absent from the jurisdiction. The exception to the hearsay rule for testimony at prior proceedings having similar issues, where the declarant is not produced at the present proceeding, requires not only substantial identity of parties and unavailability of the declarant, but opportunity for cross examination at the earlier proceeding. Barber v. Page, 390 U.S. 719, 88 S.Ct. 1318 (1968) was like *Pointer,* except the accused had counsel at the earlier proceeding, and was not restricted in cross examining there. However, use of the transcript was improper because the government failed to attempt to secure the presence of the witness, who was a federal prisoner in another state. The court held there was a violation of the right to confrontation. The requirement of unavailability probably would not be met in these circumstances under the exception to the hearsay rule, either. In Krulewitch v. United States, 336 U.S. 440, 69 S.Ct. 716 (1949) and Bruton v. United States, 391 U.S. 123, 88 S.Ct. 1620 (1968), it was considered a breach of the right to confrontation to use (or, more precisely, to take insufficient measures to insure against such use, an instruction being insufficient) a co-defendant's out-of-court confession against the defendant when, owing to the privilege against self-incrimination, the co-defendant could not be cross examined. This use of the confession did not meet the requirements of any exception to or exemption from the hearsay rule (it was not an admission of *this* party; it was not a *declaration against interest,* either because implication of another is not against self-interest or because usually penal interest, as opposed to pecuniary and proprietary interest, is not recognized; and it was not *during and in furtherance of the conspiracy* under the co-conspirator exception to or exemption from the hearsay rule, which is a branch of the party-admissions-via-an-agent principle). In a footnote in *Bruton,* the Court reserves the question whether hearsay that meets the requirements of a recognized exception to the hearsay rule could violate the right to confrontation. Notice in this connection that some jurisdictions recognize penal interest in determining delcarations against interest. Cf. Parker v. Randolph, 442 U.S. 62, 99 S.Ct. 2132 (1979) (instruction sufficient if the defendant himself has also made an admissible confession). In Dutton v. Evans, 400 U.S. 74, 91 S.Ct. 210 (1970), a statement similar to that in *Bruton* was held constitutionally proper as used against the non-confessing defendant. Georgia's somewhat atypical version of the co-

conspirator exception or exemption allowed the statement to be so used even though most jurisdictions would have held that such a statement, made after the declarant was caught, and casting blame on the other, was not within that exception or exemption, because not during and in furtherance of the conspiracy. And see Ohio v. Roberts, — U.S. —, 100 S.Ct. 2531 (1980) (comes very close to saying confrontation clause tracks the hearsay rule); California v. Green, 399 U.S. 149, 90 S.Ct. 1930 (1970) (discusses constitutionality of particular application of a California modification of the hearsay rule as it relates to prior statements of witnesses now on the stand, somewhat along the lines of the F.R.E.). See also Douglas v. Alabama, 380 U.S. 415, 85 S.Ct. 1074 (1965) where the prosecutor attempted to get a co-conspirator witness to admit to making certain statements that implicated the defendant. The prosecution read them to "refresh the recollection" of the hostile witness. The witness refused to answer on grounds of self-incrimination. These statements were inadmissible against the accused because of the lack of opportunity to "effectively cross examine one who doesn't admit or deny making the statements." The right to confrontation, like the hearsay rule, was thus violated.

The confrontation provision may go beyond what many courts would do under the hearsay rule, in that an instruction that the jury must disregard (as against the defendant) this unsuccessful attempt at "refreshment of recollection," may not be constitutionally adequate to cure the prejudice. This is also true in *Bruton,* supra.

A confrontation requirement of course is not directed only at the hearsay situation. For example, it may impose a duty to disclose identity of witnesses, e. g., Smith v. Illinois, 390 U.S. 129, 88 S.Ct. 748 (1968), or constrain the extent to which a judge may discretionarily limit (on grounds, for example, of undue protraction, confusion, prejudice, redundancy, etc.) or dispense with (on grounds, for example, that the witness has become ill or died) cross examination.

Both the constitutional provision and the hearsay rule are concerned in part with what is moral, ethical, or fair, which may to some extent diverge from what is deemed conducive to accuracy in fact finding. (This may be true of other areas of Evidence law, as well.) There is some suggestion that confrontation is considered (by the courts, the community, or the founding fathers) to be an end in itself, aside from its effect on fact-finding accuracy; and that confrontation must be enshrined, if only to promote the popular satisfaction without which the legal system could not function. There are, of course, difficulties in defining confrontation without reference to some more ulterior end.

To the extent the concern is with appearing fair rather than with accuracy, there may be additional justification for limiting the concept that conduct can be hearsay to cases in which admitting the conduct would most obviously appear to resemble testimony or accusation without confrontation: cases where the conduct is inescapably testimonial in nature, i. e., intended as a substitute for words; and for applying the hearsay rule to cases of apparent accusation without confrontation even when accuracy is fairly well assured.

The hearsay rule may have some beneficial effect on long term factual accuracy of the system statistically: it encourages lawyers and litigants over the long run to search out more reliable evidence than hearsay. But availability of other evidence is seldom individually considered (except to the stilted and limited extent the exceptions to the hearsay rule turn on unavailability of the declarant and in jurisdictions adopting the innovative so-called "catch-all" exception to the hearsay rule, infra), and thus accuracy of decision in the short run, in the particular case, is often sacrificed. This is not peculiar to this area of Evidence law.

Short Definitions of Hearsay

Consider, in the light of this chapter, the following definitions that have been used in the cases. On occasion, these different definitions can produce different results.

1. Hearsay evidence is testimony in court, or written evidence, of a statement made out of court, which statement is offered to show the truth of the matter stated therein.

a. A "statement" as used above may be either express or implied. Words or conduct from which a statement is implied need not necessarily be intended as a substitute for the statement.

b. [Alternative to "a," yielding a different result in certain cases.] A "statement" is a verbal or written assertion, and may not be implied except from something intended at the time as a substitute for the statement.

2. Hearsay evidence is testimony in court, or written evidence, of a statement made out of court, which statement depends for its value upon the credibility, veracity, accuracy, or [and] sincerity of its out-of-court asserter.

3. Hearsay evidence is testimony in court, or written evidence, of a statement made out of court, where cross examination, the oath, and the solemnity and importance of the courtroom proceedings would have been substantially helpful (as respects reliability) had the statement been subject to them when made.

4. Hearsay evidence is evidence offered to show a belief held by someone not presently testifying, which belief is offered to show the truth of the matter believed.

CHAPTER IV

TOWARD A BETTER UNDERSTANDING OF THE THEORY AND RATIONALE: THE TRADITIONAL, COMMON-LAW EXCEPTIONS TO THE HEARSAY RULE

Basis and Classification of the Common-Law Exceptions

The common-law system developed a series of exceptions to the hearsay rule that reflected considerations of necessity and trustworthiness in a very rough, generalized way. There were two classes of exceptions: those requiring unavailability of the declarant, and those not so requiring.

Many jurisdictions, of course, are still largely under the common-law system of evidence and have not codified extensively. The common-law exceptions to the hearsay rule are said to reflect two factors: special necessity for, and special trustworthiness of, the particular hearsay embraced by the exception.

Many of the common-law exceptions require that the declarant be presently unavailable to testify respecting the matter. This is said to constitute the necessity. Unavailability does not necessarily mean the same thing for all of the common-law exceptions requiring it, or in all jurisdictions. Death, absence beyond the reach of the jurisdiction (not procured by the party seeking to invoke the exception —sometimes reasonable diligence to procure presence will be required), assertion of privilege, and mental incompetence of proper magnitude have all on occasion been held to constitute unavailability. The mere fact that the declarant now tells a different or contrary story would not constitute unavailability. Faded (or failure of) memory, or present motive to falsify with the result that the hearsay, closer to the occurrence, would be more accurate than declarant's present testimony, generally would not be considered unavailability, but rather another kind of necessity, playing only a limited role and only in the fashioning of certain of the common-law exceptions (such as spontaneous declarations or admissions of a party) under which unavailability is not required.

It should be noted that all the necessity and trustworthiness in the world in a particular case will not get the hearsay in under the common-law system as it seems to have developed since the nineteenth century, if the evidence does not come within the narrow, literal terms of an exception.[1]   The hearsay may be the only way to prove a vital fact, and its trustworthiness may be beyond doubt, but if it does not come within an exception, it is not admissible under the common-law system.   Excluded hearsay is often more reliable and needed than evidence which gets in under an exception (or, for that matter, than admissible evidence that is not hearsay at all), under that system. The necessity and trustworthiness of an offered piece of hearsay is not, under this common-law system, even attempted to be measured as such in particular cases.   The assumption (often unwarranted) is made that there is special trustworthiness and necessity if the hearsay comes within the terms of an exception (and not otherwise).

There is frequently added to the usual requirements under the common-law exceptions as outlined below, a requirement that the declaration not be "self-serving" and that

---

[1] There are a few cases to the contrary, mostly dictum in decisions supportable on more conventional grounds such as the availability of an established exception.

there have been no reason or motive for the declarant to have falsified. Such a requirement is, of course, related to the trustworthiness criterion. This matter, like the matters of fading memory, trustworthiness generally, and availability of the declarant, affects the weight of the evidence as well as its admissibility.

Evidence coming within an exception to the hearsay rule may, of course, founder on some other ground, such as, e. g., relevance, prejudiciality, privilege, etc.

The following are generally characterized as principal exceptions to the hearsay rule under the common-law system. In each case, you will notice that the description (i. e., the requirements) of the exception, indeed even the very name of the exception, is in terms of some feature of or circumstance surrounding the *declarant's* statement (that is, surrounding the *declaration*), which is made elsewhere than at the current trial, not the *witness's* statement (which recounts the declaration) on the witness stand. This feature or circumstance must have been present when declarant made the statement (declaration), because that feature or circumstance is what is considered to "guarantee" (or at least indicate some probability of) the reliability of the *declaration.* (The reliability of the declaration is the concern of the hearsay rule.) In the following descriptions of the exceptions, each item in the description (including the description in the headings) is a specific requirement. It should be re-emphasized that the fact that evidence clears the hearsay rule does not mean the evidence is automatically admissible. It may still run afoul of other rules, such as the probative-prejudice balance, the character rule, relevance, etc. Some factors which impugn reliability which may not, in particular jurisdictions, render a hearsay exception unavailable, may nevertheless in a particular case tip the probative-prejudice balance against admissibility. Or, they may be used to affect weight. Here are the hearsay exceptions under a common-law system:

(1) **Testimony at Former Proceedings Where the Safeguards are Judicial in Nature (e. g., Former Trials, Depositions, etc., Not Necessarily in the Same Case).** This exception applies only if the declarant is unavailable at the later proceeding and there is an identity or substantial identity of parties, issues (legal as well as factual), and stakes, as between the two proceedings. The purpose of this requirement is that the opportunity for cross examination together with the motive or incentive to cross examine should be very much the same (both in degree and as to the issues to be focused on) in both proceedings (regardless of how the opportunity was utilized); and further, that unfairness in binding a party by another party's opportunity should be avoided. (The rationale, you see, is that a cold transcript, or a recording, or someone's recounting, of what the declarant said at the earlier proceeding, will be used in the later proceeding, without any further opportunity to cross examine the declarant.) Assuming there is no change in issues or stakes, if the earlier trial was A vs. B & C and the second A vs. C, the change in parties is probably not significant. (Some courts, however, are very strict.) However, if a new party is *added* (or substituted) in the second trial, it would be unfair to admit *against* him the earlier testimony, as he had no opportunity to cross examine. However, this may not apply if the new party is an administrator, executor or representative of the party against whom the evidence was introduced. Some courts will regard any change in parties (whether the party against whom the evidence is offered or otherwise) as significant (some only if the change is other than to an administrator, executor, or representative of one of the parties).

Some progressive courts may permit use against even a wholly new party who is not an administrator, executor, or representative, if there is a substantial identity of interests and issues as between him and the one in his shoes earlier. (Some of these courts would allow this only if the fight was in fact fought hard the first time and appears to have been at least as highly motivated on both sides as in the present controversy.)   Such was the case where suit No. 1 was a loss of consortium action brought by a husband for personal injuries to the wife, suit No. 2 was the wife's own personal injury action against the same defendant, and the husband and wife had the same lawyer.   (Some authorities adopting this view require that the opportunity to cross-examine have been utilized the first time, at least in the absence of any tactical justification for not cross-examining.)

Where the first trial is a prosecution for a crime and the second a civil suit based on the same crime (e. g., the second is a suit in which an insurance company alleges, in order to avoid payment, that the loss came about through plaintiff's own criminal act, where the alleged criminal act was the subject of the earlier criminal proceeding charging him; or the second is a tort suit against the alleged criminal for the offense), it is easy to see that one party has changed, and in addition, as respects the alleged criminal, the stakes were probably higher in the earlier (criminal) case (depending upon the criminal penalty and the civil amounts in controversy), but the burden of persuasion was lower (in the criminal case he need only raise a reasonable doubt; in the civil he must either show a preponderance of probability, or prevent the other party from doing so). Can testimony against him in the former case (criminal) be used against him in the later case (civil), assuming the witness is then dead? The party against whom the evidence is to be used has not changed from the one case to the other. If both the stakes and burdens vis-a-vis him were the same or less in the second (the civil) case as compared with the first, there might be more agreement (but not unanimity—many courts are very strict in their identity requirement) that the answer should be "yes". (Notice that we are, in this example, as always, asking a question concerning use of *evidence*, not a question concerning the binding effect of earlier judgments. And the evidence we are concerned with is a report or record of the earlier testimony of a witness, not the introduction of the earlier judgment itself. With respect to bindingness, note that in our example, the law of *res judicata* and collateral estoppel would usually hold that the first judgment did not preclude relitigation of the issue in the second case. Thus we have the question of what evidence from the first case may be introduced in that relitigation.)

Query: Why is unavailability required under this particularly trustworthy hearsay exception (attended as it is by judicial safeguards) and not under some of the others?

(2) **Dying Declarations.** This exception applies only in criminal homicide prosecutions where the declarant is alleged to be the victim, and on his deathbed made a statement implicating or exculpating the accused. At the time of making the statement, the declarant must have been *in extremis* (i. e., about to die), must have known that he was, and must have abandoned hope of recovery. He must have perished from that very injury, which must be the one alleged to have been inflicted by the accused. The theory is that one would not falsify when before his Maker and that declarant will have abandoned all hope of worldly gain. (Does this ring true to you? What about atheists? Vengeful people? People who may hope to benefit their survivors? Do people really change their "spots" at death? Is a man who is perceiving under the excitement of attack and who is so injured that he is about to die, likely to be a careful, clear, accurate, and precise observer, rememberer, and reporter; or will he be flustered and vague?)

If there is anything to this rationale that dying declarations are trustworthy, does it justify the narrowness of the exception as described above? Or is the narrowness dictated by the fact that the evidence is untrustworthy? But then, why have the exception at all? Has it been confined to the cases where it is most trustworthy? Will do the least damage? Is most needed? Is the narrowness dictated by considerations of necessity for the evidence in terms of the paucity of other evidence—no inquiry is made into whether there *actually* is any other evidence—or in terms of the seriousness of the case (homicide)? Does the seriousness of the case mean we should be *more* careful, or *less* careful, about receiving possibly unreliable evidence than we are in other cases? Does the necessity justification mean there is necessity to get someone for the crime, be he the right or wrong person?

A few jurisdictions have expanded the dying declaration exception to apply in other than criminal homicide cases.

(3) **Declarations of Pain or Other Bodily Feeling, Symptom, or Condition, that is Concurrent with the Declaration.** See p. 188 supra for an explanation of the kind of evidence that comes within this principle. The principle is alternatively recognized by courts as either an exception to the hearsay rule (thus the evidence is hearsay but not barred by the hearsay rule because of the exception) or as a principle which renders the evidence non-hearsay. In either event, the result is the same. The evidence is admissible unless barred by some other rule of evidence than the hearsay rule. The more spontaneous, non-narrative, exclamatory, ejaculatory, and not in response to questioning the declaration is, not only the more weight will it have, but the more likely it will be to come within the jurisdiction's version of this exception or principle, some courts excluding the evidence where there is any

unspontaneity and thus time to fabricate. (However, many courts do allow deliberated responses to questions, so long as the principle spontaneity requirement that applies in all cases—i. e., that the statement recounts *presently* felt pain or feeling—is satisfied.) Unavailability of the declarant is not required. Spontaneity before time to and motive to fabricate and forget is considered to make this evidence trustworthy and superior to anything the declarant might now say and hence the hearsay is regarded as "necessary" despite the availability of the declarant. (This same rationale applies to Admissions of a Party and certain other hearsay exceptions as well, infra.) The declaration need not be made contemporaneously with the infliction of the injury (if any) producing the pain or feeling—it need only be contemporaneous with the pain or feeling itself. However, a declaration made contemporaneously with the infliction of the injury is likely to be quite convincing and weighty.

(4) **Statements Relevant to Treatment Made to Physicians Consulted by the Declarant for Treatment.** The guarantee of accuracy is said to be the relationship the patient perceives between the accuracy of his statement and the quality of the treatment. Under this rationale, the significant factor would seem to be whether the patient *believed* the information to be relevant to treatment. (As a safeguard, some courts seem to require that it be *actually* or *reasonably* related to treatment. Diagnosis may also qualify.)

The rationale would seem to extend to any statements that are so motivated, including statements of both objective (outside, external) and subjective facts, both past and present, but a few courts have eliminated from coverage all but statements of present (i. e., contemporaneous with the statement) bodily symptoms, feelings, and conditions, thereby excluding, inter alia, histories given by patients to doctors. Narratives and responses to questions are permissible in nearly all jurisdictions. Unavailability of the declarant is not needed, on reasoning similar to that under the last exception above. If the physician is visited solely for purposes of preparing a case for litigation and not for treatment, nothing said to him could qualify for *this* exception. (But see, e. g., the last exception, which may be available.)

(5) **Declarations Expressing a State of Mind or Emotion Concurrent with the Declaration.** See pp. 183–90, supra, for an explanation of the kind of evidence that comes within this principle, which some courts feel renders the evidence non-hearsay; and others feel is a hearsay exception rendering admissible (insofar as the hearsay rule is concerned) evidence which is frankly hearsay. In either event, the result is the same. The "special trustworthiness" of this evidence needs no further discussion. The "necessity" is similar to that under Exception No. 3, supra, unavailability not being required. It is often said that necessity also inheres in the fact that there are few reliable alternative ways to elucidate a relevant state of mind or emotion. But evidence is usually received under this "state of mind" exception or principle regardless of the availability of alternative ways to prove the state of mind; and, with respect to another aspect of necessity, the state of mind or emotion itself is not always of critical, singular or ultimate importance in every case where the exception is applied. Sometimes it is of only circumstantial importance, and other circumstances are available. E. g., some courts permit the exception to be used where an intention is offered as evidence that the intention was carried out, as where a statement "I will deliver the deed only when paid" is offered to prove that possession of the deed without payment was fraudulently obtained; even if there is other evidence on the matter. Raborn v. Hayton, 34 Wash.2d 105, 208 P.2d 133 (1949). More straightforward examples are given in the discussion cited above.

Shepard v. United States, 290 U.S. 96, 54 S.Ct. 22 (1933) is an instructive case in this area and illustrates the metaphysical lengths the hearsay rule and its exceptions (and Evidence law in general) can go. The statement of the deceased that "Dr. Shepard has poisoned me" was admitted in the trial court under the "dying declaration" exception to the hearsay rule, in a prosecution against Dr. Shepard for killing the deceased. The Court of Appeals held that the declaration did not meet the requirements of a dying declaration (since there was no evidence of a consciousness of impending death), but that the admission of the evidence could now be sustained on the theory that the declaration showed a "state of mind" not bent on suicide in answer to the defense of suicide. The Supreme Court reversed, holding that (a) under the theory upon which the evidence was admitted, the jury was not and could not have been instructed that the statement was evidence of this state of mind only and not more directly evidence that Dr. Shepard poisoned deceased; (b) defendant could not be faulted for failing to ask for such an instruction when the theory of admission was dying declaration; and (c) even if the "state of mind" theory of admission had been the one adopted by the trial court and the jury had been instructed to confine its consideration of the evidence to that, "[D]iscrimination so subtle is a feat beyond the compass of ordinary minds. The reverberating clang of those accusatory words would drown all weaker sounds. It is for ordinary minds, and not psychoanalysts that our rules of evidence are framed." (Per Cardozo, J.)

(6) **Excited Utterances.** Out-of-court declarations about an exciting occurrence made under stimulus of the excitement in a spontaneous fashion before time for reflection and fabrication, constitute this exception, regardless of the availability of the declarant (the "necessity" being the supposed superiority to declarant's present testimony). In a

[217]

few jurisdictions the declaration need not relate to the exciting occurrence, so long as it is truly stimulated by it; but as a practical matter the declaration will normally state details of or causes of some catastrophe, collision, or accident, right on the scene. And, though it is seldom formally required, the excitive occurrence usually will also be the very occurrence ultimately in controversy. Hence, this exception is frequently titled the "res gestae" exception (the quoted term in liberal translation means "the facts of the litigated transaction or occurrence itself"); although that term is often also used for certain other exceptions, notably Nos. 2, 3, and 5, for the same reason.[2] (Nos. 3, 5 and 6 are often classified together as "spontaneous statements".) In most jurisdictions, so long as the excitement lasts, the declaration can come after the occurrence. The length of time the excitement is deemed to last depends on such circumstances as how exciting the occurrence is, and the declarant's involvement in it, etc. This also would influence weight. Some courts feel the guarantee of accuracy depends on the declaration and the facts reported (the excit-

---

[2] "Res gestae" is also sometimes used to mean out-of-court utterances which themselves have legal significance ("operative facts") or which are offered for some other similar purpose, that does not depend on the utterance's credibility or the truth of the matter stated in it. Such utterances are not hearsay in the first place (see Chapter III). "Res gestae" is not an independent principle or exception to the hearsay rule, and if evidence does not fit one of the other recognized principles or exceptions removing the evidence from the hearsay ban, such as the operative fact or "not for the truth of the matter stated" principles or the regular exceptions, then the evidence will be inadmissible. Some courts become confused and do not recognize this, and believe that "res gestae" is an independent exception covering any statement made at the time and place of an important, litigated transaction. This confusion results because many of the situations where a legitimate exception or exemption is made under exception 2, 3, or 5, or under the "operative fact" or "truth of the matter stated" principle, happen to involve "on the scene" statements, and the literal translation of "res gestae" is "things done" or "attendant circumstances."

ing occurrence) being contemporaneous, and may limit the exception to such statements, *or broaden the exception to include declarations about contemporaneous fact whether or not there was an exciting occurrence stimulating them*, provided there is spontaneity and a lack of any reason to suspect falsification. (The analogy to Nos. 3 and 5 supra is drawn for this "present sensory impression" expansion of the exception.)

Under the basic exception, special trustworthiness is said to stem from the spontaneity and the excitement. One may question whether an exciting occurrence fosters perceptual and reportorial care and accuracy, or tends to fluster. Certainly counsel in arguing weight to the jury will touch on these matters.

Suppose the existence of the selfsame exciting occurrence is not only pre-requisite to admissibility, but is the ultimate issue in controversy, is disputed, and the hearsay sought to be admitted is the only evidence thereof. An example of this might be an excited utterance following and relating to an auto collision or assault, offered in a lawsuit based on the collision or assault. A judge is usually given some discretion to receive hearsay on preliminary issues of fact, especially in circumstances like this. But this does not settle the matter, and decisions are in some confusion as to what should be done in this situation.

There is generally no inflexible requirement that the declarant himself have been *involved* in the exciting occurrence, other than as a spectator, but this factor will have an influence on the degree of his excitement and hence on the amount of time allowed between occurrence and utterance before the declaration will no longer be considered spontaneous and stimulated by the occurrence. This consideration can play a role at the level of weight, too, if the evidence is admitted.

Returning to the example used in opening the last chapter herein, if the declaration "X shot Y" were made in the heat of that very occurrence, it would in all likelihood qualify for the present exception.

(7) **Records of Past Recollection.** Normally, if a witness testifies to facts not of current memory, but on the basis that he *stated* them at some earlier time,[3] the testimony will be hearsay, in most common law jurisdictions. But the earlier statement *if written* may come within the present exception to the hearsay rule. The requirements of this exception have been set forth at pp. 44-51, supra.

(8) **Business Records.** When someone (for example a salesperson) records facts (for example a sale he has made) in a book of entry or elsewhere, if he is available and testifies to the elements enumerated at pp. 46-48, supra (though he no longer recalls the sale itself), the entry will be admissible to prove the sale under the Past Recollection Recorded exception to the hearsay rule (No. 7, supra). And there is authority that the record similarly qualifies if the salesperson, for example, reported the sale to another who made the entry and both are available and testify so that between them they satisfy those enumerated requirements, the reporter verifying that he accurately reported the sale (though he no longer remembers the sale itself) and the entrant verifying accurate recording.

---

[3] His reason for testifying in such a seemingly unusual fashion might be, for example, that he no longer remembers the facts, but can remember the statement, which he remembers making or signing, and he expresses confidence that it accorded with his perception and memory then. Another example might be that the attorney presenting him has already had him testify to the facts from current memory, and now wishes to have *additional* evidence in the form of the same witness' testimony to the effect not that he *remembers* the facts (which he already testified to earlier) but that he *stated* them when they were fresh in mind. This latter example, as we see if we follow out the reference we are coming to in text above, could *not* qualify as Past Recollection Recorded.

Suppose in the above examples, however, the required testimony cannot be obtained, because of witness-un-availability. In such a case, recourse can normally be had to the Business Records exception, which *requires* such un-availability, at least under the exception's strictest version. (In several jurisdictions, difficulty in ascertaining and pro-ducing the witness, or his inability to recall, or even his dimness of recollection, will suffice. In a number of juris-dictions, the requirement has been done away with alto-gether.)

The Business Records exception in its strictest form ad-mits a narrow class of documents: routine original entries in business books or files made systematically and in the firm's regular way in the usual course of the business, and entered at or about the time of the transaction reported, but generally only if the participants in the process have been charged by the business with the role they played.[4]

What constitutes a "business" is frequently construed broadly. In most jurisdictions it need not be a commercial or profit enterprise. Records prepared for legal purposes are often not considered to be in the "regular course of business."

[4] In several jurisdictions, an older exception to the hearsay rule for a party's own shop books introduced in his own behalf (the "shop-book" exception) remains on the books, though it is superseded by the broader present exception. In a very few jurisdictions, limitations and qualifications that appear in the jurisdiction's shop-book exception are construed to still limit a party's use of his own books despite the fact that there are no such limitations or qualifications under the Business Records exception.

While the Business Records exception we are treating in this section is very often statutory, the statutes are long standing, have acquired considerable judicial gloss, and precede the modern comprehensive codifications of evidence law generally that begin with and are based on the Federal Rules of Evidence and that cover a number of (but by no means all) the states. Thus we are justified in treating these statutes in this section as traditional exceptions to the hearsay rule as they exist under a common law system of evidence. The common law frequently involved and involves an amalgam of statutes and case law.

In personal injury cases, hospital records are often admitted as business records (although in some jurisdictions there are special statutes dealing with hospital records). In very strict jurisdictions, however, hospital records may present a possible problem in fitting under the term "business" and fitting under the term "routine" (or "regular entry"). "Non-routineness" would be a problem only in the case of entries of a non-repetitive, unusual nature, as opposed to entries of temperature, vital signs, etc. But usually this requirement is relaxed to permit any health matter. Hospital records may on occasion present a "double hearsay" problem (which can occur in many non-hospital situations, and under other hearsay exceptions, as well): A hospital record may contain a recounting of a patient's recounting of certain facts. The first-mentioned recounting may be covered by the Business Records exception. Hopefully for the offeror, an exception can also be found to cover the patient's recounting, too (e. g., Statements to Physicians, Admissions of a Party, etc.). Hospital records can also illustrate another broad problem related to business records generally: to what extent is an opinion, inference, or conclusion (e. g., a diagnosis) in a report admissible, and under what circumstances? After all, the writer is not present for cross examination. The most frequent answer under the traditional system seems to be that they are inadmissible under all conditions, but there are many permutations of view.

Some few jurisdictions have expanded the Business Records exception to include oral reports.

The requirement that entries be "original" has been relaxed in most jurisdictions to permit the introduction of either original slips (e. g., sales slips) or any permanent recordation of them done as a regular business matter. Automated methods of data keeping are thus frequently acceptable (e. g., punch-cards). The application of the Best Evidence Rule should be considered here. Normally if the hearsay exception allows a secondary copy like this, courts are reluctant to bar it with the Best Evidence Rule, and will relax the applicability of that Rule, if necessary, or will find the facts necessary to achieve the desired effect under it, e. g., that the document is original or the original is satisfactorily accounted for.

Many authorities expand the notion of "regular entries" to include even certain isolated non-routine memos, letters, reports, etc., even sometimes internal accident reports, of, say, a manufacturing company, if done in the regular course or scope of business or perhaps under standing instructions from the employer.

It is perfectly acceptable under the Business Records exception in most jurisdictions that the person making the entry had no knowledge of the facts entered so long as one having such knowledge and having the business duty to have such knowledge reported (pursuant to business duty) the facts to him (or verified them) at or near the time those facts transpired and this was the regular method. At least this is the better view. (The absence of personal knowledge on the part of the entrant may, however, affect weight.) The entry must also have been made near the time of the transaction reported.

That the document complies with all the requirements of this section is usually proved by the testimony of someone in a supervisory or custodial position.

Absence of a business record often may be evidence of the non-occurrence of an event.

(9) **Official Records.** This area is highly statutory,[5] with individual provisions tailored to particular kinds of official records. But courts also act in the area. We are speaking, of course, of official records offered as evidence

[5] See second paragraph of footnote 4, supra, the gist of which is also applicable here.

of the facts related therein, which would be hearsay requiring an exception in order to be admitted.

Included in the exception will usually be originals and officially certified copies. Marriage, birth, and death certificates and the like are generally covered. Reports of results of the more reliable varieties of official fact-investigation may also be (in a few jurisdictions), but generally not verdicts, judgments, acquittals, convictions, etc. (at least under the overwhelming majority common law view). These latter normally may not be introduced as *evidence* of the facts found, though the law of res judicata may under certain narrow conditions render them conclusive determinations of certain factual issues. (On the use of transcripts of or reports of *testimony* at earlier proceedings as evidence of facts, see pp. 211-13, supra.) Under the present exception, there must be at least some "hint" of a public or official duty to issue the writing. Private parties (e. g., physicians and clergymen) and private institutions (e. g., hospitals and churches) may be authorized or commanded by law to issue certain certificates or make certain reports, which oftentimes can be brought within the exception. No unavailability of the writer (declarant) is required under this exception. First-hand knowledge of the issuer or his authorized informant is required. This exception is poorly developed in the traditional common law, and not available on any widespread or general basis.

(10) **Treatises.** A growing but minority tendency in the more modern common law has been to treat statements in recognized treatises (and perhaps articles) as competent evidence of the facts stated by the author (a hearsay usage), subject, of course, as always, to the other rules of Evidence law such as relevancy, privilege, opinion, and the like. Compare pp. 345-47, infra (impeachment [non-hearsay] use of treatises, recognized everywhere).

Courts have generally been more receptive of mortality tables, market reports (e. g. of prices in trade journals), city directories, business registers, and the like, of an author-itative and recognized nature. Nevertheless, acceptance of even this as a hearsay exception has been far from universal.

No showing of unavailability or difficulty in producing the author is required respecting treatises, mortality tables, etc. when they are admitted under this exception.

(11) **Admissions of a Party.** This and the next excep-tion are perhaps the two most important exceptions to the hearsay rule. They are addressed at some length elsewhere in this book.

It is sufficient for now to say that under the common law system, when a party (or his agent or his co-conspirator[6] under certain circumstances) has made a statement outside the trial, that could be used against the party at trial, that statement, if offered against the party, is regarded as either not hearsay (minority common law view), or as an excep-tion to the hearsay rule (majority common law view)—in either event the result is the same. A considerable amount of opinion and even second hand knowledge has usually been tolerated in this outside-the-trial statement, at least where the party himself (rather than the agent) made it. This is either because it is believed that he would have investigated carefully, or because we don't wish to lose entirely this valuable evidence, which cannot really be re-phrased to avoid the opinion or avoid the second hand material, as a witness' statement on the stand can. It

---

[6] Do not confuse this theory of admissibility with the theory that admits against all conspirators statements of any one of them that are part of advancing the conspiracy on grounds that they are actual-ly part of the *crime* of conspiracy and are thus not offered for their truth or credibility. Admittedly the doctrines are often difficult to distinguish and have similar requirements.

should be noted, however, that the statement need not have been realized to be, nor need it actually have been, against interest when made. (Of course, such realization vel non could affect weight. So could the factor of whether opinion and second hand knowledge is in the statement.) Availability of the declarant is immaterial under Party Admissions.

(12) **Declarations Against Interest.** This distinct exception is best described by contrasting it with Admissions of a Party, No. 11, just above, *with which it must not be confused!*

A Declaration Against Interest is a statement by a declarant, who is not necessarily a party nor a person bearing any relation to a party, which statement was known by the declarant at the time of his making of the statement to be against his pecuniary, proprietary, or (in some jurisdictions) penal interest, and which statement somehow becomes relevant in a lawsuit, perhaps between two wholly other parties. Declarations Against Interest is the more stringent of the two exceptions, requiring (a) unavailability of the declarant, and (b) that he knew the declaration to be against his pecuniary, proprietary or (sometimes) penal interest; although he need not be a party or related to a party, and his statement may be used not only against him and those in some relationship with him, but against others as well. The exception for Party Admissions applies regardless of whether the statement was against interest when made, so long as it is against the party's interests now. The reader should attempt to ascertain and compare the rationales for the two exceptions. Why are the requirements, as just outlined, different? Notice particularly the requirement that the statement be *known* to be against interest when made. The opinion and first-hand knowledge rules are frequently relaxed (insofar as the out-of-court declarant is concerned) for Admissions of a Party, but at least some courts refuse to do so for Declarations Against Interest. Why?

[*226*]

Of course, a particular out-of-court statement may come within both exceptions. This would *seem* to be the case where one of two co-criminals has made an out-of-court confession or admission implicating both, and he is "unavailable" in the sense that he refuses to testify, asserting his privilege against self-incrimination. We would expect the incriminating statement to be admissible against both: against the one as his own Admission, and against the other as a Declaration Against the Interests of the declarant. But either because of a special (perhaps constitutional) criminal dispensation, or because the reference to the non-confessor is not itself against the interests of the confessor, or because penal interest does not qualify under the exception for Declarations Against Interest, the incriminating statement traditionally has been considered inadmissible against the one who did not make it. (The confessor in most jurisdictions generally could not be regarded as speaking as agent for the other criminal, for purposes of the exception for Party Admissions made by an agent or co-conspirator, since his statement would usually be made after completion of and ordinarily not in furtherance of the joint crime.) Where the two are co-defendants, and the confessor will not take the stand, and the reference to the non-confessor cannot be deleted, the inefficacy of an instruction to the jury to use the evidence against only the confessor requires a severance of the trials or a forgoing of use of the confession. (See Bruton v. United States, 391 U.S. 123, 88 S.Ct. 1620 (1968) (confrontation clause of the constitution).) However, mild reference made by a prosecutor not in bad faith, to such a confession, in a joint trial or a trial of the non-confessor, may, in some circumstances, be cured by an instruction to disregard. (See Frazier v. Cupp, 394 U.S. 731, 89 S.Ct. 1420 (1969).) The *Bruton* rule will not be applied, and the instruction will be deemed efficacious, if the "non-confessor" has also made an admissible confession. Parker v. Randolph, 442 U.S. 62, 99 S.Ct. 2132 (1979).

Under Declarations Against Interest, many situations arise where the statement is both "against the declarant's interest" and "in the declarant's interest" to make, at one and the same time, in different respects, or in different parts of the statement. One example might be the confession of a co-criminal mentioned above. Does the motive to, perhaps, please the authorities, or curry or obtain a favor, or share blame, outweigh the against-interest aspect? Another example might be where declarant's money is being held, say by a bank, and, in order to obtain his money being so held, the declarant complies with the bank's request and makes a statement damaging his spouse's claim for damages against the bank in another matter (assuming that would be considered to be against his proprietary interest). Sometimes severing the various parts of the statement can take care of the matter, but, as in at least the last case, that may be unsatisfactory. A determination has to be made as to what the preponderant motivation was and whether it acts as some substantial guarantee or indicator of reliability. Frequently also, if a statement is preponderantly against interest, a court will admit even portions that are plainly in-interest. Another kind of dual aspect statement that has often confused courts is illustrated by a statement "I owe ten thousand dollars." This statement is really two statements, one *in* the declarant's interest to make, and one against his interest to make: "I owe at least, but not more than, ten thousand dollars." The part between the commas is in his interest to make. In such a case, we should look to see which implied statement is really being offered at the trial. This depends upon whether the evidence is being offered to establish that $10,000 was owed, or to rebut the contention that more than $10,000 was owed. (I am assuming a lawsuit where, for some reason, the declarant is not considered a party or an agent of a party, so that we do not have to consider Party Admissions. For example, in some jurisdictions, this might be a wrongful death suit, where the dispute is as to the net worth of the deceased declarant, to the party plaintiff, who is his spouse.)

The objection is often made to evidence of many different sorts, that the evidence is "self-serving." Some courts seem to be under the impression that any evidence involving self-serving statements, that is, statements it is in the stater's interest to make, is inadmissible. That is not so. It is only where the evidence must be against interest to be admissible, as in the case of hearsay admissible under the present exception, that "self-serving" would be a valid objection (or in the rare case where the evidence, because of its self-serving nature, is so without value, or so likely to deceive the jury, that the probative-prejudice-time balance discussed in Chapter I tips to exclude it). As noted at the beginning of this chapter, a few courts have imposed a requirement that the declaration not be self-serving (or that there be no motive to fabricate) on several of the hearsay exceptions. These may include dying declarations, excited utterances, declarations of bodily feelings or condition, and/or declarations of state of mind. The objection should be specifically made in terms that the evidence is hearsay and ineligible for the particular exception because of its self-serving nature, rather than merely stating "objection, the evidence is self-serving."

One final note on Declarations Against Interest. By "against interest" we mean statements such as "the property is not mine" (a statement against proprietary interest), or "I have not paid yet; I still owe the money" (a statement against pecuniary interest) or, in some jurisdictions in some situations, "I obtained the money by removing it secretly from the drawer" (perhaps a statement against penal interest since it may implicate in crime; it may also be adverse to other interests). In other words, a reasonable person would not make them unless they are true. They are hurtful to

[*229*]

the stater if they are true. We do *not* mean a statement which, if true, is harmless or beneficial to the stater, but will be penalized (that is, will hurt him) if he is speaking an untruth—for example, a statement to a governmental authority which is punishable under law if false. Students sometimes become confused and believe that any statement made under penalty of law is a "Declaration Against Interest." In general under the common law system, there is no exception embracing such a statement.

(13) **Miscellaneous.** There are also certain miscellaneous exceptions to the hearsay rule, discussion of which is precluded by the economies of this short work. Among them are the exceptions for *family statements and community reputation respecting pedigree and family history,* and for *recitals in ancient writings* (usually those that meet the requirements of authentication by antiquity: i. e., at least 30 years of age, freedom from suspicion in appearance and custody, and, in some places in the case of deeds, possession given under the instrument). It should be noted that while facts which *authenticate* an ancient document may also render the document admissible to prove the truth of its recitals as an exception to the hearsay rule, the two matters are conceptually distinct.

CHAPTER V

HEARSAY UNDER THE FEDERAL RULES OF EVIDENCE AND STATE CODES PATTERNED AFTER THEM

Introduction

It has been estimated that over 60 percent of all evidence questions in trials involve the hearsay rule. Article VIII (Hearsay) of the Federal Rules of Evidence is therefore one of the most important articles in the Rules.[1]

After adopting a general definition of hearsay that declares to be hearsay any in-court evidence of a statement "made other than by the declarant while testifying at the hearing" (provided it is offered to prove the "truth of the matter asserted" in the statement), Article VIII qualifies the general definition with some special provisions or exemptions about implied statements, former statements of witnesses presently testifying, and certain other matters. In addition, two "laundry lists" of exceptions (those requiring unavailability of the declarant and those not so requiring) are also provided.

Preliminary Considerations: Rules Are An Integrated Whole

Many rules must be considered together when approaching potential hearsay. Among the rules

[1] The discussion will proceed as a discussion of the Federal Rules of Evidence, but it is to be understood that in general it also applies to codes patterned on them: the 1974 Uniform Rules of Evidence and most of the recent state codes, which state codes are largely copies of either the Federal Rules or the very similar 1974 Uniform Rules (themselves patterned on the Federal Rules), it generally making little difference which. Even the rule numbers are usually the same in all these codes. A few significant variations of substance will be specifically mentioned. We will see that the Rules considerably erode the hearsay rule (though not entirely). Thus, a party often will not be presented with the maker of a statement used against him. If this fact is to be found out and/or the evidence "debunked," the party will

likely to be important in addition to those in Article VIII (Hearsay) is Rule 403 (balance of probativity against countervailing factors). Rule 703 (permitting experts to base testimony on proper hearsay) and Rules 803(24) and 804(b)(5), the so-called "catch-all" exceptions to the hearsay rule, are frequently available as "end runs" around the hearsay rule.

Two caveats are in order before we turn to our main discussion of Article VIII:

First, as at common law, even if possible hearsay evidence clears the hearsay rule, other rules might bar its admissibility. These include, among others, the opinion rule (Rules 701 and 702), the firsthand- or personal-knowledge rule (Rule 602), the rule requiring authentication of documents (Rule 901), the best evidence or original documents rule (Rule 1002), and perhaps most importantly, Rule 403 (the "great override," which allows a judge to exclude otherwise admissible evidence on a largely discretionary balancing of probativity against prejudice, confusion, time consumption, and the like; it, like most of the other rules mentioned, is a one-way street: it does not license *admission* of otherwise *inadmissible* evidence, such as evidence inadmissible under the hearsay rule). Also consider Rule 501 (privileges) and exclusionary rules stemming from the Constitution.

Second, even if evidence is hearsay, the offeror may be able to find ways around the hearsay rule, other than what are ordinarily classed as exemptions or exceptions. Two "end runs" around the hearsay rule under the Federal Rules of Evidence—"end runs" whose status was not at all clear under the common law—are:

(1) *Rule 703* (which appears in Article VII, the "Opinion and Expert Testimony" article of the Rules). This rule pro-

have to do much pretrial investigation and discovery, and even perhaps subpoena the maker-declarant.

vides, generally speaking, that an expert may give an opinion and base it on reliable hearsay (or other reliable, though inadmissible, evidence). This is extremely far-reaching and includes the use of surveys, studies, books, polls, and a variety of secondhand statements. See generally United States v. Golden, 532 F.2d 1244 (9th Cir. 1976) (Rule 703 allows drug enforcement agent to testify to standard prices of narcotics in various cities based on hearsay of other agents).

(2) *Rules 803(24) and 804(b)(5).* These are two identically phrased "catch-all" exceptions to the hearsay rule. (For technical reasons, the "catch-all" provisions had to appear not once, but twice, i. e., in the two "laundry lists" of exceptions—those requiring unavailability of the declarant, and those not so requiring.) The "catch-alls" provide that a judge can make new exceptions under certain conditions designed to insure that the evidence is deserving and needed and that the other party has a fair opportunity to combat it. The evidence must be found to be especially trustworthy and necessary, and the party relying on the catch-all must give advance and somewhat detailed notice to the other side. This last proviso is, in reality, a new form of discovery, and can present tactical problems. For example, suppose a would-be offeror of a piece of evidence under this provision has not been required to disclose the evidence under other discovery. Suppose further that he is in doubt as to whether the evidence might be held to be within a more traditional listed exception not requiring notice. (Many candidates for the catch-all have proved to be in this ambiguous realm.) Should he give the notice or hope the evidence will be held within the more traditional exception? The answer will vary with the facts and will not always be easy of discernment.

Might extensive use of these two "end runs" or of any broad hearsay exemption or exception, violate the right to cross-examination (confrontation) under the Constitution because the hearsay declarants are not presented? See United States v. Williams, 424 F.2d 344 (5th Cir. 1970), rehearing denied 431 F.2d 1168, aff'd en banc 447 F.2d 1285, cert. denied 405 U.S. 954, 92 S.Ct. 1168, rehearing denied 405 U.S. 1048, 92 S.Ct. 1308; United States v. Lemmons, 527 F.2d 662 (6th Cir. 1975), cert. denied 429 U.S. 817, 97 S.Ct. 60; Perma Research & Development Corp. v. Singer Co., 542 F.2d 111 (2d Cir. 1976), cert. denied 429 U.S. 987, 97 S.Ct. 507.

While it now seems fairly certain that an exception to the confrontation requirement will be made where there is a hearsay exception that has at least *some* basis in tradition or reason (see Dutton v. Evans, 400 U.S. 74, 91 S.Ct. 210 (1970)), it is still possible that some of the expanded exceptions or exemptions in the Federal Rules of Evidence, or some applications, could be found violative of the right to confrontation as applied in a criminal case. There may also be an analogous right in a civil case. The Constitution, of course, can override particular applications (or all applications) of any of the Rules, as the Rules' drafters well recognized in disclaiming attempts to codify constitutional doctrines or limitations. See, e. g., Advisory Committee Note immediately preceding Rule 801, and Advisory Committee Note to Rule 804(b)(4). (The Advisory Committee Notes are the original drafters' notes that refer to a draft prior to the final draft; they appear at 56 F.R.D. 183 (1972).)

Format of F.R.E. Article VIII (Hearsay)

Article VIII can be broken down into a general definition of hearsay (utilizing the "truth of the matter asserted" concept); two exemptions (certain prior statements of witnesses, and party admissions); and two lists of exceptions (those requiring and those not requiring unavailability). Exemptions and exceptions produce the same re-

sult: the evidence is not barred by the hearsay rule.

Turning now to our main discussion and putting aside the "end runs" and the other matters just discussed, Article VIII first defines hearsay generally (Rule 801(a)–(c)), and then provides *exemptions from* (see Rule 801(d)), and *exceptions to* (see Rules 803 and 804) the hearsay rule. In actual fact, it makes no difference whether something is classed as an exemption or as an exception. It is merely the positioning in the Rules that determines what we call it. If it appears in Rule 801 it is an exemption, because that rule purports to deal with definition. If it appears in Rule 803 or Rule 804 it is an exception, because those rules purport to deal with exceptions. We will break our discussion down into exemptions first, and then exceptions, in order to approximate the format of the Rules. We will save discussion of the *general* definition of hearsay until p. 291 infra, on the assumption that the student already has at least a provisional understanding of that matter. (E. g. from Ch. 3.)

The Hearsay Exemptions

Prior Statements of Witnesses, and Party Admissions, are the exemptions. Prior Statements of Witnesses was not an exemption or exception under the prevailing common law, and is so here only if the statement is inconsistent and made at certain proceedings, or consistent and tends to rebut certain charges, or if it identifies a person. Party Admissions is broadened over the common law, as respects who is an agent of a party for admission purposes, except that predecessors-in-interest are not recognized.

Prior Statements of Witnesses

Rule 801(d)(1) covers statements made at an earlier time not a part of the present hearing, by witnesses who are now on the stand. Evidence of them is made *substantively* admissible under certain conditions. This is a change from the prevailing common law, under which they were admissible not substantively, but rather only on the issue of credibility (a non-hearsay use because then they are not offered "for the truth of the matter they assert"), unless the facts warranted application of some other hearsay exception or exemption, which would, of course, license broader use. The classic case under the traditional rule is State v. Saporen, 205 Minn. 358, 285 N.W. 898 (1939). Adherence to that rule was not unbroken, however. See, e. g., Beavers v. State, 492 P.2d 88 (Alaska 1971); State v. Skinner, 110 Ariz. 135, 515 P.2d 880 (1973); Jett v. Commonwealth, 436 S.W.2d 788 (Ky.1969); State v. Igoe, 206 N.W.2d 291 (N.D.1973); State v. Derryberry, 17 Or.App. 262, 521 P.2d 1065 (1974); Gelhaar v. State, 41 Wis.2d 230, 163 N.W.2d 609 (1969); Cal.Evid.Code §§ 1235, 1236, 1238 (West 1966). Of course, the traditional credibility use is not disturbed by the new rule.

The conditions for the new (i. e., substantive) use under the Federal Rule are as follows:

(a) *Inconsistent statements.* If the statement is inconsistent with the witness' present testimony and was made at a prior "proceeding" under oath and subject to perjury penalties (for example a grand jury proceeding, whether or not in the same case), the evidence is exempt from the hearsay rule, notwithstanding that there may not have been any opportunity to cross-examine at the earlier proceeding. An unanswered question is what types of government investigation (other than the grand jury) may be considered "proceedings" satisfying this rule. Will the swearing of an affidavit before a notary be considered a proceeding that qualifies? Is the word "perjury" in the rule confined technically to the offense of perjury or can other "false swearing" penalties qualify? In United States v. Castro-Ayon, 537 F.2d 1055 (9th Cir. 1976), an interrogation under oath by the

Border Patrol qualified. The 1974 Uniform Rules of Evidence version of Rule 801(d)(1) as it relates to prior inconsistent statements in *civil cases* does not require the statement to have been sworn nor to have been made at a proceeding nor to have been subject to perjury penalties. For criminal cases, the rule is identical to the Federal Rule. An earlier draft of the Federal Rule omitted these requirements as to both civil and criminal cases. (The Uniform Rules' position is influential in state adoptions. In *general* the Uniform Rules follow the Federal Rules of Evidence.)

(b) *Consistent statements.* If the statement is consistent with the witness' present testimony, it is exempt from the hearsay rule if it tends to "rebut" an "express or implied charge" of "recent fabrication," "improper motive," or "improper influence." It need not have been made at an earlier proceeding nor been under oath nor subject to perjury penalties. What will qualify as the requisite charge of fabrication or improper motive or influence has not been definitively determined. Is not there always such a charge implied when the facts are contested? See United States v. Iaconetti, 406 F.Supp. 554 (E.D.N.Y.1976), aff'd in part 540 F.2d 574 (2d Cir. 1976). The reason for the "charge" requirement in the F.R.E. is that under traditional law, which did not allow the evidence to come in substantively, it could come in to support credibility but (because of courtroom economies) only when there had been an attack on credibility. Under some decisions, the attack had to be in the form of the kind of "charge" articulated here. Some decisions have required that the previous consistent statement predate the alleged influence or motive to fabricate, as that would be when it is most persuasive.

There may also be a problem lurking in the provisions of the F.R.E. we are discussing, as to exactly what is a consistent or inconsistent statement. For one example, what

about a situation where the witness earlier supplied information but his present posture is that he doesn't remember
the facts; or doesn't know anything; and thus he does not
report perceiving inconsistent facts?   What if he explains
away a seeming discrepancy?   Can a statement be neither
consistant or inconsistent?   Does the statement have to be
totally inconsistent to come under the provision for inconsistent statements?   Will earlier law about what "inconsistent" means for impeachment purposes govern?   See pp.
325–26.   Will any minor discrepancy result in a finding of
inconsistency?   See generally, Gilmour v. Strescon Indus.,
Inc., 66 F.R.D. 146 (E.D.Pa.1975) (statement that crane
scratched trailer consistent with saying no one said it struck
trailer); United States v. Rogers, 549 F.2d 490 (8th Cir.
1976) (failure to recollect); United States v. Jordano, 521
F.2d 695 (2d Cir. 1975).

   (c) *Identification statements.*   If the statement is one of
identification of a person, it is exempt from the hearsay rule
(provided it is based on personal perception) regardless of
whether it is consistent or inconsistent or made at an earlier
proceeding or under oath or subject to perjury penalties or
offered in response to any charge.   There is no requirement
that the statement of identification must have been made
soon after perceiving the individual, as there is, for example,
in Section 1238 of the California Evidence Code (must be
"fresh in memory"), and as there was in an early Advisory
Committee draft of the Federal Rule.   See draft of March
1971, 51 F.R.D. 315.   Thus, there could be reliability and
influence problems.   (But perhaps such a requirement
could frequently be imposed pursuant to Rule 403 which
requires, in general language subject to considerable discretion, that as respects all admissible evidence, probativity
must be found not to be substantially outweighed by prejudice, time consumption, misleadingness, etc.)   Identification
statements are confined under 801(d)(1) to identification of

a person, as opposed to a thing. Presumably, it could be a person in a civil or criminal context and need not be any of the central actors. Exactly what is and is not a "statement of identification" may present problems, as statements conceivably within that phrase may range from naming by name a person seen committing the deed, through pointing at or describing an unknown person who committed the deed (or, even more remotely, a person who was merely present in the area), to furnishing weaker circumstantial information useful in finding the right person, such as identifying his car or giving his license plate number.

What is the net result of these new rules concerning the various kinds of prior statements of witnesses? Primarily as a result of the inconsistent-statement branch of the rule (see (a) above), grand jury statements, formerly usually usable only on credibility, will now play a much broader role. The prosecution conceivably could build its entire case on them. At the very least, they can *help* the prosecution persuade the jury or survive a motion for directed acquittal. Similar use may be made by the defense. Obviously, the grand jury has assumed increased importance. Perhaps this will provide grounds for increasing defense access thereto. An argument can be made that the new evidence rule means that there is the kind of "particularized need" the defense is required to show under discovery law to get grand jury transcripts. On "particularized need" generally, see Comment, 55 Nw.U.L.Rev. 482 (1960). Prosecutors stand most to gain from the new rule concerning the permissibility of using prior inconsistent statements made before the grand jury, since prosecutors have the burden of proof at trial, are in a position to convene and subpoena witnesses for the grand jury, and must often rely in prosecutions on perhaps criminally connected or timid witnesses who may turn (or be turned) against the prosecution between grand jury and trial, once the impact of their testimony becomes known and understood. Prosecutors can now work less with their witnesses between grand jury and trial. If the witnesses have given good grand jury statements, any inconsistency at trial will license use of relevant portions of the grand jury transcript. (And, in addition to the substantive use allowed by Rule 801(d)(1), Rule 607 removes the ban on impeaching your own witnesses.) Rule 801(d)(1) as it relates to these prior inconsistent grand jury statements has implications beyond the immediate case growing out of the grand jury proceeding wherein the testimony was given; for the grand jury testimony can be used in other cases as well—for example, a civil antitrust case. The original grand jury proceeding may, but need not have, involved antitrust. Similarly, the rule licenses the use of testimony given in one trial at a later trial, whether or not in the same case and regardless of whether the issues are totally unrelated or one was criminal and the other civil, so long as the witness testifies "inconsistently" in the second. While this all may seem to present dangers that the motivation to be accurate and careful, and to explore, was less or directed at different issues in the first proceeding than in the second, the theory is that, unlike the former testimony exception to the hearsay rule (Rule 804(b)(1)), the declarant is presently on the stand, obviating the danger.

The identification branch of Rule 801(d)(1) exempts from the hearsay rule a witness' former identification statements. This, it should be noted, includes among others, identification statements made on the street, at the stationhouse, at a lineup, or at a photographic showing. On the last, see Berrada v. United States, 45 U.S.L.W. 3349 (2d Cir. 1976), cert. denied 429 U.S. 1091, 97 S.Ct. 1102 (1977); United States v. Clardy, 540 F.2d 439 (9th Cir. 1976) (is a failure to identify at a photo array admissible?). We are always assuming, of course, that applicable constitutional safeguards have been complied with (such as the right to counsel, and to be free of unnecessarily suggestive or reliability-impairing circumstances) which apply at certain line-ups. Such constitutional cases as United States v. Wade, 388 U.S. 218, 87 S.Ct. 1926 (1967), Gilbert v. California, 388 U.S. 263, 87 S.Ct. 1951 (1967), Stovall v. Denno, 388 U.S. 293, 87 S.Ct. 1967 (1967), Biggers v. Tennessee, 390 U.S. 404, 88 S.Ct. 979 (1968), Kirby v. Illinois, 406 U.S. 682, 92 S.Ct. 1877 (1972), and their progeny, defining those safeguards, are not meant to be affected. It is also worth remembering that under appropriate circumstances a taint of this kind may render inadmissible not only the out-of-court identification, but an ensuing in-court identification as well. Congress has attempted in the Omnibus Crime Control Act of 1968 to overrule this constitutional doctrine insofar as it may prevent an eye-witness from making an in-court identification. See 18 U.S.C.A. § 3502. There is a question as to whether Congress can constitutionally do this. Cf., on a similar problem, Gandara, "Implementation of § 3501 by Law Enforcement Officials and Courts," 63 Geo.L.J. 305 (1974). On the status of constitutional safeguards at photographic spreads, see United States v. Ash, 413 U.S. 300, 93 S.Ct. 2568 (1973); cf. Manson v. Brathwaite, 527 F.2d 363 (2d Cir. 1975), rev'd 432 U.S. 98, 97 S.Ct. 2243.

The general constitutionality, under confrontation concepts, of all three branches of the prior-statements-of-witnesses rule (inconsistent statements, consistent statements, and identification statements) seems to be accepted on the basis of the generalized authority of California v. Green, 399 U.S. 149, 90 S.Ct. 1930 (1970) and Nelson v. O'Neill, 402 U.S. 622, 91 S.Ct. 1723 (1971), but even if those cases can be stretched this far, there still seem to be special situations where the adequacy of the opportunity to cross-examine the witness with respect to his former statement is questionable, both under the confrontation requirement and the rule (which requires that the witness be presently "subject to cross-examination concerning the statement"). For one example, what if the matter or statement was not directly broached on direct examination, the former statement being introduced subsequent to that exam through extrinsic evidence (by the counsel who did that exam) at a time when the witness has left the stand? The rule places no limit on how the statement may be evidenced: the witness himself need not necessarily recount or acknowledge it; instead, it may be evidenced by "extrinsic" evidence, i. e., another witness who heard it, or a document embodying it. There is no express limitation as to when this may take place. Cf. Rule 613. Is such a witness *effectively* "subject to cross-examination concerning the statement?" If he can be conveniently recalled, perhaps he is. Otherwise perhaps not. (Remember, as respects these statements, there usually will have been no opportunity to cross examine when the statement was made, so that the only opportunity will be that afforded at the present proceeding, i. e., the proceeding at which the evidence is being offered.) If the would-be cross-examiner knew or should have known, through discovery, of the statement, will it be held that he had an opportunity to examine the witness on it when the witness first appeared at the trial? What about the fact that ordinarily federal judges (under the F.R.E.) are not required to allow cross-examination to go beyond matters introduced on direct exam? Or that our cross-examiner would naturally be reluctant to introduce this matter if it was not in the direct exam?

Similarly, if a witness denies memory of whether or not he made some former statement or of the facts recounted in it, perhaps he is not "subject to cross examination concerning the statement," in any effective sense, because a lack of memory would greet every question. A similar argument might be made—this time with less justification —where the witness *denies* the statement or the facts therein. At first glance, "cross-examination" would seem ineffectual to uncover any information about the statement or the facts in it. But, in fact, the goals of a perfectly successful cross-examination have been accomplished: The witness has repudiated. Thus, in this particular instance, it should be no objection that cross-examination would be futile.

In closing our discussion of the Prior Witness Statements exemption, it should be noted that this three-pronged exemption makes it more important than ever for attorneys on both sides of cases to seek diligently to obtain early statements from witnesses and to seek to find out what statements already exist in the hands of the opponent or otherwise. (Both these points are especially applicable to grand jury statements.) Criminal discovery rules are not well suited to this new premium on discovery, since they provide for very limited discovery. Yet the relevant evidence rules apply to both criminal and civil cases. (On the subject of access to grand jury transcripts for use in civil cases, see Douglas Oil Co. of California v. Petrol Stops Northwest, 441 U.S. 211, 99 S.Ct. 1667 (1979). On access generally, see 55 Nw.U.L.Rev. 482 (1960).)

Admissions of a Party

Rule 801(d)(2) exempts admissions of a party, his agent, or co-conspirator, from the hearsay rule, if they are used against the party.

What qualifies as a co-conspirator statement? As under prevailing common law, the statement must be made in the course of and in furtherance of a conspiracy, by a fellow conspirator. (But see, for a contrary example, Georgia's co-conspirator rule, dispensing with some or all of this requirement as traditionally interpreted. It was upheld as constitutional against an attack under the confrontation clause in Dutton v. Evans, 400 U.S. 74, 91 S.Ct. 210 (1970).)

Under the better interpretation of the F.R.E., the judge determines whether, on the facts of the particular case, these requirements are satisfied, where there is a dispute of germane facts. In other words, he determines the facts for these purposes. Rule 104, prescribing the procedure for all such preliminary determinations, may have implications that differ from previous law. There is a conflict of authority, however, as to whether and exactly how Rule 104 applies and is to be interpreted. The principal questions concerning the determination of the preliminary factual issues of "conspiracy," "course of," and "furtherance" under the co-conspirator rule are: Who decides the issue; what is the burden of proof; what evidence may be heard (does it have to be admissible evidence? Can the co-conspirator statement be heard? Is it sufficient?); what if the ultimate issue in the case is the same as the preliminary issue, as would be true where the case is a criminal conspiracy case (the rule of admissibility of co-conspirator statements is not confined to such cases nor even to criminal cases); etc.? There has always been a wide diversity of views even among federal courts; and even today there is disagreement as to what effect, if any, the "new" rules (the F.R.E.) are to have. The leading views at least before the Rules, seem to have been those in Carbo v. United States, 314 F.2d 718 (9th Cir. 1963) (judge decides; evidence aside from the statement itself must satisfy him it would "support a finding"), and United States v. Geaney, 417 F.2d 1116 (2d Cir. 1969) (semble; except "fair preponderance of the evidence"). Rule 104(a) certainly seems to establish at least that the judge makes the finding, and that the inquiry is not confined to receiving only admissible evidence. Some decisions seem to doubt that Rule 104(a) (governing questions of fact determinative of issues of admissibility other than relevancy) applies, characterizing the issue instead as one under Rule 104(b) (governing questions of fact upon which relevancy hinges), and thus for the jury to determine, if there is some reasonable amount of evidence.

Turning now to another matter in Rule 801(d)(2)—that is, to the provisions dealing with party admissions *via an ordinary agent* (as opposed to a co-conspirator)—the question may be asked, "Who is an agent?" The Rules have broadened the test of agency for these purposes. An employee need no longer be authorized (neither expressly nor impliedly) to *make the statement,* so long as the statement relates to something that is part of his job (is within the "scope of his employment") and is made while he is still employed.

The older, narrower view is expressed succinctly in McNicholas v. New England Tel. & Tel. Co., 196 Mass. 138, 81 N.E. 889 (1907). Under that view, which requires express or implied authorization to make the statement, a truck driver's admission that he was going too fast would not be usable against his company in a lawsuit growing out of the collision, but the company's claims agent's statement to the family of the injured person that the driver was going too fast, would. The authority granted to the driver is to "shut up and drive," that is, not to make statements; but the claims agent is expressly or impliedly empowered to talk settlement, including discussing the facts necessary to arrive at settlement.

Under the new test of the F.R.E., both statements would be admissible against the company: the claims agent's because it is expressly or impliedly authorized to be made (Rule 801(d)(2)(C)), and the driver's because it relates to something that is part of his job—driving—though making a statement is not (Rule 801(d)(2)(D)).[2] If the driver no

---

[2] Of course, driving *too fast* is not part of his job. This raises the question of how general the characterization of what he is talking about should be: *driving*; or *driving too fast*. To avoid this problem, the rule uses the phrase "within the scope of his agency or employment," borrowing the phrase from tort and contract liability and agency law, where it has been resolved that doing an authorized act is "within the scope" even if done negligently or in a wrongful manner; rather than the phrase "part of his job."

longer worked for the company at the time of making his statement, it could not be used against the company, the rule states. This avoids the problem of grudge statements after a discharge that was perhaps motivated by his causing the injury; and reduces the likelihood of improper induce-ments to continue employment. See also United States v. Iaconetti, supra (government official makes company agent his own agent under Rule 801(d)(2)(C) for purposes of making statements, when government official solicits bribe from him and expects solicitation to be transferred to other company personnel).

The Rules appear also to abolish the common-law distinc-tion between statements made by employees or agents to their employer (or to their principal or to fellow employees or to company files) on the one hand, which so-called "in-house" statements could not qualify as admissions of the employer or principal (unless, under one view, they were final reports somehow adopted by him); and, on the other hand, statements made to outsiders, which we have just discussed. Both now seem to be governed by the same tests—those of Rules 801(d)(2)(C) and 801(d)(2)(D), dis-cussed above.

The Rules provide no guidance as to when to use the rather strict co-conspirator rule, and when to use the more liberal *ordinary* agency rules just described, if the situation is such that the declarant seems to be both an agent and a co-conspirator (which, arguably, is *always* the case with a co-conspirator!) [3]. The test cannot be "is the case a criminal case in which conspiracy between the declarant and defen-dant is charged?" For the co-conspirator rule is not con-

---

[3] If it isn't so that an 801(d)(2)(E) co-conspirator is *always* also an agent under 801(d)(2)(C) and (D), wouldn't he be both at least in a case like an antitrust violation involving a conspiracy between an employer and employee or two partners?

fined to cases where conspiracy is charged, nor even to criminal cases. See United States v. Trowery, 542 F.2d 623 (3d Cir. 1976). Nor are the ordinary agency rules made inapplicable to criminal conspiracy cases.

The Rules fail to recognize one kind of agency recognized at common law: the "predecessor-in-interest" principle, which held that if a previous titleholder of property made a statement that reflects on the property, the statement could be used against a subsequent titleholder of the same property, if the previous titleholder made the statement while he had title. See, e. g., Johnson v. Tuttle, 108 Vt. 291, 187 A. 515 (1936). In other words, the one titleholder is treated as the "agent" of the other, for party admissions purposes, though in reality he is not. (The predecessor-in-interest concept has also been applied to other interests than property title.) Although this principle, recognizing such agency for party admissions purposes, has not survived in the Federal Rules of Evidence, the "declaration against interest" exception to the hearsay rule (Rule 804(b)(3)) will frequently, though not always, admit such statements without the necessity of any "agency" theory of attribution. I say "not always," for the following reasons: Although the declaration against interest exception allows the evidence to be used for or against anyone, party or not, without the need of establishing any real or fictitious agency, and does not necessarily require that the statement be made while holding title—so that in a sense it is *broader* than the predecessor-in-interest rule—nevertheless it does require that the statement be against the speaker's interest *when made*, and *be known by him at the time to be so,* and requires that the declarant be unavailable, so that in these senses it is *narrower* than the predecessor-in-interest rule. For completeness, it should be noted that, on the facts of a particular case, the declaration against interest exception may require that the statement have been made while the speaker was holding title, in order for the statement—say, a statement disparaging title—to be truly against self-interest.

Shifting now away from the *vicarious* admissions (those made via the party's agent or co-conspirator) to admissions made by the party *personally*, we should note that one kind of admission made by a party personally can be called an "adoptive" admission. Rule 801(d)(2)(B) essentially codifies the common law concept that adoptive admissions are removed from the ban of the hearsay rule. Adoptive admissions may be illustrated by the following example. One person makes a statement damaging to another person who agrees with it, saying it is true. The second person is held to have adopted the words of the first. The principle would be the same if verbal expressions tantamount to agreement, rather than express agreement, are used by the second person. A less obvious, but still valid, example would be where the second person agrees, not verbally, but by conduct, perhaps by remaining silent where a reasonable person would contest the statement if it weren't true (usually the statement is an allegation or accusation). See generally, on adoption of another's statement by silence, United States v. Hoosier, 542 F.2d 687 (6th Cir. 1976) (defendant's silence in face of girl friend's recital of incriminating facts is an adoptive admission). In other words, an adoptive party admission is a statement of another in which the party has manifested belief.

Query whether an exemption from the hearsay rule need be found under the F.R.E. for the kind of admission by conduct illustrated by the silence example above, since conduct not *intended* by the actor as an assertion (even though it may manifest his belief in the truth of the statement or such belief may be one reasonable inference) is not a "statement" and thus not hearsay under the F.R.E. See Rule 801(a)(2), discussed infra at p. 291. It is debatable whether or not this conduct would be found by the judge, in his power to determine such preliminary facts for evidentiary purposes under Rule 104(a), to be so intended. (There will frequently be this ambiguity about conduct, and that is the problem with this "intention" test.) (Some courts feel Rule 104(*b*) is the applicable rule, rather than (*a*), in which event the judge need find only some reasonable amount of evidence of the fact. But there would be doubt as to whether or not even that lesser quantum is satisfied).

Nevertheless, the exemption for adoptive admissions under Rule 801(d)(2)(B) (statements in which the party has manifested belief) is broad enough to encompass this kind of conduct (e. g., silence in the face of accusation) if needed. The common law requirement that the circumstances be such that a reasonable person would respond if it were untrue does not *expressly* appear in the Rule, but is probably not a hearsay-related concept at all. Instead it is probably one of relevance or probativity balanced against prejudice, misleadingness, time consumption, etc., which would be imposed on the evidence whether the evidence is affected by the hearsay rule or not, by virtue of Rule 403 (general requirement that probativity must outweigh prejudice and the like) or Rule 104(b) (when relevance depends on a particular fact, jury decides whether the fact exists *if there is some reasonable evidence that it does*). Also, Rule 801(d)(2)(B) impliedly imposes this reasonable person requirement or something similar to it, when it says the declarant must be found to have *manifested belief* in the statement.[4]

---

[4] The reasonable person requirement is often said to require that the statement responded to by silence have been (1) a definite statement (2) of fact (3) understood by the other person, (4) that affected him, (5) calling for a reply if untrue, (6) concerning a matter of which the silent person had knowledge, (7) in circumstances where he was able to answer. Another phraseology requires that it be "normal, natural, and possible to respond." The whole requirement, of course, is merely a particularized application of the requirement that any

The analysis of this evidence as an implied, adopted admission on the part of the silent person, is important regardless of whether the conduct will be viewed as a hearsay statement (i. e., as a "statement" *for purposes of the hearsay rule*), because it must be made clear that it is not the speaking person's express statement that is being offered (which definitely would be excludable hearsay) but the silence of the implicated person in response. The express statement is being offered only as a predicate, to give meaning to the silence. For relevancy purposes, the conduct (silence) is offered as indicating belief in the statement —i. e., it may be viewed as an implied statement for relevancy purposes even if not for hearsay purposes.

Failure to respond to writings has been treated similarly in the decisions, and the analysis under the F.R.E. is the same. The "reasonable person" test has usually resulted in a ruling that failure to respond to bills, or to statements of account, are admissible on this theory; and failure to respond to other writings is admissible if, but only if, there have been previous dealings between the parties.[5]   It is obvious that the reasonable person test has to do with what it is safe to rebuttably assume are the likelihoods about what reasonable people do and why (i. e., what they probably mean by their actions). This law that has accumulated under the "reasonable person" test in this area prior to the Federal Rules can be expected to continue. These rulings about writings are the reason for (and probably the result of) the usual business practice of responding promptly to

words or conduct offered as agreeing with or acquiescing in a stated fact or accusation, and therefore constituting an admission, must, in the circumstances, be fairly construable as indicating belief in the facts stated.

[5] Admissibility does not necessarily mean the evidence will have much weight: it is only *evidence*, for what the jury thinks it is worth. This also applies to the silence example and all other examples. See immediately infra.

incorrect billings, and confirming oral agreements in letters on the mutual unstated understanding that the letter will be responded to only if inaccurate, and that failure to respond indicates agreement.

In these cases of "implied admission by conduct," admissibility does not necessarily mean the jury will give the evidence much weight. The jury may find other explanations for the conduct, frequently on consideration of many of the same factors considered by the judge (assuming he does it—see next paragraph) as a preliminary matter of admissibility under the reasonable person test. Just because something is offered and received in evidence as an admission, and even found to be a "party admission" for purposes of the hearsay rule, it is not necessarily going to be found to be admitting anything, by the fact finder in its capacity to decide the weight to ascribe to evidence. The fact finder may feel, on general principles, or on the particular facts, or considering this particular person, that the conduct or words offered have a different explanation.

An unanswered question is whether the reasonable person test is a preliminary fact falling under Rule 104(a) (for the judge to determine) or Rule 104(b) (for the jury to determine if the judge finds some substantial evidence). Rule 104(b) is for preliminary facts upon which relevance depends. Many preliminary facts will have an ambiguity as to whether they relate to relevance.

Other implied admissions by conduct might be bribes (or bribe attempts); suicide attempts; suppression or destruction of evidence; flight; failure to adduce certain available evidence; safety measures after an injury; offers of compromise or settlement; etc., all depending on the facts. Extrinsic policy factors might step in to bar some of these, even if there is high probativity and low prejudice, misleadingness, time consumption, etc., in certain fact situations.

See pp. 296–306.   Thus, the admissibility considerations are relevance, the probativity-prejudice-time-etc. balance (codified generally in Rule 403), hearsay (Article VIII), and extrinsic, privilege-type policies such as encouraging safety measures or settlements.   (Of course there are also problems of *weight* involving a reconsideration of many of the same facts and arguments.)   Obviously, much depends on the particular facts.   The F.R.E. have three specific rules partially resolving the relevance, probative-prejudice-time-etc., and extrinsic policy issues, as to certain of this evidence.   See Rules 407 (remedial or safety measures), 408 (settlement and compromise) and 409 (payment of medical expenses), generally rendering the covered evidence inadmissible, with certain exceptions.   Evidence within the exceptions must go through an ad hoc 403 balancing.   Usually the hearsay problem can be overcome, on the theories discussed above (party admission, or "not hearsay" because not a "statement").

In the examples given above, relating to silence in response to an accusation as being an implied admission, it follows from our discussion of the reasonable person test that the silence will not be allowed as an admission if it would be unreasonable to suppose that it connotes acquiescence, as for example where the silent person is too busy rendering aid to an accident victim to engage in denials, or is a prospective criminal defendant being questioned and accused by the police, in which case there may be many reasons besides guilt for remaining silent.   This is a question of lack of probativity which may be overlooked by the jury (high prejudice; time).   It might also be a violation of the constitutional right of silence (right against self-incrimination and right to counsel) to assume admission from silence in the police situation, even if it were highly probative, not time consuming, and not prejudicial in the evidentiary sense. Cf. Doyle v. Ohio, 426 U.S. 610, 96 S.Ct. 2240 (1976) (impermissible use of silence following *Miranda* warning; impeachment; constitutional decision); United States v. Hale, 422 U.S. 171, 95 S.Ct. 2133 (1975) (silence in police situation inadmissible as impeachment by prior inconsistent conduct; decision on ground of probativity under federal evidence law); Jenkins v. Anderson, 447 U.S. 231, 100 S.Ct. 2124 (1980) (semble; *Miranda* warning not involved; use of pre-arrest silence not unconstitutional if state evidence law wishes to permit it). (These cases generally involved failure to come forward with a defense later asserted at trial rather than silence in response to a specific statement of fact.) See also United States v. Hoosier, supra, where silence in a police custodial situation is distinguished from the situation which actually obtained in *Hoosier*, essentially a private discussion. And compare United States v. Semensohn, 421 F.2d 1206 (2d Cir. 1970), United States v. Brinson, 411 F.2d 1057 (6th Cir. 1969), Fowle v. United States, 410 F.2d 48 (9th Cir. 1969), and Johnson v. Patterson, 475 F.2d 1066 (10th Cir. 1973), cert. denied 414 U.S. 878, 94 S.Ct. 64, with United States ex rel. Burt v. New Jersey, 475 F.2d 234 (3d Cir. 1973), cert. denied 414 U.S. 938, 94 S.Ct. 243, and United States v. Ramirez, 441 F.2d 950 (5th Cir. 1971), cert. denied 404 U.S. 869, 92 S.Ct. 91.

It should be noted, in connection with this entire discussion of admissions, that "admission of a party" means any statement that can be used against him. It needn't embrace more than a minor link in the chain of evidence against him, and it needn't have been against his interest when made. Indeed, it may have been beneficial and self-serving. The only requirement is that it is to some degree damaging to his case now. In these respects, "admission," as used in the law of hearsay, does not mean "admission" as lay people use that term.

Exceptions to the Hearsay Rule

Like the common law, the Federal Rules of Evidence divide the exceptions into two groups. The exceptions listed under Rule 804 require that the declarant be unavailable to testify in court, while those under Rule 803 do not. In general, the exceptions are broadened over their phraseology at common law. And a uniform, liberal definition of unavailability is provided, applying to all Rule 804 exceptions. Rules 803 and 804 also have an innovative "catch-all" provision at the end.

"Unavailability," as defined in Rule 804, is, in general, easier to find than at common law. Unavailability under the F.R.E. embraces situations where the declarant will not testify (e. g., rightfully or wrongfully claiming privilege), cannot testify (due to death, mental or physical infirmity, or lack of memory), or cannot be obtained (being beyond process or other reasonable means; in some cases his deposition may have to be taken or used, a deposition transcript being preferred to the offered hearsay).

Rules 803 and 804 generally list the same exceptions that the common law recognized, but expressed in the new Rules in their most liberal form, favoring admissibility. The rules also have a broad, innovative provision at the end, frequently loosely called a "catch-all."

Exceptions for Which Unavailability Not Required: Rule 803

Following are some of the more noteworthy features of the more noteworthy exceptions under Rule 803:

Exception For Excited Utterances and Related Statements (Rules 803(1) and 803(2))

This exception is broadened over the form it took under the more restrictive of the traditional decisions, to include statements made at the time the declarant was perceiving the event (or immediately thereafter), even if he was not actually excited. The requirements are met, then, if the declarant was actually excited (Rule 803, subdivision 2) or if the statement was made relatively simultaneously with the event or condition reported (Rule 803, subdivision 1). For an unusual case, see United States v. Napier, 518 F.2d 316 (9th Cir. 1975) (excited utterance identifying assailant; exciting event was seeing assailant's picture in paper, not original assault).

A requirement found under most versions of the excited utterance rule is continued: The statement must "relate to" the exciting event. "Relate to" is capable of varying interpretations, broad and narrow.

State of Mind Exception (Rule 803(3))

Under the state-of-mind exception to the hearsay rule as it appears in both the common law and the F.R.E., the following statements by a declarant, reported by a witness who heard them, or evidenced some other way, would constitute exceptions to the hearsay rule: "I intend to kill you," offered to show that intent (e. g., Rosenbloom v. Metromedia, Inc., 289 F.Supp. 737 (E.D.Pa. 1968), rev'd on other grounds 415 F.2d 892 (3d Cir.)); or "I'm going to Cripple Creek tomorrow," offered to show he went (e. g., Mutual Life Ins. Co. of New York v. Hillmon, 145 U.S. 285, 12 S.Ct. 909 (1892); Raborn v. Hayton, 34 Wash.2d 105, 208 P.2d 133 (1949); United States v. Annunziato, 293 F.2d 373 (2d Cir. 1961); Nuttall v. Reading Co., 235 F.2d 546 (3d Cir. 1956); Maryland Paper Products Co. v. Judson, 215 Md. 577, 139 A.2d 219 (1958)). On the other hand, the following declaration would not come within the exception: "My state of mind contains a recollection of Mr. X going through the red light," offered to show that Mr. X did. This declaration is really offered to show the underlying fact (Mr. X going through the red light), not the declarant's state of mind.

See e. g., Shepard v. United States, 290 U.S. 96, 54 S.Ct. 22 (1933).

There is an exception to this principle of not allowing such underlying fact statements to sneak in under the state-of-mind doctrine. In the area of wills and estates litigation, statements like "I made (or revoked) such-and-such will to John," are allowed on the part of the decedent or testator, even if they are, essentially, declarations of a recollection of the underlying fact of making or revoking, offered to establish that fact. The common law (e. g., Atherton v. Gaslin, 194 Ky. 460, 239 S.W. 771 (1922)) and the new rules (Rule 803(3), last clause) recognize the admissibility of these statements for pragmatic reasons.

Suppose a declarant said "I am going with Frank to Cripple Creek tomorrow." Should this out-of-court declaration, reported in court by an overhearer or otherwise evidenced in court, be admissible to prove not only that the declarant went, but also that Frank went? See Mutual Life Ins. Co. v. Hillmon, supra (answers "yes," in dictum); People v. Alcalde, 24 Cal.2d 177, 148 P.2d 627 (1944) (seems to say "yes," but dissent by Judge Traynor says "no;" facts perhaps distinguishable from our example because statement in *Alcalde* was in the form "I'm going out with Frank" used to implicate Frank in the killing of the declarant who made the statement, so that the implications about declarant and about Frank were inseverable; Traynor would exclude whole statement while majority opinion admits whole). For interesting background of *Hillmon,* see MacCracken, "The Case of the Anonymous Corpse," American Heritage 51 (June 1968). The House legislative history of Rule 803(3) states that the state-of-mind rule is not to be used to show conduct of the other person mentioned by the declarant, notwithstanding the absence of anything definitive in the text of the rule. See H.Rep. No. 93–650, to accompany H.R. 5463, Nov. 15, 1973, Rule 803(3). The role of this Committee Report of a single House of Congress in the interpretation of this rule is yet to be determined. For a recent case going contrary to the Report, see United States v. Moore, 571 F.2d 76 (2d Cir. 1978). See also, to the same effect, United States v. Phaester, 544 F.2d 353 (9th Cir. 1976) (trial prior to Rules). Rule 803(3) also encompasses declarations of sensations and the other matters discussed on p. 214, No. (3), and p. 216, No. (5), supra.

Exception For Statements to Medical Personnel (Rule 803(4))

If a declarant knowingly states something that may influence diagnosis or treatment to a doctor he consults for a malady or for health reasons, he is probably telling the doctor the full truth on it. He would not want to risk improper medication or operation. That is the rationale of the traditional hearsay exception covering statements to physicians, which is continued and broadened under F.R.E. 803 (4). Unlike some earlier decisions, F.R.E. 803(4) expressly provides that the statement may relate to the patient's medical history, not merely his current or even past pain, feeling or conditions; may be made to, *or for transmittal to* (e. g., where a family member is used as an intermediary) any medical personnel, not merely physicians (e. g., a nurse or even an orderly); need not necessarily be made by the patient (e. g., the spouse, unbidden, may furnish information related to the patient's treatment; cf. using spontaneous utterance, Watts v. Smith, 226 A.2d 160 (D.C.App.1967), a collision case in which, in an emergency, on the accident scene, the injured, unconscious party's relative furnished medical information; we seem to have come full circle: a commonlaw exception dealing with statements by patients to physicians has been rephrased to dispense with both the patient and the physician!); and, if the Advisory Committee's gloss on the rule is to be followed, may be made to a doctor consulted solely for purposes of preparing the doctor to testify, though he never was nor will be a treating doctor, notwithstanding that such a statement appears to be outside the rationale of the rule. The reasoning advanced for the gloss is that the doctor could testify as an expert and give the statement as one of his reasons for his opinion, under the rules relating to experts, regardless of what this particular rule provided. See pp. 59–61 supra. This reasoning raises questions about the status of statements to doctors consulted for "behind the scenes" preparation of the litigation who are not going to testify, and doctors consulted for insurance or employment-clearance purposes. Perhaps the reason or rationale behind the gloss (that that doctor will testify) means these are not countenanced. (Does the phrase "*diagnosis* or treatment" in the rule cover them?)

Exception For Past Recollection Recorded (Rule 803(5))

This traditional exception to the hearsay rule is broadened under Rule 803(5). No longer need it be shown that the witness has *completely* forgotten the event. (For the older rule, see Gray v. Nathan, 221 So.2d 859 (La.App.1969).) The contents of the document may be introduced even if the witness has some recollection, so long as the recollection is not complete or clear. The rule provides that the document's contents are to be transferred to the jury by reading it aloud, and that the document may not be received as an exhibit, unless the opponent desires. This is to avoid the selective emphasis that results when the jury takes exhibits with them to the jury room during deliberations. (Query, does the judge have power to order that other received exhibits not be taken to the jury room, in particular instances? Would F.R.E. 403 or 611(a) authorize this?)

Business Records Exception (Rule 803(6))

"Business" is defined under the business records exception, codified in Rule 803(6), to include practically any organization, profit or non-profit. If, for example, a social club is thought to be too small or disorganized to come within the rule, the objection cannot be made that it is not a "business." Rather, the argument should be made that the club cannot satisfy the final substantive clause in the rule, applicable to all business records. This clause provides that the records are inadmissible if there are special circumstances of untrustworthiness, a requirement that we would also suppose is violated in a case, for example, where a company offers in its own behalf its own report of its investigation into a crime or accident or other wrong it allegedly committed. But see the contrary interpretation of a similar requirement in Rule 803(8) relating to government reports, in SEC v. General Refractories, Inc., 400 F.Supp. 1248 (D.D.C.1975) (SEC can introduce its own investigative findings against defendant).

Unlike the holding under many previous decisions, the record may contain conclusions, opinions, or diagnoses. The problem has come up most frequently in hospital records offered as business records. Some decisions barred all conclusions, opinions, and diagnoses; others seemed to allow them without limitation; and some drew a distinction between the more reliable kind, such as a diagnosis of a broken bone, measles, or perhaps leukemia (more doubtful), and the kind subject to greater debate, such as that an injury may develop into cancer. See general discussion in Loper v. Andrews, 404 S.W.2d 300 (Tex.1966). A number of decisions expressed more hesitancy about receiving opinions of absent hearsay declarant-experts coming in through a record as here than about receiving them from experts presented live on the stand, who can be cross-examined and whose opinions can thus be explored. While there seems to be no impediment under the new business records rule to receiving opinions, Rule 403 (balancing probativity against prejudice, misleadingness, confusion, etc.) and 611 (giving the judge reasonable control over proof), or Art. VII (opinions and experts), or even the confrontation clause of the Constitution, requiring opportunity for effective cross-examination, or the due process clause, could be such a bar in an appropriate case, especially where the opinion is central, of the more disputable variety outlined above, and/or highly in need of exploration. Notice that in contrast to Rule 803(6) (business records), Rule 803(8) (official records) has restrictions on opinions. See Complaint of American Export Lines, 73 F.R.D. 454 (S.D.N.Y.1977).

It is no bar to admissibility under Rule 803(6) as it was under some previous decisions that there were many participants in the process of making and maintaining the business record, as, for example, where one person observes the fact to be established (e. g., makes the sale), reports it to another, who reports it to yet another, who commits it to a computer, whose readout is offered in evidence; so long as there is sufficient evidence (as part of the "foundation") from which it might be inferred that each of these steps was done pursuant to duty in the regular course of business.

None of the participants in the process of compiling or maintaining the record is required as a witness to lay the foundation for admissibility. It is usually assumed, however, that *someone* from the business, preferably a records custodian or supervisor, is required, though he need say nothing more than that the record "appears to be one kept in the regular course of business," from which (in the view of many judges) a rebuttable inference arises that all participants in the making and maintaining of the record were acting pursuant to regular business duty and that the other requirements of the rule are met. (He need not have any *personal* knowledge of the making of the record; all he need know is the business's "system".) There is, however, authority for the proposition that the foundation can be laid by any circumstantial evidence that reasonably gives rise to at least a prima facie inference that the record was kept in the regular course of business, without anyone from the business appearing (e. g., testimony of the offering attorney's own investigator that he went to the business and was given the record by someone in authority from a records department file drawer, and the record on its face appears to be a regular account record). For a case admitting a business record on facts somewhat like this, see United States v. Quong, 303 F.2d 499 (6th Cir. 1962). Rule 803(6) says the requisite elements may be proved by a record custodian "or other qualified witness." Of course, even if a foundation is properly laid, the opponent can get the record excluded if he affirmatively shows that, notwithstanding the inference of compliance that arises from the foundation, a particular requirement of the rule is not in fact met.

Several conflicts of authority regrettably are not settled by the wording of the rule: Must the first person (the observer of the fact) in the chain described two paragraphs above (i. e., the chain consisting of an observer, who reports to another, who reports to another, etc.) have been part of the business, acting pursuant to business duty? In other words, suppose it is affirmatively shown, or conceded, or it otherwise appears, that he was not? This question is presented by cases where a policeman's report of the facts of a crime or accident, derived from a bystander's or participant's statement (not itself covered by an independent hearsay exception) is offered as a "business" record of the police department, the bystander or participant being in the shoes of the aforementioned first person. A similar situation can be presented by a hospital record compiled in part from what is said by the patient, assuming that the patient's statement (the patient being in the shoes of the aforementioned first person) is not itself covered by any independent hearsay exception such as the one for statements to medical personnel. The better view, which it is assumed is meant to be continued, is that the first person in the chain, like all the others, must be part of the business and acting pursuant to business duty, if this exception is the sole one relied upon, Wigmore to the contrary notwithstanding. 5 Wigmore, Evidence § 1530, at 379, and § 1530a, at n. 1 (3d ed. 1940). The cases under the rule, however are divided—largely because of failure to focus on the issue. Language in the rule which would have made it clear that the intention was to adopt the "better view" mentioned herein in text, was accidently dropped by Congress. See Rule 803(6), Supreme Court Draft, 56 F.R.D. 183 (1972). The congressional history suggests it unintentionally got lost in the skirmish over how broadly to define "business" and whether to scrap the term "business" and include all "regularly conducted activities" (of a business nature or not) as was originally proposed (the final broad definition of "business" accomplishes practically that result). See H.Rep. No. 93–650; S.Rep. No. 93–1277. In connection with the "first person" problem discussed here, consider that the first person who is outside the business may be deemed to be in a joint enterprise with the business and thus part of a common business, in some circumstances; or may be part of another business that is so deemed (or that may qualify for a second business records exception).

For a classic case presenting the "first person" problem, see Johnson v. Lutz, 253 N.Y. 124, 170 N.E. 517 (1930), holding a police report of the type discussed inadmissible. Should there be a distinction based on whether the bystander is under a legal duty to report?

It may be that the business records exception no longer should be used (in F.R.E.-type jurisdictions) in the police records situation, since Rule 803(8), public or government records and reports, a relatively new hearsay exception, is more tailored to them. But the same problem exists under Rule 803(8); and also exists under the business records exception as to all sorts of records other than police records. Incidentally, it is interesting to speculate whether certain kinds of police or government records which are expressly not licensed under Rule 803(8), could still arguably be a business record of the police or agency as a "business." See Complaint of American Export Lines, supra (admissibility of Coast Guard and National Transportation Safety Board investigation of accident is held to be controlled by Rule 803(8), which requires excision of opinions, not by Rule 803(6)); United States v. American Cyanamid Co., 427 F.Supp. 859 (S.D.N.Y.1977) (Justice Department internal memorandum as to antitrust matter controlled by Rule 803(8) not Rule 803(6)). And see United States v. Smith, 521 F.2d 957 (D.C.Cir. 1975) (applies the same restrictions on use of police records whether considered business record or public record). See also United States v. Cain, 615 F.2d 380 (5th Cir. 1980) (in view of congressional intention expressed in 803(8) to exclude law enforcement records offered against accused, cannot use 803(6) to admit them); cf. United States v. Oates, 560 F.2d 45 (2d Cir. 1977) (semble; other interpretation would have confrontation problems). Several decisions go the other way, but they contain little cogent reasoning on the point. See discussion of Rule 803(8), infra.

On the problem of the first person in the chain not being part of the business, see also Watts v. Delaware Coach Co., 5 Del.Super. 283, 58 A.2d 689 (1948), holding that a patient's statement (the patient being our "first person") in a hospital record is admissible for the truth of the facts it relates if they are "germane to treatment." This is conceived of as a requirement of the business records exception to the hearsay rule (as a part of "scope of business"—the hospital is the business); but a better conceptual framework would be to recognize that we have double hearsay ("hearsay within hearsay") in this kind of case (two out-of-court declarants—i. e., the report's writer and the patient)—and that a hearsay exception for each branch ("guaranteeing" the accuracy of each declarant) is required. While the business records exception covers or guarantees the accuracy of the writer of the report and subsequent steps in the maintenance of the report, it does not extend to the patient's statement. The business duty and regularity that "guarantees" accuracy under the business records exception does not attend the patient's making of the statement—he is outside the business. But another hearsay exception, with its own peculiar "guarantee" of accuracy, may apply to him—the exception for statements to physicians. But the motive to accuracy under that exception only operates if the patient perceives that his health rides on his statement, and thus there is a well-recognized requirement, under that exception, that the statement be germane to treatment. Hence, we arrive at the "germaneness" requirement of Watts v. Delaware Coach in another, sounder way.

Another conflict of authority not resolved by the rule is the question whether reports which are not routine, such as the occasional or once in a lifetime internal accident (or crime) investigation report of, say, a sales company, can qualify as being in the regular course of business like repetitive sales records. See Palmer v. Hoffman, 318 U.S. 109, 63 S.Ct. 477 (1943); Mitchell v. American Export Isbrandtsen Lines, Inc., 430 F.2d 1023 (2d Cir. 1970). It is significant that the rule changes the traditional phrase from "done in the regular course of business" to "done in the course of a regularly conducted business activity." The same decisions also indicated that "litigation" was a distinct purpose from "business," so that a report prepared with the former purpose in mind could not qualify. The change in language of the rule does not entirely settle this.

Government Records Exception (Rule 803(8))

This rule provides a far-reaching "government records" exception to the hearsay rule, not widely recognized under previous law. With some relatively minor qualifications, it renders admissible (insofar as the hearsay rule is concerned) three classes of records or reports of governmental offices and agencies: (A) reports of the "office's or agency's activities," (B) "matters observed" and "reported" pursuant to "duty," and (C) "factual findings resulting from" an authorized "investigation." (The letters here correspond to the lettered subsections of the rule.) Difficulty is sometimes encountered in deciding which of these categories a document is in. This can be important because each category has somewhat different qualifications or requirements. See, e. g., United States v. Ruffin, 575 F.2d 346 (2d Cir. 1978), where an incriminating statement by a taxpayer, recounted by an IRS agent in a report, was excluded because it was a "matter observed" by the agency and was therefore subject to that category's "law enforcement" exclusion.

Because of its relative novelty and its broad reach, and because it is a good study in the methodology of the Federal Rules generally, including the role of pre-Rules and post-Rules case law in filling in gaps and ambiguities under the Rules, Rule 803(8) deserves some discussion.

It renders immune from hearsay attack a considerable range of regulatory agency materials and determinations, and can be used, for example, by private litigants who wish to introduce agency findings (concerning, for instance, discrimination, or securities or antitrust violations, or the like) against companies in private litigation. See, e. g., Cohen v. I.T.T., 524 F.2d 818 (7th Cir. 1975), cert. denied 425 U.S. 943, 96 S.Ct. 1683 (teacher allowed to support private claim of sex discrimination, by introducing HEW finding of defendant's sex discrimination). Similar opportunities under the rule abound in other areas where public administrative regulation and private litigation remedies co-exist, such as product safety; workplace safety; environmental protection;

deceptive practices; labor; food and drugs; rate regulation; etc. See, e. g., Elwood v. City of New York, 450 F.Supp. 846 (S.D.N.Y.1978) (environmental protection). In addition, under the rule, apparently the investigative findings of an agency's staff may be used by the agency in judicial proceedings against the company, at least according to some authority. See, e. g., S.E.C. v. General Refractories, 400 F.Supp. 1248 (D.D.C.1975). Of course, the materials can be used defensively, too. We will have more to say on this later.

Investigative reports into a particular accident, crime, or occurrence—an increasingly important sort of report in today's society—are not excluded. Under business records, such a report may be considered a nonroutine, occasional, or "one-shot" matter, and this could cause a problem under some interpretations of the business records rule. Under the government records rule, however, such factors would not seem to constitute an impediment, since, at least on the face of the rule, there is no mention of the word "regular" which could imply "routine," although the report usually must be done pursuant to duty or be authorized. (At any rate, such a report will frequently be the regular business of the agency, anyway.)

(1) *Law enforcement records and the like in criminal cases.* Subsection (B) of the rule ("matters observed [and reported] pursuant to duty") expressly excludes, in criminal cases, observations by "police" and "law enforcement personnel." Subsection (C) of the rule (covering official "findings") in criminal cases can only be used "against the government." *The business records rule has no similar exclusions.* Also, the exclusion in the government records rule, you will note, reads differently depending upon whether the record is classified as containing "matters observed pursuant to duty" (subsection (B)) or "factual findings resultant from investigation" (subsection (C)). The former

forbids use "in a criminal case," presumably irrespective of which side offers it. The latter forbids use of the document only if it is offered against the criminal accused. Thus, if a police document is offered by an accused, his rights may depend upon how the document is characterized. (We will refer to both exclusions as the "law enforcement records exclusion or limitation.")

United States v. Smith, 521 F.2d 957 (D.C.Cir. 1975), holds, under both the business records rule and the government records rule, that police records concerning the case could not be introduced by the prosecution against the defendant (although defendant could introduce them). The rationale is that Congress indicated dislike of the use of law enforcement records against the accused in a criminal case by expressly mentioning such records used in such a way in the government records rule. This exclusion should thus be imported into the "trustworthiness" qualification in the business records rule as well (see business records, Rule 803(6), supra). (See also *Oates* case, supra, under our discussion of 803(6), indicating that any other interpretation might violate the confrontation clause.)

The court in *Smith* neatly avoids the difficult problem of characterizing the particular documents involved as class (B) or class (C) documents for purposes of determining which version of the exclusion applies, by finding the intention of both versions of the limitation to be the same—a libertarian intention to prevent use of police records against the accused, not an intention to disable the accused from presenting defensive material, which might present constitutional problems. See, on the burgeoning constitutional restraints on exclusion of evidence in defendant's favor, Comments, 73 Mich.L.Rev. 1465 (1975) and 9 Ind.L.Rev. 711 (1976); Chambers v. Mississippi, 410 U.S. 284, 93 S.Ct. 1038 (1973); Davis v. Alaska, 415 U.S. 308, 94 S.Ct. 1105 (1974). (Query: could favorable police documents be offered by the accused on an independent ground, i. e., as party admissions of the government via its agent under Rule 801(d)(2)?)

Contrast with *Smith* the case of United States v. Scholle, 553 F.2d 1109 (8th Cir. 1977), cert. denied 434 U.S. 874, 98 S.Ct. 432, in which a Drug Enforcement Administration record showing the composition of narcotics as customarily seized by the DEA was allowed as a DEA business record against defendant to show that his narcotics were distinctive enough to be identified, notwithstanding the exclusion from the government records rule. The two cases may be distinguishable on grounds that the information in *Scholle* was not compiled in connection with this particular case. The language of the express exclusion makes no such distinction. See also United States v. Cepeda Penes, 577 F.2d 754 (1st Cir. 1978) (evidence that there is no government [enforcement-type] record to such-and-such effect may be used against accused because there is no exclusion in the applicable rule on *lack* of government records [803(10)]; though an enforcement-type government or business record, if present, could not be so used).

Another way around the limitation that excludes law enforcement records (in addition to resort to the business records rule as in *Scholle*) was spelled out in United States v. Grady, 544 F.2d 598 (2d Cir. 1976). *Grady* makes an unwritten exception to the limitation: "routine lists" of matters observed by law enforcement personnel are admissible against the accused, apparently in contrast to more extensive or detailed recorded observations of particular criminal activity. Thus, lists kept by police of the serial numbers of weapons found in Northern Ireland were held admissible to prove defendant had illegally exported some of them from the U.S. and made false entries about them in federal firearms records. The fact that both the compiler and offeror were law enforcement interests did not result in exclusion. (It should be noted that the listings were not made specifically in connection with this particular case or defendant, and that the compiler and offeror were separate entities: the police of Northern Ireland, and the U.S. Government, respectively.) Accord: United States v. Orozco, 590 F.2d 789 (9th Cir. 1979); United States v. King, 590 F.2d 253 (8th Cir. 1978); United States v. Union Nacional de Trabajadores, 576 F.2d 388 (1st Cir. 1978).

Exactly what are law enforcement records within the limitation is considered in United States v. Hansen, 583 F.2d 325 (7th Cir. 1978), which holds that reports of building inspectors about building code violations are not such, since violations only carry a fine and are not convictions.

(2) *"Self-serving" records in general.* If the agency that prepared a report offers it in the agency's own behalf (in some context not covered by the law enforcement limitations above—for example in a civil case), is the record self-serving and inadmissible? The concept that it *is,* was developed under the business records exception to the hearsay rule under previous law. See e. g., Palmer v. Hoffman, 129 F.2d 976 (2d Cir. 1942), 318 U.S. 109, 63 S.Ct. 477 (1943); Note, 48 Colum.L.Rev. 920, 925 (1948); Annot., 144 A.L.R. 719, 727 (1943).

Such decisions indicated that a "circumstance of untrustworthiness" may be found where a business is offering its own record in its own behalf, at least if the record was prepared with litigation in mind (a factor which may also influence the determination of whether the record is a routine record in the regular course of business).

Both the "business records" rule (803(6)) and the government records rule (803(8)) are expressly inapplicable if the "circumstances . . . indicate [the record's] lack of trustworthiness." (There is a slight difference of phraseology in the two rules that may make a difference in some situations, but for present purposes it will be ignored.) This could provide the "legal handle" under the Federal Rules for continuing this requirement. Unfortunately, it is unclear under the government records rule as to whether the quoted language is meant to apply to all three classes of records embraced by the rule or just the last. (The three classes are the three lettered subsections of the rule discussed above.) The language is tacked on to the end of the sentence that in sequence describes all three, thus creating the ambiguity. See Melville v. American Home Assur. Co., 443 F.Supp. 1064 (E.D.Pa.1977), rev'd on other grounds 584 F.2d 1306 (3d Cir.) (suggests that the trustworthiness requirement applies only to the last category, and that where there is a choice, a document should thus be classed as belonging to the last category).

Nevertheless, it could be argued that Rule 403 imposes a trustworthiness requirement on all the classes of documents whether or not they are covered by the express trustworthiness requirement. Rule 403 is a general rule allowing the judge to exclude evidence on consideration of probativity, prejudice, time, confusion, misleadingness, and the like. The fact that there are two provisions applicable (403 and the quoted language) to similar effect may engender disputes as to why the duplication was thought necessary and whether there is any difference in meaning between them (for example, 403 requires that probative value be "substantially" outweighed for there to be exclusion).

Despite the beguiling nature of the proposition that the arguably "self-serving" documents we are addressing should be excluded, a number of decisions under the Federal Rules relating to business records and government records do not appear to find anything wrong with admitting them, even when there is no doubt that the "trustworthiness" language applies to their category. As mentioned above, in S.E.C. v. General Refractories, investigative findings of the SEC staff showing securities violations on the part of the defendant were held admissible in behalf of the SEC against the defendant to help prove the violations. See also United States v. Rent-R-Books, Inc., 538 F.2d 519 (2d Cir. 1976), cert. denied 430 U.S. 906, 97 S.Ct. 1175 (business records of the Post Office allowed against defendant); Seattle-First Nat'l Bank v. Randall, 532 F.2d 1291 (9th Cir. 1976) (bank offers own loan procedure manual; objected to as self-serving; excluded on other grounds); cf. Hackley v. Roudebush, 520 F.2d 108 (D.C.Cir. 1975) (Veterans' Administration, charged with discrimination in private lawsuit, can introduce administrative determination of non-discrimination).

Nevertheless, it would appear that the argument may still be open in other federal courts or on other facts. The 1974 Uniform Rules of Evidence, recommended for state adoption by the National Conference of Commissioners on Uniform State Law (and meeting considerable success) are in most respects identical to the Federal Rules. But they do provide specifically for exclusion of this variety of self-serving government document. See also the Maine Rules of Evidence.

(3) *The meaning of "factual findings resultant from an investigation."* One of the classes of documents licensed under 803(8) is "factual findings" that "result from an investigation." Thus the findings must be of "facts" and must issue from an "investigation."

The House Report on the rule urges a strict construction of the word "facts;" the Senate Report rejects such a view; while the original Advisory Committee Note to the rule speaks of "evaluative reports" as being embraced. For cases taking the more expansive view, see Baker v. Elcona Homes Corp., 588 F.2d 551 (6th Cir. 1978) (policeman's conclusion in accident report based on his shortly-after-the-fact arrival on the scene, that the car had run the red light, admissible); Melville v. American Home Assur. Co., 443 F.Supp. 1064 (E.D.Pa.1977), rev'd but this reasoning approved 584 F.2d 1306 (3d Cir.) (FAA report concluding that this particular make of plane had a certain safety problem and containing certain other expert opinions allowed on issue of whether air crash was suicide, in an insurance controversy).

In United States v. School Dist. of Ferndale, Michigan, 577 F.2d 1339 (6th Cir. 1978), findings of discrimination practiced by the school district, made by an HEW hearing examiner, were rejected by the trial judge, since they were (the trial judge said) findings resulting from "adjudication," not "investigation;" but the Court of Appeals reversed, holding that these two concepts amounted to the same thing for present purposes. In United States v. Corr, 543 F.2d 1042 (2d Cir. 1976), defendant offered an SEC release announcing the lifting of a trading suspension and listing defendant's holdings as being in a group available to the public. The court held that the record could not qualify as a "finding resulting from investigation" because it was not a determination of facts after administrative proceedings but merely an announcement made informally during the progress of investigations. (Query, could it qualify in part as a report of the "activities of the agency" under the first branch [i. e., part (A)] of the rule? On that branch see Eastern Airlines, Inc. v. McDonnell Douglas Corp., 532 F.2d 957 (5th Cir. 1976), admitting into evidence a Department of Commerce report to the Joint Committee reporting Commerce's informal policy of inducing airplane manufacturers to give priority to defense orders; offered in order to explain delay of other orders in a contract action on those other orders.)

The business records rule has no similar restriction requiring that the report relate "facts" (indeed "opinions" and

[272]

"diagnoses" are expressly embraced) or that what is reported result from investigation. Can these strictures of the government record rule be avoided by simply using the business records rule where an agency record runs afoul of the strictures, as *Scholle*, above, suggests in another context? After all, an agency is a "business" of sorts, and before the agency records rule was formulated, agency records were often received as "business records."

This problem of a document that seems to be covered by both the broad business records rule and the restrictive government records rule has been treated not only in *Scholle* and *Smith*, supra, but, more relevantly to our present context, in a pair of trial court decisions dealing directly with documents violating the "factual findings resulting from investigation" requirement.

These decisions hold that Congress intended the business records rule to be inapplicable apparently to all governmental records because Congress provided the narrower rule specifically for them, which rule must therefore be taken as the exclusive route. Thus, a report of a Coast Guard investigation of a collision, a National Transportation Safety Board report on the same collision, and (in the other case) an internal memorandum of the Justice Department respecting the antitrust matter, were treated under the standards of the government records rule. To the extent the documents could not qualify as "factual findings resultant from investigation" as required by the relevant portion of the government records rule, they could not be admitted under the business records rule either, even though the business records rule contains no restriction to "factual findings resultant from investigation" and indeed permits even opinions. Complaint of American Export Lines, Inc., 73 F.R.D. 454 (S.D.N.Y.1977); United States v. American Cyanamid Co., 427 F.Supp. 859 (S.D.N.Y.1977). Accord: that the government records rule and not the business records rule governs admissibility of Treasury Enforcement Communications System cards: *Orozco,* supra.   Cf. Melville v. American Home Assur. Co., 443 F.Supp. 1064 (E.D.Pa.1977), rev'd on other grounds but affirmed as to the reasoning on this point 584 F.2d 1306 (3d Cir.) (expert opinion in a government report is allowed in part by analogy to business records rule which expressly allows it).   Further discussion and cases on the overlap of 803(6) and (8) and the use of the former to subvert restrictions in the latter appear above in discussion of 803(6).

(4) *Records which in addition to themselves being hearsay statements made by an absent writer, also contain (recount) statements of other absent persons—in short, hearsay contained within hearsay or double hearsay.*   In both the government records and business records area, a problem of double hearsay can arise if the record contains a report of a statement by someone outside the agency or business, as in the typical case of police reports recounting statements of witnesses (e. g., Johnson v. Lutz, 253 N.Y. 124, 170 N.E. 517 (1930)), hospital records containing statements of patients (e. g., Watts v. Delaware Coach Co., 44 Del.Super. 283, 58 A.2d 689 (1948)), or records or transcripts of administrative proceedings or investigations where statements of outsiders are reported (e. g., *Hackley* and *American Export Lines,* supra).   While the business or official duty, or regularity, theoretically guarantees the reporting of the writer of the record, what guarantees the reporting of the third party, assuming another hearsay exception (e. g., spontaneous statements, statements to physicians, etc.) cannot be found to apply to his statement?

Prior to the Federal Rules of Evidence there was some diversity of authority as to whether and when to regard this as a problem, usually under business records.   See *Johnson* and *Watts,* supra; Yates v. Bair Transp., Inc., 249 F.Supp.

681 (S.D.N.Y.1965); Pekelis v. Transcontinental & Western Air, Inc., 187 F.2d 122 (2d Cir. 1951); United States v. Wolosyn, 411 F.2d 550 (9th Cir. 1969); United States v. Thompkins, 487 F.2d 146 (8th Cir. 1973), cert. denied 416 U.S. 944, 94 S.Ct. 1952 (1973); United States v. Burruss, 418 F.2d 677 (4th Cir. 1969); United States v. Bohle, 445 F.2d 54 (7th Cir. 1971); United States v. Maddox, 444 F.2d 148 (2d Cir. 1971).

The signs are that the split may persist even after the Rules. Compare *Smith* and *Hackley,* supra, recognizing it as a problem, with *Rent-R-Books,* supra, a suit for mailing pandering advertisements, wherein Post Office records containing notations sent by citizens to the Post Office stating receipt of certain mailings on certain dates were admitted to establish the mailings and dates.

While the Advisory Committee Note to original Rule 803 (6) (business records) clearly intended inadmissibility unless two hearsay exceptions could be found, Congress altered the shape of the rule (presumably for other reasons), and the applicability of this portion of the Advisory Note is now in doubt. McCormick feels this is still the only sensible interpretation of the rule. McCormick, Evidence, Sec. 310 (2d Ed. 1972). Wigmore bitterly opposed this view. 5 Wigmore, Evidence, Sec. 1530a n. 1 (3d Ed. 1940). In both the business records and government records rule, the "trustworthiness" requirement, addressed above, refers to trustworthiness "of source" as well as of "other circumstances." Is there any implication in this, on the problem we are presently discussing? See also Rule 805 (hearsay within hearsay).

The government records rule (803(8)) never contained express language either way. Of course the "findings" branch of the rule (subsection (C)) must embrace information from outside the agency, in a sense. The subsection

(B) branch requires that a matter introduced under subsection (B) must have been "observed" and "reported" pursuant to legal "duty," but does not specify that it has to be done by a person within the agency. Someone outside the government may have a "duty" under law to observe and report to the agency. There are laws that require such. Can an argument be made that, at least when this is the case, there are grounds to distinguish government records from business records, with respect to the problem dealt with here, and that such a distinction makes good policy sense?

See also Baker v. Elcona Homes, Inc., infra, where a police accident report containing statements of the truck driver was held admissible as a government record; and United States v. Davis, 571 F.2d 1354 (5th Cir. 1978), where Bureau of Alcohol, Tobacco & Firearms forms were filled out by a company. The documents were excluded as business records of the company because of insufficient foundation as to regularity, contemporaneity, and the like, and were excluded as government records because of the law enforcement exclusion, not because of the obvious fact that someone outside the agency supplied the information.

Transcripts of statements of witnesses in government agency investigations, hearings, or other proceedings present these double hearsay problems. In the present author's opinion they should not be admissible for their truth. See also language in *Smith*, supra. However, Rule 803(8) is not clear, as shown above.

(5) *Additional possible unreliabilities.* In speaking of the admissibility of so-called "evaluative" reports under the government records rule (i. e., the "factual findings" branch of the rule; but there is no reason to confine it to that branch), the Advisory Committee Note to the rule, apparently having reference to the "trustworthiness" requirement and

also to the applicability of the general "probativity-prejudice-protraction" balancing provisions of Rule 403 to this kind of evidence, states several factors relating to the agency that may influence later admissibility: "(1) [T]he timeliness of the investigation . . .; (2) the special skill or experience of the official . . .; (3) whether a hearing was held and the level at which conducted . . .; (4) possible motivation problems . . . . Others no doubt could be added." In addition, Rules 701–705 should be considered insofar as they place some (though liberalized) limits on lay persons and experts expressing opinions and conclusions. They may apply to the writer of the record. (It could even be argued that the liberalizations in 701–705 are inappropriate where, as here, the "opiner" is not on the stand for elucidation and exploration through cross examination.)

Thus, attacks on a record sought to be admitted under the government record rule (803(8)) might center on the record's overly broad, conclusory, or unsubstantiated nature; the lack of a thorough investigation; the lack of a thorough hearing; the lack of opportunity for thorough confrontation of evidence; the *ex parte* nature of the investigation, hearing, or proceeding; a difference in the issue there as opposed to the issue in the present proceeding or a difference in meaning of relevant terms (these differences may be great or subtle, perhaps likely to be overlooked or confused, or prejudicial); the undue authority likely to be attached to government pronouncements; the fact that the report contains opinions or findings of an expert of the sort that need exploration on cross examination (greater restrictions should be placed on the opinions of these experts than experts who appear at trial and can be cross examined); and the agency's interest.

For example, in Angelo v. Bacharach Instrument Co., 555 F.2d 1164 (3d Cir. 1977), pursuant to Rule 403, a determination letter issued by the Equal Employment Opportunity Commission was refused admission, since the letter was issued following an *ex parte* investigation in which the Commission conducted no formal proceedings, the letter was too conclusory, dealing with the ultimate issue, and the issue was somewhat different than in the present proceeding: the finding in the letter was only that there was "reasonable cause to believe . . . .." See, also utilizing Rule 403 to bar evidence seemingly admissible under Rule 803(8), John MacShain, Inc. v. Cessna Aircraft Co., 563 F.2d 632 (3d Cir. 1977).

Going somewhat contrary, on particular facts, to some of the suggestions above, are Baker v. Elcona Homes Corp., 588 F.2d 551 (6th Cir. 1978) (policeman's conclusion after the fact, that the car ran a red light, contained in his accident report, was admissible as a factual finding despite the lack of hearing; the court cites the timeliness of the investigation, the skill of the investigator, and the lack of bad motivational factors); United States v. School Dist. of Ferndale, Michigan, 577 F.2d 1339 (6th Cir. 1978) (trial judge ruled that the lack of subpoena power, the unavailability of discovery, and the absence of showings of expertise of the hearing examiner, rendered a finding of discrimination against the school board, which finding was made for the distinguishable purpose of termination of federal funds, inadmissible in a litigation to force adoption of a desegregation plan; Court of Appeals reverses, holding these to be merely matters of weight); Melville v. American Home Assur. Co., 443 F.Supp. 1064 (E.D.Pa.1977), rev'd on other grounds and affirmed in this reasoning 584 F.2d 1306 (3d Cir.) (broad tolerance of expert opinion in these reports should be indulged by court, in part to harmonize government records rule with the expanded reception of expert testimony under the rules relating to expert testimony (702–705); unless it can be shown there is need to have the expert present for cross examination). Compare Hecht v. Pro-Football, Inc., 570 F.2d 982 (D.C.Cir. 1977) (excludes, pursuant to Rules 403 and 702, written government legal opinion of legality of restrictive covenant, in private antitrust suit attacking covenant).

I should think a strong argument could be made in many cases, at least if there is a jury, that government records made by government experts, are likely to be considered by the fact finder as doubly infallible, involving as they do, pronouncements of both the government and of experts.

(6) *General observations.*   Rule 803(8) (government agency records) is a powerful, relatively new tool. Clients who are subject to government regulation, such as corporations, are the most affected. As pointed out, the rule provides a source of evidence against them. However, it can also be used by them where there has been a favorable agency finding—can be used either in prosecuting a claim; or in presenting a defense (see, e. g., Eastern Airlines v. McDonnell Douglas, 532 F.2d 957 (5th Cir. 1976); Cf. Lloyd v. American Export Lines, Inc., 580 F.2d 1179 (3d Cir. 1978)).

In many cases counsel may be able to resist introduction of government records, whichever side offers them, by arguing along the lines indicated above, or, as a last resort, the same arguments can be used to reduce the weight that will be ascribed to the evidence.

Several of the state codes patterned after the Federal Rules have a notice requirement in Rule 803(8). For example, North Dakota provides for advance notice of expected use of the rule and of certain particulars, and for calling of the maker of the report by the adverse party, where *fact-findings* are sought to be introduced. Nebraska provides a notice requirement for the entire Rule 803(8). The rule itself is drawn broadly.

Query: Does the "trustworthiness" of "source" requirement in both the business records and government records rules license, for example, depositions of the sources who informed the government or business? Rule 806 is a rule that states that all hearsay declarants under hearsay exceptions and exemptions may be impeached. Is this further support for this kind of investigation of source? Is there a public policy or privilege against this? Do First Amendment values get involved? Would information flow be inhibited?

Miscellaneous Rule 803 Exceptions

Rule 803(16) (statements in ancient documents) cuts the time period for documents qualifying for the ancient-records hearsay exception from thirty to twenty years.

Rule 803(17) (market reports, commercial publications) and 803(18) (learned treatises and articles) expand the list of publications that will be accepted as substantive, affirmative evidence despite the hearsay rule. Thus publications of the kind indicated in the parenthesis are not confined, as they were under many older decisions, to the issue of credibility. On the use of a treatise to forestall a directed verdict against plaintiff in a medical malpractice action, see Maggipinto v. Reichman, 607 F.2d 621 (3d Cir. 1979), on remand, 481 F.Supp. 547 (E.D.Pa.). Cf. Hemingway v. Ochsner Clinic, 608 F.2d 1040 (5th Cir. 1979). On safety codes or standards, under these and other hearsay provisions, see Johnson v. William C. Ellis & Sons Iron Works, 609 F.2d 820 (5th Cir. 1980).

Rules 803(22) (judgment of previous conviction) and 803 (23) (judgment as to history or boundaries) provide exceptions for admitting as evidence the judgments of courts, including civil judgments and convictions, in certain cases. They are admissible to prove the facts adjudged, although there are qualifications. Under Rule 803(22) relating to judgments of conviction, a judgment on a plea of *nolo contendere* may not be used, nor may a conviction of a crime punishable by one year imprisonment or less, nor may the prosecution offer judgments of conviction against other than the accused except for impeachment. The pendency of an appeal may be shown but is no bar to admissibility. Rule 803(23) relates only to judgments concerning personal, family, or general history, or boundaries.

Rule 803(24) is identical to Rule 804(b)(5). It is the so-called "catch-all" hearsay exception. We will discuss it under Rule 804, infra. Rule 803(24) appears in a rule where unavailability is not required, and 804(b)(5) appears in a rule requiring unavailability. As a practical matter it seems to make little difference which provision is used.

Exceptions for Which Unavailability Required: Rule 804

Following are some of the more important features of the more noteworthy exceptions under Rule 804, which requires the unavailability of the declarant. Rule 804(a) defines unavailability, as discussed above. Rule 804(b) sets forth the exceptions themselves.

Exception for Former Testimony (Rule 804(b)(1))

Rule 804(b)(1), codifying the exception for former testimony, does not provide that the present and former proceedings need be identical as to issues or stakes. But what is required is that the opportunity and motive to examine were similar as between the two proceedings. This can have implications concerning identity of issues and of stakes. Nor need the parties be identical: In civil cases it is sufficient that the party against whom the evidence was offered in the earlier proceeding be identical to or a predecessor in interest of the party against whom it is used in the later proceeding. In criminal cases, this party must be identical in the two proceedings. In neither case is there any express requirement relating to the other party or parties. The requirement of similar opportunity and motive may have implications as to similarity of parties, in particular cases, however.

Dying Declarations Exception (Rule 804(b)(2))

The dying declarations exception differs from the traditional rule, which applied only in homicide prosecutions. The new rule may be used in all civil cases, but in criminal actions it is still confined to homicide. Neither this nor the common-law result can be justified (as they are often attempted to be) on the basis of necessity. No inquiry is ever made into the availability of other evidence. And certainly the seriousness of the crime and the enormity of the penalty should lead to more, rather than less, caution in the reception of evidence. Is there a need to get the wrong man? The strange line drawn by the rule seems to have less rationale than the common law. The Federal Rule, unlike the common law, recognizes other forms of unavailability than death. But the declarant still must have believed he was about to die.

By continuing the dying declarations rule in *basically* its common-law shape, the Federal Rules of Evidence continue to assume (without any inquiry into religious beliefs) that persons perceiving themselves to be before their Maker somehow "change their spots" and become more honest, and that motivation to fabricate ceases; continue to ignore that persons imminently about to die (or believing themselves to be) probably have enfeebled or flustered capacity to perceive, remember, and recount; and continue the strange rule that the supposed guarantee of trustworthiness somehow ceases to operate in midsentence as soon as the sentence strays to matters other than the cause or circumstances of the death, without inquiry into the sort of matters they are. Apparently abolished is the strange notion that the guarantee ceases to operate if the dying declaration is offered in connection with another death—say, for example, in connection with a prosecution for the death of a companion killed by the same assailant at the same time as part of a common incident!

Exception for Statements Against Interest (Rule 804(b)(3))

At common law, only statements against pecuniary or proprietary interest were included in this exception. See discussion in Gichner v. Antonio Troiano Tile & Marble Co., 410 F.2d 238 (D.C.Cir. 1969), particularly the partial dissent of Judge Tamm. The Federal Rule adds penal interest and statements affecting one's claims or defenses (if not already covered by the other interests). Earlier drafts had included statements exposing their maker to hatred, ridicule, or disgrace. These are not in the final rule. If the statements are to qualify, they must be shown to be against one of the recognized interests (such as pecuniary interest) in the degree required by the rule generally—that is, in such a degree that a reasonable person would not make such a statement if he believed it untrue. The deletion of mention of statements exposing to hatred, ridicule, or disgrace was probably not intended to prevent bringing such statements within the rule, if they can be shown adversely to affect pecuniary or proprietary interest or the other recognized interests in the requisite degree on particular facts. Cf. S.Rep.No.93–1277, to accompany H.R. 5463 (Oct. 18, 1974).

There is a special class of statements against penal interest that deserves special mention: third-party confessions in criminal cases, offered to exculpate or inculpate (jointly incriminate) the accused.

The common law, suspecting their trustworthiness, refused to admit those that exculpate. See Donnelly v. United States, 228 U.S. 243, 33 S.Ct. 449 (1913). Application of this can in certain circumstances violate due process. Cf. Chambers v. Mississippi, 410 U.S. 284, 93 S.Ct. 1038 (1973). The expressed rationale for not admitting them usually was that "penal interest" was not a recognized interest under this hearsay exception, notwithstanding the obvious adverse effect the statement may have on pecuniary and proprietary interests. (The rationale was also used to exclude the inculpatory variety, too.)   But the real reason was probably suspicion of their reliability, which became generalized into doctrine.   Someone in jail, with little to lose, might be induced by improper influences to confess, it was argued. As against this, commentators argued that these statements should be treated on a par with other against-interest statements—that is, admitted into evidence if they are found to be sufficiently against interest.   The jury can assess any unreliability as a matter of weight of the evidence.   The F.R.E. adopt a compromise: The confessions are admissible if they meet the test of other against-interest statements and are clearly corroborated.

With respect to those statements that *inculpate*, an earlier draft tried to render them inadmissible.   Under the final rule, they are treated like other statements against interest: They must be truly and on balance against interest in the requisite degree, a requirement that can pose special problems here, where the motivation may not be entirely self-less.   For example, a co-criminal or alleged co-criminal might make a jointly incriminating statement implicating the accused as well as himself, in order to share or alleviate his own guilt or blame, or to obtain prosecutorial or custodial favor of some kind, or in response to threats from that source, or for some other self-seeking reason.   Where a statement has both a self-serving and a self-disserving aspect, the judge must decide whether on balance the statement is so far contrary to self-interest as to substantially insure accuracy.   Occasionally the self-serving part can be severed off and excluded (redacted).   Where the self-serving part is a minor part of the thrust, another alternative is to allow it in as ancillary to the against-interest part.   See generally Rules 804(b)(3); 104; and, e. g., Demasi v. Whitney Trust & Sav. Bank, 176 So. 703 (La.App.1937).

Of course, if there is constitutional doctrine in this area, it may modify what the rules seem to say in certain situations.

Thus, it may be that a rigid corroboration requirement cannot, consistently with due process, be used to keep from the jury a significant and relevant third-party confession exculpating the accused. Cf. Chambers v. Mississippi, supra, which held it unconstitutional to exclude the exculpatory third-party confession in that case, which exclusion was done pursuant to a state evidence rule something like that described here as the common-law rule. The particular confession was attended by some corroboration, but whether or not it amounted to the "clear corroboration" required for admission under the Federal Rule, which was not enacted yet, is undecided, so that we do not know whether the Federal Rule would have attempted to exclude. We do not know whether it would also have been held unconstitutional to exclude the evidence if there had been no corroboration—a situation where the Federal Rule would clearly attempt exclusion.

In addition, also concerning the constitution, the right to confrontation may keep certain inculpating statements of the kind we are discussing from the jury, despite what the rule says. See Bruton v. United States, 391 U.S. 123, 88 S.Ct. 1620 (1968), holding inadequate (under the confrontation clause) an instruction to the effect that the confession could be used against one defendant (the confessor, who would not take the stand) but not against the other, whom it jointly implicated. This holding was rendered against the background of an evidence rule (the traditional one), applied in the case, that did not allow use against the nonconfessing defendant. But it would seem that the necessary implication of the Supreme Court's holding is that the confrontation clause compels that there be such an evidence rule in this situation, and that thus the new Federal Rule of Evidence that purports to change that rule could not do so as applied to these facts. But there are some persons who argue that the Supreme Court's ruling was as it was only because the evidence rule was as it was, and that there is freedom to change the evidence rule. E. g., Advisory Committee Note to Rule 804(b)(3). Dutton v. Evans, 400 U.S. 74, 91 S.Ct. 210 (1970), lends support to this notion, i. e., that there is freedom to expand exceptions to the hearsay rule to let in this sort of evidence against the nonmaker, and that if the hearsay rule is so revised and the revision is not wholly without support in reason or precedent, the confrontation clause will be satisfied. In that case an untraditional expansion of the co-conspirator rule was used to admit the statement of a non-testifying cohort of the defendant against the defendant. See also Parker v. Randolph, 442 U.S. 62, 99 S.Ct. 2132 (1979), holding the instruction in the *Bruton* situation to be sufficient if both have made admissible confessions.

The Catch-all Exception (Rule 804(b)(5), also contained in identical language in Rule 803(24))

This provision allows the judge to create a new exception to the hearsay rule for particular evidence if certain conditions are met. The present author pleads guilty to coining the misnomer "catch-all" now in common use for this provision. The intention of the rule as finally drafted was most assuredly not to catch "all" or even "most." Although courts vary in their adherence to this intention, Congress clearly meant to leave the vast majority of over-the-back-fence or on-the-street or in-the-halls statements inadmissible hearsay. This is seen in the progress between the draft as it went to Congress, and as it came from Congress in its finally enacted, current form. The two provisions are set out below, together with an even earlier draft, which we may call the pre-Supreme-Court draft. I coined the term "catch-all" for the provision in a series of articles in the early 1970s, when the draft provision was much closer to a "catch-all" than the present provision.

(a) *Pre-Supreme-Court Draft (March 1969). (This language appeared as the opening phrase of both Rule*

803 and Rule 804, in lieu of a final "catch-all" exception):

"A statement is not excluded by the hearsay rule if its nature and the special circumstances under which it was made offer [strong] assurances of accuracy [not likely to be enhanced by calling the declarant as a witness even though he is available] [and the declarant is unavailable as a witness]. By way of illustration only, and not by way of limitation, the following are examples of statements conforming with the requirements of this rule:" [Here followed the list of exceptions presently contained in Rules 803 and 804. The bracketed language above concerning availability-unavailability indicates the difference in the phrase as it was used in Rule 803 and Rule 804. In addition, "strong" appeared in 804.]

(b) *Draft That Went to Congress (Supreme-Court-Approved Draft, Nov. 1972). (The above language [(a) immediately above] was deleted from the two rules; the illustrations became hearsay exceptions; and the last exception in each rule read as follows):*

"[Also excepted from the hearsay rule are] statement[s] not specifically covered by any of the foregoing exceptions but having comparable circumstantial guarantees of trustworthiness." [This, then, is the original version of Rules 803(24) and 804(b)(5).]

(c) *Current, Congressionally Enacted Version of Rules 803(24) and 804(b)(5). (Adopts the approach of (b) above, but amends the language to read as follows):*

"[Also excepted from the hearsay rule are] statement[s] not specifically covered by any of the foregoing exceptions but having equivalent circumstantial guarantees of trustworthiness, if the court determines that (A) the statement is offered as evidence of a material fact;

(B) the statement is more probative on the point for which it is offered than any other evidence which the proponent can procure through reasonable efforts; and (C) the general purposes of these rules and the interests of justice will best be served by admission of the statement into evidence. However, a statement may not be admitted under this exception unless the proponent of it makes known to the adverse party sufficiently in advance of the trial or hearing to provide the adverse party with a fair opportunity to prepare to meet it, his intention to offer the statement and the particulars of it, including the name and address of the declarant."

Although the qualifiers added in this last version are non-specific and vague, it is clear that Congress meant by them to severely limit the reach of the "catch-all." As the progress of these three drafts shows, the history of the provision has been a constant cutting back of what started out as an enormous erosion of the hearsay rule. As each of the drafts was put forward, it was met by cries of distress from the conventional bench and bar, and from politicians who did not wish to cede too much power to the judiciary. Although some such anciently exercised judicial power to create new exceptions to the hearsay rule must be responsible for the accumulation of exceptions we call the traditional exceptions, and a few modern decisions have recognized such a power prior to the Federal Rules, apparently a broad power of this kind is unacceptable to the majority of the modern bench, bar, and Congress. One objection raised was the unpredictability of such a power, and the consequent difficulty in planning, advising on, and estimating the expenses and risks of, litigation. Indeed, even under the current limited version of the power, there are widely divergent interpretations of its reach.

The "catch-all" exception in its current form may be summarized as follows: If special *need* for the evidence and special *trustworthiness comparable to the standard exceptions* can be shown, the provision empowers the judge to create an ad hoc exception to admit a particular piece of hearsay evidence in a particular case, provided that adequate *pretrial notice* has been given, including particulars of both the statement and its declarant. Available alternative proof is to be considered in deciding *need*, and the evidence is to be compared with evidence admissible under other exceptions in deciding *trustworthiness*.

On trustworthiness, necessity, and comparability to other exceptions, under this rule, see Chestnut v. Ford Motor Co., 445 F.2d 967 (4th Cir. 1971) (statement about crash made after crash while in hospital after unconsciousness covering lengthy period between crash and statement; at time of trial, whole period covered by amnesia; comparability to excited utterance or spontaneous statement; earlier draft cited, but discussion applicable to final rule in these respects). On necessity (i. e., is there other reasonably good evidence reasonably available on the matter?), see Workman v. Cleveland-Cliffs Iron Co., 68 F.R.D. 562 (N.D.Ohio 1975) (deceased declarant's statement as to what supervisor did with him is not necessary because supervisor and other eyewitnesses are available).

On the "notice" requirement, see United States v. Iaconetti, 406 F.Supp. 554 (E.D.N.Y.), aff'd 540 F.2d 574 (2d Cir.), holding that five days' notice given at trial satisfies the rule, even though the rule says pretrial notice. The 1974 Uniform Rules of Evidence have expresssly adopted the view espoused in *Iaconetti* in their "catch-all" exception.

Notice goes a long way in taking care of the problems we have with admitting hearsay. At least it does when coupled with an adequate discovery system, adequate funds for discovery, investigation, and witness-production, and a provision like Rule 806, allowing impeachment, etc., of declarants. (See, on Rule 806, United States v. Lechoco, 542 F.2d 84 (D.C.Cir. 1976).) This is so because notice enables the declarant and those who know of his circumstances to be investigated, deposed, or even brought forward at trial, if necessary, by the opponent of the hearsay. However, the risk of declarant's unavailability falls on this opponent, rather than the proponent, as does the expense of investigating, etc., and bringing declarant forward. The British make use of notice in a greater variety of situations where hearsay is used than do the Federal Rules of Evidence, which confine it to this particular exception (the catch-all); and the plan is for more hearsay exceptions, with more notice requirements, in Britain. See British Evidence Act (1968); Criminal Law Revision Comm. of Great Britain, Eleventh Report (Evidence) (June 1972). Canada has proposed a similar system. See Report, Evidence, Law Reform Comm. of Canada (Dec. 1975). Several states have made broader use of notice provisions than the F.R.E.

Can declarations that seem to be expressly excluded from a particular hearsay exception or exemption be brought within the catch-all? For example, consider grand jury statements, or prior statements of present witnesses, that do not meet the requirements of 801(d)(1); or dying declarations or excited utterances that do not relate to the occurence itself. Cf. United States v. Iaconetti, supra. Presumably, they were not intended to be excluded from the catch-all if some *additional* circumstance of trustworthiness can be pointed to (other than the circumstance that brings a statement generally within the other exemption or exception—e. g., that the statement was before a grand jury or that the witness is now on the stand [under 801(d)(1)], or is dying or is excited). What about vicarious-agency admissions that do not meet the test of agency? Cf. id; United States v. Medico, 557 F.2d 309 (2d Cir. 1977). On the "catch-all" generally, see Muncie Aviation Corp. v. Party Doll Fleet, Inc., 519 F.2d 1178 (5th Cir. 1975); United States v. Thevis, 84 F.R.D. 57 (N.D.Ga.1979) (also confrontation clause).

Limitations Inherent in Definition of "Hearsay"

An "exclusion" from the hearsay rule in addition to the above exemptions and exceptions is inherent in the F.R.E.'s basic definition of hearsay in Rule 801 (a)-(c): "Hearsay" is an out-of-court "statement" offered for its truth; "statement" is either an "express assertion" or "nonverbal conduct intended by the actor as an assertion." Thus, only assertive, as opposed to non-assertive, physical acts or omissions are hearsay. [No provision is made for words (verbal conduct) offered as amounting to another (implied) statement that is offered for its truth. The result of this omission is uncertain.]

See discussion, pp. 171–73, 177. Contra, U. S. v. Barash, 365 F.2d 395 (2d Cir. 1966) (prior to F.R.E.); State v. Menilla, 158 N.W. 645 (Iowa 1916). F.R.E. 104(a) assigns the judge the task of deciding if the act was intended as an assertion (communication). This can be difficult and may involve deciding the credibility issue! On the phrase "offered for its truth" ("truth of the matter asserted") see Ch. 3 and p. 186.

CHAPTER VI

FOCUS ON ADMISSIONS AND CONFESSIONS

Admissions and Confessions Defined

Admissions and confessions need not be distinguished for our purposes. The former term is generally used where a damaging fact is admitted; the latter where there is a complete confession of guilt (criminal guilt, usually).

Hearsay Exception

Out-of-court admissions (and confessions) of a party in civil and criminal cases are a principal exception to or exemption from the hearsay rule, and consequently are admissible against their maker unless barred by other evidentiary considerations. This exception or exemption should not be confused with that for "*declarations against interest*," which is more stringent in many respects. See discussion of these matters supra in Chapters 4 & 5. The present chapter will deal primarily with problems that surround admissions and confessions other than the hearsay problem. Some have been touched upon in those chapters.

Corroboration

Many jurisdictions will not permit conviction of an accused where the only evidence is his confession. "Corroboration" thereof is required.

The extent of corroboration required varies among the jurisdictions, from slight evidence tending to substantiate any piece of the confession, to evidence tending to establish (but not necessarily sufficient alone, without the confession, to warrant a jury in finding) one or more (even all) of the elements of the corpus delicti. The corpus delicti is variously defined to consist of any one or more of the following elements, but usually only the first two: (1) the fact that the injury or harm took place (e. g., the death or the property loss charged); (2) the fact that the injury or harm was the result of someone's criminal act; and (3) the fact that this "someone" was the defendant. The rule is often said to be that there must be independent evidence of the corpus delicti; or that the corpus delicti cannot be proved by a confession alone. The requirement of "corroboration" may reflect the questionable notion (inconsistent with the rationale of the hearsay exception for admissions and confessions) that confessions are less reliable than other forms of evidence, but it is probably more defensible on other policy grounds.

The wiser view holds that a confession cannot be corroborated by the same person's earlier or later admission, even if it is wholly separate and independent.

Some courts will not apply the corroboration rule to on-the-stand confessions.

Similar problems to those discussed in this section arise under the frequently found rule that certain (or all) sex-crimes cannot be found on the basis of the uncorroborated testimony of the complaining witness (victim). (Could an earlier, spontaneous excited utterance of the witness—made, for example, to police or passersby immediately upon escape from the alleged culprit—be used to corroborate?)

Do you suppose the jury is told of corroboration requirements, or are they only rules respecting when a peremptory ruling (directed acquittal) is in order?

A distinguishable use of the concept of corroboration, sometimes found, is to use it as a precondition to the *admissibility* of evidence that is considered somewhat unreliable (e. g., habit evidence in some jurisdictions) rather than as a notion concerning *sufficiency of evidence*.

Admissions and Confessions On and Off the Stand Distinguished from "Judicial" Admissions

A so-called judicial admission by a party or his representative forecloses the matter admitted from further debate, and concludes it against the party as though there has been a peremptory judicial ruling to that effect. An ordinary admission or confession (on or off the stand) by a party or his representative does not have that effect, but is merely evidence (though it may be evidence of considerable force, insofar as both the production and persuasion burdens are concerned).

Judicial admission status may be given by law to stipulations, statements in pleadings, attorney statements in pretrial proceedings established for the narrowing of issues, attorney statements in open court to narrow issues, responses to pre-trial requests to admit, failure to challenge a fact through a procedure specially provided therefor, failure to challenge in the pleadings where required, introduction of answers of the opponent to interrogatories, and a few other statements or actions. Occasionally it is prescribed that certain statements made on the stand under certain circumstances, will constitute a judicial admission, but this is rare.

With respect to "non-judicial" admissions made by a party while on the stand testifying, it is almost universally the law that they may be overcome by contrary evidence (e. g., evidence introduced out of his own mouth, or via documents or other witnesses, of his or of his opponent), adduced by either side. Like any witness, however, he may not be *impeached* by his own side. (Several jurisdictions, including the federal, do allow impeachment of one's own witness.) He may, of course, change his story, or make inconsistent statements while on the stand (which is, actually, a form of contrary evidence), with the same effect as in the case of any witness—that is, the factfinder may accept either story or parts of both. It is in the absence of any contrary evidence or change of story that the law may treat on-the-stand admissions or confessions of a party differently than other kinds of testimony. A court may feel that normally, reasonable people may differ as to whether an uncontradicted and unimpeached witness stating this particular fact may be believed; but where the fact is stated by the party against whom it cuts, and it is similarly uncontradicted and unimpeached, all reasonable people must believe it, with the result that it must be taken as established as a matter of law, by a peremptory ruling. Whether the "fact" admitted is indeed a "fact," or merely a conclusion or opinion, might make a difference, since the chances he is in error differ. A similar distinction may be drawn between whether he is reporting something peculiarly within his own knowledge (e. g., subjective intention or knowledge) or something about which there is a greater chance he is mistaken. It is said in some jurisdictions that an on-the-stand admission of a party will be given the effect of a judicial admission where it relates to a subjective factor such as the party's own motivation, knowledge, or intention, about which he would not be mistaken.

Wherever something is deemed a judicial admission, the party might be permitted to overcome that consequence by correcting or contradicting himself; by showing that the admission relates to something about which there is a great risk he was mistaken or inadvertent; by showing that the statement is uncertain, being opinion, conclusion, or inference as opposed to fact; or by showing that it is merely negative in effect or an omission.

Judicial admissions in pleadings and stipulations and the like may, of course, be withdrawn to the extent the law allows amendment of the pleading, stipulation, etc.

Admissions as Proof

The theory of introducing admissions is, of course, that they probably reflect accurately the underlying facts reported therein. If those facts are relevant, the admission is relevant. But that does not mean that there is no possibility of error or falsification between the fact and the admission, for the jury to appraise.

Implied Admissions

> There are many kinds of conduct that may indicate a consciousness (or belief) by a party that facts legally relevant are against him.

If an express statement of that consciousness or belief (i. e., an express admission) is admissible against him, conduct reliably evidencing that consciousness or belief would seem to be inferior in probativity only insofar as there is doubt whether the conduct really does evidence such consciousness or belief.

> Conceptually speaking, and depending on the circumstances, the conduct might be, for example, intimidation of or bribery of, or attempts to intimidate or bribe, a 'witness; other efforts to prevent evidence or facts from coming to light such as destroying or hiding evidence (including doing away with a witness) or attempting to do so; failure to produce from your own mouth or otherwise, evidence (including a particular witness or document) it would be natural for you to produce if the facts were as you contend; [1] attempting suicide while in jail awaiting trial; offering to pay something for personal injury done; safety measures (e. g., repairs, change of rules, discharge of employee, etc.) taken after injury to someone;

[1] Such evidence has similar force other than as an implied admission, as well.

**fleeing; refusal to submit to a physical examina-
tion (or a lie detector examination); silence in the
face of accusation; invocation of a privilege; etc.**

It would be rewarding for the reader to call to mind the
facts he or she would like to know or know more about in
these examples (given just above in black type) before
deciding in a particular case how reliable and forceful the
evidence is; and to call to mind factors he or she feels
should bear on admissibility, which may be quite different.
On the latter, would you confine yourself to the balancing
of relevancy (probative force) and its counter-weights discussed in Chapter I? Or are there other germane social
policies—for example, a policy to encourage settlement of
disputes (in connection with the admissibility of offers to
pay something for injury), or a policy to encourage safety
measures (in connection with the admissibility of such
measures)? There is, in a very general way, a ban on both
these lines of proof (i. e., offers to pay, and safety measures, adduced to show consciousness of guilt or of adverse
facts). Let us discuss this. Remember, however, that in all
cases, admissibility does not necessarily mean the jury will
give the evidence much weight.

Implied Admissions: Offers to Pay (Compromise, Settle)

**This kind of evidence is subject to a general ban,
but there are a number of exceptions, which differ
in different jurisdictions.**

Variously regarded as matters of weight or admissibility of
an offer to pay for injuries, are the facts that litigation is or
is not threatened, is or is not filed, or is or is not visible on
the horizon (the closer litigation, the less auspicious for the
offeror); and that the amount offered does or does not
approach the amount claimed or that realistically could be
claimed (the larger the amount, the more auspicious for the

offeror). These matters bear on the likelihood that something other than consciousness of guilt or of inculpating facts stimulated the offer to pay (e. g., a motive to buy peace, or a charitable motive), but they may also bear on the extrinsic policy mentioned in the last section. F.R.E. 408 makes these a matter of weight, although it does require that the claim be "disputed" and that the effort be to "compromise" (settle), and also uses the phrase "compromise negotiations" in defining the inadmissible evidence.

Statements of fact or opinion made during settlement discussions usually are considered to be outside the general ban that bars evidencing that discussions were undertaken and any offer made at those discussions; unless (in some jurisdictions) it is made clear that the statements of fact or opinion are hypothetical or "without prejudice"—magic phrases that are a trap for clients with unwary lawyers, and which give rise to endless disputes as to whether they were uttered. It would seem that a policy to encourage settlement would include full immunity for statements of fact and opinion (essential as they are to both sides reaching a realistic picture of relative strengths and weaknesses and thus to settlement), but such statements are perhaps distinguishable from the fact that discussions were initiated and from the offer, on grounds of probativity or relevancy and its counterweights. (F.R.E. 408 gives the statements full immunity, on a par with the other matters immunized). Would you except from the ban, settlements the defendant has concluded with or offered to *third parties injured in the same occurrence?* Generally these are embraced by the ban. (But *cf.* the apparently unintentional use of the phrase "*the* claim" in F.R.E. 408. 1974 Uniform Rule 408, and hence a number of states, add "or any other claim").

Sometimes it is argued that evidence of defendant's settlement or offer of settlement with the plaintiff or another is sought to be introduced not substantively as an admission of the defendant, but as impeachment of him: the offer or settlement made by the defendant being prior conduct (implied statement) of the defendant inconsistent with the defendant's present position, it being left to the jury to decide whether and to what extent it is inconsistent (just as the question of whether and to what extent it is an admission would be left to the jury if the evidence were admitted substantively). If the substantive use would be forbidden by considerations of relevancy and its counterweights, should *this* evidence come in provided there is a jury instruction against use as an admission? Does that make any sense? What if a policy against discouraging settlement is the relevant consideration? Generally where the evidence is forbidden in its substantive capacity, it cannot be gotten into evidence in this fashion, either. F.R.E. 408 is ambiguous but probably does not permit this use, since this kind of impeachment use is close to the *substantive* use explicitly banned by the rule (proving "liability for or invalidity of the claim or its amount"). More difficult to answer under the rule is whether a *statement of fact or opinion* made in compromise negotiations, that is directly opposite to the same party's testimony at trial, can be used to impeach him. The rule is expressed only as a ban on the *substantive* use mentioned above, not impeachment.

Settlements and settlement negotiations *between the defendant and third persons injured in the same occurrence* are often admitted *if the third person testifies* for the defendant, on a theory of impeachment of the *witness* by showing possible bias or prior inconsistent position. The jury will ordinarily be instructed not to take the evidence as an implied admission by the defendant. How do you explain admissibility here? (In this situation, some courts follow a policy of admission with instruction, some a policy of exclusion, and some a policy of ad hoc weighing and balancing in the particular case.) F.R.E 408 has an exception to the ban of the rule, in cases where the purpose of the evidence is "proving bias or prejudice of a witness, negativing a contention of undue delay, or proving an effort to obstruct a criminal investigation or prosecution," or any other purpose than proving liability for or invalidity of the claim or its amount. The "bias or prejudice" language would cover the case mentioned in this paragraph. But it is only excepted from the per se ban embodied by the rule. It is still subject to possible exclusion on particular facts under the balancing of Rule 403.

Would you include evidence of rendering aid upon injury to another, in a class with offers of settlement and safety measures after injury?

Implied Admissions: Subsequent Safety (Remedial) Measures

This kind of evidence, too, is subject to a general ban, to which exceptions are made.

F.R.E. 407 expresses the traditional doctrine:

"Rule 407.   Subsequent Remedial Measures

"When, after an event, measures are taken which, if taken previously, would have made the event less likely to occur, evidence of the subsequent measures is not admissible to prove negligence or culpable conduct in connection with the event. This rule does not require the exclusion of evidence of subsequent measures when offered for another purpose, such as proving ownership, control, or feasibility of precautionary measures, if controverted, or impeachment."

How do you explain the exception expressed by the last sentence of the rule, in the light of the rationales we suggested several sections above for exclusion of safety or remedial measures? Is evidence within that sentence automatically admissible, or is it still subject to Rule 403 balancing? Can Rule 403 be used to *admit into evidence* matters *banned* by the first sentence of Rule 407? With respect to the evidence banned by the rule, is the rule justified in expanding the ban beyond "safety measures" to the broader concept of "remedial measures"? Would remedial or safety measures be admissible in a strict products liability action? What is the issue on which they would be relevant? Is "culpability" (fault) or "negligence" in issue in such an action (see the words of the rule)? If a count in negligence is joined with the strict liability claim, could the evidence practicably be admitted only on one count? Does the *policy* of the rule seem to apply in defective products cases?

Implied Admissions: Silence in Response to an Accusation or Damaging Statement

This kind of evidence survives the probative prejudice-time-etc. balance if the conditions are such that the law deems that it could be found that a reasonable person would have responded if the statement were false, and thus deems that an inference of admission (that is, acquiescence in the facts stated) is permissible if the jury wishes to draw it. Over a period of time some of these conditions have become rather abitrarily set in some jurisdictions; hence there may be special rules about failure to respond to writings, bills, etc., and about the effect of prior dealings, and the like. If the silence is in a situation to which the privilege against self-incrimination or the right-to-counsel applies, extrinsic policy may intervene to bar the evidence even if this test is met.

In connection with silence in the face of an accusation or adverse statement, offered as implying consciousness of fault

or of adverse facts, it is generally regarded to be of significance (sometimes only for purposes of weight, but usually
for purposes of admissibility) that the silence was in response to a bill or statement of account or amount owing
(reasonable people are deemed to respond to all false billings); that there has been a regular course of dealings
between the parties (reasonable persons often do not respond to non-bill letters that are "bolts out of the blue", i. e., no
previous relations existed between the parties); that the
statement would not normally call for an answer even if untrue;
or that the person expected to respond was preoccupied with
more important or laudable activity, such as rendering first aid,
or was befuddled, or did not have knowledge of the facts stated
or of the fact that the statement was addressed to or affected
him. It may also be of significance that he was under arrest.
These affect the persuasive force of the evidence, which, as we
have seen, can affect admissibility as well as weight. But some
of them are also concerned with extrinsic policy, a matter
necessarily of admissibility. These matters are more fully
discussed at pp. 248–53 supra.

Implied Admissions: Invocation of Privilege as Im-
plying Guilt or Fault

> This area is beset by uncertainty, except as re-
> spects some applications of the federal constitu-
> tional privilege against self-incrimination. There
> the implication or inference is forbidden. The
> trend seems to be, however, toward banning the
> drawing of any adverse inference in the case of all
> privilege claims.

In considering the permissibility of the inference of implied admission or consciousness of adverse fact to be
drawn from invocation of privilege, two issues are presented: the issue of whether the invocation means what the

offeror contends, and the problem that the purposes of the privilege may be thwarted by allowing the inference (i. e., if we allow the inference, use of the privilege may in practical terms be penalized or discouraged; furthermore, use of the privilege would then itself produce the effect privileged against).

Suppose we forbid attorney and judge to tell the jury that the invocation of a privilege can furnish an inference against the party so invoking. Suppose further we permit or even require (at least if the party is so unstrategic as to want it) an instruction that the inference is *not* to be drawn. Under what circumstances would you permit argument against the privileged party to direct attention to a general dearth of evidence on his side on some issue, when that dearth is contributed to or produced by his use of the privilege? To what extent in trials generally would you permit an attorney to force an opposing party or witness to make his claim of privilege in open court? (I refer to *any* privilege.) Doesn't this invite the jury to make the inference?

Cf. Griffin v. California, 380 U.S. 609, 85 S.Ct. 1229 (1965) (federal constitution forbids state prosecutor or judge to comment adversely on *criminal defendant's* exercise of his *self-incrimination* privilege to *stay off the stand*. Would you say this has an implication concerning his other self-incrimination privilege, the privilege to turn away particular incriminating questions? Or concerning a civil or criminal *witness'* self-incrimination privilege to do so? Or a civil party's? Or concerning other privileges? Might the state law or state constitution have broader guarantees than the federal?)

A former, still influential draft (the so-called Supreme Court draft) of the F.R.E. (Rule 513), and identical Rule 512 of the 1974 Uniform Rules of Evidence (adopted in a

[*303*]

number of states) provides that judge and counsel may not comment on the fact that a privilege (self-incrimination or any other) has been claimed (whether on the present or any prior occasion) and no inference may be drawn from such claim. In addition, it exhorts procedures to avoid privilege claims coming to the attention of the jury (e. g., the opportunity to claim privilege should be given outside the jury's hearing). These rules also entitle a party, upon request, to an instruction that no inference may be drawn. (Would you want it? Is it like telling people not to think of elephants?)

Implied Admissions: Miscellaneous Matters

In each of the instances of conduct mentioned as possibly implied admissions in the black headings and subheadings above, it must be recognized that even if a judge finds them admissible (and, in so doing, may express his conclusion as to admissibility by calling them "admissions"), they are only admitted for whatever weight the jury thinks they are worth. The jury may not think they are worth much. The jurors may not feel the party was admitting anything. They may believe that for the jury's distinguishable purposes (assessing weight) they are not admissions. In making this determination the jury will consider and hear arguments on factors very like those already considered by the judge for his entirely different purposes —admissibility. To the extent possible, the judge will keep his conclusions, reached for his purposes, from the jury. Similarly, just because something qualifies for the party admission hearsay exemption or exception, does not mean it will necessarily be found to be an admission for any other purposes, by either judge or jury (weight).

Turning to another point, in each of the instances in the headings and subheadings above relating to implied admissions, it is possible to conceive of the reverse of the evidence, offered for the opposite purpose. E. g., a failure to flee offered as evidence of innocence (consciousness of favorable facts). Should this stand on a par with evidence of flight offered for the opposite purpose?

Turning our attention to yet another matter, the practice has grown up in many jurisdictions to advise the jury on the uses of particular problematic kinds of evidence, and the area of implied admissions is frequently in this class. The advice seems to be a matter handled independently of the jurisdiction's view on whether the judge may *comment on the weight of evidence.* Thus, in many jurisdictions (both "comment" and "no comment" jurisdictions), if the facts are appropriate, a judge *may* on request (rarely *must*) instruct the jury that evidence that the party attempted to flee *can* (but doesn't necessarily) mean consciousness of guilt or guilty facts (this instruction can favor either side depending not only upon the facts, but on whether the *can mean* or *doesn't necessarily mean* aspect is emphasized). (If any instruction is given, the jurisdiction may require the judge to reach a certain balance between these two aspects; or may tolerate any within a certain range. Detailing of the various motives that may account for flight may be required.)

In addition to advice or comment to the jury from the judge, attorneys' arguments and comments may be regulated. We have seen this above concerning invocation of privilege as implied admissions. Where failure to produce a witness is sought to be pointed out by one side against the other, it is usually held that no attorney comment to that effect will be heard and no instruction allowing the inference will be given, if the witness was equally available to both.

Other matters should also be considered in connection with each of the examples of conduct in the above headings and subheadings. For example, the hearsay problem they may present. See pp. 248–53 supra. And, particularly in connection with *spoliation* (i. e., the failure to adduce evidence), would you ever allow a plaintiff to make out a case (on an issue on which he has the burden) based solely on that kind of evidence? Is it merely a question of considering whether a reasonable person could believe in plaintiff's story on the basis of such evidence by itself? Or is there something wrong with requiring a defendant to respond even if a reasonable person could so believe? Would you allow such evidence to make the difference between a case that is sufficient to get to the jury, and one that is insufficient?[2] Is any of this possible procedurally?

Former Pleadings

The use, as admissions, of statements in, or connected with, pleas and pleadings that are no longer binding, is usually restricted.

Former pleas or pleadings (pleas or pleadings in other cases, whether withdrawn or not; amended or superseded or withdrawn pleas or pleadings in the present case; etc.), and statements made in connection with them, are obvious candidates for attempts to find and use damaging admissions and impeaching statements inconsistent with the pleader's present position. Generally they can be used only

[2] See Stimpson v. Hunter, 234 Mass. 61, 125 N.E. 155 (1919); Mitchell v. Silverstein, 323 Mass. 239, 81 N.E.2d 364 (1948); Wenninger v. United States, 234 F.Supp. 499 (D.Del.1964); North American Van Lines v. Heller, 246 F.Supp. 641 (W.D.La.1965); Jamison v. Sockwell, 405 S.W.2d 618 (Tex.Civ.App.1966). See also Upper Valley Aviation, Inc. v. Fryer, 392 S.W.2d 737 (Tex.Civ.App.1965).

Ask these same questions also with respect to (a) reliance on impeachment of, demeanor of, or disbelief of a witness; (b) unobjected to but inadmissible evidence of various varieties; and (c) jury views. See Dyer v. MacDougall, 201 F.2d 265 (2d Cir. 1952); and Young v. United States, 97 F.2d 200 (5th Cir. 1938), retrial 26 F.Supp. 574 (D.Tex.), new appeal 107 F.2d 490 (5th Cir.)

under certain conditions, owing to various policy considerations (such as preserving whatever freedom the law of pleading allows to make pleas secure in the knowledge they can be changed or withdrawn with no further effect) and concern over probativity and misleading the jury. Admissibility may depend upon whether civil or criminal pleadings are involved; what the plea or admission sought to be used is; whether the present proceedings are civil or criminal; what use is sought to be made of the evidence (e. g., impeachment of a contrary statement, or substantive use; or for a perjury prosecution based on the allegedly immunized statement); was the plea or pleading or statement withdrawn; was it signed or sworn to (verified) by the party or just submitted by his lawyer; was it a *nolo contendere* plea; was the statement under oath, in the presence of counsel; to whom was it made; was it technical legal jargon; etc. See F.R.E. 410. The law varies widely from jurisdiction to jurisdiction and situation to situation, and the student is only alerted here. We now turn to other subjects.

Admissibility Against the Criminal Accused of His Out-of-Court Confession: Federal Constitutional Law That Governs Both State and Federal Proceedings: (a) General Due Process—Admissibility Depends on Voluntariness as Determined from the Totality of the Circumstances

The mandate of the Constitution of the United States (as interpreted) that no court in the land shall admit an "involuntary" confession against its maker in a criminal case, deserves some examination, as there is still an area where this principle, rather than that of the *Miranda* case (infra), will apply to bar a confession. (In this short work, we are putting aside the similar guarantees that stem from other than federal constitutional law—notably state and common

[*307*]

law—since the federal constitutional law, for most practical purposes, has largely taken over the whole territory.)

The "voluntariness" of a confession is to be determined from a "totality of the circumstances" in each case, and a definition of voluntariness cannot be supplied. The best that can be done is to suggest the factors that may be considered by the Supreme Court, which makes its own factual review on the issue. Threats of, perpetration of, suggestion of, or promises not to perpetrate, the following, have been considered coercive (at least when the police were involved in obtaining the confession): physical violence, mob violence, deprivation of food, sleep, or medication, harsh confinement, stripping of clothes, lengthy detention, holding incommunicado from or denying access to friends, relatives, counsel, or other aid, excessive transferring of location, termination of public assistance, loss of custody of one's child, taking relatives into custody, increasing charges or pressing for severe penalties, excessive, lengthy, uninterrupted relay questioning, and fraudulent representations of friendship, confidentiality, or medical help. The significance of many of these may depend upon the accused's education, intelligence, youth, linguistic ability, mental or physical health, and previous experience with the police and the law. Confessions under drugs generally will not be deemed voluntary. And illegal acts on the part of the police of any kind will be closely scrutinized. A second confession that seems itself uncoerced may be considered the product of an earlier coerced confession. Evidence gained with the help of an illegal confession will be inadmissible unless the connection is very remote. These notions also apply where the confession is illegal for other reasons than coercion (see infra).

The rule against involuntary confessions is often said to be concerned with (a) the unreliability of coerced confessions, (b) the fact that where some coercion can be shown, more probably took place, and (c) regulating and "civilizing" police practice.

Admissibility Against the Criminal Accused of His Out-of-Court Confession: Federal Constitutional Law That Governs Both State and Federal Proceedings: (b) Specific Factors That Make a Confession Per Se Illegal and Inadmissible Under a Specific Constitutional Guarantee, Regardless of Voluntariness: Herein Principally of *Miranda* —Admissibility Depends on Proper Warnings

The factors mentioned in the heading may be factors that, under earlier law, only played a role in the determination of voluntariness, but have now become largely self-sufficient reasons for exclusion regardless of what the totality of circumstances may indicate about voluntariness. The specific guarantees adverted to, will normally be, in federal proceedings, one of the first ten amendments to the federal constitution (the Bill of Rights). These amendments apply only to the federal government. In the case of state proceedings, the specific federal constitutional guarantee will normally be an implied provision of the Fourteenth Amendment, which amendment applies only to state governments. Usually, however, the implied provision will correspond to one of the first ten amendments. (In this short work we are putting aside provisions of state law which might produce a similar effect. As a practical matter most cases involve the federal constitutional guarantees.)

Only one situation will be treated here: that dealt with in the case of Miranda v. Arizona, 384 U.S. 436, 86 S.Ct. 1602 (1966). The decision in that case issued out of the Fifth (self-incrimination) and Sixth (right to counsel) amendments insofar as they are deemed implied by the Fourteenth Amendment (due process applicable to state proceedings).

The principal enunciated in *Miranda* has come to largely dominate the area of confessions.

Miranda declares that statements made by an arrested person at the police station cannot be used against him unless certain conditions were met at the station house. Before being questioned, he must have been told that he need not say anything, that anything he says may be used against him, that he may consult with a lawyer before and during the questioning, and that the state will provide him with a lawyer if he cannot afford one.

His wishes on any of these matters must have been respected. No pressure of any kind, physical or psychological, may have been exerted to get him to exercise his options one way or the other. And he may remain silent on the advice of, against the advice of, or without the advice of, a lawyer.

A suspect *might* volunteer a statement without questioning (in which case the rule is inapplicable). A lawyer *might* advise his client to talk. And there may still be room for some necessary questioning on the street and a few urgent questions on the way to the police station without the warnings and without counsel. But as a practical matter, few confessions will be obtained. (The decision should not significantly hinder the obtaining of exculpatory statements.)

Miranda is an interpretation of the federal constitution. The constitution neither states that *Miranda* must be the rule, nor that *Miranda* must not be the rule. On the question of whether *Miranda* shall or shall not be the rule, the constitution had to be interpreted by the Supreme Court. The question was whether the rule of *Miranda* is required by the spirit of the constitutional provisions.

To many people it is not obvious that the Fifth Amendment's right not to incriminate oneself and the Sixth Amendment's right to counsel require that someone who has no police-prosecution affiliation be present to advise an accused in the station-house about what is incriminating and what the consequences of saying certain things will be. To such persons, the soundness of *Miranda* as constitutional interpretation depends upon whether *Miranda* is good policy for running a modern state. If it is not, the founding fathers would not have approved of this construction. Furthermore, the constitution can be changed if it is undesirable in some respect.

Miranda is not good policy if it helps only criminals. Do innocent persons benefit under *Miranda?*

An article in the Austin (Texas) American, June 29, 1966, several months after the *Miranda* decision, states:

> "Since police now know that they can no longer rely on questioning suspects to gather evidence against them, only those against whom the police have been able to gather a substantial case through other means, will be picked up. Rather than relying on picking up and questioning a number of suspects for each single crime (only one of whom can be guilty) and weeding out the guilty from the innocent on the basis of their answers, police will begin to use, perfect, and develop other methods of detection (usually scientific) which will weed out the guilty from the innocent *before* anyone is picked up. Obviously this means that there will be less interference with innocent persons. Furthermore, scientific methods of crime detection are more effective and reliable. It is doubtful that there are crimes that could not have been solved but for a confession, but if there are, there won't be for long, as new methods of crime detection are evolved under the stimulus of the decision."

The author cites to the increasingly widespread use, since *Miranda*, of techniques for taking fingerprints from forged checks.   He states that even in the short time elapsing between *Miranda* and the article, such techniques, perfected and put into common use because of *Miranda*, have enabled police in Texas in many cases to go right to the guilty party and largely abandon former practices of rounding up considerable numbers of suspects for each instance, some guilty, some innocent, and selecting on the basis of their answers.   He states that fewer forged check cases go unsolved, as well, because of the increased reliability of the technique.

The problem of large numbers of suspects being rounded up (and being subject at best to inconvenience) for each single crime, is felt most by high-crime minority groups.

With regard to the last statement in the quotation above, consider whether the real-life crime reported in Truman Capote's *In Cold Blood* could have been solved had *Miranda* been in force.

The article presents also a second way in which its author believes the innocent are benefited by *Miranda*:

> "The decision will result in fewer coerced confessions.   Coerced confessions are not reliable.   They are likely to be untrue, depending upon the degree of coercion used.   Coercion ranges from the subtle psychological pressure that can hardly be eliminated from any official questioning session absent a friendly counsellor, through stronger psychological pressure, to the use of threats or force.   The lesser degrees *generally* only break down the guilty, but not the innocent.   There comes a degree that can cause both the guilty and the innocent to confess.   [Collections of confessions by the innocent, resulting in conviction, are cited.]   It is understandable that individuals expected to solve crimes will often be mistaken as to how much pressure can be tolerated before there is a danger that

an innocent man might confess. [The author notes how belief by the questioners (who are not a judicial tribunal) in guilt, increases the amount of pressure they are willing to use; and how the police are likely to believe the questionee is guilty.] . . . It is often difficult to prove what transpired at the station-house. Aside from lying, persons perceive things differently, especially matters of degree like coercion and pressure; and one accused (but, remember, only accused) of a crime is not likely to be believed as against the representatives of the state. . . . [Thus a mere rule against coercion and coerced confessions is insufficient.] . . . Seventy years ago, the Supreme Court said: 'If an accused person be asked to explain his apparent connection with a crime under investigation, the ease with which the questions put to him may assume an inquisitorial character, the temptation to press the witness unduly, to browbeat him if he be timid or reluctant, to push him into a corner, and to entrap him into fatal contradictions [is great].' It is easy to see that the presence of a friendly lawyer in the stationhouse eases the *inherent* pressure, curbs excesses, and provides an additional witness."

But is *Miranda* the only way to safeguard against the dangers? Wouldn't it be sufficient to have a rule requiring substantial corroboration of a confession before it could be admitted—e. g., that the gun, which only the killer could locate, was found where the confession said it was buried? Would there still be danger to innocent persons, under such a rule? The article has this to say:

"Remember that many persons picked up for questioning are released as innocent shortly thereafter. These people are questioned in the hopes that a confession that can be corroborated will be obtained.

Eventually perhaps some one among them does so confess. But the others, the innocent ones, will have suffered at best a harrowing questioning session, and at worst, coercion. Often these are the very persons upon whom the police must rely for leads in other cases. In any event, they are citizens upon whose respect law and order ultimately depend. The presence of a friendly lawyer at all questioning sessions considerably improves the situation."

Does the article at large seem to assume that persons in police and prosecution work have bad motives or are incompetent? Or does it assume that they are, like all of us, trying to do their particular jobs well, which sometimes leads to excesses and forgetfulness of concerns of society that are not in the police-prosecutor province? Or does it merely assume that human beings generally tend to select the easiest way to get a job done?

Do the arguments in the article rely to any extent on any notion that criminals (or minor criminals, or those acting in extenuating circumstances) have a right to have their human dignity accorded some respect? Would such a notion be wholly concerned with solicitude for the criminal? Or might it be concerned with facilitating rehabilitation, and providing a good example for respect for the rights of others generally?

Does harsh treatment in the station-house add to the legislatively prescribed punishment for the crime?

Can a person (guilty or innocent) intelligently bargain and trade-off with the police or prosecutorial officials, without a lawyer to assess the relative strengths of the cases for and against him on various charges? Does the furnishing of a lawyer come too late after a prosecution is instituted? Is plea bargaining effectively foreclosed by an

[314]

earlier confession? Is it proper to consider plea bargaining and trade-offs?[3]

Following *Miranda,* occasionally some police were officially instructed that *Miranda* warnings are necessary only upon arrest. They were therefore urged that when they take a suspect into custody, they "detain" him without "arresting" him, until they have completed their questioning and investigation. Can *Miranda* be thus avoided? What is meant by "detaining" rather than "arresting?" Is it merely a matter of not making an entry in an arrest book? Not moving him to the station-house? Certain instructions to some police indicated that there can be "detention" at the station-house as well as on the street. Should *Miranda* and other regulations of interrogation apply whenever "suspicion has focused" on the person, or only upon "arrest?" What about before suspicion has focused? Cf. United States v. Jiminez, 602 F.2d 139 (7th Cir. 1979). What about statements given without interrogation? Or taken at the suspect's home without significant restraint? Cf. Mathis v. United States, 391 U.S. 1, 88 S.Ct. 1503 (1968) (*Miranda* applies to routine tax investigation while prisoner in custody on another charge, though interrogator not the custodian). How much is required for "interrogation?" Suppose the police merely mention that children might find the gun, and this stimulates a confession as to where it is located, to avoid children getting hurt. Is this a "volunteered" statement, admissible regardless of whether warnings were given? Cf. Rhode Island v. Innis, 446 U.S. 291, 100 S.Ct. 1682 (1980). Can a statement of an accused obtained in violation of *Miranda* be used to impeach him when he takes the stand and testifies to the contrary of the statement? See Harris v. New

---

[3] The author of the present book is also the author of the above quoted article. I wished, however, to present it here as a matter for the reader's consideration, rather than as a solution.

York, 401 U.S. 222, 91 S.Ct. 643 (1971); Oregon v. Hass, 420 U.S. 714, 95 S.Ct. 1215 (1975). Should this be treated differently than an involuntary confession, in this respect? See People v. Underwood, 61 Cal.2d 113, 37 Cal.Rptr. 313, 389 P.2d 937 (1964).

Section 701 of Title II of the Omnibus Crime Control and Safe Streets Act of 1968, 18 U.S.C.A. § 3501, "repeals" *Miranda* insofar as it applies to admissibility of evidence in United States and District of Columbia prosecutions, relegating confessions there principally to a test of voluntariness and making compliance with *Miranda* a factor to consider in determining voluntariness and weight. Can a constitutional decision be thus overcome?

Admissibility Against the Criminal Accused of His Out-of-Court Confession: Law Applicable Only to Officers and Proceedings of a Particular Jurisdiction: McNabb-Mallory Type Rules—Admissibility Depends on Speedy Presentment

In addition to the above requirements, federal courts in federal criminal cases in the past excluded confessions gained during "unnecessary delay" in bringing the accused before a commissioner or magistrate after his arrest by federal officers. The purpose of so presenting him to a judicial official was and is to set bail, set the date for a preliminary hearing (to determine if there is a sufficient case to hold him further) and to judicially inform him of his various rights. The prohibition of "unnecessary delay" appeared and still appears in Federal Rule of Civil Procedure 5(a); but the consequence of exclusion of evidence was judicial gloss and not expressly in the rule. Other evidence than a confession was also suppressible under the gloss if gained as a proximate result of the unnecessary delay or of a tainted confession. "Unnecessary" has often meant not more than a few hours (and sometimes less) except in extraordinary circumstances. Would night-time arrest be such a circumstance, or do you suppose a commissioner or magistrate is expected to be on duty? Do you suppose interrogation vel non was an issue under the exclusionary gloss? Do you suppose it was relevant whether the confession took place early, before the delay reached its illegal proportions? Do you suppose the confession must have "resulted from" the delay?

As noted, exclusion of confessions was judicial gloss placed upon the rule by McNabb v. United States, 318 U.S. 332, 63 S.Ct. 608 (1943) and Mallory v. United States, 354 U.S. 449, 77 S.Ct. 1356 (1957), pursuant to the Supreme Court's supervisory power over federal proceedings, federal officers, and the interpretation of federal rules. Many states have provisions similar to the rule, a few of which have been interpreted to require exclusion of evidence, and most of which are not interpreted to require quite such speedy presentment to a magistrate.

What was the purpose of a McNabb-Mallory type gloss before *Miranda?* After? It should be noted that one of the principal functions of the magistrate or commissioner upon presentment has been the advising of the accused of his rights, such as the right to remain silent and to have counsel, and often, arranging for counsel. See Federal Rule of Criminal Procedure 5(c). Was the McNabb-Mallory gloss designed to minimize temptation to and opportunity for intimidation and coercion? Was it necessary because of the difficulty of showing the intimidation or coercion that often takes place? If these are the reasons, why didn't the court ban *all* confessions received before presentment to the judicial official, or before presence of (or express waiver of) counsel? Are *McNabb, Mallory, Miranda,* and other rules of suppression of fruits of police illegality (like illegal searches and seizures and wiretapping), merely a socially costly way of enforcing discipline on the police? Are there other ways? Does the Court's logic lead to a ban on all pre-trial confessions, except guilty pleas taken under rigorous safeguards? Or at least a ban on all damaging pre-trial statements given in response to interrogation?

Section 701 of Title II of the Omnibus Crime Control and Safe Streets Act of 1968, 18 U.S.C.A. § 3501, "repeals" the McNabb-Mallory gloss in United States and District of Columbia prosecutions, relegating delay in presentment to whatever other civil and criminal remedies there may be, and to the position of being one factor in the determination of the voluntariness and the weight of a confession, unless the delay is greater than 6 hours and is without reasonable justification, in which event, apparently, the confession is to be excluded.[4] Since *McNabb* and *Mallory* seem at least at present to be only interpretations of a Federal Rule of Criminal Procedure or exercises of the Court's supervisory power, rather than constitutional doctrine, the 1968 Act's provision, it would seem for now, can withstand challenge in court. The 1968 Act, of course, does not affect state practice.

[4] The McNabb-Mallory rule as applied in the District of Columbia had been modified earlier by Congress along similar lines, providing a period of 3 rather than 6 hours and conditioning it on the proviso that the warnings "required by law" were given. See Title III, District of Columbia Crime and Criminal Procedure Act of Dec. 27, 1967, P.L. 90–226, 81 Stat. 734, now apparently superseded by the 1968 Omnibus Crime Control and Safe Streets Act. In 1967 the police and prosecutors in D. C. were taking the position (see supra, p. 315) that a detention was different than an arrest, so that if a mere detention were involved, no warnings were required and neither the McNabb-Mallory nor the 1967 D. C. Crime and Criminal Procedure Act limit on permissible delay between arrest and presentment would apply. Is this a tenable position? Could a similar argument be made to avoid the 6-hour limit under the 1968 Act?

The repeal of McNabb-Mallory by the 1968 Act was not inspired by the thought that *Miranda* rendered McNabb-Mallory unnecessary, inasmuch as the same Act also attempts repeal of *Miranda*.

What would be the effect of the Federal Rules of Evidence on a supervisory exclusionary principle like the McNabb-Mallory doctrine? What would it mean that it is not expressly mentioned in the text of the F.R.E.? See discussion of the exclusivity of the F.R.E. at pp. 4–6, note 1, supra.

CHAPTER VII

IMPEACHMENT OF WITNESSES

Impeachment: Some General Principles

"Impeachment" is the term for attacks on the credibility of witnesses.

"Impeachment" encompasses attempts to show lying, mistake, poor memory, inept reporting, perceptual, recollective or reportorial defects or incapacities, obstructions of perception, or any other factor, innocent or not, increasing the likelihood that the facts vary from the story perceived or told. The terms "veracity," "credibility," "truthfulness," "falsehood," etc., and their opposites, as used herein, are also each meant to encompass all these factors and not merely purposeful deception. Evidence adduced for impeachment purposes is often distinguished from the more affirmative, principal kind of evidence in a case ("substantive" evidence). The distinction can be drawn on the basis of whether the evidence is designed primarily to operate by means of lessening the personal credibility of a witness.

In general, the rules governing the impeachment of party and non-party witnesses are the same.

However, notwithstanding the principle in black letters here, where there is discretion, courts are especially careful to see that a party-witness' substantive case is not undeservedly prejudiced under the guise of impeachment of him, e. g., where the witness is the defendant in a criminal case and his impeachment is attempted by showing his bad character (propensity for falsehood). More will be said about this later.

Impeachment of an opponent's witness may take place upon cross examination of the witness, or through the introduction of so-called "extrinsic" evidence.

Extrinsic impeachment evidence is evidence elicited not on cross examination (from the witness' own mouth or suggested by the cross examiner) but rather through the introduction of the testimony of independent witnesses (or perhaps tangible evidence such as documents) directed at attacking the credibility of the witness being impeached. Extrinsic impeachment evidence is normally introduced at the stage in the litigation when it next becomes the impeacher's turn to put on his case, rather than during or immediately following the examination or cross examination of the witness to be impeached.

Sometimes a particular statement made by a witness is to be the focus of impeachment, and the emphasis is not primarily on discrediting the person generally. (See, e. g., contradiction and inconsistency, infra.)

The statement (whether it is to be impeached on cross examination or with extrinsic evidence) may have been made by the witness during either his direct or his cross examination, and it may or may not have been elicited by the examiner (statements are frequently volunteered). In general, it makes no difference.

Under the traditional rule still prevailing in many jurisdictions (but not those following the F.R.E. or the 1974 Uniform Rules), you may not impeach a witness you yourself have called, unless he is "adverse" (ordinarily this means he must be an adverse party) or the testimony to be impeached both surprises and damages you beyond merely failing to help.

"Surprise" generally means that the witness maintained otherwise before trial and gave no notice, actual or constructive, of a change of heart. The requirement of some positive or affirmative damage is more difficult. If your witness turns coat and now disclaims knowledge of the occurrence in controversy, he is regarded as failing to give helpful testimony, but not as providing affirmatively damaging testimony. It is otherwise if he still reports observing the occurrence but states what transpired quite differently now.

If the trial judge retains his common law power to call witnesses of his own, a party may get around the rule against impeaching his own witness by inducing the judge to call him, in which event both parties may examine, cross examine, and impeach. Compare Young v. United States, 97 F.2d 200 (5th Cir. 1938), retried 26 F.Supp. 574 (D.Tex.), re-appealed 107 F.2d 490 (5th Cir.), with Dyer v. MacDougall, 201 F.2d 265 (2d Cir. 1952).

While one ordinarily may not impeach his own witness, he may *contradict* him. Since contradiction can conceivably be regarded as a form of impeachment (see infra), this requires explaining. What it means is that a party may introduce evidence of substantive facts (i. e., facts relevant to the legal issues in the case) that are at variance with the substantive facts as reported by another of his own witnesses, but he may not more directly attack the perception, memory, honesty, knowledge, consistency, or reportorial powers of the witness.

The rule against impeaching one's own witness will not preclude reasonable efforts on direct examination to "refresh the witness' memory" or "awaken his conscience," perhaps by reference to former statements of the witness that conflict with the present testimony, so long as the ostensible purpose is not to discredit.

(It may be well to recall here, when we are talking about impeaching or "bringing around" your own witness, the situations where one is permitted to prompt his own witness with leading questions, viz., when the witness is hostile, or cannot remember, or seems to remember something contrary to what he has induced counsel to expect, or must be specially directed to the matter inquired into. In situations where there seems to be a relatively minor danger of the witness distorting truth to please the examiner, or where there is special need, leading questions are permitted. Thus, they are widely permitted upon cross examination of opponents' witnesses or on direct examination where one has called the adverse party or perhaps a witness associated with an adverse party, or a witness who is hostile. Cf. F.R.E. Rule 611(c).)

The F.R.E. and the 1974 Uniform Rules, and rules patterned after them, allow impeachment of one's own witness as freely as any other witness. See Rule 607.

With that preliminary discussion, we now proceed to the principal kinds of impeachment or lines of attack on credibility of witnesses.

Lines of Attack: (1) Proving Statements Made Prior to the Present Hearing by the Witness-to-Be-Impeached Which Conflict or Tend to Conflict with His Present Testimony (Hereinafter Referred to as "Prior Inconsistent Statements")

These statements are usually proved up by testimony of someone who overheard them, or by documentary proof, or by the witness admitting, upon cross exam, to having made them. If offered as evidence that they are true (i. e., as substantive evidence) they would in most cases under the traditional system be inadmissible as hearsay for which no exception or exemption would be available. (But see F.R.E.

801(d)(1)(A)—partly expanded in the 1974 Uniform Rule of similar number which has been adopted in a number of states—that makes a limited inroad on this as discussed at pp. 235–37 supra. The inroad under the Federal Rule applies only if the former statement was made at a proceeding under oath subject to perjury penalties. The Uniform Rule in civil cases applies the inroad regardless of this condition). When offered as impeachment, however, they are admissible, even under the traditional system, despite any danger of misuse by the jury for the impermissible substantive purpose just mentioned. (Impeachment use is outside the definition of hearsay, under the "truth of the matter asserted" concept or whatever equivalent concept the jurisdiction uses.) It is considered a sufficient safeguard, that when the prior statement is admitted (and admissible) only as impeachment, the trial judge, if requested, must instruct the jury as to the only permissible usage; and the attorney offering the prior statement will not be permitted to argue its impermissible capacity to the jury. The jury is instructed that the statement can cast doubt on each of the two statements made by the witness, create a doubt as to which is true, and shake confidence in one who tells inconsistent stories, but it cannot be credited or taken as evidence of the facts related in it (always assuming that we are not in a jurisdiction and situation covered by a rule such as F.R.E. 801(d)(1)(A) or other hearsay exemption or exception). Whether and to what extent the statement has these impeaching effects is left up to the jury. It is doubtful that the limiting instruction makes sense, especially to a jury, and its efficacy is extremely questionable. The most that can be done is to caution the jury about possible probative infirmities in connection with the prior statement, and while the traditional instruction may obliquely achieve some such effect, an instruction more expressly fashioned for that purpose would be more heeded because more comprehensible.   (The impracticality of the distinction has been a principal argument for broadening the traditional rule, to allow both substantive and impeachment use.)

If the prior statement is the only evidence of an essential fact, the ban on substantive use will mean the case of the party with the burden fails.   The result is similar if the other evidence of the fact would be insufficient without the prior statement.   See Dyer v. MacDougall, 201 F.2d 265 (2d Cir. 1952).   But compare the Young v. United States chain of litigation, 97 F.2d 200 (5th Cir. 1938), retried 26 F.Supp. 574 (D.Tex.), re-appealed 107 F.2d 490 (5th Cir.).

To be admissible as impeachment, the prior statement need not actually be logically inconsistent (that is, irreconcilable) with the present testimony.   It need only *seem* or *tend* to be somewhat contrary.   It need only be such that a reasonable juror might find that it tended in some significant degree to impeach, unless the danger of unwarranted prejudice, misleading impression, time consumption, or confusion is deemed great.   It is for the jury to decide if and how inconsistent the statement is—what impeachment weight it has.   (Under the F.R.E. and similar state codes this matter as respects impeachment is governed only by the general provisions of Rules 401–403, dealing generally with balancing relevancy and its counterweights, as supplemented by Rule 104(b) providing for jury determination of facts upon which relevance depends.   Thus, the traditional common-law principles, concerning this kind of impeachment, discussed here, arising as they do from 401–403 and 104(b) type considerations of previous law, are continued under the F.R.E. and its progeny, despite failure to mention the matter specifically under any rule.)

Suppose a collision has taken place between a car and a truck.   In the personal injury litigation arising therefrom, a witness testifies for the trucker, stating certain facts as true which tend to exculpate the trucker: that the truck was proceeding at 20 m. p. h. on the correct side of the road, etc., etc. On a former occasion following the accident, the witness had said, "The truck was to blame." The former statement is not actually logically inconsistent with the present testimony. The two are reconcilable. They are not totally opposite each other. Nevertheless the former statement is admissible as impeachment. (Notice this is true despite what would seem to be a violation of the rule against opinions, especially those opinions sounding of legal conclusions. The opinion ban is lifted for impeachment by prior inconsistent statement, presumably because the opinion is for impeachment purposes and not to be credited, and also because application of the opinion rule would work a total exclusion rather than the rephrasing it would normally work. A similar relaxation often takes place for a similar reason where hearsay is admitted substantively under an exception to the hearsay rule.)

Whether a similar definition of "inconsistent" obtains in the case of prior inconsistent statements admissible *substantively* under rules like F.R.E. 801(d)(1)(A) is somewhat problematical and beyond the scope of the present discussion, which is confined to impeachment. On that matter, see pp. 237–38 supra.

It should be noted that in federal criminal trials, Rule 26.2 of the Federal Rules of Criminal Procedure, whose constitutionality has yet to be determined, provides that each side is entitled to have access to written statements, and reports of statements, of witnesses for the other side, that are in the possession of that other side, and that relate to the witness' testimony. Such right to access is accorded at the time that the witness testifies (as opposed to in advance). What constitutes a statement or report thereof is defined so as to get at substantially verbatim writings and avoid judgmental writings of the statement-taker. The judge is to make a

[*326*]

determination of whether it relates to the testimony. The primary purpose is to uncover, for use at trial in accord with the principles described above, prior inconsistent statements. The rule is modelled on the Jencks Act, 18 U.S.C.A. § 3500, which codified and limited earlier case authority; and gave the right only to the defense. Some states have similar provisions or cases.

The Required Manner of Introducing the Former Statement

We will refer to all impeachment statements of the kind described in the last subsection of our text, as prior inconsistent statements, realizing that they need not be totally or logically inconsistent or irreconcilable.

In traditional jurisdictions the following procedure must be followed by an attorney who seeks to impeach with a prior inconsistent oral statement.

> **A foundation must be laid on cross examination of the witness who is to be impeached by his prior oral inconsistent statement. In this context this means, in traditional jurisdictions, that the impeaching attorney must on cross examination ask the witness he seeks to impeach whether (1) he made such-and-such a statement (2) to such-and-such a person (3) at such-and-such a time and (4) at such-and-such a place. Of course the attorney must be referring to the prior inconsistent statement that is to be used.**

The purpose of the foundation is to furnish the witness with specific enough information about the former statement so that he can recall. If the witness admits having made the statement, the impeaching attorney cannot press the matter any further: he cannot adduce any extrinsic evidence of the prior inconsistent statement. If the witness admits having made the statement but offers an explanation for the apparent inconsistency (for example, that the former statement was a joke or was merely signed by him unread, having been prepared by another), the explanation will be permitted, for what the jury thinks it is worth. The impeaching attorney may not be permitted to attempt any rebuttal of the explanation, at least with extrinsic evidence, although there is some discretion on the part of the trial judge. (Similarly, the explanation ordinarily must be made *by the witness* during his *cross examination,* if it is to be made at all; but there is some discretion to allow extrinsic explanation. So, too, is there discretion concerning the allowability of extrinsic rebuttal of an allowed extrinsic explanation.) If the witness denies having made the statement, or states that he doesn't remember whether he did or not, the attorney may, but need not ever, prove up the statement and its making with extrinsic evidence such as a witness who overheard it. (Normally, if the attorney is going to so prove, he must wait until it is his turn to put on witnesses and evidence). The attorney will not be allowed to prove up the statement unless the witness-to-be-impeached has first been given the opportunity just described, during his cross examination. There is temptation here for dishonest practice by unscrupulous attorneys. On cross examination the impeaching attorney could ask about a prior inconsistent statement he knows was never made, and having planted the seed of doubt in the jury's mind, he can fail to follow up the witness' denial with any extrinsic proof. There is very little remedy for this, other than the jury's sophistication (perhaps solicited by counsel). The impeaching attorney technically has not asserted that such a statement was made. Rather, he is merely inquiring whether one was made. Can he thus escape a charge of dishonesty? Occasionally attorneys have been judicially requested on motion and out of the hearing of the jury, to show that they had at least some reason to believe there may have been a prior inconsistent statement. Occasionally the question put to the witness has been ordered stricken, or, more effectively, the jury has been instructed that there is no basis for the inference. Even more rarely some action has been taken against the attorney, a mistrial declared, or a case dismissed or judgment entered. "Bad faith" may have to be shown in order to obtain a remedy. (F.R.E. 613 gives opposing counsel the right to call for disclosure to him of any prior statement being inquired into by the impeacher, but it does not say what should happen if the impeacher responds at the bench that he has none (or no reason to believe there is one) and is just inquiring, as per his right to cross examine. Is there an implication that he must have one? Or reason to believe there is one?)

The procedures for introduction described in this section are in some imprecise way the products of policies we see at work in other areas of evidence law. The mandatory warning on cross examination and the regulation of extrinsic proof are said to minimize surprise; to economically provide the witness a chance to defend himself and supply the jury with information for evaluating the impeachment; and to minimize protraction, misleadingness, confusion, and distraction into collateral issues. The effort is to minimize the impeacher's chance of blowing "nothing" up into "something"—"something" that would be hard to reduce back down to "nothing" later. On the other hand, it gives a clever mendacious witness a better chance to make "something" look like "nothing." In addition, the foundation frequently saves the time that extrinsic proof might necessitate: If the witness admits making the statement on cross, time consuming extrinsic evidence is not permitted. Furthermore, any explanations and counter explanations will take place more economically, conveniently, and less confusingly, when the witness on cross admits the statement, explains it, and the explanation is perhaps countered, all during the cross exam; as compared with the matter not being mentioned on cross, the extrinsic evidence being introduced at a later stage, and then the witness being recalled to explain, followed by counter-explanations. As always in evidence law, where the judge is given discretion, it is to be exercised on the basis of these and other objectives of the law, laid down earlier.

Suppose the prior inconsistent statement was written rather than oral? It would seem that it should make no difference to the application of the foregoing rules. In general this is so, with only the following modification.

It is usually held in traditional jurisdictions, that the foundation requirement can be satisfied in the case of a prior written statement only by permitting the witness to examine, during cross examination, the writing or such part of it as the impeacher seeks to use (so long as it is a sufficient part for identity, etc.) before any reference can be made to it.

The impeaching attorney, by complying with the procedure in the black letters, will obviously have warned the witness sufficiently to enable the witness to possibly recall. The cross examiner thus is not required to put the specific questions reminding of time, place, and substance, required in the case of a prior oral statement. (He may wish to establish time, place, and substance, however, through questions at some point.) By way of foundation, then, the attorney merely presents the document to the witness, and asks whether he made the statement. If the witness admits making the statement, the attorney will read or have the witness read the statement to the jury (or enough of the document to obviate the danger of non-contextual quotation). [As a mechanical matter, the document will have been marked for identification (before presented to the witness) and moved into evidence (after it is acknowledged by the witness) before reading. The attorney will be required to show the document to opposing counsel, but not too much before the point at which it is to be shown to the witness (usually it will be somewhat simultaneously). The document will ordinarily be received into evidence as an exhibit after acknowledgment by the witness. This generally means it can be circulated to the jury when received, and taken with them at the end of the case during deliberations. Sometimes reading aloud and physically circulating the exhibit or taking into deliberations are deemed redundant, and one or the other may be disallowed. In some courts exhibits such as documents may not be admitted during cross examination, and the physical introduction must wait until the introducer's turn to put on his case. As indicated, the document generally will be marked for identification just before it is presented to the witness, to alleviate confusion in referring to it, whether or not it is to be offered in evidence during the examination. Marking at any earlier point (e. g., in a session just before trial) is generally regarded by attorneys as providing too much advance notice of impeachment, since opposing counsel normally asks to see what is being marked.]

If the witness denies making the statement, the impeaching attorney may but need not, prove up the document and its authorship through another witness when it is his turn to put on his case. The document itself then goes into evidence as an exhibit. The dishonest practice of some impeachers spoken of above can be more effectively policed here, where there is a writing.

Whenever the document itself is to go into evidence as an exhibit, the rules of Authentication (taken care of by the maker admitting the statement or by the independent witness) and Best Evidence are applied. See pp. 72–78 supra.

In some jurisdictions the requirement that the writing must be shown to the witness is applied in such a fashion

as to require that it be shown before any line of questioning leading to the inconsistent statement can be undertaken
(on pain of disallowing use of the inconsistent statement if
the requirement is breached).   Thus, one very effective
cross examination technique is foreclosed: getting an un-
suspecting witness to repeat on cross, in detail, the story he
told on direct, and to deny any possibility or error, before
the attorney springs the writing.   It is submitted that applying the foundation requirement, which was designed only
as a precondition for the introduction of extrinsic evidence,
in this fashion, destroys a very effective tool for revealing
the true dimensions of a witness's mendacity; allows him
too much opportunity to "wriggle out" of a real inconsistency; and is essentially misguided.

If a witness can be induced to acknowledge a previous
inconsistent oral statement or writing as a correct recital of
the facts related therein (which, practically speaking, is
sometimes only possible before the inconsistency with the
present testimony is emphasized), the previous statement is
regarded as incorporated into the witness' present testimony, with the result that it becomes part thereof, and
stands on an equal footing with the rest.   Assuming the
present version has not been retracted, the inconsistency
becomes an internal inconsistency in the present testimony,
for whatever impeachment value the jury may wish to give
it.   But more importantly, the information in the previous
statement can be taken substantively as evidence of the
truth of the matter related therein, even in traditional jurisdictions.   If the witness is the attorney's own, but seems to
have turned coat, the attorney *might* use this technique to
avoid the traditional ban on impeaching his own witness,
on the theory that the attorney is not impeaching, but rather
contradicting by providing conflicting evidence of the underlying substantive facts (albeit via different portions of the
same witness' testimony).   Alternatively, the attorney on

[*332*]

cross examination might refer to the former statement ostensibly to "refresh the witness' memory" or "awaken his conscience," to get him to change his present story. This would not be considered "impeachment," either. While the attorney could in no event under this procedure introduce extrinsic evidence of the statement, and the jury technically can make no use whatever of the former statement unless the witness "corrects" his present testimony or incorporates the former statement, nevertheless it is before the jury. If a witness can be induced to admit having made the statement and to report circumstances under which his former statement was made which would satisfy the requirements for some exception to or exemption from the hearsay rule, of course the evidence will be *substantively* admissible.

The F.R.E. (and codes modelled on the F.R.E.) radically alter the foundation required for both the oral and the written statements, by abolishing any requirement of confronting the witness with the oral or written statement before examining him on the matter or before introducing extrinsic evidence, so long as, at some point, the witness is afforded an opportunity to explain or deny any such matter that is evidenced and the opposite party to examine him on it. The opposing attorney is entitled on request to have any prior statement a witness is being examined on, disclosed or shown to the attorney. These rules seem to apply to prior statements introduced substantively as well as for impeachment, with the exception of party admissions.

This is F.R.E. 613. An important aspect of the rule is that the "foundation" (confronting the witness with the statement) may come *after* the extrinsic evidence, for example by recalling the witness. The reasons for the change are several. While the traditional rule is said to prevent in advance attorneys from exaggerating an inconsistency that has an innocent explanation, it also warned mendacious witnesses early enough to prevent the true dimension of their mendacity from being impactfully demonstrated. In addition, the new rule allows several witnesses co-operating in a lie to be examined before alerting them (in the cross examination of the first of them) to a prior inconsistent statement exploding their story. Several questions arise, however, under the new rule. What if a witness tells his story, cross examination is waived, and the witness then leaves the jurisdiction, or it is inconvenient to recall him, or he dies. The attorney who is against the witness then wishes to introduce later in the trial, a prior inconsistent statement of the witness. The rule says it cannot be done (or if done, the statement is to be stricken), if the witness is not afforded an opportunity either before or after, to explain or deny it and his attorney to examine him on it. But the judge is expressly given discretion to waive this if the interests of justice demand. The judge will have to weigh the importance of the prior statement, the inconvenience of recalling the witness, and the nature of what it is the witness would likely say if recalled. Which attorney should have the obligation to see that the witness remains around?

Presumably the rule's requirement that the opposing counsel be given the prior statement applies only at the point where the cross examiner actually begins inquiry into the statement itself, not when the cross examiner first gets into a line of questioning that appears to be leading to the statement. But in the light of the prior misguided practice under the traditional foundation as applied in some places (see pp. 331–32 supra), this is not entirely clear.

The entitlement of opposing attorney to get the statement seems also to apply to prior statements (consistent or inconsistent) used substantively, as well.

Further Limitation on Extrinsic Evidence of Former Statement: "Collateral Matters" Rule

During cross examination of the witness to be impeached, the impeaching attorney, within limits, is usually allowed to attempt to uncover any previous statement at all in conflict with the present testimony. But when it comes to introducing extrinsic evidence of a prior inconsistent statement (which can only be done under the conditions already outlined), the inconsistency he seeks to demonstrate must not be on a "collateral matter." A "collateral matter" is something that is not of real importance to the litigation (and frequently may defy precise definition, being left to sound judicial judgment).

If a witness to an automobile collision irrelevantly relates that he happened to be wearing a red sweater on the day of the accident, he cannot be impeached by extrinsic proof that he had formerly said he was wearing a blue sweater. While in some slight way this kind of impeachment indicates something about the witness' credibility as to matters of detail, the additional light it sheds over and above what the jury already knows of human nature is certainly not worth the investment of time and energy and the distraction into collateral issues. There may be discretion in the judge to curtail an inquiry obviously running in this direction even on cross examination. The red sweater example is, of course, an easy case. Other fact situations present closer questions. If W identified the car or light by color, his sweater mistake would be more important.

Were the color of the sweater independently provable regardless of the inconsistency (as, for example, if it were the color of the driver's sweater where identity is disputed), the prior inconsistent statement (still offered and offerable only as impeachment) would not be collateral. Nor would it be collateral if the witness had said he remembers the

[*335*]

accident because it was the day he bought and wore home his new red sweater.

The principles of this section arose out of a general principle like that expressed in F.R.E. 403 (relevance and its counterweights) and thus are continued under the F.R.E. and codes modelled on the F.R.E., even though there is no specific rule on the matter.

Lines of Attack: (2) Specific Contradiction

This is the second principal line of attack on credibility that we will take up. "Specific contradiction," "contradiction," and "specific error" are interchangeable terms. Despite some judicial usage to the contrary, "contradiction" as a term should not be used to cover *prior inconsistent statements,* discussed above.

> **When your witness testifies to the same transaction as your opponent's witness, which transaction is the subject of the litigation, but your witness reports the facts of that transaction inconsistently with the facts thereof as reported by your opponent's witness, you are in effect not only building your substantive case, but also challenging (impeaching) the credibility of your opponent's witness. This is an example of "specific contradiction." Specific contradiction occurs wherever there is a difference like this over substantive facts in controversy.**

We have already touched upon this (i. e., contradiction) where it is done by a party to his own witness. We said there it is not regarded as "impeachment" for purposes of the rule against impeaching one's own witness. But in actual fact it has an element of impeachment to it. We will here exclude the situation of contradicting your own witness. We will also exclude from consideration the situation where evidence given by a witness at one time (on direct or cross) conflicts with evidence given by him at another time in the same proceeding (on direct or cross), even though this is both contradiction and inconsistent statement (though not "prior" inconsistent statement in the sense used above, which was limited to statements outside of the trial), and is both substantive and impeaching.

In the present discussion we will be concerned only with *extrinsic* evidence of a *fact incompatible with* or *in conflict with* a fact reported by an opponent's witness. (As in the case of prior inconsistent statements, absolute irreconcilability is not required, and the conflict may be in the circumstantial inferences to be drawn.) The attempt under this line of attack is to show that some *fact* is different than reported by the witness who is being impeached. It is *not* to show that conflicting *statements* about some underlying fact have been made by the witness. That is within the topic of prior inconsistent statements, just completed. Under the present line of attack, the attempt is to show that the *facts* are not as reported by the witness, whether or not he has consistently maintained his position. If the attempt is to show that whereas the witness states the killer was wearing a red sweater, he was in fact wearing a blue sweater, and the latter fact is attempted to be proven by the testimony of other witnesses who also saw the killing, we are dealing with specific contradiction. If the attempt is to show that whereas the witness now says the killer was wearing a red sweater, formerly the same witness said the killer was wearing a blue sweater, we are dealing with impeachment by prior inconsistent statement.

Evidence specifically contradicting the witness is admissible only if it would have been independently admissible for a substantive purpose, regardless of the contradiction. If the evidence overcomes this hurdle, its proponent will then be permitted to argue both its impeachment and its substantive value to the jury. The impeachment aspect of the evidence may permit its introduction during rebuttal where otherwise it would be confined to the case in chief.

Under this requirement of independent substantive admissibility, if a witness to an automobile collision quite irrelevantly states that he was wearing a red sweater on that day, the impeaching attorney will not be permitted to show that he was in fact wearing a blue sweater. The color of the sweater the witness was wearing would not affect damages, liability, or any material issue, other than perhaps the credibility of the witness regarding unimportant detail. We have already seen that the rule against impeachment by prior inconsistent statement on "collateral matters" would prevent the introduction of a prior *statement* by the witness that he was wearing a blue sweater. The reasoning in both cases is very much the same, and the rule here also may be articulated as a ban on impeachment on "collateral matters." In both instances the ban may be more stringently administered where the fact to be attacked was elicited by the impeaching party upon cross examination. In both areas, if a statement by the witness is damaging, though irrelevant, immaterial, or otherwise incompetent, and the damaged party has not solicited the statement, fairness may dictate that refutation by specific contradiction or prior inconsistent statement be allowed ("the door has been opened"), although one could argue that objection to the original statement should be the exclusive remedy. It may make a difference whether the statement was made on direct or cross examination; but the real consideration should be whether the damaged party solicited the statement. (In the example I assumed the witness did not also purport to identify a car or light by color.)

The reasons for the rule against collateral contradiction suggest certain exceptions to it:

(1) Where a witness purports to have been an eyewitness in a position to accurately report the occurrence, the oppo-

nent may attempt to show he is mistaken about some fact concerning which he could not be mistaken were he an eyewitness and possessed of sufficient perceptual, memorative, and reportorial powers to recount the occurrence. Thus, if he has testified to witnessing an assault and states there was an enormous crowd at the scene, the opponent will be allowed to produce witnesses to the fact that the place was virtually deserted, though their testimony be irrelevant but for the contradiction.   (A prior inconsistent statement on this would also be allowed.)

(2) Where the witness to be impeached testifies to a fact that, while not competent on any substantive issue, is relevant as to the credibility of himself or another witness, the opponent may rebut (contradict) that fact with extrinsic evidence, even though the extrinsic evidence would not be competent on any substantive issue.   Thus, if the witness expressly denies having made a former inconsistent statement, or denies a certain bias or connection with the case (e. g., that he is the brother of the party for whom he is testifying), the opponent may specifically contradict him by showing the facts to be otherwise—by adducing extrinsic witnesses or documents to prove, for example, that he *is* the brother of the party for whom he is testifying, or *has* made the inconsistent statement denied.   In such a case the impeachment is not only by specific contradiction, but by prior inconsistent statement or bias as well.   The rules under the latter two headings would govern.   If the fact to be contradicted relates, say, to the bias, powers, consistency, or character of *another* witness than the one testifying, it is within the present heading, and under the present exception (i. e., permitted; but subject to a considerable amount of judicial discretion to curtail).   No. (2) also covers W's mistake on his sweater-color if he purports to identify car or light by color.

Despite failure to mention any of the matters discussed in this section under any specific rule in the F.R.E., it is generally assumed that the broad provisions of Rule 403 (relevancy balanced against counterweights) of the F.R.E. and similar codes, are meant to incorporate and continue the law stated in this section, which law originally evolved in response to policies like those expressed in Rule 403.

Lines of Attack: (3) Bias

Anything that suggests the witness may have an interest in, or improper incentive or motive for testifying in, the controversy, or may harbor other conscious or unconscious bias or prejudice for or against a side, witness, party, or counsel, or may be subject to improper influence, reflects on credibility. The circle of the admissible to impeach here is drawn broadly, and goes under the heading of "bias".

Permissible impeachment under this heading, generally speaking, encompasses anything which raises a suspicion that there could be a motive to fabricate or to consciously or unconsciously "slant" matters. Nothing as marked as bribery is required. Included are showings of family relationship; past or present employment; litigation involving the witness and a relevant person or a similar issue; common or antagonistic political or religious or social affiliation; quarrels; compensation or monetary expectation or lack thereof;[1] prior settlement of a claim between the wit-

---

[1] Lay witness fees are generally prescribed by law. They usually include an allowance for travel and a daily or hourly wage or fee which may or may not be linked to what the witness actually normally earns. Usually they are not so linked. The party calling the witness pays. These fees *may* be included as part of an award of costs against the losing party if costs are awarded at all. Where such an award is permitted, it is frequently discretionary. Amounts paid in excess of those prescribed may or may not be illegal. But the witness is entitled to at least the prescribed fee, at least if he is subpoenaed. Ordinarily a day's pay and travel expense must be tendered the witness with the subpoena, and must therefore be paid in advance by the party calling the witness. It should be noted that

ness and the party for whom he is testifying; feelings for or against the victim of the crime in issue or a party or a class or category of person or organization; prior testimony for the same or similar party or of the same kind; pending, possible, or dropped charges against a witness for the prosecution; psychologic or ideologic predilections; and many, many more. This matter and that of the next section are governed by no specific rule in the F.R.E. and its progeny.

subpoenas are often issued in quantity to lawyer's offices in blank but signed by the judge or clerk, to be filled in and served by the attorney or his agent as particular cases as needs arise. There is usually the option to have a marshal serve them instead. The same procedures ordinarily apply both for trials and depositions. A subpoena by custom is usually good for date specified or any reasonable later date if the witness' appearance is delayed because of the progress of the trial or other similar reason and the witness is properly notified. The issue of whether a subpoena presents the witness with undue hardship can be raised upon motion by the witness. Issuance of a subpoena itself is virtually automatic and no showing is required therefor. A subpoena may require that a witness bring documents, as well. It would generally not be permitted to show for impeachment that an ordinary witness is receiving only his prescribed fee. An expert witness, if he is to testify in the capacity of an expert, is entitled to additional compensation, but often this is the case only if he must prepare specially. Expert fees may be unregulated (i. e., the subject of private bargaining) or they may be regulated in that they must be "normal" or "reasonable" charges; or regulated in some other way. It is relevant to note that a rule is frequently found to the effect that expert testimony, insofar as it *is* expert testimony, cannot be compelled under subpoena or otherwise, neither at deposition nor at trial. The reach of this rule is not always clear, but facts within the expert's firsthand knowledge can be compelled as distingushed from facts requiring extra work, or opinions on facts or on hypotheticals (at least where fashioning an opinion requires extra work). Expert fees may or may not be awardable as costs. His compensation generally may be shown to the jury by way of impeachment. A counter-explanation as to normal fee rates in the field, and what the law allows, may be permitted where fees are shown by way of impeachment. A witness' (particularly an expert's) failure to take compensation or the full extent of compensation may in certain circumstances indicate a bias. A fee contingent on the outcome of the litigation may be permissible, at least in the case of experts; but the potential for impeachment in such a situation is obvious.

At least as respects the present section, the traditional law as outlined here is continued by virtue of the general provisions of Rule 403 (relevance and its counterweights) which contains the general policies that originally gave rise to this law.

Bias: Foundation Required?

Some courts require a foundation—of the type described above as traditional in the case of prior inconsistent statements—for the introduction of both forms of bias impeachment: conduct (or facts) evincing bias, and prior statements evincing bias. Others do so only for the latter form. Some do so for neither form.

(a) *Out-of-court conduct or fact indicating bias.* Suppose as impeaching attorney you wish to show via your own witnesses or documents that a witness for the other side is the brother of the party for whom he is testifying, or has had a quarrel with your client. Under one view you need give the witness no warning on cross examination: You need not ask him if the matters you wish to prove are true, or even refer to them. In short, you need lay no *foundation* in the sense used in connection with other forms of impeachment. You may prove directly by extrinsic evidence (when it is next your turn to put on your own evidence), without any prelude on cross examination, the quarrel or the kinship. If you *do* ask him about the matter on cross examination and he denies it, your extrinsic evidence will tend to show him to be not only biased, but a liar as well (or at least mistaken). That is, you will have impeached by bias and by specific contradiction.[2] This is permitted, but you run the risk that he will admit the bias in response to your question on cross examination, which

---

[2] The same would be true had he denied the fact indicating bias during his direct examination.

will take some of the wind out of your sails. Worse, he may explain it away or say that he is impartial anyway. (If not deemed too far ranging and collateral, explanation may be allowed in any event, but more freedom of explanation is accorded during cross examination, and further, it has more impact then.) Worse still (from your viewpoint), courts, to avoid unnecessary protraction and distraction, will bind you by an answer admitting the bias, i. e., they will prevent your introducing your extrinsic evidence, especially if it would add little or nothing of legitimate value.

Some courts impose (in the example set out at the beginning of the last paragraph) a foundation requirement that the witness must be confronted with the fact on cross examination, and if he admits the fact (whether or not he concedes bias) the extrinsic evidence may not be introduced.

(b) *Prior out-of-court statements of the witness evidencing bias.* Not all courts draw a distinction between this and the evidence of bias described in (a) immediately above. They either do or do not impose the foundation requirement on both alike, without distinction. Those that do draw a distinction do so in order to impose on prior biased statements, but not on biased fact or conduct, the foundation requirement and the ban on extrinsic evidence (after an answer confessing the statement) described above. A declaration falling under this subsection (b) (prior out-of-court statement evidencing bias) might be, "I hate the defendant [against whom the witness is presently testifying] and want to see him burn," or, "I had a quarrel with the defendant," or, "I am employed by Mr. X [the party for whom the witness is testifying]," or, "I am Mr. X's brother," the declaration in each case having been made by the witness at some time prior to his present testimony. (Might a court feel some of these are hearsay?)

(If the witness, having made this statement, makes or is induced to make a conflicting statement on the stand, and then the earlier statement is revealed, we would have impeachment by prior inconsistent statement as well as by a showing of bias. A court that would not otherwise require a foundation might apply the rules for prior inconsistent statements in such a case. The impeaching attorney, by characterizing the evidence more in terms of bias than in terms of inconsistent statement, may minimize the chance of this happening. But, as noted, many courts apply a foundation requirement to prior biased statement, regardless.)

(In a rare case, a court might permit the introduction of both the prior biased statement and evidence of the facts stated in the statement, as, e. g., both the statement, "I am the brother of X [for whom the witness is now testifying]," and documentary or other proof that he is indeed the brother. And, if there is in addition a conflicting *present* on-the-stand statement by the witness, the impeachment would suggest not merely that the witness is biased, but that he is lying or mistaken and inconsistent about it. It might very well be made to appear that the witness and his side deem the bias important enough to cover up. At one and the same time there would be impeachment by bias, specific contradiction, and prior inconsistent statement.)

The status of a foundation requirement under bias impeachment is uncertain under the F.R.E. and its progeny. The foundation could be imposed on either or both forms of bias impeachment by virtue of Rule 403, since the foundation supposedly was designed to satisfy factors like those listed in that rule. Rule 613 addresses the foundation in the case of prior inconsistent statements, to modify it, and makes no specific mention of it for bias, although some language of 613(a) seems possibly to apply to it. (What may be inferred from all this?) The foundation requirement in the case of bias originated first in connection with biased statements; probably is a confusion with prior inconsistent statements; and should be abandoned.

Lines of Attack: (4) Establishing the Witness' Propensity for Being Non-Credible

This line of attack—attacking the witness' propensity or character for credibility—is dealt with in Chapter 8, infra, dealing with the subject of character or propensity evidence generally, i. e., for substantive and credibility purposes. In summary, and within certain limitations, this line of attack may consist of showing (1) reputation for non-veracity; (2) specific instances of conduct evincing non-veracity, including wrongs that (a) were and (b) were not convicted for; and (3), in F.R.E. type jurisdictions, opinions on the witness' veracity.

Lines of Attack: (5) Impeaching Experts From the Literature

Statements from treatises, articles, and other reference works traditionally are hearsay if offered for their truth. Some jurisdictions have a special exception to the hearsay rule to cover certain classes of source materials.[3] In the

---

[3] For example F.R.E. 803(17) is an exception for "market quotations, tabulations, lists, directories, or other published compilations generally used and relied upon by the public or by persons in particular occupations;" and F.R.E. 803(18) is a hearsay exception allowing the reading to the jury (but not introduction as an exhibit) of "statements in published treatises, periodicals or pamphlets [in] history, medicine, or other science or art . . . to the extent called to the attention of an expert upon cross examination or relied upon by him in direct examination . . . [if] established as reliable authority by . . . testimony or judicial notice." The tendency of the rules to defer to the judgments of trades or professions is manifest here, as well as in Rule 703, which allows experts to base opinions on the kind of materials used in the profession. As in Rule 801(d)(1)(B), relating to prior consistent statements, restrictions that applied to the evidence formerly, when it was admissible only on credibility, are extended into the new substantive use (i. e., the restrictions relating to reliance and "calling to attention" in 803(18)), probably because one of the

absence of such an exception, the statements are generally admissible, if at all, only as *impeachment* of a witness who purports to be an expert in the field, and not for their truth. I. e., they may be offered to show that the witness has disregarded or overlooked or is at variance with a passage from a work he has relied on or should be familiar with. Is this distinguishable from offering the statement for its truth? Because of the danger of improper substantive hearsay use by the jury despite the cautionary instruction that is granted, many courts place one or more of the following restrictions on this type of impeachment:

(1) Before the impeachment will be allowed, the expert must, in his testimony, have indicated reliance (a minority view suggests this may not be elicited, or purposely elicited, by the cross-examiner initially) on the work or, in some jurisdictions, on works of the same general type. In some jurisdictions the expert's mention of a particular work or type of work relied on may license elicitation of reliance on a particular work not mentioned if it is of the same class (assuming such would not otherwise be permitted).

Cf. pp. 55–56, 59–61, supra, for an expert witness' right to rely on and mention his literary sources.

(2) The expert must recognize the work that is to be used for impeachment, as a "leading," "authoritative," or

rationales for substantive admissibility is that since the evidence comes in on credibility it might as well come in substantively. An additional reason here is that the restrictions insure some expert explication of the material. As in the case of Rule 803(5) (hearsay exception for past recollection recorded), Rule 803(18) has a restriction on use as an exhibit, to avoid undue emphasis and indiscriminate jury use of other pages. The requirement of reliance or acknowledgement by an expert, and the need to show the treatise is authoritative, will make it difficult, although not impossible, for someone like a medical malpractice plaintiff to use a treatise in lieu of a standard-of-care expert witness (such witnesses being hard to get). Under former law, where substantive use was not permitted, this was impossible.

"recognized" work. Usually this may take place on direct or cross examination. In a number of jurisdictions it may not be established by extrinsic evidence. Reliance on the work in his testimony sometimes suffices. A clever or "primed" expert sometimes can avoid having a treatise used against him under this requirement by refusing to admit that the treatise is "leading," "authoritative," or "recognized." Saying that it is "used" in the profession, or that *some* of it is good, has been held on occasion not to be enough. (Even if the treatise can still be used, this expert has considerably blunted the force of the impeachment: He can always say he disagrees with the particular part cited. This technique is adaptable to (1) above, too.)

(3) There must be judicial notice or evidence establishing that the work is leading, authoritative, or recognized.

(4) Actual use of the work must be confined to cross examination.

(5) There may be limitations on how extensively the passage may be referred to or read from aloud, and on whether the treatise can be marked as an exhibit and formally put into evidence.

See, for one approach to the matter, Abrams v. Gordon, 276 F.2d 500 (D.C.Cir. 1960).

Other Kinds of Impeachment

The reader can readily imagine other forms of impeachment, e. g., any showing of defect of mental, perceptual, mnemonic, or recounting capacity; any showing of obstruction of perception; any showing of lack of proper positioning or location to observe; anything that detracts from an "expert" witness' "expertise;" etc. The principles already discussed should suggest the boundaries within which these may be done. (An extreme showing along any of these lines might totally disqualify, rather then merely impeach, the witness unless the law in the particular jurisdiction on the particular point regards the witness as qualified upon a *prima facie* showing by the offeror, regardless of what is shown later.)

In the case of an expert, lawyers opposing the expert frequently ask leave to "voir dire" the expert after the portion of his direct exam devoted to his qualifications, before he gets into his opinion. "Voir dire" is, essentially, early cross examination, in theory confined to attempting to show that the expert is not at all qualified to testify on the subject he will testify on. But if unsuccessful in excluding the testimony, the questioning still stands, for whatever impeachment value it has—that is, whatever value it has in effecting the weight the jury wishes to ascribe to the expert's testimony.

Support of Witness' Veracity

The reverse of each of the impeachment lines of attack on credibility can be conceived of: prior *consistent* statements, propensity for *veracity* (good reputation, good opinions, instances of honest conduct, lack of a pertinent criminal record), lack of bias, etc., each contributing to credibility. These would be known as credibility "support," the opposite of "impeachment." Speaking very generally, and realizing the trial judge is accorded much leeway in either direction in this area (he will seldom be reversed), and also realizing that something may depend on the lengths to which the supporting attorney wishes to go in order to prove the supporting facts (e. g., does he wish to introduce extrinsic evidence?), we can generalize and say that normally these lines of support will be allowed, if at all, only to the extent that a *precisely opposite counterpart* has been advanced against the witness' credibility. Thus, prior inconsistent statements *may* license the use of prior consistent statements to some extent,[4] but not the use of evidence of propensity for veracity.

This principle may not go so far as to hold that impeachment by a showing of propensity (character) can only be met by showing opposite propensity (character) *proved in the same manner* (i. e., instances of conduct met by instances of conduct rather than reputation).[5]

We have said in this section that the only "support" of a witness that is allowed is "rehabilitation" after attack. This may be somewhat relaxed to permit a cursory showing of *lack of bias* (impartiality) when a witness is first introduced. In addition, showings of a witness' background, profession, residence, etc., are customarily allowed, though they may reflect to his credit. Also, specific contradiction cannot be literally subject to the rule described in this section.

[4] In some jurisdictions prior consistent statements are allowed if and only if they tend to rebut (which usually means they must predate) an expressly or impliedly alleged fabrication or motive to fabricate or improper influence or motive. General notions of courtroom economy, of course (as codified, for example, in F.R.E. 403), are responsible for all the restrictions on support. Does the mere fact that a witness has an interest in the litigation (he may be a party), or has been cross examined, or has been attempted to be impeached under any of the forms of impeachment, mean that there is an implied allegation of fabrication of the kind we have just mentioned? Also note the similar requirement with respect to *substantive* use of prior consistent statements under F.R.E. 801(d)(1)(B). The use discussed *here* is a *credibility* use.

[5] Could it be argued that the introduction of a prior inconsistent statement, or indeed any allegation or argument that the witness has not reported the facts correctly (even just introducing contrary facts, let alone a vigorous cross exam or any of the forms of impeachment), is an attack on propensity or character for veracity, and thus licenses showings supporting propensity or character for veracity? Might this be so at least on some particular facts? Does merely being made a civil or criminal defendant in the case constitute such an attack? Is F.R.E. 608, quoted just infra, clear on these matters? Notice the phrase "or otherwise."

One entirely distinguishable notion ought to be mentioned. Within realistic limits of time and similar practical considerations, refutation of the truth of *specific facts* alleged by way of impeachment is usually permitted. Thus, it may be shown that the particular conviction was not in fact had, the particular prior statement not made, or a particular familial relation evidencing bias does not in fact exist.

The F.R.E. have very little to say on the matters dealt with in this section, except for the following provisions of Rule 608. Thus these matters are left largely to the broad policies of Rule 403 that may be expected to continue the general outline of existing decisional law. The relevant provisions of Rule 608 (which essentially bear out the main principles of this section to the extent they are addressed) are:

Rule 608(a)(2):

"[Opinion or reputation] evidence of truthful character is admissible only after the character of the witness for truthfulness has been attacked by opinion or reputation evidence or otherwise."

Rule 608(b):

"Specific instances of the conduct of a witness, for the purpose of . . . supporting his credibility . . . may not be proved by extrinsic evidence [but] may, . . . in the discretion of the court, if probative of truthfulness . . . be inquired into on cross-examination [6] of the witness . . . concerning his character for truthfulness . . .." [Query, will the judge exercise this discretion to continue traditional law to the effect that ordinarily there must first be an attack on credibility character?]

---

[6] *Cross*-exam makes no sense here. It must mean either direct or redirect exam.

CHAPTER VIII

PROPENSITY OR CHARACTER OF-FERED FOR SUBSTANTIVE OR CREDIBILITY PURPOSES

Preliminary Theory: General Considerations

In determining whether a person acted in a certain way on a particular occasion—for example, whether a witness has reported correctly or lied or made a mistake, or whether a particular person did or did not commit a rape, or was or was not careful, or turned a corner in an automobile in a particular way—it is logical to reason that one who has exhibited a pattern of behavior of the kind in question or a propensity for it is more likely to have acted in accord with that pattern or propensity on the occasion in issue, than someone who has not exhibited the pattern or propensity or has exhibited a contrary one.

At least as a matter of logic, a pattern or propensity can be proved, with varying persuasiveness, by showing specific instances of like conduct on the part of the person; by showing the person's reputation in the relevant respect; or by introducing the personal opinion of those who know him, as to the relevant characteristic. Further, logically speaking, the persuasiveness of the evidence will vary according to how precisely like the conduct in issue the other instances of conduct, or the quality reputed or opined, are. Instances of, or a reputation for, parking violations will not be particularly persuasive on the issue of credibility or the issue of whether the defendant committed the rape charged. Instances of, or a reputation for, lying or sex crimes, might be.

We see, therefore, that it is always *relevant* to prove a pattern of, or propensity for, the kind of conduct in issue, on the part of the person whose conduct is in issue (although there will be varying degrees of relevance or probativity). If this mode of proof, argument, or reasoning is objectionable, it must be for some other reason than that it is irrelevant. The dangers in it may be that the jury will over-emphasize its logical force, become unduly emotionally disposed in favor of or against one side or the other, punish or exact payment for past sins regardless of findings concerning the present one, or (where a witness is involved) hold a party responsible to an undue extent for the sins of his witnesses. Further, witnesses and parties may be humiliated and discouraged from coming forward. And there is the danger that what is at most a subsidiary inquiry will become too time consuming or central or will protract, distract, and confuse, with respect to the main issue. It may engender its own rebuttals and explanations, carrying the inquiry even farther afield, yet into areas that will be difficult to keep distinct from the main inquiry. To allow the evidence without the rebuttals and explanations may produce its own distortions, dissatisfactions, and unfairness. In addition, introduction of particular instances selected from a person's entire life can catch opposing counsel (or the witness or party) unawares, and place upon him a tremendous burden to anticipate which instances will be selected, and to prepare for them, without which preparation the evidence could be very misleading. There is also the desirability of encouraging reform and rehabilitation by letting people know that it is not futile to change their ways —that they can live down past derelictions and that they will not be unnecessarily dogged by them the rest of their lives. All these factors must be weighed in the particular context. In the calculus it should be recognized that the evidence may have only an attenuated logical tendency to establish the proposition for which it is offered, again depending upon the context. Finally, the efficacy of cautionary instructions in reducing the dangers is a factor to be considered in the balance.

Additional considerations may be: (1) In a criminal case "it is better that many guilty go free than that an innocent be punished." Might this mean that a kind of evidence barred to the prosecution might be acceptable when introduced in defense? (2) Is a jury especially prone to overemphasize propensity evidence introduced by the prosecution? (3) Is a propensity to abstain from certain acts probative or persuasive in the same degree as a propensity to commit certain acts? (4) Of the three forms of propensity evidence (reputation, personal opinion, specific instances), which it the most probative? Which is the least probative? Which is most likely to unduly prejudice the jury? The least? Which is the most time consuming? The most likely to distract the inquiry into collateral incidents likely to be confused with the main inquiry? Which the least? There might be a reluctance to permit the most probative evidence if at the same time it is the most unduly prejudicial and time consuming.

A system of rules and exceptions have evolved in response to these considerations. These rules and exceptions, at least as they appear in the F.R.E., are briefly suggested in Figure 2 below. A more thorough discussion of them, in all jurisdictions, appears in the text in the remainder of this chapter.

Fig. 2
F.R.E. 404: The General Prohibition

The chart below shows the chain of inference prohibited in general under the F.R.E. because of the considerations outlined above. These matters are

[Fig. 2 continued]
    more fully explored in the text that follows this figure.

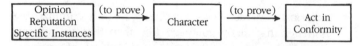

Description for Fig. 2:

The above chain is the generally prohibited chain under the F.R.E. (Rule 404). The principal question is "What is meant by 'character'?" Is it *any* propensity, whether general or specific? Whether considered good, bad, or morally neutral? Does the answer depend upon what danger the rule is meant to guard against: the inspiring of moral approval-disapproval; or a deceptive appearance of strength on the part of a weak inference; or both?

As we stated, the pictured chain is the generally prohibited chain under the F.R.E. However, F.R.E. 404(a)(1)–(3) list some special exceptions allowing (when read together with F.R.E. 405(a)) *opinion* and *reputation* for the purpose expressed by the chain, *in certain circumstances* (character of accused, of victim, etc., as defined and regulated there). *Specific instances* offered for the purpose expressed by the chain are inadmissible (except for the impeachment allowed by F.R.E. 608–609 dealing with convictions and with misconduct bespeaking falsity that has not resulted in conviction). (All uses of specific instances allowed by F.R.E. 404–405 [other crimes, wrongs, acts, for certain purposes, specific instances used to challenge or test a character witness, and situations where character or a trait are "elements"] are *not* for the purpose expressed by the chain depicted above, except perhaps that an argument could be made that, although the drafters did not realize it, some of the permitted purposes under the last sentence of 404(b) [which sentence deals with other crimes, wrongs, acts, for certain permitted purposes] are the same as the

[Fig. 2 continued]

prohibited purpose [i.e., the purpose expressed by the above chart]). Specific instances, opinion, and reputation, not offered for the purpose expressed by the depicted chain, are not subject to any per se ban and thus are governed by the ad hoc balancing of the general provisions of Rule 403 (probativity to be balanced against prejudice, time, misleadingness, etc.). Such evidence, then, need not be recognized expressly by any provision or exception in Rules 404–405, but for tidiness the drafters did mention in 404–405 a few types of such evidence as not being within the per se ban of 404–405. Be aware that evidence allowed by 404–405 (whether expressly or by implication) is still not automatically admissible, but rather is subject to the balancing of Rule 403.

If "habit" is substituted for "character" in the above chart, the chain is then usually permitted (F.R.E. 406). Is there a propensity that is neither "habit" nor "character", that might appear as the middle term in the chart, at least conceptually speaking? [End of Fig. 2]

The Evidentiary "Rules" in the Area

"Rules" (including "exceptions") have evolved supposedly in response to the various considerations discussed in the text preceding Figure 2, which considerations are in major part the considerations discussed under the "balancing" process in Chapter One, supra. These "rules" (and their "exceptions") may be summarized (in perhaps slightly more categorical fashion than is precisely warranted on the current somewhat fuzzy and diverse state of the law, even under the codifications) by the following black letters:

The term "propensity" means a "tendency" or "penchant". "Character" is a propensity that is both general (i. e. propensity for "honesty" or

"dishonesty," "violence" or "non-violence") as opposed to specific (i. e., propensity for executing certain kinds of violent or dishonest acts, or for executing them in a certain manner) and possessed of good or bad moral connotations. "Habit" is a very strong and very specific propensity in which acts occur somewhat invariably and automatically and which take some deliberation to vary, qualities which we may take "character" not to have. Propensities of each of these types, at least conceptually if not under the law, could be established by proof of specific instances of conduct, by proof of reputation for the propensity, or by someone's opinion about whether the propensity is possessed or not. There is a general legal ban on establishing propensity in any fashion, unless (1) the propensity is not offered to show an act in conformity with the propensity, or if so offered, (2) it is not a character type of propensity (i. e., is not a general propensity [as in many cases where the evidence is allowed to establish "identity, motive, knowledge, intent, plan" etc.] or does not have good or bad moral connotations or is a habit), or, if it is a character-type propensity offered to show an act in conformity with it, it fits the special rules for exceptions generally known as character of the accused (substantive evidence), character of the victim (substantive evidence), or credibility-character of witnesses (credibility evidence). In such cases, there is no automatic ban and admissibility is determined based upon consideration of the general factors and policies (relevancy and its counterweights) listed in Chapter One, supra, and F.R.E. 403 (perhaps more specifically codified by particular rules or rulings). However, the form of the evidence used to establish the propensity is often limited to reputation evidence (in some jurisdictions, reputation and opinion evidence), with specific instance evidence frequently banned, al-

**though this varies with the situation and the juris-
diction. In addition, a few jurisdictions place special limits on habit evidence, requiring corroboration or lack of eyewitnesses to the occurrence.
Showings concerning the victim in rape and similar cases is often the subject of separate, special
regulation. Generally speaking, F.R.E. 404–406
(substantive use of character and habit), 412 (victim in rape), and 608–609 (witness's credibility-
character), and the codes modelled on the F.R.E.,
codify, perhaps cryptically, all this traditional law.
Significant changes in the F.R.E. and its progeny,
from the law of many other jurisdictions, are the
general licensing of both reputation and personal
opinion testimony where the line of proof is permitted; an attempt to disapprove the qualifications
on habit that relate to eyewitnesses and corroboration; and a broadening of the form of question
permitted to challenge a character-witness's
knowledge, allowing "did you know" of certain
contrary instances, as well as the traditional "have
you heard." The rape evidence is also restricted.**

Let us explain in slightly different form some of the
matters summarized in this black letter:

There is a general ban on proof of propensity adduced
for purposes of soliciting the sort of reasoning we have
been discussing—that is, establishing a propensity *in order
to show an act in conformity with it*—but the exceptions
are many. First of all, a question can be raised, at least in
many jurisdictions, as to whether the ban applies at all to
propensity that cannot be called "character." (Although
there is not universal agreement, "character" may be defined as a propensity that has a "good" or "bad" moral
connotation; and is general rather than specific, i. e., a
propensity for dishonesty rather than for using a particular
modus operandi in conducting a particular type of
fraudulent scheme. "Character" appears also to be distinct
from the propensity known as "habit," which, in addition to

being specific, is not necessarily morally tinged, and is in some degree automatic.) [1] A number of other exceptions are commonly found, among them the following: [2]

(a) *Certain Kinds of Substantive Evidence (As Opposed to Credibility Evidence).*

(i) *Good character showing by criminal defendant.*

In a criminal case, the defendant may reduce the likelihood that he committed the crime by showing his good character (propensity for not committing the crime). This principle is called "character of the accused." The showing is usually confined to testimony as to his *reputation* for the *particular trait in issue* (e. g., reputation for peaceableness or non-violence in an assault or homicide case; reputation for trustworthiness with property in an embezzlement case), given by a person familiar with his reputation in his community reasonably near the time of the crime. Personal opinion evidence is also permitted in some jurisdictions. (E.g. F.R.E. 404(a)(1) as qualified by 405(a).) The evidence will be given by someone other than the defendant; thus the defendant does not open himself up to character assassination under the guise of impeaching defendant. But his character witnesses may be subjected to not only the more customary varieties of impeachment, but also to a kind of impeachment potentially exceptionally damaging to the defendant: the defendant's prior derelictions are introduced ostensibly not to reflect on the defendant, but to

---

[1] "Character" and "character trait," are probably alternative ways to say nearly the same thing. "Character" seems to refer to a very very broad or general propensity such as "he is a good man" made up of a sum of "character traits" such as propensity for non-violence, honesty, law abidingness, etc., also general and also tinged with moral approbation, but slightly less general than character. In any event, both are characterized by their generality and moral tinge, as compared with propensities we would not put in the realm of character, and neither has the automaticity and specificity of habit.

[2] The special subject of showings concerning the *victim in rape and similar cases* is deferred until the end of this chapter.

show that the witnesses are not actually familiar with that whereof they speak. (See, e. g., F.R.E. 405(a), second sentence.) This in theory does not involve the kind of propensity reasoning under discussion (although in practice, despite cautionary instructions, it tends to blacken defendant along propensity lines). The prosecution usually will be confined to asking the witness, on cross examination, "*Have you heard* that the defendant did X [a wrong, not necessarily a conviction or crime, directly relevant to the character trait testified to by the witness]?". (But the Advisory Committee Note to F.R.E. 405(a) also allows the question to be put in the form "Did you *know* that . . .".). The prosecution will not be permitted to introduce extrinsic evidence in any event. This approved procedure presents a very serious danger of unsubstantiated imputation of wrongdoing. Cf. pp. 328–29, supra, for possible solutions. This license to impeach good character witnesses should be distinguished from the other license given the prosecutor upon the introduction by defendant of good character witnesses: the right to show bad character (propensity) substantively —i. e., to directly and frankly demonstrate that the defendant is the sort of person who will have committed the crime—discussed at (ii) infra. It is also to be distinguished from the license given the prosecutor if the defendant takes the stand: The license to impeach the defendant's veracity to the same extent as any witness' veracity may be impeached, including a showing of a propensity for falsehood, except in rare circumstances where an instruction is deemed insufficient to guard against undue prejudice. (Any witness, of course, in a civil or criminal case, party or not, may turn away impeachment questions *to him* attempting to elicit crimes for which he has not yet been convicted nor granted immunity, on the basis of the privilege against self-incrimination, assuming the statute of limitations has not run out on the crime. But the accused's fear of incrimination in the *present* prosecution, from an impeachment question, e. g., the fear that his word will be impeached or he will be made to seem like a criminal type, is not assertable under the privilege if he has taken the stand.) If the defendant himself were to take the stand and testify to his own good propensity (character) he would be open not only to personal impeachment, but to the substantive rebuttal mentioned at (ii) infra, which rebuttal is in order whoever testifies to the defendant's good propensity (character).

(ii) *Responsive substantive showing by prosecution.*

Although the prosecution normally may not (but note items (iii) and (vi) below) *initiate* substantive bad character showings about the defendant in order to suggest he acted in conformity with it and thus to increase the likelihood he committed the crime, nevertheless the prosecutor may *respond* to defendant's substantive good character evidence ((i) above) with such evidence—he may show bad character in rebuttal, frankly to establish that the defendant is the "kind of guy" who would commit the crime. This rule also goes under the name "character of the accused." This evidence would be similarly limited as expressed in the third and fourth sentences in (i) above, with the same augmentation in the case of the F.R.E. that is noted in parentheses at that point in our text.

(iii) *Prosecution initiating similar showing.*

The prosecution may *initiate* a substantive propensity showing something like those above in certain very persuasive and necessitous circumstances, usually where it seems imperative to use the evidence to show identity, motive, knowledge, or intent, or where there is a single scheme embracing several wrongs or several wrongs have a common "blueprint" or "plan" or "modus operandi." Admissibility is frequently confined to showing specific instances of conduct very like that charged. This gateway to admissibility is often referred to as the "identity, motive, knowledge, intent, plan or scheme" principle, or some variant of those catchwords; or simply the "other crimes, wrongs, or acts" principle.

In a prosecution for the bathtub drowning of the defendant's present wife, the fact that several of his former wives had also been found drowned in the bath was admitted against him. In another case, the defendant was a supermarket customer on a day when the supermarket received a check signed with a fictitious name from some one of its customers. The fact that the defendant had passed similar bogus checks in similar circumstances in the past, was admitted to help show that he was the one (from among the many customers of the supermarket that day) who had passed the bogus check. A plan to commit a series of interdependent crimes embracing the one charged may be shown by proving up the other crimes (e. g. bank robberies used to get money to obtain narcotics) and the plan may be admissible on the issue of the commission of the present crime, or on the issue of intent. In addition crimes bearing an earmark in common with the present crime are often admissible even regardless of a "common plan or scheme" in the sense of all of them falling within a single master plan formulated at one time for all of them. The concept of "plan" or "common plan" will be extended in such cases to mean wrongs having a similar but separate plan or "blueprint" underlying each.

(Note: the reader should be reminded that we are not talking about *impeaching* a witness or the accused, but about substantive use.)

F.R.E. 404(b) expresses the principle we have labelled (iii) by declaring that specific instances ("other crimes, wrongs or acts") offered to prove "motive, opportunity, intent, preparation, plan, knowledge, identity, absence of mistake or accident" or other similar purpose is not, at least in theory, offered for the prohibited chain of reasoning (that a person acted in conformity with a propensity of his that can be characterized as *character*, although character is not specifically defined). The prohibited chain under the F.R.E. is "to prove the character of a person in order to show that he acted in conformity therewith." Since evidence offered to prove "motive, opportunity [etc.]" is declared not to be, in theory, offered for that purpose, it is thus not subject to the automatic ban on evidence offered for that chain of reasoning, but is rather subject to the ad hoc balancing of Rule 403 (including an assessment of the danger the jury may use it for impermissible purposes). An examination of many of the traditional cases where evidence has come in under similar catchwords ("motive," "opportunity," etc.), meant to be codified by F.R.E. 404(b), reveals that the permitted purposes are indeed purposes involving proving propensity in order to prove an act in conformity with the propensity; but the propensity is probably too specific to be called character. "Plan," for example, is frequently used to admit other crimes (by the same person) having a similar modus operandi to the present charged crime (the "Brides of the Bath" is but one example); or, in sex crime or child abuse cases, to admit other similar incidents against similar victims, perpetrated by the same individual. In each instance they are admitted to increase the likelihood that the person is the present culprit —that is, to show propensity to do a certain thing in a certain way, in order to establish likelihood he did it that way again. So, too, in the classic instance of the "identity" gateway: the supermarket case, just above. Similarly, if instead of a check with a fictitious name, the supermarket case had involved a check with insufficient funds, other similar incidents by the same person could be offered to show it was intentional rather than a case of accidental overdrawing or mistaken estimate of the amount in the bank, pursuant to the catchwords "intent," "knowledge," "accident," or "mistake." There is considerable overlap in all the terms. The "Brides of the Bath" case, for example, could also involve the same four catchwords. "Motive" has also been used to admit repeated attacks against the same person or class of person, and thus might embrace the "Brides of the Bath" case, too, especially if the wives were all wealthy and the husband inherited. "Motive," however, has frequently been used to admit the other crime in, for example, cases where a person is accused of killing another because of a grudge arising as a result of another criminal transaction, e. g. a failure to split bank robbery proceeds; or where the accused allegedly killed because of a grudge against the victim, say a policeman, for action the policeman has taken in connection with another crime allegedly committed by the accused—perhaps the policeman was pursuing or helping prosecute him. Of course our examples do not exhaust the possibilities of these terms. Except for cases of the type of the last two cases it is difficult to discern a theory of admission under the catchwords that does not implicitly rely on the argument that a propensity has manifest itself. For a discussion of the theory of some of the catchwords and whether, under at least some of them, the prosecution must wait until the issue is disputed in the defendant's case before the prosecution's evidence is admissible, see United States v. Danzey, 594 F.2d 905 (2d Cir. 1979). The cases (with their facts) under the various catchwords are extensively collected in Rothstein, Federal Rules of Evidence at 81 et seq. and 105 et seq. (Clark Boardman Co., 2d ed. 1980 and annual updates). The situations are many and varied.

Should the evidence discussed under this heading (iii) be limited to evidence of other *crimes?* Convictions? With what degree of certitude must wrongs not convicted for be proved in order to be admissible? Must they have been the subject of an inculpatory judgment? Suppose they have been the subject of an *exculpatory* judgment? In the "Brides of the Bath" case, supra, do you suppose it was necessary to actually *show* that the defendant was responsible for the former deaths? How many "other instances" are needed? Would one other suffice in some circumstances? The F.R.E. and most codifications have no specification on these matters, and they are thus left to the general, non-specific policies of a rule like F.R.E. 403 (relevance and its counter-weights), to be computed on the facts of the particular case, frequently with somewhat wide discretion allowed. Thus, all of the factors just mentioned will be merely factors to be weighed with other factors and circumstances, but not automatically conclusive.

The F.R.E., like some previous cases, do not limit showings under the principle discussed under this heading (iii) to the prosecution. Thus, the defense could invoke it, too. But as a practical matter such cases are rare. And see (v) here.

How would you justify the common reception of evidence of other similar crimes to show "predisposition" to commit the present crime, where police entrapment is raised as a defense? Under the law of entrapment such "predisposition" negates the defense. Cf. F.R.E. 404(b), 405 (b).

(iv) *Self defense.*

In a criminal case where self defense is put in issue by the defendant, the question whether the victim was the aggressor can be illuminated with showings concerning the victim's propensity for violence, but in many jurisdictions only if such showings are initiated by the defendant. In certain jurisdictions the permission would be confined to homicide cases (where, of course, the deceased victim is unavailable). In others, it might encompass prosecutions for the various kinds of assault as well. In some juris-dictions, the analogy would extend to permitting such a showing in civil assault, battery, and/or wrongful death cases involving an issue of self defense. The principle of this subsection (iv) is often generalized and called the "character of the victim" principle (but it must be remem-bered that the special subject of showings concerning the victim of a sex crime such as rape is usually dealt with separately; see pp. 387–406). F.R.E. 404(a)(2) permits "evi-dence of a pertinent trait of character of the victim of the crime offered by an accused, or by the prosecution to rebut the same; or evidence of a character trait of peacefulness of the victim offered by the prosecution in a homicide case to rebut evidence [for example, evidence given by a witness who saw the victim attacking the defendant] that the victim was the first aggressor." Notice that the "door opener" by the defendant that licenses the prosecution to show charac-ter of the *homicide* victim may or may not itself be a character showing. For other crime victims, it must be a character showing. For crime victims other than homicide, the issue is not confined to self-defense and first aggressor. Note that the whole rule is confined to criminal cases. Rule 405(a) limits evidence admissible under 404(a)(2) to opinion and reputation evidence. Some jurisdictions allow specific instance evidence. Some confine the evidence to reputation evidence. The quoted language of 404(a)(2) looks like it would encompass showings about the victim in rape cases, but that is covered by a special rule, Rule 412. Showings of that nature are the subject of pp. 387–406, infra.

Evidence of violent acts, reputation, character, etc., of an assault or homicide victim, that were known to the defen-dant, offered to render self-defensive measures of the defen-dant reasonable in the light of this knowledge, looks as though it would be covered here. But in fact the rules and rulings we are discussing are exceptions to the ban on a certain chain of propensity reasoning (that a person acted in conformity with his propensity). This evidence in no way involves that prohibited chain of reasoning, and so needs no special exception. It would be governed by an ad hoc consideration of the factors enumerated in Rule 403. It is usually found to be admissible.

(v) *Civil analogies to the above.*

Where the commission of a crime is in issue in a civil case, as where the complaint charges defendant with a tort that is also a crime or where life insurance depends (pursuant to the terms of the policy) upon whether the insured deceased met his demise through his own criminal act, some courts will permit evidence of his good and bad propensities to the same extent as if he were being tried criminally. It would seem also that the "identity," "motive," "intent," "plan," or "scheme" categories have their analogies in civil cases not involving crimes, although they may go under different appellations. (F.R.E. 404(b), however, applies these same catchwords to civil and criminal cases alike, without distinction.) Thus there are many civil cases where the evidence consists of specific instances sufficiently similar to the dereliction to be established, that in the particular circumstances the evidence is regarded as rationally highly persuasive of the dereliction and admissible.[3]

[3] Prior false claims brought by the plaintiff, of the same sort as the present claim, stand a good chance of being admitted to show the falsity of the present claim. How numerous must the claims be? Can they become too numerous? Must they be shown to be false, or will numerosity supply the inference? If falsity must be shown, to what degree of certitude? Do you think such evidence would be more favorably received if offered to *impeach* a witness-plaintiff? Prior frauds perpetrated by the defendant may be admissible to increase the likelihood that he committed the fraud charged, or did so with intent, if they are of what is regarded as a proper number and quite similar to the present charge, or are part of a common plan or scheme with the present one.

(vi) *Habit; routine practice.*

The concept of *habit,* as that term is used in evidence law, originated in civil cases. A strong, specific, consistent, somewhat involuntary or automatic habit, shown by sufficiently numerous instances or by the opinion of someone who is in a position to know, is usually admissible in a civil case to establish an act, whether it is inculpatory or exculpatory or merely circumstantially relevant in some way. The habit must consist of repetition of a very particular act nearly identical to that in issue. There would seem to be little basis for a distinction between civil and criminal cases,[4] except perhaps when the habit is a bad habit of the defendant. F.R.E. Rule 406 dealing with habit draws no distinction between civil and criminal cases. However, it does not say habit to show an act in conformity is *"admissible,"* but only *"relevant,"* something that was always known. The problem with habit, from the standpoint of both civil and criminal cases, if problem there was, stemmed from the countervailing factors of prejudice, misleadingness, time consumption, etc.—not relevance. Thus, under 406, admissibility would still seem to be controlled by ad hoc consideration of those factors (pursuant to the general listing of those factors in Rule 403). Previous law, more favorably receiving habit than character, may be expected to continue pursuant to these factors. On occasion these factors may allow some distinction between a civil and a criminal case. The rule also declares that the evidence is "relevant" despite such factors as eyewitnesses (to the act sought to be established by the habit) and corroboration (of the testimony establishing the habit or of the act sought to be established

---

[4] Perhaps because it was not "automatic" enough in the context, one case held that defendant's regular attendance every week at religious services at the time of the crime was not admissible to establish that he was most probably at those services rather than at the scene of the crime.

by the habit). Some jurisdictions admit habit to establish an act only if there are no eyewitnesses and/or there is such corroboration. The language of 406 does not insure that these requirements may not be re-imposed by a court either on the facts of a particular case or in general. For no one ever doubted what the rule declares: that the evidence is "relevant" regardless of eyewitnesses and corroboration. The eyewitness and corroboration requirements were imposed pursuant to the countervailing factors now listed in Rule 403, which may still be considered.

Routine business practice amounting to the "habit" of an organization—for example, that letters put in a certain place are regularly mailed, proved by the testimony of someone in a position to know, for the purpose of establishing that a particular letter was mailed—is ordinarily admissible if sufficient regularity is adequately proved. Some jurisdictions again impose a requirement concerning eyewitnesses and/ or corroboration. As in the case of habit, even though the favorable attitude towards reception of routine practice originated in civil cases, there seems no reason to distinguish civil from criminal cases except perhaps where the practice is a "bad" one of the criminal defendant. F.R.E. 406 treats *habit* and *routine practice* identically in all respects, including the matter of eyewitnesses and corroboration and the matter of no express distinction for criminal cases. One is the term used for individuals, the other for organizations.

As under previous law, there is no specification in the F.R.E. as to how to establish the habit or practice—by reputation, opinion, or specific instances—and the matter seems to vary from case to case, controlled only by the general language of Rule 403, which probably serves, among other things, to require enough evidence to establish relative invariability of the habit or practice without excessive redundancy of the evidence.

(vii) *Summary of Substantive Evidence.*

As we have seen, the most outstanding instance of a ban on use of propensity or character evidence is in a criminal case, where the prosecution may not initiate a showing of the defendant's propensity or character except as indicated above. In a civil case, negligence or care may not be shown by a general propensity for negligence or care.[5] But, in accord with the principles above, a habit may be introduced to establish the likelihood of a specific act of negligence or care on the occasion in issue. Other of the above principles may on occasion also serve as a way around the ban.

To be distinguished from evidence offered for purposes of the propensity reasoning under discussion in this entire chapter, is evidence of propensity, character, reputation, particular instances of conduct, etc., offered to prove the truth or falsity of an alleged libel or slander representing the propensity, character, reputation, or conduct to be such-and-such. This is normally admissible pursuant to the general rules relating to relevancy and relevancy's counterweights. Its admissibility *vel non* is not usually the subject of a specific rule. Cf. F.R.E. 405(b). Similarly beyond the scope of the discussion are cases where the issue of damages for defamation engenders a comparison of the plaintiff's reputation before and after the defamation. Again, this is general-

---

[5] Although it is not precisely germane, one common question asked at this point is: Can a criminal conviction (or a fine or ticket), say for a traffic offense, be introduced in a subsequent civil suit based on the same incident? In most jurisdictions, the answer is no, even if a violation of traffic law is per se negligence. Nor will the conviction or fine or ticket have any res judicata effect on the civil case normally. Everything must be proved anew. The situation is usually the same for most offenses, traffic or otherwise. There are a few special statutory and other exceptions. But compare F.R.E. 803(22). Cf. 803(8). If, however, there has been a plea of guilty (or the ticket equivalent), that *may* be admissible as an admission; but usually not *nolo contendere* pleas.

ly not the subject of any specific rule and its admissibility would normally depend upon how the relevancy-and-its-counterweights factors and other rules not specifically addressed to the problem (hearsay, privilege, etc.) may happen to line up on the facts of a particular case. (It is generally admissible.) Cf. F.R.E. 405(b). Also distinguishable as not involving our "propensity reasoning," and as therefore governed like the other matters in this paragraph, and often admissible, are the following: (1) Previous dangerous conduct (or a reputation therefor) on the part of some person, offered to establish that the defendant was negligent in entrusting a dangerous instrumentality to that person when he knew or should have known of the conduct or reputation. See Richmond v. City of Norwich, 96 Conn. 582, 115 A. 11 (1921); Clark v. Stewart, 126 Ohio St. 263, 185 N.E. 71 (1933). (2) Other accidents on the premises introduced either to show that the defendant should have been on notice of the dangerous condition and was therefore negligent in failing to repair, or to show that there was a dangerous condition. See Sullivan v. Detroit & Windsor Ferry Co., 255 Mich. 575, 238 N.W. 221 (1931); Taylor v. Northern States Power Co., 192 Minn. 415, 256 N.W. 674 (1954). (But *safe* condition generally may not be shown by absence of accident. Why not?) (3) Practices of others introduced to show what reasonable men in the circumstances do, for purposes of establishing a standard of care. See Brigham Young Univ. v. Lillywhite, 118 F.2d 836 (10th Cir. 1941); Garthe v. Ruppert, 264 N.Y. 290, 190 N.E. 643 (1934).

It may happen that evidence permissible under one of the theories will also be susceptible of an impermissible use along the lines of another of the theories discussed above, for example where both principal and agent are being sued for some atrocity committed by the agent with a firearm or automobile, and a theory of negligent entrustment is used, which licenses introducing prior instances of or reputation for reckless conduct with other firearms or automobiles on the part of the agent that would not otherwise be admissible (see *Richmond* and *Clark* cases, supra). In such a case, the court, upon request, will normally instruct that this evidence can be used to help establish that the principal knew or should have known of the prior acts or reputation and was negligent in entrusting the agent; but it cannot be used against either the principal or the agent on a theory that it renders it likely that the agent was guilty of the particular instance of misfeasance charged. Only occasionally will the risk of misuse be considered great enough and incurable enough to bar the evidence entirely. Note that the instruction allows the jury to find that the defendant should have made the very inference the jury is forbidden to make.

Another kind of evidence that must be carefully distinguished that does not involve the kind of propensity reasoning under discussion is where prior convictions of a criminal defendant are introduced in enhancement of the penalty, under a statute so providing. Cf. F.R.E. 405(b). Must evidence introduced for this purpose be barred from presentation to the jury before verdict? If not, is a limiting instruction required? Desirable? How would you phrase such an instruction? Is it likely to be efficacious?

Is the (limited) protection from inferences from prior wrongdoing discussed earlier a constitutional matter, at least in criminal cases? See Spencer v. Texas, 385 U.S. 554, 87 S.Ct. 648 (1966); cf. Burgett v. Texas, 389 U.S. 109, 88 S.Ct. 258 (1967).

Also not involved in the present discussion is a situation where the crime charged consists of several component crimes, each of which must be proved. Cf. F.R.E. 405(b).

In some jurisdictions, otherwise inadmissible prior mis-conduct or convictions may be admissible if punitive dam-ages are bona-fidely in issue. How do you account for this? Is there a criminal analogy? Should this be allowed only after a finding of liability has been returned?

(b) *Credibility Evidence.*

In the area of impeachment of witnesses,[6] testimony in the form of *reputation* for a propensity (character) of non-veracity is permitted to be shown; *personal opinion* on the witness' propensity (character) for non-veracity traditionally has not been allowed (but F.R.E. 608 and codes based thereon are contra); and *specific instances of conduct* bespeaking propensity (character) for non-veracity must be divided in two (each admissible according to its own pecul-iar rules, to be discussed later): (1) *misconduct not result-ing in a conviction* (at least semantically the fact that it did not result in a conviction could come about because it was wrong but not illegal, or because it was civilly but not criminally wrong, or because it never became the subject of judicial proceedings, or because there was an acquittal, or because it became the subject only of a civil adjudication either of "guilt" or "innocence," or because an arrest was made and no charges brought, or charges were brought and dropped, etc.); and (2) *convictions* (at least semantically this would include non-final convictions, appealable convic-tions, convictions on appeal, collaterally attackable convic-tions, and convictions being collaterally attacked, as well as other convictions).

The reputation must be for *telling falsehoods or untruths* (honestly mistaken or not); the personal opinion, if per-

---

[6] *Support* of a witness' credibility character or propensity, which is generally allowed only after it has been attacked (impeached), is also part of the subject of this heading; but will not be treated here because its principles are analogous to impeachment and have been considered supra at pp. 348–50.

mitted, has to be *of his veracity* (lying, mistake, etc.); and the specific conduct must be of a sort that evidences a propensity for *non-veracity* (lying, mistake, etc.). Thus, we would expect that instances of fraud or misrepresentation could be shown, as opposed to rape, although some jurisdictions take such an expansive view regarding what reliably and non-prejudicially evidences non-veracity, that virtually any serious wrong is encompassed. How broadly or narrowly the circle of permissibility is drawn must be ascertained from the cases, rules, and statutes in the particular jurisdiction. The law in a given jurisdiction may not be consistent, excluding some wrongs that evidence greater mendacity than some of those included (differences in "prejudiciality" being only sometimes an explanation). And the kinds of convictions permitted may be defined in such vague or illogical terms as "crimes," "infamous crimes," "crimes of moral turpitude," "felonies," "felonies or misdemeanors," or may be more specifically enumerated. One of the more petty disputes engendered by such language has been whether traffic offenses are included. The kinds of crimes allowed may be different for convictions and non-convictions.

In at least one case decided before the new wave of regulation of evidence concerning the victim's sexual character, conduct, etc. in rape cases (discussed infra), reputation for nymphomania was allowed to impeach the complaining witness in a rape case. This illustrates the principle that reputation evidence may not be literally confined to reputation for truthfulness or accuracy, but may extend to other traits or propensities the court thinks are closely relevant to truthfulness or accuracy on the particular facts. The same would be true as to opinion evidence and specific instance evidence as well.

While all the forms of propensity impeachment evidence (reputation, opinion, specific instances of conduct) present considerable danger of undue prejudice where a party-witness is being impeached, the danger seems greatest where specific instances are alleged, particularly where they are convictions, and most particularly where that witness is the defendant in a criminal case. Nevertheless, the probativity is generally considered to outweigh this consideration, if the evidence otherwise complies with the rules applicable to that category of impeachment, although cautionary instructions are required if requested and the judge frequently has discretion to disallow the evidence in an aggravated case, and a duty to do so in some particularly aggravated cases. The law, however, varies on this from jurisdiction to jurisdiction, and many gradations and variations are found.

Let us examine more specifically each of the permissible forms of propensity impeachment evidence: *reputation; opinion;* and *specific instances of misconduct* (the latter breaking down into *misconduct resulting in conviction;* and *misconduct not resulting in conviction*). These areas (particularly convictions) tend to be highly and diversely codified in the various jurisdictions, so that at most we can express some generalizations that are not entirely valid everywhere.

(i) *Reputation (and opinion where allowed, as under the F.R.E.).*

At this juncture it is well to recall a point made earlier: reputation as to propensity for non-veracity is an allowable form of impeachment in most jurisdictions, including those adopting the F.R.E. or its progeny. But only a few jurisdictions, notably F.R.E.-type jurisdictions, also allow *opinion* as to propensity for non-veracity. In general, the rules as to both types of impeachment (where allowed) are the same. No foundation need be laid on cross examination of the witness-to-be-impeached, in the sense used in connection with impeachment by prior inconsistent statements (see pp.

327–335 supra). In other words, extrinsic evidence may be introduced when the time comes, without any preparation of the witness-to-be-impeached. However, a foundation must be laid in the sense that the reputation (or opinion) witness must be shown to be familiar with the reputation (or with the person he is opining about).

If the matter of the reputation *is* approached on cross-examination of the witness being impeached, the cross-examiner may be estopped from introducing the extrinsic evidence, since it may be redundant, depending upon what happens on that cross examination.

F.R.E. 608 codifies the matter of impeachment by opinion and reputation evidence as follows (the emphasis is supplied to indicate the significant change from traditional law):

> "The credibility of a witness may be attacked . . . by evidence in the form of *opinion or* reputation, but . . . the evidence may refer only to character for . . . untruthfulness. . . . Specific instances of . . . conduct . . . may, . . . in the discretion of the court, if probative of truthfulness . . . be inquired into on cross-examination of [a] witness . . . concerning the [veracity-] character . . . of another witness as to which character the witness being cross-examined has testified."

The last quoted sentence is not directly concerned with how to impeach by opinion or reputation for non-veracity, but rather with how to attack, by testing his familiarity with the subject of his testimony, the credibility of a witness *who has attempted such impeachment.* It is included to complete the picture and indicate what an attorney opens the door to by attempting impeachment by opinion or reputation for non-veracity. Note that the specific instances are not conduct of the witness being cross-examined, but of the person he testified about.

(ii) *Misconduct resulting in conviction.*

No foundation need be laid in the sense used in connection with prior inconsistent statements. If the cross-examiner does inquire into the conviction on cross examination of the witness-to-be-impeached and the witness admits the conviction, the impeacher can go no further and cannot introduce extrinsic evidence. Absent extraordinary circumstances, the only extrinsic evidence permitted in any event is just the record of or the fact of conviction (with no aggravating details). Mitigating details are rather freely admitted, more so if the matter comes up on cross examination and the witness at that time wishes to state them. The trial judge is sometimes given considerable discretion to exclude this kind of impeachment on the basis that the misconduct is too remote in time. Where impeachment of a non-party witness is involved, the trial judge ordinarily has little discretion respecting exclusion on the basis of prejudice, need for the evidence, or relevance of the kind of crime to truth-telling ability. The statute or rule usually is deemed to preclude such discretion by enumerating kinds of crimes that may be used. (There may be room for argument based on policy, respecting what crimes are intended where the statute or rule speaks in broad categories.) However, where a party-witness is being impeached, particularly a criminal defendant, discretion of some kind is often accorded by rule, legislation, or judicial fiat.

It is instructive to examine how one jurisdiction (the F.R.E.) codified this kind of impeachment. It is useful also to examine the provision's evolution through various selected versions, i. e., two earlier drafts (the so-called "Supreme Court" draft and the March 1971 draft); and the modifications made in the F.R.E. rule by the 1974 Uniform Rules. All represent respectable American positions currently found somewhere in the U.S., at least in essence. Below is

F.R.E. 609(a), with the variations represented by the earlier drafts and the 1974 Uniform Rules indicated:

"Rule 609.   Impeachment by Evidence of Conviction of Crime

"(a) General Rule.—*For the purpose of attacking the credibility of a witness, evidence that he has been convicted of a crime* [except on a plea of nolo contendere] *shall be admitted* [is admissible] [*if elicited from him or established by public record during cross-examination] but only if the crime (1) was punishable by death or imprisonment in excess of one year under the law under which he was convicted [and the court determines that the probative value of admitting this evidence outweighs its prejudicial effect [to the defendant]* [to a party or witness]] *or (2) involved dishonesty or false statement, regardless of the punishment* [unless in either ·case the judge determines that the probative value of the evidence of the crime is substantially outweighed by the danger of unfair prejudice]."

All the words in italics, bracketed or not, constitute *current* F.R.E. 609.   Bracketed language that is also italicized is language that is omitted from one or more of the other versions of 609 (*i. e.,* the March, 1971 F.R.E. draft, the "Supreme Court" F.R.E. draft, or the 1974 Uniform Rules of Evidence, commended to the states).   Bracketed unitalicized words are present in one or another of the other versions of 609, but are not present in current F.R.E. 609.   The "Supreme Court" F.R.E. draft had neither of the two clauses relating to balancing probativity against prejudice.   But it did have the "is admissible" language rather than "shall be admitted"—did this mean Rule 403 could be used to keep out the evidence under that draft but not under the present draft?   Rule 403 on its face would seem to reach the two categories of crimes enumerated in 609(a).   On the question whether 403 could be used to bar 609(a)(2) convictions despite Congress' failure to subject them to the balancing language in 609(a)(1), see United States v. Toney, 615 F.2d 277 (5th Cir. 1980) (under enacted draft of rule). Notice also, from the wording of 403, that the "presumption" or "priority" is in favor of admissibility. Is that so under the first bracketed "weighing" clause quoted above? Is it so under the second, i. e., the very last bracketed, unitalicized clause in the rule above? (Is it so under the weighing clause in 609(b), quoted below?) No version of 609(a) has *both* of the bracketed weighing provisions. Notice, in the first "weighing" clause in 609(a) quoted above, that there are alternative formulations there concerning whom prejudice must accrue to (defendant; or party or witness). Current F.R.E. 609(a) says "defendant;" the Uniform Rules say "party or witness." Why this special, favorable, unequal treatment of the "defendant" in the F.R.E.? Should the provision say "criminal defendant" instead? Does a limited weighing provision placed specifically in the rule, preclude application of the more general Rule 403? Is it wise to restrict the proof to the time of cross examination and allow no other proof than the witness' word or the public record, as current F.R.E. 609 does? Suppose the witness denies the conviction and the record is unavailable?

It is also worthwhile reproducing the remainder of current F.R.E. 609, this time without any other versions, and (owing to space limitations of this short volume) without comment as to how other jurisdictions may differ:

> "(b) Time Limit.—Evidence of a conviction under this rule is not admissible if a period of more than ten years has elapsed since the date of the conviction or of the release of the witness from the confinement imposed for that conviction, whichever is the later date, unless the court determines, in the interests of justice, that the probative value of the conviction supported by

specific facts and circumstances substantially outweighs its prejudicial effect. However, evidence of a conviction more than 10 years old as calculated herein, is not admissible unless the proponent gives to the adverse party sufficient advance written notice of intent to use such evidence to provide the adverse party with a fair opportunity to contest the use of such evidence.

"(c) Effect of pardon, annulment, or certificate of rehabilitation.—Evidence of a conviction is not admissible under this rule if (1) the conviction has been the subject of a pardon, annulment, certificate of rehabilitation, or other equivalent procedure based on a finding of the rehabilitation of the person convicted, and that person has not been convicted of a subsequent crime which was punishable by death or imprisonment is excess of one year, or (2) the conviction has been the subject of a pardon, annulment, or other equivalent procedure based on a finding of innocence.

"(d) Juvenile Adjudications.—Evidence of juvenile adjudications is generally not admissible under this rule. The court may, however, in a criminal case allow evidence of a juvenile adjudication of a witness other than the accused if conviction of the offense would be admissible to attack the credibility of an adult and the court is satisfied that admission in evidence is necessary for a fair determination of the issue of guilt or innocence.

"(e) Pendency of Appeal.—The pendency of an appeal therefrom does not render evidence of a conviction inadmissible. Evidence of the pendency of an appeal is admissible."

These provisions indicate some of the complexity of impeachment by conviction. Let us turn now to impeachment by misconduct not resulting in conviction.

(iii) *Misconduct not resulting in conviction.*

Many courts do not permit this line of impeachment at all. Those that do, permit it upon cross examination of the witness-to-be-impeached only. No extrinsic evidence is permitted. The witness' answer must be accepted (although not necessarily his first answer: some "badgering" seems to be permitted so long as it is confined to the cross examination). The trial judge is given enormous discretion to permit or disallow the inquiry based upon (a) the relevance of the kind of misconduct to truth-telling ability, (b) proximity or remoteness of the misconduct in time, and (c) all of the other factors we have discussed that influence the exercise of a judge's discretion in matters of evidence, including prejudice, need, time, confusion, etc. He will seldom be reversed, particularly if he opts to exclude. A very few jurisdictions are more liberal than this and permit this evidence on a basis similar to that under convictions (heading (ii) immediately above) or require the trial judge to permit very wide inquiry into all kinds of misconduct not resulting in conviction upon cross examination (while at the same time still forbidding extrinsic evidence). F.R.E. 608(b) codifies the matter as follows:

> "Specific instances of the conduct of a witness, for the purpose of attacking . . . his credibility, other than conviction of crime . . . may not be proved by extrinsic evidence. They may, however, in the discretion of the court, if probative of . . . untruthfulness, be inquired into on cross-examination of the witness . . . concerning his character for . . . untruthfulness . . .."

A witness being impeached by this method of impeachment may have a self-incrimination privilege to refuse to answer the impeachment questions. See pp. 43–44, 462–65.

(This does not apply to impeachment by *convictions,* pursuant to (ii) above, because conviction ordinarily removes the possibility of further incrimination.)

Some Common Principles of These Substantive and Credibility "Rules" Relating to Propensity Evidence: Instructions

Where propensity evidence is offered on and meets the requirements of one of the permissible propensity theories, but there is a danger of one of the impermissible uses being made by the jury, the evidence usually will be admitted, but the opponent of the evidence is entitled to an instruction attempting to forbid the jury from making the impermissible use, and, as always, to a parallel limitation on argument. (A frank explanation to the jury of the dangers and probative shortcomings of the evidence would serve much better than such an instruction.) In an aggravated case, however, where the legitimate value of the evidence is considered to be greatly outweighed by the risk of misuse or when the real purpose of the offering party is manifestly illegitimate, and a cautionary instruction is deemed insufficiently efficacious, the evidence will be excluded.

The problem addressed in the black letters just above is most acutely presented where a criminal defendant takes the stand as a witness for himself, and the prosecution seeks to impeach him by showing his propensity for falsehood, for example by prior convictions, which could easily be taken as evidence of propensity to commit crimes including the present one, or could cause the jury to convict for past badness. See, for one approach to this problem, Luck v. United States, 348 F.2d 763 (D.C.Cir. 1965) (cited for its approach, not as authority), giving the judge exclusionary power. A compromise approach is found in current F.R.E. 609(a), set forth several pages supra. An analogous problem is presented where the accused's good character witnesses are sought to be impeached by inquiry into their knowledge of former derelictions of the accused. This is generally permitted in the form stated earlier in this chapter (pp. 358-9), with cautionary instructions against any other use of the evidence, but on occasion it may be excluded for reasons like those just noted. See Awkard v. United States, 352 F.2d 641 (D.C.Cir. 1965) (impeaching value slight because the witness-to-be-impeached did not testify as to familiarity with defendant in the locale of or at the time of the purported wrongdoing of defendant).

Even where there is only one possible use of propensity evidence, and that a permissible one, the opponent is frequently entitled to an instruction cautioning against the danger of overemphasis, and to some regulation of argument.

Common Principles Continued: Remedies for Introduction of Impermissible Propensity Evidence

As in the case of other impermissible evidence, where a propensity has been impermissibly introduced by one side, without the fault of the other (i. e., the other could not have been expected to object sooner before it was introduced), an argument can be made that a contrary propensity (or one that tends to dispel the effect of the impermissible evidence) should be allowed to be shown even though it would not otherwise be allowed to be shown. The court will consider, however, the comparative adequacy and desirability of other remedies, such as a motion to strike (which results in an instruction to the jury to disregard) or a mistrial.

See for an example of the problem addressed in the black letters, Hudson v. Hightower, 394 S.W.2d 46 (Tex.Civ. App.1965). Defendant in an auto collision case testifies seemingly somewhat accidentally and unexpectedly that he normally entered the relevant intersection slowly. Plaintiff then produces a witness who states that defendant normally went through that intersection "too fast—50 or 60 m. p. h." The judge instructs the jury that the sole purpose of the latter testimony is to "rebut [defendant's] testimony as to how he customarily entered the intersection . . . and it is no evidence of the speed or the manner in which [defendant] entered the intersection on the date of the collision in question." Assuming adequate requests were made, was the instruction sufficient to protect defendant? Was it phrased meaningfully? Should the "rebuttal" of what defendant said have been ruled inadmissible when the judge previewed it out of the hearing of the jury? Should neutralization of defendant's testimony by instruction of some kind have been considered in order and sufficient without allowing defendant's testimony to be rebutted? Was a new trial in order at some point, rather than what was done? A new trial either upon defendant's testimony, plaintiff's witness' testimony, the end of the case, or some other point?

Common Principles Continued: Two Helpful Questions

It will be noted from the "rules" governing propensity evidence set forth earlier in this chapter, that when character evidence is offered and is not inadmissible per se, there are two questions the offering attorney frequently must ask himself regardless of whether he plans to use the proof for impeachment or substantively: "Is the propensity I am seeking to prove, of the requisite specificity (i. e., in a theft case, tendency with respect to stealing rather than with respect to fighting or lawlessness generally)?" and, assuming that it is, "Am I proving it with the proper kind of evidence (i. e., opinion, reputation, or specific instances)?"

In general, as we have seen, the law allows only the more specific and frequently only reputation (and opinion under the F.R.E. and rules patterned thereafter).

As we have seen, even in areas of evidence law where character proof is not per se forbidden, the dangers involved have rationally or irrationally inclined the law to place restrictions on both the degree of generality of the propensity, and the kind of evidence used to prove the propensity. For example, with reference to the degree of generality, if a witness is sought to be impeached, can a propensity for criminality or immorality in general be shown (there may be some slight tendency for dissolute persons to be more mendacious than others), or must it be a propensity for telling falsehoods, more specifically? In a criminal rape case, if the prosecution is permitted to increase the apparent probability of guilt by showing the defendant's character for such acts (assume defendant has triggered this), will a propensity for criminality in general suffice, or must it be a propensity for rape? [7] It is true that "generally lawless" persons may be somewhat more disposed to rape than others. But significantly so? Enough to outweigh the dangers? In an assault or homicide prosecution, may the accused show his general good character, morality, and law abiding nature, or is he confined to showing his non-violence and peaceableness? These are all examples of the first question the attorney must ask himself, supra, which relates to the generality or specificity of the propensity. The law will ordinarily allow only the more specific. Thus, for example, in the area of impeachment, we have seen that *usually* the witness' propensity only for non-veracity (honest

---

[7] Notice that neither of the two alternatives in each of our examples is *so* specific as to take the matter out of the realm of character. See discussion at pp. 355–59 supra. What we are saying is that within the realm of character, the more specific character (character "trait?") is required.

error as well as dishonest deception) may be shown. The specific is also required in the other examples just posed. For a more precise answer, see the "rules" under the italicized headings "substantive evidence" and "credibility evidence" in this chapter above.

Once the generality or specificity that is required by the law is ascertained and the attorney proposes to prove (for his substantive or impeachment purpose) a propensity that meets the requirement, he is confronted with the second question: What kind of evidence may be used to establish that propensity? As we have seen, conceptually there are at least three feasible varieties: Testimony by someone as to that someone's perception of the subject person's reputation for the propensity; testimony by someone as to that someone's own personal opinion of the subject person in the relevant respect (that is, with respect to the propensity); and testimony or other proof of specific instances of conduct evidencing the propensity.

Generally speaking, the "rules" discussed above in this chapter reveal that the law has been more receptive to reputation evidence (for which a tacit exception to the hearsay rule must be made) than to either opinion or specific instance evidence. Can you say why? But see F.R.E. 405 and 608 generally allowing reputation *and* opinion evidence, but still generally barring specific instance evidence. We have seen above, however, that there are occasions under traditional law and the F.R.E., where specific instances are allowed. (Opinion seems to mean lay opinion.)

Common Principles Continued: Reputation, Opinion, Specific Instances: The Required Foundation

Under all three of the forms of evidence (reputation, opinion, specific instances), there is a requirement that the person testifying must be familiar with that whereof he speaks. Thus, in the case of

> reputation testimony, courts normally require that the witness and the subject have lived or done business in reasonable proximity to each other for a substantial period in the fairly recent past, and that the reputation reported be the reputation in that community and be relatively current. A prerequisite for personal opinion testimony would be that the witness and the subject person have had some substantial recent intercourse together that would furnish a reasonable basis for a current opinion. Recent or current means near the act to be established by the propensity.

If this foundation appears, weaknesses in the evidence in terms of *degree* of the witness's exposure would be matters of weight and not admissibility.

Common Principles Continued: Specific Instances: Further Restrictions

> Respecting specific instances of conduct, while there is little uniformity, courts usually restrict the adduction of details (perhaps favoring mitigating details) and in addition there is often a preference for the most economical and trustworthy form of proof available: a record of the conviction, etc. There is also frequently a requirement of temporal proximity between the conduct sought to be put into evidence and the conduct in issue. Additionally, there may be authority relating to the effect of formal legal dispositions that may have occurred with respect to the specific instance.

With respect to the last point in the heading, while there is little uniformity, some authority suggests that mere charges that have been dropped and arrests that have not resulted in charges, are barred as evidence of misconduct, and may even prevent the underlying misconduct from being evidenced even if it is evidenced by some other means, such as a witness. At the very least, the favorable (or at least not unfavorable) legal disposition of the incident ought to be allowed to be shown to curtail or destroy the force of the evidence, with perhaps an instruction cautioning about what can be deduced from a mere charge or arrest. We would expect a similar result where the alleged misconduct was the subject of an exculpatory civil or criminal adjudication, or, perhaps, a pardon, or, on a proper occasion, where an appeal, say of a conviction, is pending. Would you say the presence of a ground for collateral attack (e. g., habeas corpus) of a conviction should have a similar effect? Some of these matters are dealt with, as respects convictions used for impeachment, in F.R.E. 609(c)–(e). But in general they are not subject to rule and are handled on a more ad hoc basis.

Even if some of these matters do not affect admissibility, they are certainly fertile ground for arguments to the factfinder respecting weight.

Special Regulation of Propensity or Character Evidence (Whether Offered for Substantive or Credibility Purposes) as it Relates to Certain Sex Crime Victims: F.R.E. 412 Typical

A recent movement toward special, separate regulation restricting evidence of the character, conduct, or propensity of the victim of certain sex crimes such as rape is illustrated by F.R.E. 412, enacted several years after the other rules in the F.R.E. This new rule prohibits the introduction of opinion or reputation evidence about the past sexual behavior of an alleged victim of rape or assault with intent to rape. Other kinds of evidence to the same effect (principally evidence of specific instances) are also inadmissible except in three listed circumstances: (1) when the evidence is "constitutionally required to be admitted;" (2) when the accused offers evidence of sexual behavior between

the victim and a third party to show whether the accused "was or was not, with respect to the alleged victim, the source of semen or injury;" or (3) when the accused introduces evidence of the alleged victim's past sexual behavior with the accused relevant to the issue of consent.

Among the more obvious unanswered questions that may be asked concerning the above categories of potentially admissible evidence listed in the rule are why the "constitutionally required" category was not also made applicable to *opinion* and *reputation* evidence, instead of being confined to *specific instance* evidence; and would the category "injury" embrace pregnancy and/or disease, as well as whatever else it may embrace. Some of the state provisions are more explicit on these scores. Of course, the constitution prevails to admit "constitutionally required" evidence, whatever the rule states. Thus the constitutional provision is at once too narrow, and unnecessary (except perhaps as a reminder to trial judges).

It is clear that the provisions of 412 apply to both substantive and credibility evidence; that they apply whether the evidence is offered on a propensity or character theory or not; and that they apply only to the crimes of rape and assault with intent to rape. The evidence relating to victims of other sex crimes (and to victims of non-sex crimes) is left to the less restrictive, more discretionary, and more ambiguous provisions of Rules 404–406 (character and habit), particularly 404(a)(2) (character of victim, as restricted by 405(a) relating to form of proof), Rules 608–609 (credibility character and conduct), and Rule 611(a) (judge's responsibility to prevent unnecessary harassment and embarrassment), all as conditioned by 403 (relevance and its counterweights). These were also the governing rules as to the victims of rape and assault with intent to rape before enactment of Rule 412. These rules are discussed earlier in this chapter.

It is also clear that the *prohibitions* of Rule 412 apply regardless of other F.R.E. rules.

But certain severe questions of scope remain. Is evidence listed as *allowable* under Rule 412 subject also to screening under Rules 404–406 relating to character and habit generally, with the result that it might be prohibited by those rules? For example, those rules provide that *specific instances* of conduct on the part of a victim generally cannot be introduced to show a pattern of conduct or character of the victim in order to show an act by the victim in conformity with it (though reputation or opinion may). Those rules do, however, allow specific instances if they can qualify as showing "motive, intent, plan," etc., or habit, or an element of a crime (as where it is a crime for a convicted felon to possess a weapon—the conviction may be shown). See F.R.E. 404(a)(2); 405(a); 404(b); 405(b); 406. Yet Rule 412 seems to indicate (pursuant to category (3) in our heading) that specific instances of the victim's sexual behavior with the defendant may be allowed to show consent, apparently regardless of these requirements, although this is not clear—one permissible reading is that the category is meant merely to except from the ban of Rule 412 and not any bans of any other rules. (Interestingly enough, 404(a)(2) and 405(a) would allow reputation and opinion for these purposes, whereas 412 would not. In the case of a *prohibition* in 412, the prohibition clearly controls as against all other rules.)

The relationship to yet other rules is also obscure, particularly Rule 403 (balancing of relevancy and its counterweights). Although, as we shall see below, a similar balancing is provided under Rule 412, it does not mention all the factors of Rule 403, so a question could arise as to whether it is meant to be exclusive.

Returning now to the express provisions of Rule 412, evidence that is encompassed within one of the categories of admissible evidence listed in the rule (i. e., (1), (2), or (3) in our black letters above) must go through certain procedures to be admissible: In all three situations, the rule provides that at least fifteen days before the date on which the trial is scheduled to begin, the accused must file with the court and serve upon the alleged victim and all other parties a written motion to offer such evidence. The court may permit the motion to be made at a later date, including during trial, if the evidence is newly discovered and could not with "due diligence" have been obtained previously, or if the issue to which the evidence relates has newly arisen. The motion must be accompanied by a written offer of proof. Upon a determination that the offer of proof contains evidence described in one of the three exceptions noted above, the court must order an in-chambers hearing to determine the admissibility of the evidence. If the relevance of the evidence depends on the fulfillment of a condition of fact, the court must at this or at a subsequent in-chambers hearing accept evidence on and determine whether the condition of fact is satisfied, notwithstanding the provisions of Federal Evidence Rule 104(b) (which generally allows contingently relevant evidence to be admitted subject to jury determination of the fact upon which relevance hinges, provided there is *some* evidence of that fact or *some* evidence of it is promised to be introduced later). If the court determines on the basis of the hearing that the evidence is probative enough to outweigh the danger of unfair prejudice,[8] it may be admitted in the trial, but only in

---

[8] Although the rule is unclear and sidesteps the issue, the concern for victims that prompted the rule would indicate that "prejudice" is not confined to prejudice to the determination of the case or to one side or the other, but includes the interests of the victim-witness and society, something left ambiguous in the usual evidentiary "balancing"

accordance with a court order specifying the evidence that may be offered and the areas with respect to which the alleged victim may be examined or cross-examined. The weighing and court-order procedure, however, is not, at least under the terms of the statute, applicable to evidence "constitutionally required to be admitted." The notice, motion, offer of proof, hearing, and fact-finding procedure, however, is applicable to such evidence. Can a constitutional right be so conditioned?

It is not made clear in the text of the rule whether the in-chambers proceedings can be off the record (or the record sealed) and the public and press barred access. Conceptually, access could be part of the defendant's constitutional right to a public trial; or a First Amendment "freedom of press" matter involving the right of the public and press to have and give information. Analogies may be found in the fact that informers' privilege and state and military secrets privileges are often determined in secret. The access situation concerning other suppression hearings and other similar contexts has not yet been definitively settled although recent Supreme Court authority suggests that at least in some situations (e. g. certain preliminary proceedings as opposed to the trial itself) the right belongs to the defendant and cannot be asserted by the press under the First Amendment if the defendant and prosecution agree to closure. Those preliminary proceedings did not involve the kind of delicate privacy rights of third persons that we have here, and there is reason to believe closure could be ordered here regardless of the wishes of the defendant. See Gannett Co. v. De Pasquale, 443 U.S. 368, 99 S.Ct. 2898 (1979). Cf. Richmond Newspapers v. Virginia, — U.S. —, 100 S.Ct. 2814 (1980).

provision. See F.R.E. 403; cf. F.R.E. 611(a). Does this interpretation raise constitutional questions from the standpoint of the defense?

The advance notice provisions may present some problems concerning compelled advance disclosure of the defendant's case, which could be of constitutional dimension. There is precedent, however, in provisions requiring advance disclosure of alibi and insanity defenses, but the Supreme Court seems to require some sort of "reciprocity" on the part of the prosecution. See Wardius v. Oregon, 412 U.S. 470, 93 S.Ct. 2208 (1973); Williams v. Florida, 399 U.S. 78, 90 S.Ct. 1893 (1970); Fed.R.Crim.Proc. 12.1, 12.2. A number of states have such provisions.

Special Regulation of the Evidence as it Relates to Certain Sex Crime Victims, Continued: Selected State Statutes

Rule 412, in limiting the use of evidence about the sexual history of the victim, comports with a modern statutory trend in the states. Let us examine a representative sampling of such statutes.

In Michigan (Mich.Comp.L.Ann. § 750.520j (West Supp.1977)), opinion or reputation evidence about or specific instances of a victim's sexual conduct is inadmissible except to the extent that a judge finds that evidence of the victim's past sexual conduct with the actor or evidence of specific instances of sexual activity showing the source or origin of semen, pregnancy, or disease, is material to a fact at issue in the case. In addition, the judge must find that the prejudicial or inflammatory nature of the evidence does not outweigh its probative value. Within ten days after arraignment, the defendant must file a written motion and offer of proof. The court may order an in-camera hearing to determine whether the evidence is admissible.

In New York (N.Y.Crim.Proc.L. § 60.42), evidence of a victim's "sexual conduct" (apparently this includes reputation evidence as well as evidence of particular instances, with personal opinion evidence continuing to be banned in

New York by virtue of the common law) is not admissible in a prosecution for a sex offense unless it (1) tends to prove specific instances of the victim's prior sexual conduct with the accused; (2) tends to prove that the victim has been convicted of a prostitution offense within three years prior to the present offense; (3) rebuts (not "tends to rebut") prosecution evidence that the victim has not engaged in sexual activities during a given period of time (it is not clear whether this provision would cover evidence showing that the victim has engaged in it *more often* than admitted); (4) rebuts prosecution evidence that the accused is the cause of the victim's pregnancy or disease or the source of the semen found in the victim (what about rebutting evidence that the accused caused other physical evidence of intercourse, such as local bruising, etc.? What about showing that the victim *thought* she was pregnant by another act of intercourse, and charged rape to cover up? —cf. State v. DeLawder, 28 Md.App. 212, 344 A.2d 446 (1975)); or (5) is found by the court to be relevant and admissible "in the interests of justice" after (a) an offer of proof outside the hearing of the jury, or such other hearing as the court may require, and (b) a statement by the court of its findings of fact. See, on (5), People v. Mandel, 61 A.D. 563, 403 N.Y.S.2d 63 (1978), rev'd 48 N.Y.2d 952, 425 N.Y.S.2d 63, 401 N.E.2d 185, cert. denied 446 U.S. 949 (1979), reh'g denied 448 U.S. 908 (1980).

Colorado (Colo.Rev.Stat. § 18-3-407 (1976 Cum.Supp.)) imposes a presumption that specific instances of prior or subsequent sexual conduct as well as opinion or reputation evidence of this nature are irrelevant. (While "*or subsequent*" is omitted from many of the codifications, it is probably meant to be understood; in addition, some formulations omit "prior" or "other" as well, but obviously evidence of the very incident in issue is not meant to be barred). This presumption does not apply to evidence of a

victim's prior or subsequent sexual history with the defendant or to evidence (offered to show the defendant did not
commit the alleged rape) of specific instances of sexual
activity showing the source or origin of semen, pregnancy,
disease, or the like.   If an accused proposes to present
evidence overcoming, or under an exception to, the presumption, or evidence that a victim has a history of falsely
reporting sexual assaults (a kind of evidence not specifically
licensed in the other enactments but probably not needed
to be because such evidence may not be within the ban on
evidence of "sexual behavior or conduct"), the defendant
must make a written motion thirty days before trial to the
court and to the opposing parties stating that the moving
party has an offer of proof of the relevance and materiality
of such evidence.   An affidavit in which the offer of proof is
to be stated must accompany the written motion.   Upon a
finding that the offer of proof is sufficient, the court must
set a pre-trial in-camera hearing.   (The pre-trial procedure
can be dispensed with, and the matter handled by in-
camera proceedings at trial, if good cause is shown.)
If the court finds at the conclusion of the hearing that the
proposed evidence is "relevant to a material issue" in the
case, the court must order that the evidence can be introduced and prescribe the nature of the evidence or questions to be permitted.   "Relevant to a material issue" seems
a lax standard.   On its face, probativity and prejudice are
not compared.   There obviously was constitutional or other
sensitivity to restricting relevant defense evidence.

Other states have also enacted statutes that limit the use
of evidence about a rape victim's sexual history.   These
include, among others, California, Florida, Iowa, and South
Dakota.   Several courts have imposed similar restrictions
judicially.   See, e. g., United States v. Driver, 581 F.2d 80
(4th Cir. 1978) (prior to F.R.E. 412); United States v. Kasto,
584 F.2d 268 (8th Cir. 1978) (prior to F.R.E. 412; contrary

case overruled); State ex rel. Pope v. Superior Court, 113
Ariz. 22, 545 P.2d 946 (1976) (en banc); State v. Geer, 13
Wash.App. 71, 533 P.2d 389 (1975). For more traditional
cases, but expressing limits on the evidence, see People v.
Stephens, 18 Ill.App.3d 971, 310 N.E.2d 824 (1974); State v.
Yowell, 513 S.W.2d 397 (Mo.1974). An important case re-
stricting the evidence is McLean v. United States, 377 A.2d
74 (D.C.App.1977).

Special Regulation of the Evidence as it Relates to Certain Sex Crime Victims, Continued: Protecting the Victim vs. Protecting the Accused's Right to Defend: Policy and Constitutional Considerations

The impetus for the new federal and state regulation,
above, was a general feeling that in rape cases there was
too much indiscriminate cross examination about and other
evidence relating to the sexual behavior of the victim.
Unquestionably, this "second attack" on victims in the
courtroom, in addition to severely affecting their psyche and
privacy, made them reluctant to report the crime, testify at
trial, or otherwise cooperate with the police and prosecution. Frequently, the evidence contributed little of legitimate value to the trial. On the other side, however, is the
consideration that restricting this evidence could deprive a
defendant of some item of proof which could legitimately
lessen the probability of his guilt. At some point, such
restriction, at least if not intelligently drawn, may impact on
the constitutional right to defend.

Some defense lawyers would argue that the Constitution
(when it confers rights to jury trial, to compulsory process
to secure the attendance of favorable witnesses, to confrontation, to a fair trial under general due process, and the
like) confers a right on the defense to introduce all defensive evidence that a reasonable juror might feel bears in

any measure on defendant's legal guilt or innocence. (See particularly the Sixth Amendment for these guarantees.) In other words, relevance (and perhaps undue prejudice instilled in the tribunal) is all that can be considered. After all, all that need be raised is a reasonable doubt. If this is so, any restrictions on defense evidence that issue out of *other* considerations—such as solicitude for the interests of victims and witnesses or the extrinsic policy of encouraging them to come forward, upon which all these regulations must at least in part depend—would have to fall.

But so, too, would many ordinary rules of evidence when used against the defense: for example, the doctor-patient privilege; the spousal confidentiality privilege; the attorney-client privilege; the rule banning evidence of safety measures taken after an injury; the rule banning evidence of offers of compromise; the character rules; even the hearsay rule. For in each of these instances, evidence which some reasonable juror could think raises a reasonable doubt or advances the probability of innocence some percentage points over what it appeared to be before, is kept out because of some extrinsic social policy, such as encouraging patients or spouses in the community to communicate in order to promote better health care or marriages, or encouraging safety measures or settlements in the public interest.

Even the hearsay rule keeps out evidence of a type we all think useful and relevant in daily life. For example, we rely on hearsay when we invest, or look up a telephone number, or even read the clock—all the people whose credibility we rely on are not present at that time for questioning. The law excludes hearsay because the evidence could be improved, perhaps by producing the declarant, or because better evidence is available, and because attorneys in general (not just in this case) should be encouraged to produce the declarant or the better evidence. In this way, the accuracy of decisions *in general* will be increased. Evidence that could be legitimately useful to the accused is sacrificed for a broader social policy.

The character rule similarly excludes evidence rational people may think reduces the probability of guilt. The evidence is excluded for other reasons—in part for reasons related to the undue imposition the evidence places on the person whose bad character is injected. The evidence may come as a surprise to him; and also, the law wants to give him a chance to reform and "live it down." Only in part is exclusion motivated by probative infirmities in the evidence (i. e., jury exaggeration). Thus, a defendant might be prevented from proving, via evidence of the character of a third party, some relevant act of that third party—for example that the third party was at the critical place rather than defendant. In some jurisdictions, a homicide defendant or simple assault defendant could even be prevented from adducing certain forms of proof (e. g., specific instances) of the victim's character for aggressiveness to make it more likely that the victim attacked *him.* Indeed this seems to be the result of reading F.R.E. 404(a)(2) with 405(a). Or the defendant may be prevented from showing the bad character of a prosecution witness, to attack credibility, at least in certain jurisdictions as to some forms of character evidence.

The attorney-client privilege is a clear example. Suppose defendant is prevented by the privilege from showing some relevant act of a third party because defendant seeks to prove it by means of a confidential letter between the third party and that party's attorney. The privilege exists to protect the third party's confidentiality and the social interest in encouraging clients in general to communicate with their lawyers. It exists to foster informed legal services generally—not because of any problem with cogency, etc. Can we constitutionally hobble the defense out of solicitude for these interests? Cf. United States v. Buckley, 586 F.2d 498 (5th Cir. 1978); People v. Maynard, 80 Misc.2d 279, 363 N.Y.S.2d 384 (1970).

Even the work-product privilege (for example invoked by prosecution against defense) is based on a social policy of encouraging thorough case work-ups in general, and not relevance, etc.

Also very much in point is the universally recognized evidence rule expressed by F.R.E. 611(a) that the trial judge may regulate the mode and order of interrogation of witnesses and presentation of evidence to "protect witnesses from harassment or undue embarrassment."

A less extreme version of our defense lawyers' constitutional argument would say that *significantly* relevant defensive evidence may not be kept out in the absence of *compelling* reasons.

The much publicized *Farber* case (so-called because the reporter involved was named Farber) may support one or other of these views of the Constitution. In that case, New Jersey's journalist privilege statute protecting a reporter's notes and sources from disclosure, embodying first amendment values, was held by the New Jersey court to be inapplicable when used to bar a criminal murder defendant's access to potential sources of exculpatory evidence. The reporter had covered the murder, and defendant believed the reporter's investigation might have contained some leads to evidence useful to the defense. New York Times v. New Jersey (New Jersey v. Jascalevitch), 78 N.J. 259, 394 A.2d 330 (1978), cert. denied 439 U.S. 997, 99 S.Ct. 598.

A number of other decisions seem to reinforce the notion that there is some sort of emerging constitutional right to introduce defensive evidence. An Alaska statute protecting

the confidentiality of juvenile records was held constitutionally inapplicable to prevent' a criminal defendant from
impeaching a prosecution witness with the witness' juvenile
record. Davis v. Alaska, 415 U.S. 308, 94 S.Ct. 1105 (1974)
(right to confrontation). And a familiar evidence rule that
declared an out-of-court confession of sole guilt by a third
party to be inadmissible hearsay when offered in behalf of
the defendant was similarly stricken down, at least when
coupled with the familiar rule that one cannot impeach
one's own witness (so that the defendant could not call the
third party and impeach him with the confession). Chambers v. Mississippi, 410 U.S. 284, 93 S.Ct. 1038 (1973) (confrontation; compulsory process; fair trial under general due
process). See also the handful of cases that do hold that
various confidential communications privileges of witnesses
have denied defendants constitutional rights to effectively
cross examine, or to call favorable witnesses. E. g., Salazar
v. State, 559 P.2d 66 (Alaska 1976); State v. Hembd, 232
N.W.2d 872 (Minn.1975); State v. Roma, 140 N.J.Super. 582,
357 A.2d 45 (1976), aff'd 143 N.J.Super. 504, 363 A.2d 923.
Cf. State v. Myers, 115 R.I. 583, 350 A.2d 611 (1976);
Chesney v. Robinson, 403 F.Supp. 306 (D.Conn.1975), cert.
denied 429 U.S. 867, 97 S.Ct. 177; United States v. Cardillo,
316 F.2d 606 (2d Cir. 1963), cert. denied 375 U.S. 822, 84
S.Ct. 60; State v. Walters, 528 S.W.2d 790 (Mo.App.1975);
People v. Flores, 71 Cal.App.3d 559, 139 Cal.Rptr. 546 (3d
Dist. 1977); Commonwealth v. Michel, 367 Mass. 454, 327
N.E.2d 720 (1975); State v. Macumber, 112 Ariz. 569, 544
P.2d 1084 at 1088 (1976) (concurrence).

A number of decisions have considered the constitu-
tionality of rape evidence provisions, with mixed results.
In addition to People v. Mandel, supra, see, e. g., State v.
Jalo, 27 Or.App. 845, 557 P.2d 1359 (1976). Cf. People v.
Blackburn, 56 Cal.App.3d 685, 128 Cal.Rptr. 864 (1975);
Lynn v. State, 231 Ga. 559, 203 S.E.2d 221 (1970); State v.
Geer, supra.

What probably will emerge is that there is a right to introduce defensive evidence, but that some "reasonable" amount of restriction of defense evidence will be allowed ("reasonable" to be determined by case development), even when the restriction is based upon considerations of extrinsic social policy, such as the functioning of the criminal justice system or protection of witnesses' privacy. The importance to the particular case of the barred evidence and the importance of the reason for the restriction will be scrutinized. Consideration of these factors finds some support in the areas of informer's identity privilege and state and military secrets. The typicality or atypicality of the restriction in state law around the country may also play a role. The decisions will be ad hoc, and will, of course, in particular cases, override the applicable rule, whether the rule provides specifically for the Constitution or not. In general, most of the Federal Rules of Evidence have been drafted on the assumption that the Constitution may override a particular application of a rule and that this need not be expressly stated in the rule. The rules seldom make specific reference to the Constitution (although as Rule 412 shows, this is not uniformly the case).

Special Regulation of the Evidence as it Relates to Certain Sex Crime Victims, Continued: A Problem for Student Analysis

Considering all that is said above concerning the special regulation of the evidence in sex crime cases, and considering the general desirability of giving litigants, victims, and the judge specific guidance rather than referring merely to general desirable policies or to the Constitution, would you recommend the following hypothetical rule for adoption instead of F.R.E. 412 in states having rules modelled on the F.R.E. who have not yet adopted F.R.E. 412? In your view, does it improve upon Rule 412 or does it introduce more problems? To aid in your analysis, hypothetical "Drafters'

Notes" are provided to explain the hypothetical rule, following the rule:

"**Rule xxx: Character and Conduct of Victim in Sex Crime Cases**

"(a) In a prosecution for a sex offense, evidence relating to the victim's other sexual conduct or the victim's sexual character or sexual propensities is not admissible unless it complies with the *Rules of Evidence* and is in the form of specific instances of conduct, and such conduct:

(1) is relevant to the issue of consent and involved participation by the accused;

(2) is part of a definite pattern of conduct which, in the circumstances of the case, is substantially indicative of consent;

(3) was part of the circumstances immediately surrounding the offense with which the accused is charged;

(4) is offered to show an alternative source of the victim's pregnancy or disease or of medical or other evidence of the commission of a sexual act;

(5) is offered on the issue of sentencing in an offense involving consent of the victim;

(6) is offered to impeach the victim's testimony, or other evidence, indicating the extent to which the victim has engaged in other similar conduct; or

(7) is substantially probative of a reason for false accusation."

[In addition, the rule would contain a notice and hearing provision, with the hearing not on the public record to the extent feasible. And Rules 404–406 (relating to character, habit, other wrongs, etc. used substantively) and 608–609 (relating to similar matters offered on the issue of credibility), would contain a cross-reference to indicate that this new rule limits them. The exemption from Rule 104(b) noted in connection with actual Rule 412 above would also be provided in both this rule and Rule 104(b).]

Hypothetical "Drafters' Note" Explaining Rule:

The proposed rule conforms to the recently enacted federal law (i. e., actual F.R.E. 412) by excluding opinion and reputation evidence as too unreliable. Note that, unlike the federal rule, our rule is not confined to cases of rape and assault with intent to rape. In addition the first few lines more clearly spell out the precise variety of evidence addressed.

The first exception parallels the congressional rule (i. e., actual F.R.E. 412) in that it permits the introduction of evidence of the victim's sexual behavior with the accused on the issue of consent. The fact that a victim has consented to intercourse with the accused on previous occasions is often strongly relevant because it enables the fact finder to properly evaluate the likelihood that consent was given on the particular occasion that the victim claims was a rape. The opening mandate in our draft rule that the evidence must comply with other rules means that a balancing of probativity against prejudice (Rule 403) would be done before the evidence was admitted under any of the seven gateways, and that Rule 611, banning undue harassment, etc., of witnesses, would apply. If the facts showed the rape to have been at knife point, or if the victim is severely beaten preliminary to the rape, or if the victim and the accused were strangers, or had no previous relationship, the evidence of consent may well be found to be inadmissible under these principles, consent being unlikely.

The second exception provides for the admission of evidence of sexual conduct of the victim involving persons other than the accused when the conduct constitutes part of a definite pattern which under the circumstances of the case is substantially probative of consent. For example, if evidence indicates that the alleged victim is a prostitute and that the act took place under conditions and at a place that strongly indicate that the alleged rape was in fact a regular "business transaction" for her, this bears on the defendant's guilt or innocence. Another example would be evidence that the alleged victim was following a pattern of trading sexual favors for narcotics, perhaps because she is addicted. Under the new federal law (actual Rule 412) these matters could not be evidenced unless the court finds it to be required by the Constitution. A possible expansion of our second exception might be to not always require a "pattern" of conduct in the sense of more than one incident, if a single incident is very probative of consent. For example, suppose complainant had published a lewd picture of herself soliciting group sexual intercourse. In certain circumstances this could strongly suggest consent. Cf. People v. Mandel, supra.

The third exception is designed to cover, for example, proof by the defendant of group intercourse with the victim, voluntarily, in which the accused may or may not have participated, on the occasion of the alleged rape by the defendant. (Cf. Powell v. Alabama, 287 U.S. 45, 53 S.Ct. 55 (1932) and details in Carter, Scottsboro, A Tragedy of the American South (1971).) Evidence of this nature would not be admissible under the federal act (actual Rule 412) unless offered to explain "semen or injury" or unless constitutionally required.

The federal law (actual F.R.E. 412) provides for the admission of evidence of the kind that would be permitted under our *exception four* (evidence of alternative sources of certain telltale signs of intercourse), but our proposed rule expands the telltale signs from "semen or injury" to "pregnancy, disease, or . . . medical or other [similar] evidence," including semen, injury such as local bruising, etc.

Exception five is designed for statutory rape cases in which the victim consented. Although the accused is still guilty, a victim's consent may affect the severity of the sentence imposed, especially when the victim was very active sexually or was engaged in prostitution. Although in federal cases there is judge-sentencing, and the Federal Rules of Evidence are expressly inapplicable to sentencing (see Rule 1101[d][3]), this provision is for the benefit of states which may have a different practice.

The federal law (actual F.R.E. 412) does not adequately permit the introduction of evidence of the kind envisioned in exceptions six and seven. *Exception six* is a provision permitting contradiction. If, for example, the alleged victim testifies that she never has had or rarely has had sexual intercourse, the defendant in appropriate circumstances may, under this exception, contradict this statement of her by putting on evidence of her more frequent sexual conduct that tends to disprove her statement. Other possible situations exist where it might be thought desirable to allow impeachment of the victim as a witness by showing matters related to her past sexual conduct. For example, it might be thought desirable to show that she has lied at other hearings about sexual matters, or that the complete picture of her mental health, including her abnormal sex life, adds up to a person who is not a reliable witness on this kind of matter. These are purposely not included except as exception seven may embrace the latter. Cf. People v. Mandel, supra.

The federal law (actual F.R.E. 412) fails to specifically provide for evidence that is substantially probative of a reason for false accusation, our *exception seven*. A motive to falsely accuse is covered by this exception and might occur, for example, in the case of a woman who suspects (incorrectly) that she is pregnant by her boy friend and who accuses someone other than her boy friend of having raped her in order to provide an explanation to her family for her suspected pregnancy. Cf. State v. DeLawder, supra. It would not fall within *exception one* because the sexual conduct to be evidenced is not with the accused. It would not fall within *exception four* because the pregnancy is not real. Exception seven would in appropriate circumstances also permit proof that a complainant has a grudge against the accused because the accused has humiliated her by rejecting her sexual advances; or proof that the complainant suffers from a specific psychological condition, if such can be documented, involving a history of abnormal sex practices and fantasizing about sex that leads to the repeated making of false sexual charges. Cf. People v. Cowles, 246 Mich. 429, 224 N.W. 387 (1929).

There is no category of admissible evidence under our model, that would specifically admit evidence of the victim's bad reputation (or bad acts) known to defendant, as reflecting on defendant's state of mind (e. g., giving rise to a reasonable belief in consent), nor do we have a general catchall category of admissibility like the New York Act ("interests of justice") or like the federal one ("constitutionally required" evidence) which perhaps arguably could on occasion embrace such mental state evidence. If the Constitution requires admission, that would override the rule anyway. The strongest case for making the "state of mind" evidence just mentioned an admissible category would be in an assault with *intent to rape* case. It may be that our proposal here could desirably add such a category to include reputation, specific instances, and even the defendant's opinion, in this connection, in case the Constitution did not cover it. But we think not. Cf. People v. Mandel, supra.

A question may be raised as to whether there is any room in the criminal law of rape for implied consent where there is no actual consent—for example, a woman who advertises for group violence-oriented intercourse, with pictures of herself, has a well-known reputation for it, comes to defendant, and indicates willingness to be forced, but at the actual moment changes her mind. Should there be a category to allow into evidence the indicia of implied consent? Might exception two cover it if the defense is allowed under the substantive law? What of a *single* incident, not a pattern? Cf. People v. Mandel, supra.

We deem it advisable not to provide specifically for the evidence raised in the last two paragraphs. It is worth noting, however, that a recent as yet unenacted recodification of federal criminal law seems to require that defendant have actual *knowledge* of the victim's lack of consent in rape. See S. 1722, section 1641, as interpreted in the Senate Report to its predecessor. Senate Report No. 95–605, Pt. 1, 95th Cong., 1st Session, to accompany S. 1437.

CHAPTER IX

SOME SELECTED EVIDENTIARY PRIVILEGES

Introduction

The term privilege as used in Evidence law means a freedom from compulsion to give evidence or to discover-up material, or a right to prevent or bar information from other sources, during or in connection with litigation, but on grounds extrinsic to the goals of litigation.

In the absence of privilege, citizens, be they parties or not, can be compelled by process of law to give evidence and surrender up items a court requires for the resolution of a controversy, subject to certain legal safeguards that need not concern us at present. Furthermore, in the absence of privilege, a person cannot prevent the obtaining and use in such resolutions, of material from other sources, unless he can assert one of the ordinary rules of inadmissibility. Not all the various privileges can be gone into here. But principles learned in connection with one privilege are often transferrable to others. This is especially true of privileges designed to foster, by promise of secrecy, more or less confidential disclosures, e. g., disclosures to government agencies, or to one's spouse, doctor, or lawyer. The required report privilege has been selected to be representative of such privileges herein, with some of the others being merely touched upon. The privilege against adverse spousal testimony (i. e., the so-called "anti-marital facts privilege") has been chosen to illustrate another sort of policy. It should always be borne in mind that privileges operate to exclude good proof, in the name of some other social objective. Does this mean that the ascertainment of truth is compromised in trials? Have we already come across matters that might be deemed privileges?

The Required Report Privileges (Herein Also of Some Other Governmental Privileges) *

> **Certain records required by the government to be kept or submitted may be attended by a "required report privilege." Although on occasion they may overlap, this privilege is to be distinguished from the privileges protecting certain other governmental matters: state secrets, certain official information, and the identity of informers.**

A typical statute found in many jurisdictions requires a motorist involved in a collision to report that an accident has occurred, and later to report the facts; requires the investigating officer to report the facts (from observation and/or interviewed persons); and may require persons (perhaps the motorist) to give information to the officer for his report. An accompanying statutory privilege usually renders confidential one, some, or all of these required reports (and perhaps even an unrequired statement by the motorist, especially if given in aid of the preparation of a required report). The privilege is an example of a class of statutory privileges providing for non-disclosure of certain reports, oral or written, which individual citizens, companies, or government employees are required by law (either absolutely or as a condition of receiving certain societal, financial, or business advantages) to submit to state and federal governmental agencies.[1] These are the "required report privileges" with which this section deals.

---

* Portions reproduced by permission of the Northwestern University Law Review (Copyright © 1961) and my co-author on that piece, Mr. Donald Funk. See 56 Nw.U.L.Rev. 283.

[1] For the application of the privilege against self-incrimination to such reports, see Leary v. United States, 395 U.S. 6, 89 S.Ct. 1532

(1969) (requirement that marijuana transferee report as such for purposes of imposing tax, violates privilege); Marchetti v. United States, 390 U.S. 39, 88 S.Ct. 697 (1968) (requirement that gamblers register); Haynes v. United States, 390 U.S. 85, 88 S.Ct. 722 (1968) (registration of firearms). See also United States v. Freed, 401 U.S. 601, 91 S.Ct. 1112 (1971) (amended firearms registration provision); Grosso v. United States, 390 U.S. 62, 88 S.Ct. 709 (1968) (gambling registration); Albertson v. Subversive Activities Control Bd., 382 U.S. 70, 86 S.Ct. 194 (1965) (communist registration). A requirement that motorists involved in accidents leave their names and addresses was upheld in California v. Byers, 402 U.S. 424, 91 S.Ct. 1535 (1971). In Garner v. United States, 424 U.S. 648, 96 S.Ct. 1178 (1976), accused's tax returns were held admissible to show a criminal business since privilege was not claimed in the returns.

Occasionally a statute merely requiring or soliciting a report and saying nothing about a privilege or about confidentiality will give rise to an implied required report privilege.

When used as substantive evidence, required reports like other out-of-court communications covered by confidential communications privileges, are usually hearsay. They often qualify for an exception to or exemption from the hearsay rule, however. In the case of required reports, the following exceptions or exemptions are most frequently applicable: (1) excited utterances; (2) admissions of a party; (3) declarations against interest made by a non-party; (4) past recollection recorded; (5) entries made in the regular course of business; (6) government records; (7) dying declarations; (8) declarations relating to physical or mental condition to doctors or others; (9) declarations about family history.

It should be noted that when a reporter submits a report and the reporter's statements of fact (rather than his report of what someone said) in the report are sought to be introduced into evidence as true, there will ordinarily be a "single hearsay" problem; the sincerity and accuracy of the reporter are in question. (In this situation the admissions of a party and declarations against interest exceptions or exemptions to the hearsay rule are often called into play. The excited utterance exception ordinarily would not be applicable where there is a formal, meditated report, since such a report may not be considered spontaneous enough.) On the other hand, it may be that the reporter is reporting a statement made by another person. When that statement is sought to be introduced as true, via the report, there is a "double hearsay" problem. The original statement of that other person must fall within an exemption from or exception to the hearsay rule, since his sincerity and accuracy are in issue. Furthermore, the reporter's report of that statement must also fall within an exemption or exception, since the reporter's sincerity and accuracy are also in issue. A common double hearsay situation is where a motorist, fol-

Required report privilege statutes differ widely in form, substance, and judicial interpretation. They are normally individually tailored to a particular regulatory area: income tax returns, census reports, claims for veteran's benefits, patent applications, filing of corporate trade or securities or financial or product or work-conditions information with various agencies, unemployment compensation claims, public assistance records, selective service records, social security records, information obtained from citizens in conjunction with health service plans, public health records, adoption records, various types of accident reports, etc.

Although the policy behind a particular required report privilege is rarely clearly articulated in the statute or judicial interpretations thereof, the privileges generally seem to be founded upon *either one or both* of two rather distinct policies: (1) *Encouragement.* The intent here is to encourage citizens (or companies) to accurately report potentially self-damaging information which they would otherwise hesitate to furnish for fear of the consequences resulting from later uses of such information. It is this kind of statute that will principally concern us. (2) *Housekeeping.* The concern here is with the government's "housekeeping;" i. e., (a) preventing disclosure of government officers' and investigators' notations or opinions; (b) preserving documents from loss, destruction, alteration or wear; (c) avoiding the general inconvenience resulting from frequent de-

---

lowing an automobile accident, makes an on-the-spot declaration relating to facts of the accident, and an officer takes down that statement and submits it as (or in) the officer's required report. The officer's report of the statement may be admissible, since the motorist's statement may fall within the excited utterances, admissions of a party, or declarations against interest exception or exemption; and the officer's report may fall within the government records exception or business records exception. (There is some authority for an alternative theory of admissibility—that government or business records may utilize third party statements that are related to the government or business activity without the necessity of a second hearsay exception.)

mands for disclosure; or (d) preventing direct exertion of judicial power on executive personnel, a policy with "separation of powers" overtones. Rarely will housekeeping be the only or the principal concern under the privileges discussed here.

The required report privileges may be analytically distinguished from four other privileges or non-disclosure principles applicable to information in the hands of the government. These four somewhat overlap one another and the present privilege. Two of them have their origin at common law: the governmental privileges not to disclose military or diplomatic secrets of state (and, perhaps, certain other official information) ² and not to reveal the identity of

---

² The exact parameters of the state secrets and official information principles are unknown because of the infrequency of definitive cases involving them. The most recent attempt at formulating them from existing law and principles was Supreme Court draft F.R.E. 509 (1972). Rule 509 was not enacted, but not necessarily for reasons that would invalidate it as a kind of "restatement" authority. It codifies and amplifies, in part, the principles expressed in the most definitive case, United States v. Reynolds, 345 U.S. 1, 73 S.Ct. 528 (1953). In effect, the rule states two privileges, one for "Secrets of State" and one for "Official Information." The case of United States v. Nixon, 418 U.S. 683, 94 S.Ct. 3090 (1974), suggests that privilege in these areas is qualified, and gives way upon a judicial assessment that there are more important interests to be served by disclosure in a particular case. Unenacted Rule 509 reads as follows:

"**Rule 509: Secrets of State and Other Official Information**

"(a) Definitions.

"(1) Secret of state. A 'secret of state' is a governmental secret relating to the national defense or the international relations of the United States.

"(2) Official information. 'Official information' is information within the custody or control of a department or agency of the government the disclosure of which is shown to be contrary to the public interest and which consists of: (A) intragovernmental opinions or recommendations submitted for consideration in the performance of decisional or policymaking functions, or (B) subject to the provisions of 18 U.S.C.A. § 3500 [Jencks Act], investigatory files compiled for law enforcement purposes and not otherwise available, or (C) information within the custody or control of a governmental department or agency whether initiated within the department or agency or acquired by it in its exercise of its official responsibilities and not otherwise available to the public pursuant to 5 U.S.C.A. § 552 [Freedom of Information Act].

"(b) General rule of privilege. The government has a privilege to refuse to give evidence and to prevent any person from giving evidence upon a showing of reasonable likelihood of danger that the evidence will disclose a secret of state or official information, as defined in this rule.

"(c) Procedures. The privilege for secrets of state may be claimed only by the chief officer of the government agency or department administering the subject matter which the secret information sought concerns, but the privilege for official information may be asserted by any attorney representing the government. The required showing may be made in whole or in part in the form of a written statement. The judge may hear the matter in chambers but all counsel are entitled to inspect the claim and showing and to be heard thereon, except that, in the case of secrets of state, the judge upon motion of the government, may permit the government to make the required showing in the above form *in camera*. If the judge sustains the privilege upon a showing *in camera*, the entire text of the government's statements shall be sealed and preserved in the court's records in the event of appeal. In the case of privilege claimed for official information the court may require examination *in camera* of the information itself. The judge may take any protective measure which the interests of the government and the furtherance of justice may require.

"(d) Notice to government. If the circumstances of the case indicate a substantial possibility that a claim of privilege would be appropriate but has not been made because of oversight or lack of knowledge, the judge shall give or cause notice to be given to the officer entitled to claim the privilege and shall stay further proceedings a reasonable time to afford opportunity to assert a claim of privilege.

"(e) Effect of sustaining claim. If the claim of privilege is sustained in a proceeding to which the government is a party and it appears that another party is thereby deprived of material evidence, the judge shall make any further orders which the interests of justice require, including striking the testimony of a witness, declaring a mistrial, finding against the government upon an issue as to which the evidence is relevant, or dismissing the action." [The reader should also consult the recently enacted an informer.[3] The third is the federal statutory privilege of government agency heads to make rules (respected in

> Classified Information Procedures Act, Public Law 96–456, Oct. 15, 1980, establishing a procedural framework for the handling of classified information in federal criminal litigation.]

A somewhat narrower draft of the privilege (also an honest attempt like the above to faithfully codify existing principles) appeared earlier, and should be contrasted to get a feel for the areas of uncertainty that exist in the uncodified law. See F.R.E., Revised Draft of March, 1971, 51 F.R.D. 315 (1971). The principal differences there are the omission of the "official information" privilege, a requirement under state secrets of reasonable likelihood of *injury or detriment to national defense or international relations,* and less protection against disclosure in the course of determining the privilege claim.

The 1974 Uniform Rules (Rule 508) attempt to codify what the law is on the state level, as follows:

> "(a) If the law of the United States creates a governmental privilege that the courts of this State must recognize under the Constitution of the United States, the privilege may be claimed as provided by the law of the United States.

> "(b) No other governmental privilege is recognized except as created by the Constitution or statutes of this State.

> "(c) Effect of Sustaining Claim. If a claim of governmental privilege is sustained and it appears that a party is thereby deprived of material evidence, the court shall make any further orders the interests of justice require, including striking the testimony of a witness, declaring a mistrial, finding upon an issue as to which the evidence is relevant, or dismissing the action."

---

[3] See in connection with the latter Smith v. Illinois, 390 U.S. 129, 88 S.Ct. 748 (1968) (right to confrontation infringed by this privilege in case where informer was put on as a government witness). See also Roviaro v. United States, 353 U.S. 53, 77 S.Ct. 623 (1957) (informer's identity must be disclosed where, though he was not put on as a witness, he was a participant, and could testify to possible entrapment and other important matters); McCray v. Illinois, 386 U.S. 300, 87 S.Ct. 1056 (1967) (not necessary, ordinarily, to reveal identity of informer who furnished the probable cause that makes a challenged search and seizure legal).

The unenacted Supreme Court Draft of the F.R.E. attempted faithful codification of the existing law of informers' privilege as follows. Congressional rejection was for reasons not necessarily related to the merits and the provision may still have some "restatement"-like authority:

"Rule 510: Identity of Informer

"(a) Rule of privilege. The government or a state or subdivision thereof has a privilege to refuse to disclose the identity of a person who has furnished information relating to or assisting in an investigation of a possible violation of law to a law enforcement officer or member of a legislative committee or its staff conducting an investigation.

"(b) Who may claim. The privilege may be claimed by an appropriate representative of the government, regardless of whether the information was furnished to an officer of the government or of a state or subdivision thereof. The privilege may be claimed by an appropriate representative of a state or subdivision if the information was furnished to an officer thereof, except that in criminal cases the privilege shall not be allowed if the government objects.

"(c) Exceptions.

"(1) Voluntary disclosure; informer a witness. No privilege exists under this rule if the identity of the informer or his interest in the subject matter of his communication has been disclosed, to those who would have cause to resent the communication, by a holder of the privilege or by the informer's own action, or if the informer appears as a witness for the government.

"(2) Testimony on merits. If it appears from the evidence in the case or from other showing by a party that an informer may be able to give testimony necessary to a fair determination of the issue of guilt or innocence in a criminal case or of a material issue on the merits in a civil case to which the government is a party, and the government invokes the privilege, the judge shall give the government an opportunity to show *in camera* facts relevant to determining whether the informer can, in fact, supply that testimony. The showing will ordinarily be in the form of affidavits, but the judge may direct that testimony be taken if he finds that the matter cannot be resolved satisfactorily upon affidavit. If the judge finds that there is a reasonable probability that the informer can give the testimony, and the government elects not to disclose his identity, the judge on motion of the defendant in a criminal case shall dismiss the charges to which the testimony would relate, and the judge may do so on his own motion. In civil cases, he may make any order that justice requires. Evidence submitted to the judge shall be sealed and preserved to be made available to the appellate court in the event of an appeal, and the contents shall not otherwise be revealed without consent of the government. All counsel and parties shall court) prohibiting subordinates from disclosing intra-departmental communications, agency files, and information obtained by agency investigation; although the head himself may have to disclose unless the matter comes within another privilege. See 5 U.S.C.A. § 301. The reach of this statute has been considerably contracted by later amendment and by the Federal Freedom of Information Act, 5 U.S.C.A. § 552, providing broad public access to administrative documents, with certain exceptions. The fourth privilege encompasses some of the fundamental principles of the three above mentioned privileges and is embodied in state statutes which provide that "a public officer cannot be examined as to communications made to him in official confidence, when

> be permitted to be present at every stage of proceedings under this subdivision except a showing *in camera*, at which no counsel or party shall be permitted to be present.
>
> "(3) Legality of obtaining evidence. If information from an informer is relied upon to establish the legality of the means by which evidence was obtained and the judge is not satisfied that the information was received from an informer reasonably believed to be reliable or credible, he may require the identity of the informer to be disclosed. The judge shall, on request of the government, direct that the disclosure be made *in camera*. All counsel and parties concerned with the issue of legality shall be permitted to be present at every stage of proceedings under this subdivision except a disclosure *in camera*, at which no counsel or party shall be permitted to be present. If disclosure of the identity of the informer is made *in camera*, the record thereof shall be sealed and preserved to be made available to the appellate court in the event of an appeal, and the contents shall not otherwise be revealed without consent of the government."

An earlier draft (Revised Draft of March, 1971, 51 F.R.D. 315), also purporting to be a faithful rendition of the somewhat uncertain existing law, provided a narrower privilege, principally (1) in part (a), where the information had to purport to "reveal a violation of law" and legislative inquiries were omitted; (2) in part (c)(2), which was considerably curtailed (to the advantage of the government) in the draft reproduced above; and (3) in the procedural parts in (c)(2) and (c)(3), where the draft reproduced above increased the protections against disclosure in the course of determination of the privilege claim.

the public interest would suffer by the disclosure." A some-what analogous judge-made rule exists in some jurisdictions. (Can a privilege that leaves this much judgment to a court after the report has been made, encourage to the extent of a required report privilege? Is it intended as encourage-ment?) These four non-disclosure principles, which we must needs place beyond the scope of our inquiry, are extensively qualified.

The breadth of the cloak of secrecy accorded by a privilege often is the product of an amalgam of statutory language and judicial gloss, and of a tension between policies like those described above and the need of the public, the government, and the courts to be informed. For the privilege frequently operates to secrete reliable, admissible, relevant information in the name of some higher policy. Further, in the required report privilege area, the policy of the legislature in requiring the submission of the report in the first instance must be considered. It would make no sense to handcuff the very governmental agency for whose use the legislature required the report, by preventing access to and use of the report by that agency.

In the present area, as with most other privileges designed principally to promote potentially damaging confidential communications, the determinations of coverage *vel non* are not made on an *ad hoc* balancing of the competing considerations on the facts of each case, after the manner of a qualified privilege. For uncertainty of coverage at the time of the communication reduces the encouragement to communicate. Therefore, we find in this area that if, for example, a motorist's report is the subject of a statutory privilege, the reporter may, generally speaking, prevent it from being disclosed in court, whatever the circumstances, and, at least in most instances, he is the final arbiter of whether disclosure would be against his interests or not.

Required Report Privileges: Coverage: When and from Whom the Report is Secret

At least theoretically, access to privileged information may be denied to the judicial tribunal, parties, the general public, certain members thereof, certain administrative agencies, or any one or combination of these. Disclosure for purposes of litigation is what concerns us as Evidence lawyers. Some statutes provide very generally that the government shall not publicly disclose the required report. Courts have often held that such a statute will not prevent use of the report in litigation. Other statutes specifically provide that the record shall be kept confidential except when ordered produced by a court of law. On the other hand, a number of statutes provide that the record shall not be produced for use in any court proceedings, shall not be referred to in court, shall not be used in civil cases, or shall not be used in any litigation except that involving the governmental department to which the report is required to be made. Some statutes provide that the report may be released to specified government agencies; used for specific regulatory purposes; or used in court by a specified agency. Still another approach has been to prohibit disclosure if the report will be used to the reporter's prejudice; or to prohibit "use against" the reporter. A few statutes provide that they apply in "actions arising out of the facts on which the report is based." If disclosure is not permissible in trial, it is generally considered barred for all litigation purposes, including discovery. It would seem that no distinction should be drawn on the basis of whether the report is used in the capacity of discovery, substantive evidence, impeachment, or refreshment of recollection. Some decisions suggest that a report that could not be used in a substantive capacity may be used to refresh the memory of a witness; or to impeach the reporter by a prior inconsistent state-

ment, on a theory that "the door has been opened."[4]
What remedies might be invoked if a report is used not in
evidence, but rather only to uncover other evidence against
the reporter? Is this a prohibited use?

Required Report Privileges: Coverage: Items Other Than the Report Document

No existing required report privilege prevents disclosure
of the facts of the reported occurrence by sources that can
supply them wholly regardless of any privileged report.
Such would be, for example, the testimony of first-hand
witnesses to the occurrence. It is no objection to such
evidence that the same facts happen to be mentioned in the
required report. In other words, the facts are not privi-

---

[4] The "Jencks" evidentiary rule may suggest this latter result as
respects impeachment of government witnesses, in criminal cases
where the rule applies. Generally speaking, under the federal "Jencks
rule" (a Jencks-type principle is adopted by statute in the federal
jurisdiction, 18 U.S.C.A. § 3500, and by decision in a few states), a
criminal defendant may call for production of substantially verbatim
written records of pertinent prior statements of government witnesses.
(It provides that statements of government witnesses may *not* be
called for, however, in advance of the witness testifying, though prosecutors often will *voluntarily* supply such statements of prospective
witnesses in advance). If a statement called for under Jencks is
privileged (under the present privilege or any other), either the privilege must yield, or the witness must not testify, or the Jencks rule
itself must yield. Consider a somewhat analogous situation: what
would be the right to discovery under F.R.E. 612 where a witness uses
a report, privileged for some reason (such as the present privilege), to
refresh his recollection for trial? Rule 612 provides that documents so
used can be subject to discovery. But, like the Jencks Act, Rule 612 is
silent as to what the result of privilege is. Would privilege be
waived? To what extent the federal constitution protects the accused
along the lines of the Jencks rule or Rule 612 is uncertain. There
must be at least some situations where suppression of such documents
pursuant to a privilege like the present one or attorney-client or work-
product privilege will unconstitutionally interfere with the right to defend
or confront. Rule 26.2 of the Federal Rules of Criminal Procedure
incorporates the Jencks Act and extends its benefit to the prosecution, as
well.

leged. Thus, even the reporter himself could be asked for his first-hand observations of the occurrence, though he has previously put them in a privileged report. I am assuming there is no reference to the report.

Suppose the reporter or someone authorized to have (or somewhat unavoidably having) access to the report is asked, "What did the report submitted by X contain;" or "What were the facts" where he knows them only from the report; or suppose government reports, made up from the reporter's original privileged report, are sought for use in court. Individuals and companies might not be encouraged to report or report accurately if these things could not be prevented. Some courts have nevertheless held that where a motorist is required to submit an accident report to a policeman, who is thereafter to make his own report, and a privilege statute forbids use of the former report, the latter may be disclosed, even if it contains reference to the former.

It should be noted that even where certain facts are known independently of the report, it may be additionally damaging to have it revealed that they are also in the report. Would this be privileged? [5] Would the fact of making a report—that is, that a report was made or filed, without revealing anything about its contents—be privileged?

Courts have often been troubled with the problem of whether or not the privilege should extend to copies of required reports, particularly tax returns. Some cases seem to distinguish between whether the copy is in the

---

[5] If yes, then where the witness is both a first-hand witness to the occurrence and has knowledge of the report, he should be prevented from indicating that the facts also appear in the report. The reporter (who, incidentally, may also be the witness), could anticipate additional prejudice from that revelation (e. g. the evidence may take on additional credibility, as an admission that has been made in a formal, official-type report).

possession of the reporter, or the government. What policy does this reflect? A further distinction might be drawn respecting whether the reporter himself can obtain copies from the government. If he can, can he be compelled to do so and compelled to produce them? Would an encouragement policy suggest a different result than a housekeeping policy? Does it depend on *which* housekeeping policy? Strikingly different results have been reached under virtually identical statutes, and there has been a conflict even under the federal tax law, where it has been usually held, however, that copies of taxpayer returns in the hands of the taxpayer, or compelled by the court to be gotten by the taxpayer from the I.R.S., are admissible, though the I.R.S. cannot be made directly to produce to the court originals or a copy. Obviously housekeeping seems paramount.[6]

Following an automobile accident a motorist may give information to an officer who thereafter uses this information either to help prepare the officer's required report or to

---

[6] Some authority has held that a privilege granted by the state legislature for state income tax returns may be invoked to prevent disclosure in state court of any copies of federal income tax returns when the state returns require substantially the same information as the federal returns.

Federal law on the tax returns matter is discussed in Required Report Privileges, 56 Nw.U.L.Rev. 283 at 295 (1961). More recent amendments have not entirely clarified things. See generally Internal Revenue Code § 6103. It operates by regulating government employees, allowing them to make disclosure for a wide range of law enforcement functions and proceedings (including, incidentally, certain state child support efforts). A prohibition directed to government employees is often interpreted to create a privilege against use in court, in addition to whatever civil or criminal penalties may lie against the employee.

It might be thought that a required report privilege statute providing in general terms for non-disclosure of the "information" supplied by the reporter would indicate an intention to encompass copies (regardless of whether they are in the hands of the government or the individual). But conflicting results have been reached on such language.

aid in the preparation of the motorist's required report. The motorist may be under no legal obligation to make the earlier statement to the officer. Should the privilege extend to such an unrequired report, made in aid of a required report, in the absence of statutory language on the matter? Should anything turn on whether the policeman requested the information? Or gave the impression that it was required, or privileged? Often the statute will privilege "all reports required under section . . . ." If there can be no contention that the motorist's first statement constitutes a *required* report under the statute (statutes are often unclear as to what reports are *required*), then the motorist must rely on an implied privilege for the unrequired report.

It seems reasonable to say that a reporter ordinarily should be protected when he makes an unrequired statement to some governmental official who aids the reporter in preparing his, the reporter's, required report. This subserves the legislative intent to have the required report filed accurately, promptly, and in the correct form; and avoids the general distaste and future reticence that might otherwise be engendered. The privilege, however, could safely exclude excited, spontaneous utterances, statements to third persons, and other statements not intended to aid in the preparation of the required report.

Where an unrequired oral report has been given by a motorist involved in an accident, to aid in the preparation of the *officer's own* required report, are the considerations the same? Some courts have inferred from the privilege surrounding the officer's report a legislative policy to encourage accurate reporting by the motorist (with the consequence that the privilege has been extended to the motorist's report); while others have inferred only a housekeeping policy to protect the officer's report.

In certain complex situations where both the giver and receiver of the volunteered unrequired statement are under a duty to submit required reports about the occurrence, the facts might not indicate for whose privileged, required report the unrequired statement was made. In such a case what should be the result?

In the situations discussed in the last several paragraphs, some courts have accorded privilege status to a motorist's volunteered statement or report insofar as disclosure by the government or its agents is concerned, while allowing third-party overhearers to testify. Does this subserve the relevant policies?

Required Report Privileges: Assertion and Waiver

On the question of who may assert or waive a confidential communication privilege, the statutory language is the starting place, but it is often uncertain or not deemed controlling, as is frequently the case with many other questions concerning privilege as well. The court's notion of policy (often unexpressed) and the position of the common law, if any, play an influential role on most privilege issues. Since the required report privilege did not exist at common law, however, the influence of the common law here is minimal except insofar as analogy to other privileges is used. Many other communications privilege statutes, however, are deemed to be codifications of the common law, and are often read in the light of that common law.

For purposes of analysis it is helpful to suggest that there may be two types of "holders" of a privilege that is intended to encourage accurate communication of potentially self-damaging information. The primary holder is the one whose immediate interests are harmed if disclosure occurs. He is the communicator. It is he whom the law seeks to encourage. His express assertion or express waiver of the privilege should thus always prevail over anyone else's wishes, including those of a secondary holder. A secondary holder is one who is allowed to assert the privilege in certain instances where the primary holder is unable to assert the privilege for himself. Consider, for example, litigation to which the reporter is not a party, and of which he is not aware, where someone is called to give evidence of the reporter's privileged report to the government of a loathsome disease. The encouragement policy would be furthered if reporters knew that someone (e. g., the witness, or one of the litigants in the action, or the government, or the judge) would be likely to assert the privilege for him.

An encouragement type privilege should be raisable by a secondary holder only when it can be safely assumed that the primary holder would not wish disclosure. If the primary holder knows that his report is being sought for disclosure, and is able to but has not asserted the privilege, this condition may not be met. (Where he does not so know, should the nature of the report and the suit be considered? On an ad hoc basis?)

McCormick says the following of the privilege covering confidential attorney-client communications, which is instructive here:

> "While once it was conceived that the privilege was set up to protect the lawyer's honor, we know that today it is agreed that the basic policy of the rule is that of encouraging clients to lay the facts fully before their counsel. . . . Accordingly it is now generally agreed that the privilege is the client's and his alone. . . . [T]his would be recognized even in those states which . . . codified the rule in terms of inadmissibility of evidence of communications, or of incompetency of the attorney to testify thereto. . . . [Thus the following may be said:]

> "First, it is clear that the client may assert the privilege even though he is not a party to the cause wherein the privileged testimony is sought to be elicited.

Second, if he is present at the hearing whether as party, witness, or bystander he must assert the privilege personally or by attorney, or it will be waived. Third, if he is not present at the taking of testimony, nor a party to the proceedings, the privilege may be called to the court's attention by anyone present, such as the attorney for the absent client, or a party in the case, or the court of its own motion may protect the privilege. Fourth: While if an asserted privilege is erroneously sustained, the aggrieved party may of course complain on appeal of the exclusion of the testimony, the erroneous denial of the privilege can only be complained of by the client whose privilege has been infringed. This opens the door to appellate review by the client if he is a party and suffers adverse judgment.

"If he is not a party, the losing party in the cause by the better view is without recourse. Relevant, competent testimony has come in, and the privilege was not created for his benefit. But the witness, whether he is the client or his attorney, may refuse to answer and suffer a commitment for contempt and may, in some jurisdictions at least, secure release on habeas corpus if the privilege was erroneously denied.[7] This remedy, however, is calculated to interrupt, and often disrupt progress of the cause on trial. Does a lawyer on the

---

[7] But probably not if the client is a party and so has an adequate remedy by appeal. See Ex Parte Lipscomb, 111 Tex. 409, 239 S.W. 1101 (1922) (attorney for one of the parties refused to obey judge and testify to confidential lawyer-client communication; attorney committed for contempt; attorney's application for writ of habeas corpus asserting judge's erroneous refusal to accord privilege denied because client had adequate remedy by appeal).

A witness will seldom refuse to obey the judge. As a result, where there is no party in a position to assert the error on appeal, the judge is considerably induced to deny the privilege claim, whether it is valid or not, and receive the relevant evidence. What about mandamus? [Footnote not part of quotation.]

witness stand who is asked to make disclosures which he thinks may constitute an infringement of his client's privilege, owe a duty to refuse to answer and if necessary to test the judge's ruling on habeas corpus? It seems clear that, unless in a case of flagrant disregard of the law by the judge, the lawyer's duty is merely to present his view that the testimony is privileged, and if the judge rules otherwise, to submit to his decision.[8]"

---

[8] This view, if carried to its logical extension into a rule of law rather than merely ethics, means that an attorney refusing to answer is rightfully held in contempt even if he is correct that the judge should have accorded the privilege and even though the client has no remedy by way of appeal because he is not a party.

Would it be sensible to hold that unless a privileged party-witness refuses to testify and braves a contempt citation after the judge has denied his privilege claim and ordered him to testify, he waives his right to assert on appeal that the judge was in error? This once was the practice in some states regarding the privilege against self-incrimination.

On other points in the quotation, it should be noted that statutory language cast as a *prohibition* of the evidence rather than taking the form of granting a privilege, suggests not only that others than the client or attorney may assert the ban, but that neither the client nor a party can waive it; that the judge *must* raise it regardless of whether anyone else does or wishes to; that his improper failure to allow it can be asserted as error on appeal by the aggrieved party whether or not he is the client or attorney and even though the question may not have been raised below; and, possibly, that the appellate court is required to raise it of its own motion. This sort of language, however, has never been interpreted so extensively, and is usually treated as granting only a privilege. Language cast in terms of *admissibility* would suggest that any party to the suit can assert the privilege regardless of the wishes of the client and that a party losing the suit (whether or not he is the client) can claim (on appeal) error in the denial of the privilege if the denial was prejudicial to his case and he properly raised the matter below and preserved his rights. Again, in this area such language is generally interpreted so as to grant a privilege. Most other rules of evidence than privilege are treated as speaking in terms of *admissibility*, even if language of prohibition is used. (*Incompetency* is a term that suggests prohibition of the evidence, but is usually taken to mean *inadmissibility* or *privilege*, depending on the context.) [Footnote not part of quotation.]

Handbook of the Law of Evidence 195-6 (1st ed., 1954) (a similar passage appears in the 2d edition, 1972, pp. 192-93 as well). McCormick does not purport to say that this is law everywhere, or that it is beyond change by argument where it is the law, or that it is true of all evidentiary privileges. The principles, however, would seem to be applicable at least in theory to many of the privileges in this chapter.

When the policy of a required report privilege is solely housekeeping, the government should be the sole holder of the privilege. The government is always in a position to know when a particular report in its files is sought for disclosure, and what its housekeeping interests are. Consequently there seems to be no reason to give anyone else the status of secondary holder of the privilege.

Under a statute which embodies both encouragement and housekeeping policies, both the reporter and the government may be considered primary holders of the privilege, and consequently conflict could arise where they take adverse positions regarding assertion or waiver of the privilege. What should be the result? It would seem that either one would be able to raise the bar of privilege despite the wishes of the other.

What considerations should govern whether an encouragement privilege should survive the death of the reporter? Would it be the nature of the material, i. e., whether disclosure after death is likely to matter to the reporter when reporting (or to reporters of this kind of material)? Should this determination be made on the facts of each case? What would afford maximum encouragement? Is it worth it?

The right to assert an encouragement-type required report privilege may be lost by *voluntarily* bringing into issue a matter which can best be proved by information contained in the required report. One example may be where the reporter testifies contrary to his report. Another might be where he sues for damages based on loss of earnings, and defendant seeks to have plaintiff's income tax returns produced for inspection. (Assume they would be privileged had he not put his financial situation in issue.) Another might be where he voluntarily embarks on a discussion of part of the report (or part of the facts therein?) and later (in the same proceeding only?) seeks to keep another part secret. But when a reporter is cross examined in court about his report, some decisions have held that a failure to object to such questions will not result in a waiver of his privilege to prevent later disclosures. The theory is that an objection during cross examination would have been prejudicial, so that the waiver cannot be *voluntary*. (This argument might be raised as to any assertion in open court of the privilege. Is it sound?) There are other applications of the principle that a person does not lose his privilege by being compelled to do some act which if done voluntarily would result in a loss of the privilege. E. g., assuming that copies of income tax returns are within the privilege, if a taxpayer is erroneously compelled by a court over his objection to produce such copies for discovery purposes, he will not lose his privilege to prevent later introduction of such copies into evidence.

Under an encouragement-type privilege, if the reporter voluntarily allows disclosure in one action, should the privilege be held to have been waived in subsequent litigation? If disclosure in the subsequent action would be harmful, should prior waiver in a situation where the disclosure was not so harmful bind him? Would a rule of once-and-for-all waiver actually inhibit disclosure? Should a distinction be made between whether the content of the earlier disclosure, or the privileged report itself (or portion thereof), is the thing sought to be introduced in the subsequent proceeding? What about voluntary disclosure at some preliminary proceeding in connection with a trial? Would that constitute a waiver of the right to assert at trial the privilege to bar disclosure of what was said at the preliminary proceeding? To bar another revelation of the statement in the report itself at trial?

The encouragement and housekeeping-type required report privileges are sometimes said to differ from certain "personal" privileges such as the husband-wife, attorney-client, and physician-patient privileges, in that they do not depend upon the communication being secret. Normally, under those privileges, a reasonably avoidable third person, unnecessary to the communication, who is present at or gains access to the communication, can render unavailable a confidential communications privilege. It may render it unavailable to suppress just the third party, or both the third party and any other evidence, such as testimony of a party to the communication. Which of these effects is given depends upon the jurisdiction, the privilege, and the circumstances. Generally, *negligence* of the communicator, as respects access by the third party, allows only the third party to testify; but the communicator's *intentionally* giving access destroys confidentiality and hence the privilege to suppress anyone or anything. If, however, the third party obtained access solely through actions of a party to the communication who could not himself waive the privilege for the communicator, the privilege remains intact as to all forms of evidence. Third persons are more often viewed by the law as "necessary" to or desirably facilitative of the lawyer-client or doctor-patient relationship, than they are of the husband-wife relationship. Thus, other lawyers working on the matter, clerks, secretaries, telephonists, and co-clients will often be tolerated under the lawyer-client privilege; and nurses, friends of the patient, etc., may be allowed under the doctor-patient privilege. The presence of minor children has been a matter of some dispute under the husband-wife privilege. If a third person is deemed necessary or facilitative, his access will have no effect on the privilege and all forms of evidence will remain suppressible. Is this body of learning inapposite to the present privilege?

While the decisions are by no means uniform, some have held that a particular required report privilege will not ordinarily be waived or lost by the fact that an unneccessary third person has been privy to the report, even if the access was intentional on the reporter's part. (Of course, persons within the government who necessarily have access are not considered third persons.) Thus, if a motorist tells or shows a friend what he reported in a written highway accident report, the privilege, which extends to the written report, may not be destroyed and may be assertable later. Or, when a motorist makes an oral report to a police officer following an accident, the known presence of a third person who overhears the oral report may not destroy whatever privileges are accorded in the absence of the third person. However, in both these situations, it is possible that the third person may be allowed to testify as to the report.

Required Report Privileges: Some Questions Relating to Encouragement Under Communications Privileges in General

Are citizens aware at the time they are making a privileged communication, that it is privileged? Of the extent of coverage of the privilege? (Consider not only the present privilege, but the husband-wife, physician-patient, attorney-client, etc., privileges.) Thus, would a rule of no privilege, or exceptions to coverage adversely affect future reporting? Might a feeling of unfair deception and consequent over-caution neverless be ultimately engendered by exceptions and gaps? How would elimination of gaps and exceptions affect future reporting? Does the report form provide an opportunity for informing of privilege, that is not present in the case of other confidential communications privileges? Assuming citizens are unaware of a privilege and its scope when communicating, so that the privilege's existence and its lack of gaps and exceptions would not seem to encourage, would publicized repeal of the privilege or publicized creation of gaps and exceptions nonetheless discourage communication? Are such things likely to be publicized? See "Ancient Marital Privilege Cast Aside—Court Frees Spouses to Testify Against Each Other," Washington Post, p. A–1, Feb. 28, 1980; "Court Upholds Spouses' Right to Testify," Washington Star, p. A–1, Feb. 27, 1980; "Mate vs. Mate—Spouses Can Spat in Court," Time Magazine, p. 49, March 10, 1980, all reporting the Supreme Court's decision in *Trammel v. U. S.,* discussed infra under *Marital Privileges.* Are all privileges and all courts likely to receive equal press coverage?

Are criminal and civil sanctions for disclosure an adequate substitute for privilege? Could a public official resist compulsory disclosure of a report in court on grounds it would be a crime to disclose?

Would the standard rules of evidence (e. g., the hearsay rule) or the general privilege against self-incrimination adequately prevent disclosure in most cases, without a special privilege? Would these be anticipated by the communicator at the time of communicating?

Would it be wise to provide in a report privilege statute that the report may not be introduced by the reporter, in order to forestall self-serving falsifications? Under other rules of evidence (e. g., the hearsay rule and its exceptions and exemptions), would self-serving out-of-court statements be admissible in his favor? Is he likely to know this when he is reporting?

Do criminal sanctions against failing to report and against inaccurate reporting render the encouragement-type privilege unnecessary? Can such sanctions encourage accuracy respecting matters the reporter knows only he can know? Can the privilege?

Marital Privileges: Two Privileges Distinguished

> The ancient common law incompetency of one spouse to testify for or against the other in legal proceedings eventually eroded into two broad privilege principles, the confidential marital communications privilege, and the privilege against adverse spousal testimony.

These two privileges are now widely accorded by statute (essentially codifying the common law development described in the black letters) except in a few states and in federal courts, where they are still a matter of common law.

The 1974 Uniform Rules, Rule 504, adopted in a number of states, provides only the confidential marital communications privilege, and somewhat atypically confines it to criminal cases, where it may be raised by or on behalf of the accused only. The unenacted Supreme Court Draft F.R.E. 505, which still may be influential (see infra, *Privileges Under the F.R.E.*; but see *Trammel* case, infra, which provides for a different holder of the privilege than draft F.R.E. 505), grants only the adverse spousal testimony privilege, which may be raised by or on behalf of the accused in a criminal case only.

In the area of the spousal communications and the adverse spousal testimony privileges, as with most privileges, the statutes and their judicial interpretations must be examined closely, but certain generalizations can be made:

The *confidential marital communications* privilege permits the suppression in any civil or criminal case of so much of a spouse's testimony (or other evidence such as

[*431*]

documents or a third person's testimony in some circumstances) as may reveal confidences passed between the spouses by reason of the marital relationship. The privilege thus only applies to a "confidential communication." (Would it apply to avoid disclosure of the fact that a communication occurred, without revelation of its contents? This question, like most hereunder, occurs under other communications privileges, as well.) A cluster of problems arises surrounding both the requirements of "confidentiality" and of "communication." Can the act of placing money in a bank account, observed by a spouse, be an implied "communication?" Is it confidential, where others could see it but only the spouse knew its significance in a course of criminal dealings? Is the act of putting something in a drawer at home privileged insofar as viewed by the opposite spouse? Does it matter whether the spouse placing it in the drawer would not have done so openly but for the marital relation? Does it matter if he meant to hide it from the spouse? That he could have anticipated she would find it? Would anything depend on which spouse was called to testify? Are we concerned here with "confidentiality," "communication," or yet another requirement: that it be a "marital" communication? Is it appropriate to ask of verbal communications whether they would have been made but for the marital relation?

Concerning "confidentiality" in more orthodox contexts, where a third person overhearing or otherwise obtaining simultaneous or subsequent knowledge of the contents of an interspousal communication did so with the knowledge, negligence, consent or complicity of a spouse (or even sometimes in the absence of these things), the confidentiality of the communication, and hence the privilege, may be entirely destroyed, or the privilege to keep a spouse silent may still prevail, but not to keep the third party silent, or nothing at all may happen, depending upon the court, upon which spouse (communicant or communicatee; the spouse claiming the privilege or the other spouse) was responsible for the disclosure to the third party, upon the degree of that responsibility, upon who the third party was (child of the family, etc.), and upon the aggravation of the circumstances. The communicant's and communicatee's privileges may be affected differently, according to their relative responsibility for the disclosure to the third party.

And there are questions under this privilege as to who may normally assert the privilege—are both communicator and communicatee spouses primary holders with the result that either can raise the bar despite the wishes of the other? Or should the communicatee be a secondary holder only, able to raise it only on behalf of the communicator and not able to override his wishes? But consider that a previous communication of the communicatee spouse may be revealed in a communication by the communicator (as, e. g., where the communicator is responding—perhaps in a give-and-take conversation). Does that affect your answer? On an *ad hoc* basis only? Some decisions even hold that the privilege is destroyed if either one waives. Some hold that positive waiver (or consent) of a specified one, or perhaps of either one, or perhaps of both, is required. In other words, instead of the privilege being inapplicable until raised, it is applicable until waived by a positive act. Some allow one or the other or both untrammeled control over whether he will testify to the communication, but not over whether the other will.

Because the tendency of statutes is to speak in terms of husband and wife, and spouses, rather than communicator and communicatee, and in terms of prohibition rather than privilege, some confusion results. Consider what it is that seems to be privileged (e. g., what person's or persons' testimony, including overhearers; whether exhibits can be suppressed) and who (communicator or communicatee)

[*433*]

would seem to hold the privilege under the following statutes: (1) "Neither spouse shall be compelled to testify as to
a confidential communication made to him by his spouse."
(2) An identical statute except "be compelled to" is omitted.
(3) An identical statute except "made to him by his spouse"
is omitted and "marital" inserted before "communication."
(4) "Neither spouse shall testify to confidential marital communications without the consent of the other." [9] Does this
mean either spouse may waive and override the wishes of
the other? Does it mean the privilege is automatically asserted unless affirmatively waived (by positive consent)?
(5) Suppose "against the will of" is substituted for "without
the consent of." (6) Suppose "be compelled to" is inserted
before "testify." (7) Suppose "without the consent of the
other" is added to the statute quoted at (1) above. Courts
do not always feel bound by statutory language. The privilege's purpose or shape at common law has often provided
justification for "interpreting" away variant language. One
example would be that it is usually implied that the communication must be "confidential," whether or not the statute says so. Note that some of the statutes refer only to
testimony of a spouse; yet the privilege often will be construed to cover any evidence of the contents of the communication. On the other hand, some courts are strict
slaves to the statutory language.

The other marital privilege, the *adverse spousal testimony*
privilege, permits the suppression of all testimony of one
spouse against the other (often only in the latter's criminal
prosecution). The distinctions between the two privileges,

---

[9] Under this statute might the communicator spouse be compelled
(say in a civil case) to testify against himself (that is, to disclose a
communication he made that hurts his case) if the communicatee
spouse wished it? And might the communicator spouse be prevented
by the communicatee from voluntarily disclosing (in a civil or criminal
case) the communicator's own message in a case in which the communicator wishes to so disclose because it helps his case?

where the privileges remain "pure," may be generalized in the following fashion: The *communications* privilege applies only to prevent disclosure of confidential marital communications; the *adverse spousal testimony* privilege can entirely prevent the spouse from taking the stand as a witness adverse to the other connubial partner, regardless of the subject matter of the expected testimony. The communications privilege applies in civil and criminal litigation; the other privilege is frequently confined to criminal. The communications privilege applies regardless of whether the testimony is for or against the spouse; the other privilege can prevent only testimony adverse to him. The communications privilege may apply to bar testimony of both members of the couple; the other privilege, only one member. The communications privilege may cover evidence other than spousal testimony; [10] the other privilege cannot. The communications privilege applies whether or not a spouse is party to the litigation; the other privilege requires it. Indeed, the communications privilege generally applies even where neither of the spouses is a party or a witness. Only the adverse spousal testimony privilege applies when the testimony does not relate to a matter transpiring during the marriage; the communication under the communications privilege must have transpired during the marriage. And finally, only the adverse spousal testimony privilege is destroyed by divorce. This is because the marital communications privilege is said to be intended to encourage spouses *in the population generally*, to confide in each

[10] Such "other evidence" might be the letter that constitutes the communication, testimony of third persons having knowledge of the communication's contents, etc. What about evidence of actions taken by a spouse (after a communication to him) which reveal inferentially what the contents of the communication were (e. g., spouse buys stock after communication; communication probably advised such a course)? If this is permissible, could the acting spouse be asked in addition whether the action was stimulated by or was the product of the communication?

other; whereas the aim of the privilege against adverse spousal testimony is said to be to preserve and promote harmony *in the particular marriage before the court.* (Would it really harm marital harmony for one spouse to testify *under compulsion of law* against the other? One suggestion has been that the real reason for the privilege is that adverse spousal testimony offends our "sense of justice.")

Because we have already dealt somewhat in depth with one privilege intended to encourage communication (required reports, supra), we will direct our attention to the privilege against adverse spousal testimony.

The Privilege Against Adverse Spousal Testimony: Who Holds It?

A number of jurisdictions where this privilege exists, still adhere to the traditional rule that both spouses (witness and defendant) are primary holders, with the consequence that each may assert it regardless of the wishes of the other. Should this rule be abandoned for one more responsive to the policy of the privilege (assuming the privilege and its policy are worth preserving)? In many of these jurisdictions, under the wording of their statutes or the liberality of their interpretive process, no legislative change would be necessary. Such would also be true where the matter is not statutory. Consider the wisdom of the following proposal appearing in an article entitled "A Re-Evaluation of the Privilege Against Adverse Spousal Testimony in the Light of Its Purpose," 12 International and Comparative Law Quarterly 1189 (1963). It concerns the privilege in federal courts. The federal privilege is non-statutory in form and confined to criminal cases where one spouse is to testify against the other, who is the defendant. The author assumes a "marital harmony" rationale for the privilege. Federal law at that time embodied the traditional position that both spouses are primary holders, still found in many states, of which he is critical. He sets forth how he believes the matter should be handled:

> "In the very rare situation where the defendant-spouse does not care to raise the privilege, there is little risk of marital discord in taking adverse spousal testimony, regardless of the wishes of the witness-spouse. Other situations become more complex. Consider first situations in which the only information practicably cognisable by the court concerning harmony in the marriage, are the positions taken by the spouses on the privilege issue. Assume also that there is no extraordinary necessity for the testimony. Where the defendant-spouse cares to exclude the testimony (which is virtually always the case), the testimony should be received if the witness-spouse so wishes, inasmuch as the witness-spouse thereby indicates that there is little marital harmony to preserve or salvage, absent other circumstances indicating that the witness's willingness to testify is more likely the manifestation of a temporary spurt of anger or moral compunction, as might be the case where the defendant had seriously wronged the witness shortly before the trial. [Similarly, other such circumstances making the willingness to testify an unreliable indicator of lack of marital harmony, which the article could have added, would be where the prosecution has threatened that, unless the witness spouse testifies, charges will be brought against the witness spouse; or has promised leniency, reduced charges, or immunity for the witness spouse, if the testimony is given.] The witness's *un*willingness to testify should be respected because it indicates harmony in the marriage, absent circumstances suggesting that the unwillingness was procured by fear and coercion exerted by the defendant . . . ."

[437]

The article goes on to examine situations where other facts concerning harmony in the marriage, than the positions of the spouses on the privilege issue, are "feasibly cognisable" by the court:

> "In certain circumstances, there will be little marital harmony of the type the law strives to preserve: serious wrongs committed by the defendant-spouse against the witness-spouse; prolonged and continuous adultery or prostitution; separation or divorce; sham marriage or marriage contracted in order to acquire the privilege. Under the first and second categories, it is irrelevant whether the wrong is the one being tried in the case at bar. The 'victim' witness-spouse's un-coerced marriage to or cohabitation with the defendant after the wrong, or her voluntary acquiescence in, consent to, or co-operation in the wrong, would tend to nullify the indications of marital strife produced by the wrong. Her unwillingness to testify would not necessarily have this effect. For, unwillingness when there has been such a wrong is more likely the product of fear and coercion wrought by the defendant, than of strong marital ties; unless accompanied by one of the acts of forgiveness just mentioned. Willingness to testify would seem to corroborate the presumption of marital discord arising from the wrong."

Notice that in the opening phrase of this last quotation, it is suggested that the law should consider not only the possibilities for marital harmony in the marriage, but whether the marriage is the *kind* that ought to be preserved. The suggestion made later in the article is that where the marriage is used to facilitate a prostitution business (with the husband as procurer for the wife), it ought not to be fostered.

With respect to the author's suggestion concerning separation and divorce, it could be argued, contrary to his suggestion, and to the law everywhere, that the marital harmony policy should be extended to attempt to nurture possibilities of *reunion*, in addition to its present aim of avoiding creating rifts, at least where there is some substantial chance of reunion. But the cost of having a privilege must be remembered. And, is it practicable for the law to get into gauging the possibility of reunion? Could it be done for broad categories of cases? For example, one may argue that divorce and separation are distinguishable in that the hope of reunion is more realistic in the case of separation.

Let us put aside divorces and separations, and return to subsisting marriages. It may not be feasible for courts to inquire into marital harmony to the extent the author suggests. On the other hand, it could be argued that there should be even *deeper* inquiry into marital harmony in each case, including actual testimony and evidence on the matter, in an effort to ascertain even more accurately whether there is any harmony to preserve by granting privilege. This would increase the contingency of the applicability of the privilege even beyond the large measure of it introduced by the author. Contingency of applicability (which occurs whenever the particular facts of each case are given a large role) would not encroach upon the policy of this privilege to the extent that it would in the case of a confidential communications privilege, where the purpose is to foster communications, which will not be fostered unless the communicator is relatively certain of secrecy in advance. But aside from contingency, would it be feasible to make such an inquiry?

The author goes on to suggest that perhaps there should be an even further contingency in the applicability of the privilege: that there may be cases in which the need for the testimony overrides any consideration of marital harmony. He suggests that these cases would become more defined as precedent becomes established; and that judges are often called upon to balance need for a particular disclosure against the reasons for secrecy, on an *ad hoc* basis, on the facts of the particular case. He cites the examples of discovery (where often "good cause" must be shown before disclosure will be ordered), qualified privileges (state secrets, informer privilege, etc.), the work-product rule, and the probative-prejudice balancing described in Chapter I, supra.

Traditionally the defendant-spouse loses his privilege where the charge upon which he is being tried is one of physical violence [11] against his spouse. The reader should consider carefully how this does not "square" with what the author sets up as desiderata above: Notice that under the traditional rule in this situation, the witness-spouse still retains her privilege—i. e., retains an unqualified right to admit or exclude, apparently regardless of the possibility of fear or coercion or any other circumstance.[12] Notice also that only a *violent crime* that is the subject of the *present charge* is considered; and that no determination of whether or not the crime was committed is made preliminary to admissibility. The reason for the abrogation of the defendant's privilege in these cases is often said to be "special necessity" for the testimony of the victim, who may be the only witness—but nothing hinges on whether or not there were in fact other witnesses. Furthermore, crimes against the spouse may not be as heinous as crimes of a more distributive effect. Is not this an element of "necessity"

[11] Somewhat atypically, violation of the Mann Act, 18 U.S.C.A. § 2421, which proscribes interstate transportation of women for immoral purposes, has been held to come within this category when the witness-spouse is the woman transported, even if she consented.

[12] But see Wyatt v. United States, 362 U.S. 525, 80 S.Ct. 901 (1960) (Mann Act prosecution against husband for prostituting his wife interstate; she compelled to testify; her raising of privilege *presumed* to be the product of coercion on his part and thus an indirect exercise of his lost privilege, despite contrary indications).

too? One can think of an abundance of fact situations and crimes where there is more "necessity" for the spousal testimony, both from the standpoint of availability of other evidence and the standpoint of need for conviction, than in the cases comprehended by this so-called "necessity exception" to the privilege. Further, it must be remembered that the witness-spouse, in these cases, retains the option not to testify. If the testimony is necessary, is it not equally so even if the witness desired not to testify? Why is only the defendant deprived of his privilege? The entire "necessity exception" seems really to be the product of some rough sense of justice that says the victim-witness-spouse ought to have the power to damn or forgive. But then why not have a substantive rule that forgiveness is a defense? The article summarizes the disparities between the traditional "necessity exception" and the way things "ought to be," as follows:

"[T]he necessity exception treats improperly the witness's willingness or unwillingness to testify, where there has been a serious wrong committed by the defendant against the witness. In a necessity exception case where that witness is willing to testify, the traditional rule properly allows the testimony. But where, in the same situation, the witness is unwilling, that wish is, improperly, respected automatically under the rule. Where the wrong by the defendant against the witness is serious but does not come within the literal terms of the necessity exception, the defendant is, quite irrationally, able to defeat the willingness of the witness to testify. Unwillingness to testify in such a case is, improperly, respected.

"The standard necessity exception is occasionally defended on the ground that even though the accused has lost his privilege, the witness-spouse must retain hers to avoid the perjury that compelled testimony is likely to entail in such a situation. [Indeed, the danger of perjury has been cited as a prime justification for privileges generally.] But there is always the danger of perjury when testimony is compelled, and especially is this true where one sibling is compelled to testify against another or against his own parent, or a parent against her own child, or any relative against relative, or friend against friend. And yet, such witnesses are not accorded privileges."

In 1980, the view espoused in this article, that the witness-spouse alone should normally control the privilege, was adopted by the U.S. Supreme Court for all federal prosecutions, in Trammel v. United States, 445 U.S. 40, 100 S.Ct. 906 (1980). By that date, approximately half the states had also modified the traditional rule in a similar direction. Whether some of the refinements in the article will be adopted remains to be seen. The Supreme Court decision did not place significance on the fact that the spouse's willingness to testify, which was taken as an indicator of little marital harmony, may instead merely have been the product of the promise of leniency and immunity that was frankly granted her by the prosecution in this case. The court did not note the "Hobson's choice" thus given her (testify or be tried yourself); the strain on a harmonious marriage this can produce; the incentive to prosecutors to place in this dilemma future witness-spouses whom they would not otherwise have thought of charging; and the strain on marital harmony this could produce in future cases.[13]

[13] The author of the present volume also wrote the article quoted. I wished to present it here as material to be objectively analyzed rather than as a somehow preferred solution, at least until the reader had gone through the problems and issues.

Doctor-Patient Privilege

In a majority of states there is a privilege covering private communications from a patient to his doctor if the information is germane to the purposes of a consultation for treatment, prescription, or cure, as opposed to preparation for litigation, application for insurance, etc.

The aim of the law here is to facilitate informed medical care. (Doesn't society have an interest in informed insurance application and informed preparation for litigation?) Because of this policy, the privilege is sometimes, although not universally, extended to cover matters in the doctor's files that were not communicated by or to the patient, things obtained or found out by the doctor concerning the patient from other doctors and hospitals, uncommunicated opinions, facts observed by the doctor, communications by the doctor to other doctors, and communications passing from him to the patient (as well as the reverse), in some jurisdictions only to the extent these things may inferentially reflect communications from the patient. In each instance, of course, the information must relate to the patient's case. Where permission or information is needed from the patient for the doctor to gather a complete file on the patient from other doctors or hospitals, the patient may be encouraged to give it by a promise of confidentiality. He may also be more forthcoming about communicating facts if he knows that things the doctor says or has in his file that could reflect them, are secret. And other doctors, hospitals, etc., may be more forthcoming about supplying information if they know it is protected. See generally Doctor-Patient Privilege, 56 Nw. U.L.Rev. 263 (1961). Problems very similar to all of these come up under the attorney-client privilege, as well, and there is a similar diversity of views there. A diversity of authority also exists concerning the related matters of whether the privilege (doctor-patient or attorney-client) should cover the fact that a doctor (or lawyer) was visited (or retained); the fact that a communication was made; etc. Query: is there a policy not only to encourage information, but also to encourage the seeking of professional help? Would you privilege the date of a visit or communication under both privileges?

In view of the purpose of the privilege, the test of whether information is germane to treatment should be whether the patient *thought* it was germane. Would the fact of *where* an injury occurred ordinarily be germane? *How* it occurred? Would alcohol smelled by the doctor on the patient's breath be germane? (Should this be ruled out because it is not a communication?) In a given case the sanitary conditions of the place of occurrence, or the presence of alcohol in the body, might influence the choice of medication. The manner of infliction might influence treatment. What role should be played by the fact that a reasonable person would or would not have thought a matter germane to treatment?

In view of the purpose of the privilege to improve treatment, the presence of a nurse at the consultation would not ordinarily destroy the privilege. Something may depend upon the dispensability of her role. (What about the presence of a friend brought by the patient for moral support?)

Should the privilege terminate upon the patient's death? Assurance of secrecy even after death may significantly encourage some kinds of patient-to-doctor disclosure.

The bringing of a personal injury action by the patient will generally accomplish a waiver at least as respects the physical condition he puts in issue and probably as respects all doctors and medical conditions in the patient's life that may be relevant, which is usually a very broad waiver indeed.

On all these questions not only must the policy of the privilege be considered, but the degree of encouragement to patients must be weighed against the hindrance to trials. Furthermore, it is not the effect on *this* patient that is to be gauged, but rather the effect on patients generally, as in the case of most communications privileges (but not the adverse spousal testimony privilege).

If the visit to the doctor is for purposes of preparing litigation or preparing the doctor as a witness, the information will be outside the scope of this privilege, but may be within the attorney-client privilege if the doctor can be viewed as an agent (for purposes of the privilege) of the attorney or of the client, standing between the two. (Does that privilege take care of the question raised above concerning whether society has an interest in having litigation prepared well?) Consider also the attorney work-product privilege.

There is an exception to the hearsay rule for declarations to doctors in certain situations where the motive of seeking care is deemed to guaranty accuracy. Thus the applicability of the doctor-patient privilege and of the hearsay rule may both turn upon the purpose of the consultation in a given case (i. e., treatment or preparation for litigation). Does the rationale of the hearsay exception suggest that the privilege is not needed—i. e., that a patient is not going to falsify or leave things out where he knows it might mean his health will suffer?

A doctor (like a lawyer) has an ethical duty of non-disclosure roughly analogous to the privilege. But a conflict between a doctor's legal duty and ethical duty can arise, especially in a jurisdiction or situation where the law recognizes no doctor-patient privilege. Psychiatrists, especially those working for government institutions, have been greatly concerned. Testimony under compulsion probably does not violate the doctor's ethical duty, but it discourages visits and helpful patient-to-doctor disclosures, especially in the field of mental health, where the seeking of help and candor in interviews are very contingent things.   Because of this last point, a number of jurisdictions recognize only a psychotherapist-patient privilege, rather than a general physician-patient privilege.   This was the original position of the F.R.E., see unenacted Supreme Court Draft Rule 504, 56 F.R.D. 183 (1972), although the definition of psychotherapist there might have been broad enough to include an ordinary doctor treating a broken bone if he was sufficiently attentive to the emotional or mental state of his patient.

Unlike the husband-wife and lawyer-client privileges, the doctor-patient privilege (including any psychotherapist-patient privilege), did not exist at common law, and is generally deemed to require special enactment.   (This leaves its status under the current provisions of the F.R.E., which refer privilege questions to an evolving common law process and state law, somewhat in doubt.   See infra, *Privileges Under the F.R.E.*)

The privilege is usually not available in workman's compensation cases and certain enumerated (or all) criminal actions (e. g., abortion).   There may be certain other enumerated exclusions as well, e. g., cases involving homicide, the validity of a will, medical malpractice, mental illness, etc.

1974 Uniform Rule 503 provides a good statement of the physician-patient and psychotherapist-patient privileges.   The Rule is a psychotherapist-patient privilege with an optional provision extending coverage to also include an ordinary physician-patient privilege for those jurisdictions that choose. It has been adopted in alternative forms by a number of jurisdictions.

Attorney-Client Privilege

To facilitate informed legal services, there is in all jurisdictions a privilege covering private communications [14] between client and attorney made pursuant to professional consultation.

The purpose is similar to that of the doctor-patient privilege. Because of the "pursuant to professional consultation" requirement reflecting a policy to foster legitimate legal services, advice to commit a crime would not be privileged, nor would things said by a client seeking such advice. Similarly, attorneys who get involved in activities for a corporation of a "business" as opposed to "professional legal" nature, frequently find that the communications made pursuant thereto are held not privileged.

Courts are divided as to whether and when the mere *fact* of consultation, retention, or employment of a lawyer, and the identity of a lawyer's client, may be privileged. So, too, with requiring a description of the general nature or amount of the legal services rendered, including fees and time. See *Privileges Under the F.R.E.,* infra. Where these things could be used to the detriment of the client, should they be privileged? What does the policy of the privilege suggest?

In comparison with the other privileges, it is equally or more likely here that a communication from lawyer to client will inferentially reveal a communication from client to lawyer, with the result that communications both ways should be covered as a general matter or at least in many particular cases.

One rule dictated by practical considerations in this area has been that documents existing before or not arising out

---

[14] A number of jurisdictions privilege quite a bit more than communications from client to attorney. See opening paragraphs of *Doctor-Patient Privilege* above. The positions found are the same, for similar reasons. See also infra, pp. 457–58.

of the lawyer-client relationship, that are subject to discovery in the hands of the client, cannot be brought within this privilege or the work product privilege (see infra) by delivery to the lawyer.

In some kinds of cases, notably those involving wills of the client or intestate succession to his property, the lawyer-client privilege has on occasion been held to die with the client.

Not infrequently several parties have been regarded as "the client" for purposes of assertion or waiver of the privilege. This can occur, e. g., where they all claim under the original client making the communication (as his successors, heirs, grantees, etc.), or where they have consulted the attorney together. Usually the problem arises where these parties are on opposite sides of the litigation or are otherwise not in agreement on the exercise of the privilege. The consequences in this situation of regarding several such parties as "the client" have not always been uniform. (Consider what they might be.) Another approach to the same problem has been to regard the material as "not confidential," or "not confidential as between these parties." (What are the consequences of these?) The tendency seems to be to hold that the material should not be disclosed, except where the two "clients" are litigating with each other, in which case the material is generally held unprivileged.

One area of considerable controversy is the extent to which the client's agents' or employees' reports to the client (who is usually a company), or to the lawyer, are privileged as attorney-client communications or legal work-product (see infra). Under both, a distinction is often drawn on the basis of the extent of the lawyer's participation in ordering (or receiving) the report; or on the basis of the existence of litigation, legal controversy, or a legal or litigation motive, at the time of the report. In addition, sometimes a distinction is drawn based upon whether the employee has authority to seek and/or act upon legal advice for the company. (This would limit it to a rather high group of officials; or at least ones with considerable authority as respects that particular operation.) At the very least, it would seem, the employee would have to be authorized or directed to speak to the company's lawyer or agent he spoke to; and perhaps it would be required that the communication relate to his job and to the legal business of the company. (See footnote 15, infra.) If a communication goes to the lawyer through intermediaries, or is otherwise made known to agents within the company, they must be considered necessary in some sense, if privilege is to endure. A related problem comes up in the form of insurance agents' reports when there has been an automobile collision. The agent will have interviewed the insured, and included the information in the report. He will also have generated information of his own. Is such an agent an agent of the insured? Of the attorney? Of the insurance company? Who is the client? Does it matter if the report goes to the company or the attorney? What effect will all this have? Answers have varied, but there is a marked tendency toward privileging these if other requirements are met.

Corporations clearly may avail themselves of the attorney-client privilege. See Radiant Burners, Inc. v. American Gas Ass'n, 320 F.2d 314 (6th Cir., 1963). But questions have arisen as to who is in the shoes of the client—the stockholders? or the management? which group of shareholders?—especially when they are at odds. See Garner v. Wolfinbarger, 430 F.2d 1093 (5th Cir. 1970). On communications between corporate in-house and out-of-house counsel, see Natta v. Zletz, 418 F.2d 633 (7th Cir. 1969). On the privilege of government agencies communicating with their own lawyers, see Coastal States Gas Corp. v. Department of Energy, 617 F.2d 854 (D.C.Cir. 1980).

Following is a good statement of the lawyer-client privilege. It appears in the 1974 Uniform Rules, adopted in a number of states. Brackets indicate significant material not included in Supreme Court Draft F.R.E. 503 (which was not enacted but which may still be persuasive authority—see *Privileges Under the F.R.E.,* infra), upon which the Uniform Rule is modelled:

"Rule 502.   Lawyer-Client Privilege

"(a) *Definitions.* As used in this rule:

"(1) A 'client' is a person, public officer, or corporation, association, or other organization or entity, either public or private, who is rendered professional legal services by a lawyer, or who consults a lawyer with a view to obtaining professional legal services from him.

"[(2) A 'representative of the client' is one having authority to obtain professional legal services, or to act on advice rendered pursuant thereto, on behalf of the client.] [15]

[15] Supreme Court Draft F.R.E. 503 deleted any provision on this because previous authority was not clear. The Uniform Rule codifies the more restrictive of the two prevailing views as to which employees of the corporation may make protected communications to the corporation's lawyers—the "control group" view which confines it to those persons authorized to seek and/or act on legal advice (City of Philadelphia v. Westinghouse Elec. Corp. 210 F.Supp. 483 (E.D.Pa.1962)) as opposed to the "directed, job related" view which expands it to encompass, additionally, any employee communication of a legal nature directed to be made by corporate authority if related to the employee's work (Harper & Row Pub., Inc. v. Decker, 423 F.2d 487 (7th Cir. 1970) affirmed by equally divided court without opinion, 400 U.S. 348, 91 S.Ct. 479, rehearing denied 401 U.S. 950, 91 S.Ct. 917 (1971)). Under the "control group" test, it is possible to take the view that there is one control group in a corporation; or that different transactions have different control groups. The Supreme Court has, since *Harper & Row,* rejected the control group test, in a decision concerning the availability of the privilege to resist a subpoena in a federal tax investigation, which will probably be given broad effect, and will influence even the states. See Upjohn Co. v. United States, — U.S. —, 101 S.Ct. 677 (1981). On the privilege in the corporate context generally, see 56 Nw.U.L.Rev. 235 (1961); Rothstein & Brunner, Corporate Information: Confidentiality & Disclosability (West, 1982).

[Footnote continued next page.]

"(3) A 'lawyer' is a person authorized, or reasonably believed by the client to be authorized, to engage in the practice of law in any state or nation.

"(4) A 'representative of the lawyer' is one employed [by the lawyer] to assist the lawyer in the rendition of professional legal services.

"(5) A communication is 'confidential' if not intended to be disclosed to third persons other than those to whom disclosure is [made] in furtherance of the rendition of professional legal services to the client or those reasonably necessary for the transmission of the communication.

"(b) *General rule of privilege.* A client has a privilege to refuse to disclose and to prevent any other person from disclosing confidential communications, made for the purpose of facilitating the rendition of professional legal services to the client, (1) between himself or his representative and his lawyer or his lawyer's representative, (2) between his lawyer and the lawyer's representative, (3) by him [or his representative] or his lawyer [or a representative of the lawyer] to a lawyer [or a representative of a lawyer] representing another party in a [pending action and concerning a] matter of common interest [therein], (4) between representatives of the client or between the client and a representative of the client, or (5) among lawyers [and their representatives] representing the [same] client.

"(c) *Who may claim the privilege.* The privilege may be claimed by the client, his guardian or conservator,

Query: Does Section (b)(4), after the "or," negate the attempt to mandate the "control group" test? The "client" may speak to the control group ("representative of the client"—see definitions) through a lower employee authorized to speak. The lower employee is the voice of the "client," communicating with the "representative of the client" (i. e., with the control group).

Second query: Can one get around the narrowness of a control group test by having the attorney represent the employees, too, so that they are also clients? [Footnote not in original.]

the personal representative of a deceased client, or the successor, trustee, or similar representative of a corporation, association, or other organization, whether or not in existence. The person who was the lawyer [or the lawyer's representative] at the time of the communication is presumed to have authority to claim the privilege but only on behalf of the client.[16]

"(d) *Exceptions.* There is no privilege under this rule:

"(1) *Furtherance of crime or fraud.* If the services of the lawyer were sought or obtained to enable or aid anyone to commit or plan to commit what the client knew or reasonably should have known to be a crime or fraud;[17]

"(2) *Claimants through same deceased client.* As to a communication relevant to an issue between parties who claim through the same deceased client, regardless of whether the claims are by testate or intestate succession or by inter vivos transaction;

"(3) *Breach of duty by a lawyer or client.* As to a communication relevant to an issue of breach of duty by the lawyer to his client or by the client to his lawyer;[18]

---

[16] Does this mean the parties to the action or the judge cannot raise it on the client's behalf if he is not a party and is unaware that the information is being called for? Incidentally, the F.R.E. draft says presumed *in the absence of contrary evidence.* On another point, note that § (b) eliminates the old "eavesdropper" rule allowing third parties to testify to the communication in some circumstances where lawyer or client need not. [Footnote not in original.]

[17] Note that this refers to a future crime or fraud. Defending a *past* crime or fraud is just the sort of thing the privilege is designed to cover. [Footnote not in original.]

[18] Would this cover in addition to a malpractice claim, a claim of ineffective assistance of counsel made in order to get a criminal conviction reversed? A suit by a lawyer for fees? A disciplinary proceeding? Is there a privilege in a case where the client raises a defense "I relied on advice of counsel?" [Footnote not in original.]

"(4) *Document attested by a lawyer.* As to a communication relevant to an issue concerning an attested document to which the lawyer is an attesting witness;

"(5) *Joint clients.* As to a communication relevant to a matter of common interest between or among two or more clients if the communication was made by any of them to a lawyer retained or consulted in common, when offered in an action between or among any of the clients [or]

"[(6) *Public officer or agency.* As to a communication between a public officer or agency and its lawyers unless the communication concerns a pending investigation, claim, or action and the court determines that disclosure will seriously impair the ability of the public officer or agency to process the claim or conduct a pending investigation, litigation, or proceeding in the public interest.]"

A number of important questions that have troubled courts over the years are not satisfactorily addressed by this draft, or the Supreme Court F.R.E. draft upon which it is modelled. See Rothstein, The Proposed Amendments to the F.R.E., 62 Geo.L.J. 125, particularly 133–34 (1973) (also discusses the other privileges in that draft F.R.E.), reprinted 9 J. of Reprints for Antitrust L. & Econ. 157, 165–66 (1979) (special attorney-client privilege issue, containing a collection of informative articles on that privilege, particularly in the corporate context).

Work-Product Privilege

This privilege prevents access to matters considered part of a lawyer's work-up of a case for (or already in) litigation. It is a qualified privilege giving way for "good cause," a sliding concept that requires more, the closer to the heart of a lawyer's creative contribution the material sought comes.

The theory is that better law results where lawyers do not fear to work up their cases thoroughly and to put things down on paper.

Suppose a client prepares a work-up on a certain aspect of a case, but not on the direction of his lawyer? Suppose a lawyer prepares a legal work-up, but not for litigation? Can work-product for one litigation be required to be disclosed in another? Courts have differed on these, but there is a substantial risk that these matters will not be privileged.

Somewhat atypically as respects privileges generally, the Federal Rules of Civil Procedure codify this privilege separately for discovery (F.R.Civ.Pro. 26(b)(3)), rather than relying on the general provisions of F.R.Civ.Pro. 26(b)(1) and F.R.E. 1101(c) to the effect that trial privileges apply during discovery. A work-product privilege of approximately the same shape applies as a matter of common law at trial. See infra, *Privileges Under the F.R.E.*

Other Similar Privileges

Are there other socially desirable relationships or professions whose work or solidarity ought to be facilitated in a fashion similar to that extended to doctors, lawyers, and spouses? To name just a few possibilities, how about a priest-penitent, journalist-informant, or accountant-client privilege? Why isn't it considered as desirable to foster, with privilege, communications between other family members, as it is between husband and wife? Wouldn't it be desirable to foster the work of the boss-secretary or social worker-client relationship? What about a researcher-subject privilege? A number of jurisdictions have some form of the penitent, journalist, and/or accountant privileges. There is scant authority for the others, although the social worker and researcher privileges are not unknown. See the next section herein for the status of these more remote privileges under the F.R.E.

Privileges Under the F.R.E.

Article V of the F.R.E. is the article that deals with privilege. It consists of one rule: Rule 501. Instead of providing specific rules of evidentiary privilege (a rejected earlier draft had expressly formulated a required-report, lawyer-client, psychotherapist-patient, adverse spousal testimony, clergyman-communicant, political vote, trade secret, state secret, official information, and identity-of-government-informer privilege, plus some general provisions on such matters as waiver and comment on invocation),[19] Rule 501 provides that "privilege" is to be governed by "the principles of the common law as they may be interpreted by the courts of the United States in the light of reason and experience," except in certain state law cases, where state privilege law is to apply.[20]

---

[19] The 1974 Uniform Rules, Article V, intended as a model for the states and adopted by several of them, has a very similar list of expressly formulated privileges, except that it has no specific formulation of a required report privilege and there are some differences in the husband-wife, physician, and governmental privileges, and a modification of the lawyer-client formulation, all noted above, and a few other more minor differences. The general provisions are also quite similar.

[20] Normally this will be the law of the state in which the federal court is sitting (or, in the case of transfer between federal courts, the state in which the transferor court is sitting), including its applicable choice-of-law rules, if any.

This deference to state law is found in nearly identical form in three places in the Federal Rules of Evidence: Article III (effect of presumptions), Article V (privileges), and Article VI (competency of witnesses). (In Articles III and VI, when federal evidence law is to govern, the federal evidence law is specifically prescribed, rather than left to federal common law as in Article V.) In these three areas (the only areas of express deference to state evidence law), the state evidence law governs only when the matter sought to be proved is an "element" of a "claim or defense" as to which state law supplies the "rule of decision." What would *not* be an "element?" Does it mean *ultimate* element as opposed to a mediate step?

[Footnote 20 continued next page.]

It is not entirely clear what is encompassed by the term "privilege" as used in F.R.E. 501, but probably outside the term as used there are rules banning the evidencing of such things as remedial measures, compromise or settlement efforts, insurance, character, and the like, because they are in F.R.E. Article IV (Relevancy and Its Limits); and matters usually classed as *incompetencies* of witnesses, dealt with in F.R.E. Article VI (Witnesses).[21] F.R.E. Article V (Privileges), consisting of Rule

---

[Footnote 20 continued from last page.]

Diversity cases are the usual cases in which state law comes into play, as opposed to, for example, federal prosecutions, or civil actions under such laws as the federal securities, tax, and antitrust laws. What of cases with joined federal and state issues—that is, issues of both types mixed? Might not the same piece of evidence have a dual capacity? Might not the fact issues be the same under both? Instead of an instruction to use the evidence on one issue but not the other (if the state and federal evidence law differed), might the judge use Rule 403 to exclude the evidence altogether? Or apply the law favoring admissibility? Or try to determine the predominant character (state or federal) of the action? Or refuse to join certain state and federal claims?

The F.R.E. and the Rules of Procedure provide that the privileges that would apply at trial pursuant to the F.R.E. also apply during discovery. Is it always possible during discovery to identify whether it is a state law issue or a federal law issue that will be sought to be proved at the trial with the evidence? And yet that might be necessary, to decide which privilege law applies.

[21] Witness incompetencies—i. e., automatic disqualification of a witness for interest in the case, commission of a felony, mental incapacity, youth, drug or alcohol intoxication or addiction, marital relationship to a party, etc.—are largely becoming things of the past, these matters now being left mainly to the probative-prejudice-etc. balance (see Chapter I) and to the realm of impeachment and weight. See In re R. R., 79 N.J. 97, 398 A.2d 76 (1979) (4-year-old competent). However, the Dead Man Rule (see p. 72) still widely survives as an incompetency among the states. F.R.E. 601 adopts the local state incompetencies in certain state law cases. In all other instances it abolishes incompetencies except for the few mentioned specifically in Article VI (lack of personal knowledge; failure to take the oath or make an affirmation; and disqualification of judges and jurors as witnesses). F.R.E. 610 states that beliefs on matters of religion can no longer be shown as matters of competency or credibility. Would this prevent showing that a witness against a party was a member

501, covers such questions as the existence and scope of marital and medical privileges, privileges related to attorneys, accountants, journalists, and informants, and privileges covering governmental matters and required reports. Since in many instances Congressional disapproval of the earlier draft that codified particular privileges seems to have had little to do with the merits of the particular privilege provisions (with some exceptions), there is disagreement in the cases as to the extent to which that draft (drawn up by leading scholars, lawyers, and judges, and approved by the Supreme Court) may help in fashioning a modern "common law" of privileges under the federal law branch of present Rule 501.

Several cases illustrate the operation of this branch. In Gannet v. First Nat'l State Bank, 410 F.Supp. 585 (D.N.J.1976), rev'd on other grounds sub nom. United States v. First Nat'l State Bank, 540 F.2d 619 (3d Cir.), and aff'd in part sub nom. Gannet v. First Nat'l State Bank, 546 F.2d 1072 (3d Cir.), cert. denied 431 U.S. 954, 97 S.Ct. 2674, an anonymous cashier's check was sent to the Internal Revenue Service to cover overdue tax payments. Through an administrative summons (subject to Rule 501) the I.R.S. sought from the lawyer the identity of his client on whose behalf the check was sent. The court overruled a claim of attorney-client privilege, holding that a federal tax matter was among those areas governed by the "common law . . . reason and experience" standard in Rule 501, and that, whatever state privilege law may say, a client's identity is not covered by the attorney-client privilege under what the court apparently feels is the better view under the split of authority in federal jurisprudence. (The states, incidentally, are also divided on this question—i. e., the question of

of a religious group, that believed what the party stood for was evil, or whose church had a stake in the litigation?

whether the fact that there was an attorney-client relationship can be shown—as they and federal courts are on such questions as showing the fee or the general nature of services rendered, or matters not strictly communications *from the client.* Some of the split no doubt arises from factual differences.) In the case of In re Grand Jury Investigation (Sturgis), 412 F.Supp. 943 (E.D.Pa.1976), involving a federal criminal grand jury proceeding (to which Rule 501 applies), the qualified privilege for an attorney's work-product, covering materials prepared in anticipation of litigation, was adopted pursuant to the "common law . . . reason and experience" standard. The privilege adopted was modelled on the one formulated in Federal Rule of Civil Procedure 26(b)(3) which applies to discovery in civil cases. Incidentally, the formulation of a privilege in that rule is unusual, because most privileges applicable during discovery are not expressly formulated. They are taken over by reference to the evidentiary privileges that would apply at trial under the Federal Rules of Evidence. The court relied in part on a Supreme Court ruling prior to the F.R.E., United States v. Nobles, 422 U.S. 225, 95 S.Ct. 2160 (1975), which recognized the privilege as a matter of judge-made law in the trial of a criminal case. No such privilege was recognized at the old common law. See also *Upjohn,* supra.

The case somewhat obliquely suggests a broader question: Does Rule 501 use the term "common law" strictly to require direct federal authority, or direct common-law precedent (either of which would preclude new, previously unrecognized privileges), or does it use the term in the looser sense of a common law process permitting recognition (or even creation) of new privileges based on general policies found in the common law. If what we termed the "looser view" obtains, is it confined to privileges that have substantial precedent in modern cases, statutes, or rules, amongst the states (although, of course, such precedent would be advisory only, since it is federal law the court is expounding under this branch)? It is on this latter basis that a claim of physician-patient privilege, for example, can be distinguished from a claim of parent-child or researcher-source privilege, all three privileges being unknown at common law. For although general policies of confidentiality and encouragement of communication, information, and professional or personal relationships can be found in the common law—for example in the marital communications and attorney-client privilege area—tending to support all three of these claims, nevertheless modern statutes, and decisions, among the states, tend to support the physician-patient privilege but not the other two privileges. Thus, the result depends on how broadly one reads the "common law" standard of Rule 501. On accountant-client privilege, which did not exist at common law or under federal decisions and which federal decisions still usually refuse to recognize (some states have it), cf. United States v. Arthur Andersen & Co., 612 F.2d 569 (1st Cir. 1980). On the status of a clergyman-penitent privilege, recognized in a number of states, and, unlike the accountant-client privilege, recognized in the Supreme Court draft F.R.E., see United States v. Webb, —— F.2d —— (9th Cir. 1980).

In this writer's opinion, it should be remembered that Rule 501 refers not to the "common law," but rather to "*principles* of the common law" as they "may be *interpreted* . . . in the light of *reason and experience.*" These words I have italicized suggest an expansive reading. In addition, it is significant that "*may be* interpreted" is the phrase used, rather than "*have been* interpreted." This indicates a future tense, a kind of future-looking freedom: that it is an evolving common law that we are after, or an interpretation done in the light of *modern* reason and experience.

The language taken as a whole, then, would seem to license at least *some* new privileges, not previously recognized, in cases where they share common policies with existing privileges. The same would apply to new exceptions to privileges.

It is also interesting to note that the phrase is "as they may be interpreted by the courts *of the United States,*" not merely "federal courts." This may open the way for consideration of what state as well as federal courts are doing, when a federal court is asked to fashion this modern federal common law. Of course, as already indicated, what the states are doing is advisory only, since it is *federal* law that the courts are fashioning under *this* branch of the rule.

The following cases illustrate the varying approaches of federal courts to the problems posed in the last several paragraphs. In each case, the court was asked to recognize a new privilege, or a new exception to a privilege, under the federal common law branch of Rule 501:

United States v. Allery, 526 F.2d 1362 (8th Cir. 1975) (extending the common law exemption from marital privilege for crimes against a spouse, to cover crimes against a child of a spouse); United States v. Meagher, 531 F.2d 752 (5th Cir. 1976) (refusing to recognize a federal physician-patient privilege); In re Grand Jury Impanelled Jan. 21, 1975 (Freedman, Cortese), 541 F.2d 373 (3d Cir. 1976) (refusing to recognize a prothonotary privilege); United States v. Cortese, 540 F.2d 640 (3d Cir. 1976) (same); United States v. Craig, 528 F.2d 773 (7th Cir. 1976) (recognizing a state-legislator privilege but holding it waived on the facts), rehearing en banc, 537 F.2d 957 (refusing to recognize such a privilege) (see also on this one, United States v. Gillock, 445 U.S. 360, 100 S.Ct. 1185 (1980)); F.T.C. v. T. R. W., Inc., 628 F.2d 207 (D.C.Cir. 1980) (refusing a privilege for "self-evaluative" reports); United States v. King, 442 F.Supp. 1244 (E.D.N.Y.1976) (recognizing a qualified privilege for state income tax returns); Edney v. Smith, 425 F.Supp. 1038 (E.D.N.Y.1976) (recognizing a *qualified* psychotherapist privilege). Cf. Richards of Rockford, Inc. v. Pacific Gas & Elec. Co., 71 F.R.D. 388 (N.D.Cal.1976) (creating a new privilege —a researcher's privilege—in discovery stage of case that would seem to involve the state-law branch of Rule 501, where state law would not recognize; invokes inherent power of court over discovery to do so; but see Rule 1101, which seems to make Rule 501, and, thus, state privilege law, binding in this type of case). See also United States v. Penn, —— F.2d —— (9th Cir. 1980) (refusing to create a "family" privilege).

Gillock, supra, contains some interesting, though inconclusive, language on the general subject of the extent of judicial flexibility under the federal branch of F.R.E. 501, and also on the role of Supreme Court draft F.R.E. Art. V. Concerning judicial flexibility, though the Court found policy reasons for refusing to recognize the particular privilege claimed, the opinion seems to authorize new privileges in appropriate cases.

"Privileges" Relating to Grand and Petit Juries

Testimony or affidavits of a petit juror showing impropriety in jury deliberations or in jurors, will not be received to impeach (overturn) a verdict he participated in rendering, with certain exceptions in various jurisdictions.

The exclusionary principle here is usually termed an "incompetency" rather than a privilege. See F.R.E. 606(b). The policy is to prevent approaches to jurors, avoid juror harassment or intimidation, and forestall a chilling effect on jurors' freedom to deliberate and willingness to serve. Usually other methods of proof than juror testimony or affidavits will not be barred.   These others will be received to show whatever would constitute legal grounds for overturning a verdict under the substantive (non-evidence) law of the jurisdiction.   These grounds are often severely restricted under the substantive law, in the interests of finality of judgments.

> **Grand jury proceedings (including witness-testimony received there and the deliberations of the jurors) were originally privileged (except for the government's access to such testimony) but today good cause or particularized need for access to a transcript of the witness-testimony or portions thereof will result in access thereto by the accused.**

Such need has been shown where grand jury statements of key trial witnesses, made some years nearer to the witnessed incident, were sought for possible impeachment by inconsistency.   The witnesses were presently exhibiting some confusion and possible bias, and their testimony was uncorroborated.   This was considered sufficient grounds. An accused is usually entitled to a transcript of his own grand-jury testimony.

The reasons for privileging grand jury matters are very similar to those noted for petit juries above.

The Privilege Against Self-Incrimination

> **The privilege against self-incrimination as guaranteed in all American courts by the federal constitution is actually two privileges: one of the criminally accused, which includes both a right to stay off the stand and a right to turn away certain questions; and one of a civil or criminal witness (who may or may not be a civil party but is not at least presently a criminally accused) to turn away particular questions that might increase his**

exposure to criminal prosecution or criminal liability. The two are, of course, similar in many ways.[22]

Unless waived, the witness' privilege can be invoked by any civil or criminal witness to resist giving testimony in court, whenever it can be made to appear to the judge that there is some substantial likelihood that information disclosed by the invoker might be used either investigatively or as evidence, in a way that would substantially increase the probability of the invoker's prosecution for or conviction of some crime under any law anywhere. If that possibility is removed, for example by a grant of immunity, by the expiration of the statute of limitations, or by the fact that conviction or acquittal has already taken place, there is no privilege.[23]

[22]Malloy v. Hogan, 378 U.S. 1, 84 S.Ct. 1489 (1964) and Griffin v. California, 380 U.S. 609, 85 S.Ct. 1229 (1965) established that both privileges are part of the Fourteenth Amendment and therefore applicable to the states.

[23] See generally Counselman v. Hitchcock, 142 U.S. 547, 12 S.Ct. 195 (1892); Murphy v. Waterfront Commission of New York Harbor, 378 U.S. 52, 84 S.Ct. 1594 (1964). *Murphy* seems to recede from the position expressed at least at one point in *Counselman* that the immunity grant must guarantee *against prosecution* for the crime feared rather than against *use of the disclosure.* (That *Counselman* view was probably based on possible difficulty to the accused of proving behind-the-scenes investigative use.) The two cases are distinguishable, however. *Counselman* deals solely with federal compulsion in federal proceedings. *Murphy* deals with the question whether a state grant of immunity and ensuing state compulsion, where one justifiably fears federal incrimination, ought to be legal and what effect it ought to have on later federal prosecution. The answer given is that it is legal and there is then an automatic immunity from *use* of the disclosure (rather than from prosecution) by the federal government. Subsequent to *Murphy*, however, the Supreme Court has held that "use" immunity is all that is required under the constitution, in the *Counselman* situation as well. Kastigar v. United States, 406 U.S. 441, 92 S.Ct. 1653 (1972). The federal act conferring "immunization" authority on federal officials authorizes only "use" immunity, 18 U.S.C.A. §§ 6001–6005. It should be noted that violation of the privilege (or giving an immunity grant and then compelling the testimony) by one jurisdiction may now mean an automatic immunity from use by another jurisdiction, even though no jurisdiction (except the feder-

Notice that sometimes at least peripheral aspects of the allegedly privileged information may have to be revealed to the judge in order to enable him to decide whether the information is incriminating within the above definition and therefore privileged. Sometimes the circumstances surrounding the case and the face of the question will be sufficient to show a valid fear of incrimination, without more. Courts must tread the thin line between allowing a mere claim of the privilege to be sufficient in every case, and prying too deeply into allegedly privileged matter.

The privilege applies to enable testimonial silence other than in court. Comprehended are governmental hearings, police interrogations, and other situations where the government requires information. See, respecting required reports, note 1, supra. On the testimonial privilege as applied to police station confessions, see pp. 309–16 supra. A second violation of the privilege may take place where information wrongfully compelled at one time is later sought to be used, as where a police-extracted confession is sought to be introduced against the confessor in court.

al) has the power to grant directly an immunity from use in other jurisdictions.

On the entirely separate matter of waiver, it should be pointed out that the privilege against self-incrimination may be lost insofar as the privilege claim is based on fear of incrimination respecting a crime the story of which has been voluntarily touched upon by the claimant earlier in the same proceedings, provided that at that earlier point he could properly have refused to do so on grounds of incrimination respecting the same crime and he could reasonably have been expected to have known that he could have so refused.

Express and implied waivers of the privilege against self-incrimination are usually effective only for the duration of the immediate proceedings. Suppose the privilege is waived during the hearing of some preliminary matter. Is it waived for the trial proper? Cf. F.R.E. 104(d).

See p. 43, n. 5 supra, for the effect of taking the stand on the privilege of the criminal defendant. What is said in the present section about the witness' privilege generally has an analogue under the accused's privilege to turn away particular questions; but consider the waiver accomplished by his taking the stand.

On the issue of non-testimonial self-incrimination in and out of court (blood tests; breath tests; fingerprints; writing and other specimens; bodily displays; vocal identification; requiring certain action; line-ups) under the Fourth and Fifth Amendments, see generally Schmerber v. California, 384 U.S. 757, 86 S.Ct. 1826 (1966) (blood test for intoxication not covered by the privilege at least insofar as federally guaranteed); United States v. Euge, 444 U.S. 707, 100 S.Ct. 874 (1980); United States v. Dionisio, 410 U.S. 1, 93 S.Ct. 764 (1973); In re Kelley, —— A.2d —— (D.C.App.1980).

The privilege against self-incrimination affects many areas of Evidence law. No attempt is made in the present work to cover the field. The matter of adverse inference from invocation of the privilege is briefly considered at pp. 302–04 supra. The role of the privilege in police line-ups is suggested at pp. 240–41 supra.

Illegally Seized Evidence

Evidence obtained as a not-too-remote or not-too-attenuated result of violation of the federal constitutional prohibition against illegal government-sponsored searches and seizures (which prohibition is applicable against agents of the federal government by virtue of the Fourth Amendment, and against agents of the states by virtue of the Fourteenth Amendment—the two provisions being probably co-terminous as interpreted in the present respect) cannot be admitted as substantive evidence in a criminal case in any court in the land (again by virtue of the Fourth and Fourteenth Amendments, which are again probably co-terminous for these purposes) against the person whose rights were invaded.

Thus, there will be not only whatever ordinary civil, criminal, and equitable sanctions are provided for violation of constitutional rights, but also a privilege to exclude evidence. The prohibition of conduct and the privilege to exclude evidence are probably co-extensive. There is an exception to the privilege (as there is to many privileges to exclude evidence, constitutional or otherwise, particularly as respects illegally obtained evidence) for *impeachment* use of the evidence, where the defendant, who has been the victim of the illegal search or seizure, takes the stand and in either direct examination or cross examination denies possession of the materials seized from him or testifies contrary to the statement obtained from him as a result of the illegal search or seizure. See United States v. Havens, 446 U.S. 620, 100 S.Ct. 1912 (1980). See also Walder v. United States, 347 U.S. 62, 74 S.Ct. 354 (1954).

Some jurisdictions extend a similar privilege to civil cases. But cf. United States v. Janis, 428 U.S. 433, 96 S.Ct. 3021 (1976). The privilege has also been denied, at least insofar as federal or constitutional law might grant it, in grand jury proceedings. United States v. Calandra, 414 U.S. 338, 94 S.Ct. 613 (1974).

What constitutes an illegal search and seizure is not strictly a matter of evidence law, but briefly a search and/or seizure will be illegal if unreasonable as to the grounds of suspicion stimulating it (even if the search thereafter uncovers sufficient grounds), the manner of its execution, the range of the search, or the items seized. (Incidentally, an arrest is a seizure of the person, so that it must comply with these requirements in order to be constitutional and in order for evidence obtained in consequence to be legal.) If these things are complied with, a warrant (arrest or search) is not necessarily required. A warrant is required (in addition to these other requirements) in special areas that the courts deem to be high in privacy expectations (provided getting a warrant would not entail substantial law enforcement problems) such as defendant's home, assuming there are no special exigent circumstances. See generally United States v. Chadwick, 433 U.S. 1, 97 S.Ct. 2476 (1977);

Arkansas v. Sanders, 442 U.S. 753, 99 S.Ct. 2586 (1979); Payton v. New York, 445 U.S. 573, 100 S.Ct. 1371 (1980).

A warrant requires that the grounds for suspicion and the areas to be searched and things to be seized be specified in advance to the issuing magistrate. See Lo-Ji Sales, Inc. v. New York, 442 U.S. 319, 99 S.Ct. 2319 (1979). The standard of reasonableness of grounds and the like, for the issuance of a warrant, is the same as will be applied retroactively to determine the validity of the action if done without a warrant. Whether done with or without a warrant, the reasonableness of the grounds the police had or presented to the magistrate, and the other reasonableness requirements, will be determined upon a motion to suppress the evidence at the trial. Only in a close case will any slight presumption of validity attach to the judgment of the magistrate. There is a split of authority as to whether and when the accuracy of the facts alleged in the affidavits submitted by police to the magistrate to obtain a warrant, can be inquired into at the motion to suppress. In other words, is the defendant confined to challenging only whether the allegations in the affidavit constitute sufficient grounds? Or can he challenge the bona-fides and accuracy of the affiant (usually a policeman)? Of the informer to the affiant? Clearly, facts constituting the police's reasons to believe in (or disbelieve in) the informer's reliability are provable to the issuing magistrate or at a motion to suppress where there has been no warrant. And it is clear that the question of whether and what facts of this kind were shown to the issuing magistrate may be inquired into at the suppression hearing. But to what extent, if any, may the accuracy of those facts be gone into at the suppression hearing? See, on the general subject of questioning the affidavit, Franks v. Delaware, 438 U.S. 154, 98 S.Ct. 2674 (1978). Even if the constitution requires only limited ability to question it, might a jurisdiction accord more?

The advantages of a warrant, from the standpoint of civil libertarian social policy, is that the first-instance or advance judgment, rather than having been made by interested parties (the police), will have been made by an independent person (the magistrate). If the impartial judicial officer only gets to make the judgment after-the-fact, in a suppression hearing, there will always be some measure of justification by hindsight and of the fallibility of after-the-fact reconstruction that must inevitably infect any later judicial determination of the issue. Under the warrant procedure, the magistrate will have made a record of the facts as they appeared *at the time*, for review at the suppression hearing. As a practical matter, the warrant situation seems to be the less important to discuss in a work on evidence. Most evidence is obtained through the non-warrant procedure, and the factual questions are closer there.

Can non-compliance with non-constitutional law (e. g., additional state guarantees) covering arrest, search, or seizure, render police action constitutionally illegal? (By constitution I mean federal constitution.) Or at least result in the application of a privilege to exclude? Would it be the constitutional privilege? See United States v. Grajeda, 570 F.2d 872 (9th Cir. 1978). For example, what if a state requires a knock and announcement before entry to search, in a situation where decisions under the federal constitution, coming to the federal court from states having no such requirement, have said knock and announcement is not constitutionally required? Cf. Ker v. California, 374 U.S. 23, 83 S.Ct. 1623 (1963).

Once there is justification for a search and it is properly conducted, evidence coming to the attention of the searchers and thereupon seized may be used even if it relates to a crime other than the one stimulating the search. And a justifiable search may uncover unsuspected evidence justifying a broader search. Health, fire, and sanitation inspectors, border and customs officials, etc., may not be subject to precisely the same strictures as police. Cf. Marshall v. Barlow's, Inc., 436 U.S. 307, 98 S.Ct. 1816 (1978) (warrantless inspection provisions of Occupational Health and Safety Act); Marshall v. Nolichuckey Sand Co., 606 F.2d 693 (6th Cir. 1979) (Mine Safety and Health Act); United States v. Brignoni-Ponce, 422 U.S. 873, 95 S.Ct. 2574 (1975) (border search); United States v. Ramsey, 431 U.S. 606, 97 S.Ct. 1972 (1977) (semble); Torres v. Puerto Rico, 442 U.S. 465, 99 S.Ct. 2425 (1979) (neither border exception nor health and safety exception applies to Puerto Rico border).

A rich patina of case-law has been laid down in the area of illegal searches and seizures, covering a great variety of fact situations. Particularized research is required on the part of any attorney handling such a matter. E. g., searches of (or subpoenas to) newsrooms, offices of professionals such as lawyers, and other third parties not involved in the crime, to gather leads and evidence, present special problems, resulting in special federal legislation. Cf. privilege.

A common practice is for searches and seizures to be justified as reasonably incident to a valid arrest. See, discussing the permissible scope of such a search, United States v. Robinson, 414 U.S. 218, 94 S.Ct. 467 (1973); and People v. Clyne, 189 Colo. 412, 541 P.2d 71 (1975), People v. Brisendine, 13 Cal.3d 528, 119 Cal.Rptr. 315, 531 P.2d 1099 (1975), State v. Kaluna, 55 Hawaii 361, 520 P.2d 51 (1974), and Zehrung v. State, 569 P.2d 189 (Alaska 1977) (these state cases define a narrower scope under their own constitutions).

But if the arrest is made on insufficient grounds, the search and seizure will be illegal. At common law, and hence under the constitutional standard (as well as under local arrest requirements and any local rulings restricting admissibility), the grounds that will suffice have come to be expressed as "probable cause," rather than mere suspicion.

"Probable cause" in these contexts has come to mean, generally speaking, such grounds as a reasonably cautious person would require.

We have seen above (pp. 315–16) how attempts have been made to avoid the thrust of *Miranda* by creating a status of "detention" that is not "arrest." By creating a status of "detention" that is not "arrest," some quarters hoped also to evade the full requirement that there be "probable cause," not merely suspicion, before there can be an arrest.

The cause or grounds required should vary with the magnitude of the interference with freedom or privacy and the exigencies of the circumstances (officer's safety, magnitude of the crime, etc.); and if what is called a "detention" really is less than arrest, perhaps less "cause" should be required. See Terry v. Ohio, 392 U.S. 1, 88 S.Ct. 1868 (1968) (suspicious activity not amounting to probable cause to arrest justifies stopping and frisking; evidence uncovered in course thereof amounting to probable cause justifies arrest and full search); Dunaway v. New York, 442 U.S. 200, 99 S.Ct. 2248 (1979) (taking into custody for interrogation rather than arrest, not permitted on less than probable cause); Ybarra v. Illinois, 444 U.S. 85, 100 S.Ct. 338 (1979) (limits of *Terry*). How would you rank the following in terms of magnitude of interference with privacy: search of car; home; person; office; locker? Is stopping a car to check licenses a great interference with freedom? See Delaware v. Prouse, 440 U.S. 648, 99 S.Ct. 1391 (1979). Cf. Michigan v. De Fillippo, 443 U.S. 31, 99 S.Ct. 2627 (1979); Brown v. Texas, 443 U.S. 47, 99 S.Ct. 2637 (1979) (grounds to ask I.D.).

On airline terminal stops based on the fact that the passenger fits a hypothetical suspect "profile," see United States v. Mendenhall, 446 U.S. 554, 100 S.Ct. 1870 (1980).

Electronic and Mechanical Eavesdropping (Including Wiretapping)

This kind of eavesdropping is now subject to comprehensive federal prohibitory legislation, including a broad exclusionary evidence rule, covering federal and state proceedings and officials (as well as private persons), but with a warrant exception. These matters are also covered by the constitutional search and seizure provisions, which the statute is meant to satisfy. See interpretations, below.

The phrase "electronic and mechanical eavesdropping" encompasses many ways a message or information can be obtained by devices augmenting the range of the human ear: wiretapping (i. e., the interception of a message carried by wire), overhearing conversations from long distances or through barriers, intercepting airwave broadcasts, recording, etc. Electronic and mechanical eavesdropping, being incursions into privacy, are now deemed "searches and seizures" when committed by agents of government, without the necessity of a physical trespass being perpetrated in connection with them. They are thus subject to the constitutional requirements surrounding searches and seizures, but with some adjustment for the new context. See Berger v. New York, 388 U.S. 41, 87 S.Ct. 1873 (1967); Katz v. United States, 389 U.S. 347, 88 S.Ct. 507 (1968); United States v. White, 401 U.S. 745, 91 S.Ct. 1122 (1971). See also Desist v. United States, 394 U.S. 244, 89 S.Ct. 1048 (1969) and Kaiser v. New York, 394 U.S. 280, 89 S.Ct. 1044 (1969) (both holding the rule prospective only). Cf. Smith v. Maryland, 442 U.S. 735, 99 S.Ct. 2577 (1979) (installation of "pen register" at phone company offices and using it to record numbers dialed from particular phone not governed by these guarantees). Court rules and statutes permitting these practices or permitting such evidence, on a basis inconsistent with the constitutional standards, are as illegal as the practices themselves, as in any case of conflict of this kind.

Ch. 9   *SOME EVIDENTIARY PRIVILEGES*

Formerly, Section 605 of the Federal Communications Act of 1934, 47 U.S.C.A. § 605 (1964), passed pursuant to Congress' power to regulate interstate transmissions, made it a crime for *anyone* to *divulge* information he obtained by interception of a wire or radio message absent proper consent (in advance?) to the interception (or to the disclosure?) by a party ("the sender," but some cases interpreted this away; some required either party, some both) to the communication. Wholly intrastate transmissions were considered indistinguishable from interstate ones. Eavesdropping by extension telephone, by party line, by overhearing the spill-over from the receiver or overhearing one of the parties (even if the ear was aided mechanically), or by receiving a message intended for another by impersonating that other or hiding one's status as informer, were often considered not to be "interceptions." Federal courts, at the behest of a party to the communication, excluded (usually in federal criminal cases) evidence obtained as a not excessively remote or attenuated "but for"-type result of an interception (of the kind wherein the information obtained could not be divulged under Section 605), usually regardless of whether federal officers, state officers, or private citizens had done the intercepting. Authority was diverse regarding whether, why, and to what extent state courts must follow suit and what should be done about it if they did not. Finally it was determined that exclusion in state courts was mandatory, too, probably to the same extent as in federal courts. Lee v. Florida, 392 U.S. 378, 88 S.Ct. 2096 (1968). See also Fuller v. Alaska, 393 U.S. 80, 89 S.Ct. 61 (1968) (rule is prospective only).

Under Section 605 "unauthorized" disclosure by one charged with aiding transmission or reception was forbidden except in response to judicial process and in certain other similar situations. Except for this provision concerning aiders of transmission and reception, Section 605 has been amended by Title III of the 1968 Omnibus Crime Control

[472]

and Safe Streets Act, 18 U.S.C.A. §§ 2510-20, and is now confined to radio communications. This Title III is the comprehensive legislation spoken of above.

Title III of the 1968 Act encompasses all forms of electronic and mechanical eavesdropping on oral and wire communications where a party to the communication has not authorized the eavesdropping in advance. (A number of states have a more stringent requirement, requiring *both* [or all] parties to consent.) Oral communication is defined as any oral communication about which there is a justifiable expectation it will not be intercepted. All jurisdictions are covered. The Act permits governments to authorize such eavesdropping by government agents upon application by law enforcement officials to the judiciary for warrants to be obtained upon a showing of probable cause to suspect certain serious crimes and of need for the eavesdropping, in the particular case. The warrant is to specify a time limit on the eavesdropping it authorizes, that must be reasonable under all the circumstances. The warrant must specify as particularly as possible just what may be eavesdropped upon under it. In certain emergency situations, where a warrant would have issued if there had been time, a short period of properly limited eavesdropping may be done before applying for a retroactive authorization (warrant). Evidence obtained from eavesdropping that complies with the Act may be used in evidence or as leads, etc. With minor exceptions, *all other* electronic and mechanical eavesdropping *by anyone,* on oral or wire communications, is forbidden, criminally punishable, and may be the subject of private litigation; and evidence obtained thereby or as a reasonably proximate result thereof is inadmissible in any local, state, or federal governmental forum, including civil, criminal, and administrative proceedings. Unlike the Fourth Amendment exclusionary rule, this one is held to apply to grand jury proceedings, as well. Gelbard v. United States, 408 U.S. 41, 92 S.Ct. 2357 (1972).

On the statute generally, see United States v. United States Dist. Court for Eastern Dist. of Michigan, 407 U.S. 297, 92 S.Ct. 2125 (1972); United States v. Donovan, 429 U.S. 413, 97 S.Ct. 658 (1977); United States v. Giordano, 416 U.S. 505, 94 S.Ct. 1820 (1974); United States v. Chavez, 416 U.S. 562, 94 S.Ct. 1849 (1974). Cf. United States v. New York Tel. Co., 434 U.S. 159, 98 S.Ct. 364 (1977) (recording numbers dialed from a phone is o.k.).

Does a warrant to eavesdrop under the Act carry with it authority to commit a trespass to execute the eavesdropping? Would that be constitutional under the Fourth Amendment? See Dalia v. United States, 441 U.S. 238, 99 S.Ct. 1682 (1979).

The warrant requirement under the Act is very detailed and specific, with a number of safeguards, to minimize abuses. The provisions regulate, and/or require specification of, who must authorize an application for a warrant; the grounds for issuance; to and from whom the eavesdropped messages will pass; the premises involved; the time, scope, range, and parties; the custody of the tapes; disclosure; etc.; and require necessity (will other investigative techniques do?), and notice to parties afterwards. Do you think such matters can be adequately safeguarded? See generally 26 Stan.L.Rev. 1411 (1974).

Other Invasions of Privacy

It would seem that unauthorized electronic or mechanical visual surveillance, unauthorized listening by the unaided ear, and unauthorized spying by the unaided eye, if perpetrated by agents of the state and involving a physical trespass, can clearly be constitutionally illegal searches. Where there is no physical trespass, there may still be an invasion of privacy to such an extent as to amount to a constitutionally illegal search. The cases suggest that anything seen because it is visible to the naked eye without a physical trespass, say through an automobile window, would not constitute an illegal search, even if the seeing required approach to the automobile. Peering through the window of a home, however, may be such an invasion of privacy as to be treated differently, even if no physical trespass is involved. Cf. People v. Arno, 90 Cal.App.3d 505, 153 Cal.Rptr. 624 (2d Dist. 1979) (use of binoculars to see things in office building that could not otherwise be seen is illegal under federal and state constitution). Several cases have divided on the question whether peering through holes in public washrooms to spy homosexual acts can be an unconstitutional search. Consider manner and grounds for body cavity searches or taking blood.

Evidence Obtained as a Result of Other Kinds of Misconduct

We have elsewhere examined other privileges against illegally obtained evidence than those just discussed. E. g., illegally obtained confessions, Chapter VI supra. There are others. Indeed, some jurisdictions may have a broad privilege against all illegally obtained evidence.

There may on occasion be such a privilege where technically no illegality has been committed in obtaining the evidence, e. g., where the conduct was morally wrong, or would have been impermissible if committed by *police*, or by police of another jurisdiction than the one these police were actually from (for example, the court's home jurisdiction or the jurisdiction in which they acted). Cf. Stevenson v. State, 43 Md.App. 120, 403 A.2d 812 (1979) (D.C. officers in Md. acting as private citizens; thus illegality in arrest that would result in excluding evidence does not so result).

Rochin v. California, 342 U.S. 165, 72 S.Ct. 205 (1952), should also be regarded as establishing a privilege of the sort we are discussing. It holds that evidence obtained as a result of violation of a criminal accused's due process right to be free of abusive treatment at the hands of the state would itself be a violation of his right to due process if introduced against him in the case. There the accused was made to vomit up incriminating evidence that he had swallowed. Had testimonial statements rather than physical evidence been coerced out of the defendant, this principle would overlap those for coerced confessions and the privilege against self-incrimination. The case has not yet been applied where the abuse was not perpetrated by or for or with the complicity of the government, or to civil cases.

Federal courts have generally refused to create evidence-exclusionary privileges for official misconduct that is not the subject of some specific statutory, constitutional, or court-rule provision. E. g., *Payner*, just below; United States v. Caceres, 440 U.S. 741, 99 S.Ct. 1465 (1979) (I.R.S. fails to follow its own regulations in investigation); United States v. Penn, — F.2d — (9th Cir. 1980) (police bribe 5-year-old to lead them to mother's heroin). Cf. People v. Green, 405 Mich. 273, 274 N.W.2d 448 (1979) (violation of Code of Professional Responsibility when prosecutor interviewed defendant without his lawyer's consent). Let us now turn to the policies of the last several sections.

Policy of Privileges to Exclude Evidence Obtained by Misconduct

The policy in most cases seems to be to increase the inducement to public officials, police, or others subject to the regulation, to act properly in carrying out investigations, etc., by providing a remedy in addition to other remedies available to deter the misconduct. Why, then, is it that generally only he whose rights were invaded may invoke the privilege, and only to suppress evidence against himself? See Rawlings v. Kentucky, — U.S. —, 100 S.Ct. 2556 (1980) (defendant has no standing to challenge search of third party's purse that contained narcotic of defendant); United States v. Salvucci, — U.S. —, 100 S.Ct. 2547 (1980) (defendant can't complain of illegal search of his mother's apartment that yielded evidence against him); Rakas v. Illinois, 439 U.S. 128, 99 S.Ct. 421 (1978) (semble; passengers can't complain of search of car); United States v. Payner, 447 U.S. 727, 100 S.Ct. 2439 (1980) (defendant can't complain of search of another's briefcase; court won't create a privilege under its supervisory power either).

In the case of wiretapping under old Section 605 of the Federal Communications Act, another policy was often mentioned: disclosure of a wiretapped message was a crime, and courts did not wish disclosure (a crime) to be perpetrated in the courtroom or by law officers.

Where the policy is merely to discipline police, an argument could be made that the discipline must be confined to police of the court's jurisdiction, if the exclusionary rule is peculiar to the law of that jurisdiction.

Privileges against illegally obtained evidence usually exist only in criminal cases (e. g., United States v. Janis, 428 U.S. 433, 96 S.Ct. 3021 (1976), declining to apply the exclusionary rule relating to illegally seized evidence to at least certain civil cases), but in any event, they often will be limited to protecting only against officially (governmentally) perpetrated or instigated misconduct. (Contra, under the 1968 Omnibus Crime Act's electronic eavesdropping provisions discussed several sections above. See United States v. Rizzo, 583 F.2d 907 (7th Cir. 1978).) However, it is possible for a private citizen to be deemed an agent of government for these purposes, if he is complicitous with government officials, at least if he is so complicitous before or during his suspect conduct. See Marsh v. Alabama, 326 U.S. 501, 66 S.Ct. 276 (1946). Cf. State v. Helfrich, —— Mont. ——, 600 P.2d 816 (1979) (under Montana constitution, evidence barred regardless of any complicity where private person obtained evidence by trespass and turned it over to police); People v. Jones, 47 N.Y.2d 528, 419

N.Y.S.2d 447, 393 N.E.2d 443 (1979) (private guard treated like private citizen making arrest, unless police help, in which case *Miranda* would apply).

Note that the privileges discussed in this book do not bar prosecution, but merely evidence. If there is sufficient other evidence, the case may proceed.

For a discussion of and challenge to the current policy of deterring illegal police conduct (unconstitutional searches and seizures) by creating an evidence-exclusionary rule, see dissent in California v. Minjares, 443 U.S. 916, 100 S.Ct. 9 (1979). Alternative remedies are there discussed. See also "Impact of the Exclusionary Rule on Federal Criminal Prosecutions," U. S. Gov't General Accounting Office Study, Document GGD–79–45 (April 19, 1979).

Proof that Evidence is the Result of Misconduct

Once the criminal defendant proves there was a search and seizure or electronic eavesdropping that might have yielded the prosecution evidence or leads in the case, the government may be required to disclose fully all facts and circumstances in its knowledge that might reflect on whether the conduct was legal and whether it led to or contributed to any of the evidence in the case against the defendant. This would include disclosure to defendant's counsel of the information overheard, for example, through electronic eavesdropping, even, it would seem, if that information must remain confidential in the interests of national security. Refusal might mean that the government would have to forego the benefit of any evidence that could conceivably be tainted; or, indeed, forego the prosecution completely because of the possibility that all of the evidence might be tainted or resultant from tainted leads. See, concerning electronic eavesdropping, Alderman v. United States, 394 U.S. 165, 89 S.Ct. 961 (1969).

In addition, once the defendant has made the showing mentioned above at the opening of the last paragraph, the government may be required to assume the burden of proof on the issues of legality of the conduct, relationship of it to the evidence, remoteness thereof, etc. There is, however, considerable conflict of authority on this. Clearly at some point, perhaps after a prima facie showing of illegality of the conduct and some connection to the evidence, the burden shifts to the prosecution. See Brown v. Illinois, 422 U.S. 590, 95 S.Ct. 2254 (1975).

Attenuation Doctrine Where Evidence Obtained as Result of Misconduct

On the general doctrine that the relationship between the evidence objected to and the misconduct alleged to trigger the privilege must not be too attenuated or the privilege will not apply, see Silverthorne Lumber Co. v. United States, 251 U.S. 385, 40 S.Ct. 182 (1919) and Costello v. United States, 365 U.S. 265, 81 S.Ct. 534 (1961) (search and seizure); Harrison v. United States, 392 U.S. 219, 88 S.Ct. 2008 (1968) (fruit of confession); Smith v. United States, 324 F.2d 879 (D.C.Cir. 1963) (McNabb-Mallory violation; confession leading to eye-witness; eye-witness not barred); Lyons v. Oklahoma, 322 U.S. 596, 64 S.Ct. 1208 (1944) and Leyra v. Denno, 347 U.S. 556, 74 S.Ct. 716 (1954) (second confession given after coerced one); United States v. Bayer, 331 U.S. 532, 67 S.Ct. 1394 (1947) and Killough v. United States, 315 F.2d 241 (D.C.Cir. 1962) (semble; McNabb-Mallory situation). For a thorough relatively recent discussion of the problem, somewhat changing the emphasis of the inquiry to include consideration of the purposes to be served by exclusion and the type of evidence (eyewitness evidence being somewhat favored as compared with physical evidence) see United States v. Ceccolini, 435 U.S. 268, 98 S.Ct. 1054 (1978) (illegal search and seizure arguably led to eyewitness; degree of witness' willingness to testify is also part

[*479*]

of the calculus). In United States v. Crews, 445 U.S. 463, 100 S.Ct. 1244 (1980), a robbery victim's in-court identification of an illegally arrested defendant, was held to be too remotely related to the arrest to be considered a suppressible fruit of the arrest. There is some good discussion in the opinion.

Section 701(a) of the 1968 Omnibus Crime Control and Safe Streets Act seems to provide that nothing shall bar an eye witness in a federal court from testifying that he saw the accused participate in or commit the crime. This cuts across all areas of the law where heretofore such testimony might have been barred because of its method of obtention (e. g., an illegal confession or search furnished a lead to the uncovering of the witness). 18 U.S.C.A. § 3502. Is this entirely constitutional?

Some Additional Comments about Constitution-Based Privileges

We have seen that often misconduct that results in exclusion of evidence is unconstitutional conduct, although not always, and that in either event exclusion of the evidence may or may not be a constitutional matter, at least conceptually. Let us examine some special aspects of those privileges where the constitution plays a role.

A Supreme Court decision finding a guarantee in the Bill of Rights to be present also in the Fourteenth Amendment not only permits states to be more favorable to the defendant than the federal decisions ostensibly applying the Bill of Rights guarantee; but also does not *necessarily* foreclose state autonomy to be less favorable in many particulars on grounds either that the constitutional guarantees are not identical in the two places, or that a particular federal decision (or rule or statute) is at most auxiliary to, but not part of, the constitutional provision. Thus, the decision that the Fourth Amendment prohibition of illegal searches and seizures applies to state officers through the Fourteenth did not automatically mean illegally seized evidence had to be excluded in state proceedings, as it was in federal proceedings. See Wolf v. Colorado, 338 U.S. 25, 69 S.Ct. 1359 (1949). A later decision was required to effectuate that. Mapp v. Ohio, 367 U.S. 643, 81 S.Ct. 1684 (1961). (Indeed, the Fourth Amendment prohibition, like the prohibitions against coercing confessions, unnecessary delay, failure to warn, and other prohibitions, does not necessarily imply an exclusionary rule in *any* court. There are other civil and criminal sanctions or means of enforcing them.) Furthermore, neither of these decisions meant that the federal statutory rule ordinarily requiring a knock, announcement, and request before entry, and incorporated by decision into the federal exclusionary rule, was mandatory upon the states. Ker v. California, 374 U.S. 23, 83 S.Ct. 1623 (1963). See also Sabbath v. United States, 391 U.S. 585, 88 S.Ct. 1755 (1968). Nor did *Mapp* necessarily mean that the federal procedure for suppressing the evidence in advance of trial (Criminal Procedure Rule 12(b)) had to be followed by the states insofar as favorable to the defendant. (This Rule 12(b) procedure can also be applied to other areas than search and seizure. Legislation allows the government to appeal a 12(b) ruling at the time it is made). The extension of the federal privilege against self-incrimination to state prosecutions (Malloy v. Hogan, 378 U.S. 1, 84 S.Ct. 1489 (1964)) did not necessarily mean the states had to follow the federal rule of no-comment on invocation (but see Griffin v. California, 380 U.S. 609, 85 S.Ct. 1229 (1965) extending that rule to the states), or had to follow, insofar as they favor defendants, the federal rules of waiver, or those regarding whether and how the privilege protects against incrimination under the laws of another jurisdiction (but see Murphy v. Waterfront Comm'n of N. Y. Harbor, 378 U.S. 52, 84 S.Ct. 1594 (1964) establishing at one time the new federally mandated rules for both federal and state proceedings), or the federal rules regarding grants of immunity. Nor did the decisions requiring exclusion of involuntary confessions and confessions without warnings necessarily mean that the federal rules regarding how the preliminary facts were to be determined (judge, jury, or some combination; burdens) had to be followed by the states insofar as favorable to the defendant. But cf. Jackson v. Denno, 378 U.S. 368, 84 S.Ct. 1774 (1964), placing limits on the states along the lines of the federal procedure. When it was decided in a federal prosecution that the constitutional confrontation requirement (previously extended to state proceedings) forbade admitting a jointly implicating confession of a co-accused who could not be cross-examined, even though jury instructions were given to the effect that the confession could not be used against the other accused, since such instruction was unlikely to be followed (Bruton v. United States, 391 U.S. 123, 88 S.Ct. 1620 (1968)), did it necessarily follow that such an instruction would not be adequate in a state proceeding? [24] And what about the federal decision in a federal prosecution, that testimony of the accused at a motion to suppress illegally seized evidence cannot be used against him at his trial assuming he does not take the stand and testify to the contrary and assuming he asserts the privilege against self-incrimination? (Both the search-and-seizure and anti-self-incrimination guarantees had previously been extended to the states.) Simmons v. United States, 390 U.S. 377, 88 S.Ct. 967 (1968). Other similar areas can be mentioned. E. g., the question whether unconstitutional evidence that cannot

[24] While it has since been determined that *Bruton* in principle applies to the states, the facts to which *Bruton* applies have been consistently narrowed. See Frazier v. Cupp, 394 U.S. 731, 89 S.Ct. 1420 (1969), Dutton v. Evans, 400 U.S. 74, 91 S.Ct. 210 (1970), and Parker v. Randolph, 442 U.S. 62, 99 S.Ct. 2132 (1979). Would the narrowing apply equally to federal and state proceedings?

be used substantively can be used to impeach. [In several fields this question is now foreclosed because it has been held that even in federal proceedings the evidence can be used for impeachment. For example, in the field of search and seizure the answer in federal prosecutions has been "yes," in certain situations. E. g., accused swears he had no narcotics and illegally seized narcotics are introduced to contradict this; or a statement contrary to his trial testimony has been obtained in consequence of an illegal search and seizure. See generally on this whole matter, including some state and some federal prosecutions, Walder v. United States, 347 U.S. 62, 74 S.Ct. 354 (1954) (impeachment allowed, search and seizure); United States v. Havens, 446 U.S. 620, 100 S.Ct. 1912 (1980) (semble); Harris v. New York, 401 U.S. 222, 91 S.Ct. 643 (1971) (similar; *Miranda*); Oregon v. Hass, 420 U.S. 714, 95 S.Ct. 1215 (1975) (semble); New Jersey v. Portash, 440 U.S. 450, 99 S.Ct. 1292 (1979) (self-incriminatory grand jury testimony, obtained by grant of immunity from use, cannot be used to impeach at trial) (cf. United States v. Apfelbaum, 445 U.S. 115, 100 S.Ct. 948 (1980) (use of immunized testimony, beyond part charged false, at later perjury prosecution)); Jenkins v. Anderson, 447 U.S. 231, 100 S.Ct. 2124 (1980) (pre-arrest failure to come forward with defense of self defense, which defense is asserted at trial, can be used to impeach, despite right to remain silent); Doyle v. Ohio, 426 U.S. 610, 96 S.Ct. 2240 (1976) (post-arrest silence after *Miranda* warnings cannot be so used); cf. United States v. Hale, 422 U.S. 171, 95 S.Ct. 2133 (1975) (silence during police interrogation not probative impeachment as matter of federal evidence law, not constitutional law).]

Another similar area is whether there can be, and what constitutes, harmless error. See, e. g., Spano v. New York, 360 U.S. 315, 79 S.Ct. 1202 (1961) (error in admitting a coerced confession); Chapman v. California, 386 U.S. 18, 87 S.Ct. 824 (1967) (erroneous comment on failure to take stand; general discussion as to constitutional errors; what law, federal or state, governs); Fahy v. Connecticut, 375 U.S. 85, 84 S.Ct. 229 (1963) (error in admitting illegally coerced evidence).

In the same vein, is the definition of "involuntariness" as respects confessions necessarily the same for state and federal prosecutions? If federal courts had a liberal federal rule regarding who may assert a violation of another's constitutional rights, would it have to be followed by the states? (But see the search and seizure cases discussed several sections supra under "Policy of Privileges to Exclude Evidence Obtained by Misconduct.") If federal courts allowed objections to unconstitutionally obtained evidence to be asserted in civil cases; or had a liberal definition of what is state as opposed to private searching or coercing; or extended the ban to coercion or searching by private parties; or were ready to find police participation in ostensibly private searching or coercing; or had narrow rules of what constitutes consent to otherwise illegal actions; or were very favorable to defendants in determining when a "fruit" of police illegality is too remotely related to the illegality to forbid it in evidence, would the states have to do likewise to precisely the same extent? If federal courts in certain circumstances impose the burden of proving voluntariness, or of proving evidence was not a "fruit" of the illegality, or of proving some other preliminary fact, or of proving error harmless, on the prosecution, must the states do likewise? See Harrison v. United States, 392 U.S. 219, 88 S.Ct. 2008 (1968) (burden of proving that defendant's inculpatory testimony at a prior trial was not the result of an illegally obtained confession that was admitted).

In the absence of a decision expressly in point, the decision involving the federal prosecution must be closely examined to ascertain whether its reasoning, basis, and citations suggest it has implications beyond federal proceedings.

Questions often arise concerning whether new evidentiary rulings are retroactive. The question arises acutely respecting Supreme Court rulings of constitutional law regulating evidence in criminal cases. See Roberts v. Russell, 392 U.S. 293, 88 S.Ct. 1921 (1968) (retroactivity of co-defendant confession ruling); Johnson v. New Jersey, 384 U.S. 719, 86 S.Ct. 1772 (1966) (retroactivity of ruling regarding right to counsel and warnings upon interrogation); Linkletter v. Walker, 381 U.S. 618, 85 S.Ct. 1731 (1965) (retroactivity of search and seizure ruling); and Tehan v. U. S. ex rel. Shott, 382 U.S. 406, 86 S.Ct. 459 (1966) (retroactivity of ruling regarding comment on failure to testify). A distinction has sometimes been drawn between rulings designed to assure accuracy in the particular case and those designed to pressure enforcement personnel to conduct themselves in a certain fashion.

Another question that is in the process of receiving an answer is the extent to which the constitutional criminal evidence guarantees are applicable to military trials, to the juvenile process, and to other areas that seem similar to criminal proceedings. Cf. In re Gault, 387 U.S. 1, 87 S.Ct. 1428 (1967); In re Whittington, 391 U.S. 341, 88 S.Ct. 1507 (1968).

*

INDEX

References are to Pages. Where a reference is principal as compared to others, it is italicized. See also Table of Federal Rules, Table of Cases, and Table of Contents. Page references are generally to initial pages only. Federal Rules on each subject are discussed even where not specifically so noted in this index.

INDEX

References are to Pages

INDEX
References are to Pages

INDEX

INDEX
References are to Pages

[*494*]

INDEX
References are to Pages

INDEX

HANDWRITING, 19–20, 72–74, 465
See also Authentication; Scientific Evidence

HARMLESS ERROR
See Error

HEARSAY, 31, 33, 34, 53, 74, 75, *Chapters III, IV* and *V*, 409
Agency, 198
Conduct as, omissions as, and other implied hearsay, 171, 172, 174, 179, 181–182, 206, 248–253, 291, 296–306
Contract as, 196, 231, 291
Defamation as, 195, 201, 202, 231, 291
Definitions, 207 231, 291. See, also 234 et seq.
Double hearsay, 222, 261–264, 274, 409
Exceptions, opinion in, 53, 222, 259, 271–273, 277–279
Exceptions and exemptions, 167, 182, 188, 206, 208–210, *Chapter IV, 235–291*

    See, also, Admissions; Ancient Documents; Business Records; Catchall or Residual Hearsay Exception; Conspiracy; Declarations Against Interest; Dying Declarations; Excited Utterances; Former Proceedings, Testimony at; Identification; Inconsistent (And other Prior) Statements; Official Records; Pain and Other Bodily Feelings, Declarations of; Past Recollection Recorded; Pedigree and Family History, Statements of; Physicians, Statements to; Prior Consistent Statements; Prior Statements of Witnesses; Reputation; State of Mind

Expert's opinion, hearsay in, 55–56, 59–61, 183, 232–234, 286–291
Federal Rules, 231
First-hand knowledge rule distinguished, 53
Gift, words constituting, 196, 231, 291
Hearsay-within-hearsay. See Double hearsay
Intention, hearsay offered to prove carried out, 192, 193, 207, 216, 231, 256, 291
Non-hearsay out of court statements, 195 et seq., 231, 235 et seq., 291
Operative facts, 196–197, 231, 291
Prior statements of witnesses. See Inconsistent (And Other Prior) Statements
Rationale, *161*, 167, 179, 181–182, 185–186, 202, 203, 206, 251
Reputation. See Reputation
State of mind. See State of Mind
Surveys, 55–56, 59–61, 183, 232–234, 286–291

INDEX

INDEX

INDEX

INDEX

References are to Pages

STATE RULES

See specific subjects; Federal Rules of Evidence; Table of Rules.; Uniform Rules of Evidence. State law is included even when not cited

STATEMENTS

See Admissions; Confessions; Declarations Against Interest; Inconsistent (And Other Prior) Statements; Jencks Rule; Line-Ups; Pain and Other Bodily Feelings; State of mind; Writings; and other particular kinds of statements. Also, e. g., instead of "Statement Against Interest", the phrase "Declarations Against Interest" would often be used in this index, or "Against Interest, Declarations of". So also for certain other entries

STATEMENTS TO PHYSICIANS (AND FOR PURPOSES OF MEDICAL DIAGNOSIS OR TREATMENT)

See Physicians, Statements to

STIPULATIONS, 24, 74, 294, 295

STRIKE, MOTION TO, 4, 30, 88, 329

SUBPOENA OF WITNESSES, DOCUMENTS, 340–341

SUBSTANTIVE EVIDENCE, DEFINED, DISTINGUISHED FROM CREDIBILITY EVIDENCE, 41, *320*, 325, 333, 336, 345–346, 483

SUFFICIENCY OF EVIDENCE

See Peremptory Rulings

SUICIDE, 251, 296

SUMMARY JUDGMENT, 102, *104*

SUPPORT OF CREDIBILITY, 164, *348*

SUPPRESSION AND HIDING OR DESTRUCTION OF EVIDENCE, 251, 296, 305, 306

See also Objections And Offers; Pre-Trial; as well as specific grounds, for suppression by legal procedure

SURPRISE, 10, 11

See also Relevancy And Its Counterweights—Balancing

INDEX
References are to Pages

[*513*]

INDEX
References are to Pages

†